REA's Test Prep Books Are The Best!

(a sample of the <u>hundreds of letters</u> REA receives each year)

" I did well because of your wonderful prep books... I just wanted to thank you for helping me prepare for these tests. "

Student, San Diego, CA

" My students report your chapters of review as the most valuable single resource they used for review and preparation. "

Teacher, American Fork, UT

" Your book was such a better value and was so much more complete than anything your competition has produced — and I have them all! "

Teacher, Virginia Beach, VA

" Compared to the other books that my fellow students had, your book was the most useful in helping me get a great score. "

Student, North Hollywood, CA

" Your book was responsible for my success on the exam, which helped me get into the college of my choice... I will look for REA the next time I need help. "

Student, Chesterfield, MO

" Just a short note to say thanks for the great support your book gave me in helping me pass the test... I'm on my way to a B.S. degree because of you! "

Student, Orlando, FL

(more on next page)

(continued from front page)

" I just wanted to thank you for helping me get a great score
on the AP U.S. History exam... Thank you for making great test preps! "
Student, Los Angeles, CA

" Your *Fundamentals of Engineering Exam* book was the absolute best
preparation I could have had for the exam, and it is one of the major
reasons I did so well and passed the FE on my first try. "
Student, Sweetwater, TN

" I used your book to prepare for the test and found that the advice and the
sample tests were highly relevant... Without using any other material, I earned
very high scores and will be going to the graduate school of my choice. "
Student, New Orleans, LA

" What I found in your book was a wealth of information sufficient to shore up
my basic skills in math and verbal... The section on analytical ability was
excellent. The practice tests were challenging and the answer explanations most
helpful. It certainly is the *Best Test Prep for the GRE*! "
Student, Pullman, WA

" I really appreciate the help from your excellent book. Please keep up
the great work. "
Student, Albuquerque, NM

" I am writing to thank you for your test preparation... your book helped me
immeasurably and I have nothing but praise for your *GRE* preparation."
Student, Benton Harbor, MI

(more on back page)

The Best Test Preparation for the

AP English

Literature & Composition Exam

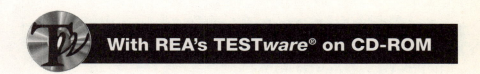

With REA's TEST*ware*® on CD-ROM

Pauline Beard, Ph.D.
Instructor of English
Portland State University, Portland, OR

James Maloney, M.A.
Chairperson of English Department
Ewing High School, Trenton, NJ

Robert Liftig, Ed.D.
Adjunct Assistant Professor of Writing
Fairfield University, Fairfield, CT

Joanne Miller, M.A.
Chairperson of English Department
Harrison High School, West Lafayette, IN

James Malek, Ph.D.
Chairperson and Professor of English
DePaul University, Chicago, IL

Peter Trenouth, M.A.
Teacher of English
Silver Lake Regional H.S., Kingston, MA

Mattie Williams, M.A.
Chairperson of English Department
Walter F. George High School, Atlanta, GA

Research & Education Association
Visit our website at
www.rea.com

Research & Education Association
61 Ethel Road West
Piscataway, New Jersey 08854
E-mail: info@rea.com

The Best Test Preparation for the
AP ENGLISH LITERATURE & COMPOSITION EXAM
with TEST*ware*® on CD-ROM

Library of Congress Control Number 2002114238

ISBN-13: 978-0-87891-129-5
ISBN-10: 0-87891-129-4

CONTENTS

AP ENGLISH COURSE REVIEW

SIX PRACTICE EXAMS

About Research & Education Association

Founded in 1959, Research & Education Association is dedicated to publishing the finest and most effective educational materials—including software, study guides, and test preps—for students in middle school, high school, college, graduate school, and beyond.

REA's Test Preparation series includes books and software for all academic levels in almost all disciplines. Research & Education Association publishes test preps for students who have not yet entered high school, as well as high school students preparing to enter college. Students from countries around the world seeking to attend college in the United States will find the assistance they need in REA's publications. For college students seeking advanced degrees, REA publishes test preps for many major graduate school admission examinations in a wide variety of disciplines, including engineering, law, and medicine. Students at every level, in every field, with every ambition can find what they are looking for among REA's publications.

REA's practice tests are always based upon the most recently administered exams, and include every type of question that you can expect on the actual exams.

REA's publications and educational materials are highly regarded and continually receive an unprecedented amount of praise from professionals, instructors, librarians, parents, and students. Our authors are as diverse as the fields represented in the books we publish. They are well-known in their respective disciplines and serve on the faculties of prestigious high schools, colleges, and universities throughout the United States and Canada.

Today, REA's wide-ranging catalog is a leading resource for teachers, students, and professionals.

We invite you to visit us at *www.rea.com* to find out how "REA is making the world smarter."

Acknowledgments

In addition to our authors, we would like to thank Larry B. Kling, Vice President, Editorial, for his overall direction; John Paul Cording, Vice President, Technology, for coordinating the design, development, and testing of REA's TEST*ware*® software; Pam Weston, Vice President, Publishing, for setting the quality standards for production integrity and managing the publication to completion; Project Managers Amy Jamison and Reena Shah, for their tireless work in the testing and development of the TEST*ware*®; Diane Goldschmidt, Senior Editor, for post-production quality assurance; Molly Solanki, Associate Editor, for coordinating revisions; Rachel DiMatteo, Graphic Designer, for typesetting revisions; and Joanne Morbit and Martin Perzan for typesetting the manuscript.

ABOUT THIS BOOK AND TEST*ware*®

This book, along with our exclusive accompanying TEST*ware*® software, provides you with an accurate and complete representation of the Advanced Placement Examination in English Literature and Composition. Inside you will find topical reviews designed to equip you with the information and strategies needed to pass the exam. REA also gives you six full-length printed practice tests and four topical review sections, all based on the most recently administered AP exam and covering every type of question that you can expect to encounter on test day. As with the actual test, each of ours takes three hours to complete. Following each practice test, you will find an answer key with detailed explanations designed to help you better grasp the test material.

ABOUT THE TEST

The Advanced Placement Program is designed to allow high school students to pursue college-level studies while attending high school. The AP English Literature and Composition exam is usually taken by high school students who have completed a year's study in a college-level literature and composition course. The results are then used for awarding course credit and/or placement level in college.

The AP English Literature and Composition course is designed to represent college-level English studies. Students are expected to leave the course with college-level writing skills, knowledge of literary terms, and an ability to read prose and poetry critically. The course is intended for students with a strong background in literature and writing.

The exam is divided into two sections:

1. **Multiple-choice:** This section is composed of approximately 60 multiple-choice questions designed to measure the student's ability to understand and analyze English literature. The questions are based on two poems and two prose passages. This section tests the student's ability to understand and analyze passages of prose and poetry, rather than calling on knowledge of literary history. The questions vary in complexity and difficulty, and require the student to make critical judgments about the language, structure, tone, imagery, etc., of poems and prose written in English from the Renaissance to the present. The student has 60 minutes to complete this section of the exam, which counts for 45 percent of the final grade.

2. **Free-response:** This section is composed of three essay questions designed to measure the student's ability to write coherent, intelligent, well-organized essays on literary topics. Two of the essays are based on given texts (one prose passage and one poem), and the third essay requires the student to discuss a general topic in relation to a selection from a given list of works. The student has 120 minutes to complete this section, which counts for 55 percent of the final grade.

ABOUT THE REVIEW SECTIONS

The reviews in this book are designed to further students' understanding of the test material. Each review includes techniques students can use to enhance their reading and writing abilities to earn higher scores on the exam. Each review contains several sample essays with explanations of the analytical skills and writing techniques that will lead to success on the test. The reviews also discuss extensively the variety of literary genres, terms, and devices that the student will be required to know for the exam. The four review sections in this book correspond with the four topics covered on the AP exam:

READING PROSE This review covers the various forms of prose the student may encounter on the AP exam, including novels, short stories, essays, and satire. Also included is a section covering general rules and ideas about fiction and non-fiction, as well as tips on how to analyze prose passages for the test.

READING POETRY Every type of poetry the student can encounter on the AP exam is described in detail with examples. Genre, structure, convention, and poetic form are all given ample discussion. Definitions and examples appear in this section for such terms as onomatopoeia, masculine/feminine rhyme, paradox, allusion, and many others, as well as study hints to help the student analyze poetry for the test.

READING DRAMA This review gives extensive examples of the types of questions which could be asked about drama on the AP exam. Sample essays discuss various types of drama, including conflict, character, and types of plays. Classic works such as *Antigone*, *The Glass Menagerie*, and *Death of a Salesman* are used to illustrate the topics covered.

WRITING ESSAYS The Writing Essays review gives a comprehensive overview of the skills needed to write clear, coherent, and intelligent essays which meet the standards of the AP graders. Sections on form, structure, and punctuation guide the student and instruct him on how to write the best essay for the AP. Also included are tips for writing outlines for better essay organization. A sample topic and essay show the tools discussed in use.

HOW TO USE THIS BOOK AND TEST*ware®*

The practice exams in this book and software package are included in two formats: our TEST*ware®* software on the enclosed CD, which features three computerized tests, and six model tests in printed form in this book. **We recommend that you begin your preparation by taking the AP English Literature & Composition Practice Exam 1 on your computer.** The software provides timed conditions, automatic scoring of the multiple-choice section of the exam, and scoring information that makes it easier to isolate your strengths and weaknesses. This exam should serve as a diagnostic test for you, so that you know how to best utilize your study time. This is especially important if your preparation time is limited.

ABOUT THE INDEX OF LITERARY WORKS

In the back of this book you will find an extensive index which lists all of the literary works which are mentioned in this book. In addition to helping you find where specific works are located in the tests, this index also serves as a suggested reading list of many of the literary classics you should read to help familiarize yourself with all the terms and genres you will need to know. Reading these works is excellent preparation for taking the AP English Literature test.

SCORING THE EXAM

The multiple-choice section of the exam is scored by crediting each correct answer with one point and deducting one-fourth of a point for each incorrect answer. Unanswered questions receive neither a credit nor a deduction. The free response essays are graded by over 1,500 instructors and professors who gather together each June for a week of non-stop AP essay grading. Each essay booklet is read and scored by four graders. Each grader provides a score for the individual essays. This score is a number on a scale from 0 to 9, 0 being the lowest and 9 the highest. These scores are covered up so that the next grader does not see them. When the essays have been graded four times, the scores are averaged, one score for each of the three essays, so that the free-response section is composed of three scores.

The three essays are weighted equally, and the total weight of the free-response section is sixty percent of the total score. The multiple-choice section comprises forty percent of the total score. Each year the overall grades fluctuate because the grading scale depends upon the performance of students in past AP administrations. The following method of scoring and the corresponding chart will give you an **approximation** of your score. It does not indicate the exact score you would get on the actual AP English Examination, but rather the score you achieved on the sample tests in this book.

SCORING THE MULTIPLE-CHOICE SECTION

For the multiple-choice section, use this formula to calculate your raw score:

$$\underset{\substack{\text{number} \\ \text{right}}}{\underline{\hspace{2cm}}} - (\underset{\substack{\text{number} \\ \text{wrong}}}{\underline{\hspace{2cm}}} \times 1/4) = \underset{\substack{\text{raw} \\ \text{score}}}{\underline{\hspace{2cm}}} \text{ (round to the nearest whole number)}$$

SCORING THE FREE-RESPONSE SECTION

For the free-response section, use this formula to calculate your raw score:

$$\underset{\substack{\text{essay} \\ \#1}}{\underline{\hspace{2cm}}} + \underset{\substack{\text{essay} \\ \#2}}{\underline{\hspace{2cm}}} + \underset{\substack{\text{essay} \\ \#3}}{\underline{\hspace{2cm}}} = \underset{\substack{\text{raw} \\ \text{score}}}{\underline{\hspace{2cm}}} \quad \text{(round to the nearest whole number)}$$

You may want to give your essays three different grades, such as a 5, an 8, and a 6, and then calculate your score three ways: as if you did well, average, and poorly. This will give you a safe estimate of how you will do on the actual exam. Try to be objective about grading your own essays. If possible, have a friend, teacher, or parent grade them for you. Make sure your essays follow all of the AP requirements before you assess the score.

THE COMPOSITE SCORE

To obtain your composite score, use the following method:

$$1.0 \times \underset{\substack{\text{multiple-choice} \\ \text{raw score}}}{\underline{\hspace{2cm}}} = \underline{\hspace{2cm}} \quad \text{(weighted multiple-choice score—\textbf{do not round})}$$

$$3.333 \times \underset{\substack{\text{free-response} \\ \text{raw score}}}{\underline{\hspace{2cm}}} = \underline{\hspace{2cm}} \quad \text{(weighted free-response score—\textbf{do not round})}$$

Now, add the two weighted sections together and round to the nearest whole number. The result is your total composite score. Compare your score with this table to approximate your grade:

AP Grade	Composite Score Range
5	100-150
4	86-99
3	68-85
2	46-67
1	0-45

These overall scores are interpreted as follows: 5-extremely well qualified; 4-well qualified; 3-qualified, 2-possibly qualified; and 1-no recommendation. Most colleges will grant students who earn a 3 or above either college credit or advanced placement. Check with your guidance office about specific school requirements.

AP ENGLISH LITERATURE STUDY SCHEDULE

Here is a suggested six-week study schedule for the AP Examination in English Literature. In order for this schedule to benefit you the most, you should follow it carefully. You may want to condense or expand it depending on how soon you will be taking the AP exam. Set aside time each week, and work straight through the activity without rushing. This way, you'll boost your confidence and be thoroughly prepared for the exam.

Week	Activity
1	Acquaint yourself with the AP English Literature Exam by reading the book's introduction. Take Practice Test 1 on CD-ROM as a diagnostic exam in order to determine your strengths and weaknesses. After checking the score report and detailed explanations, highlight the items that prove difficult. Review the specific area of difficulty by using the appropriate textbooks, notes, or the AP course review included with this book, as you prepare to take Practice Test 2.
2	Take Practice Test 2 on CD-ROM. Carefully read through all the detailed explanations (not just those for your incorrect answers), and highlight any sections that prove difficult for you, or any questions that remain unclear after reading the explanations. Use textbooks, notes, or course materials to review those areas that need clarification.
3	Take Practice Test 3 on CD-ROM. Carefully read through all the detailed explanations, and highlight any sections that prove difficult for you, or any questions that remain unclear after reading the explanations. Use textbooks, notes, or course materials to review those areas that need clarification.
4	Take Practice Test 4 in your book. Carefully read through all the detailed explanations, and make a note of any sections that prove difficult for you, or any questions that remain unclear after reading the explanations. Use textbooks, notes, or course materials to review those areas that need clarification.
5	Take Practice Test 5 in your book. Carefully read through all the detailed explanations (not just those for your incorrect answers), and make a note of any sections that prove difficult for you, or any questions that remain unclear after reading the explanations. Use textbooks, notes, or course materials to review those areas that need clarification.
6	Take Practice Test 6 in your book. Carefully read through all the detailed explanations, and make a note of any sections that prove difficult for you, or any questions that remain unclear after reading the explanations. Compare your progress between exams. Note any sections where you improve your score, and sections where your score remains the same or declines. Allow yourself extra study time for those areas that require more attention. For additional review, take printed tests 1 – 3, which are identical to the CD-ROM-based exams.

CHAPTER 1

PROSE

GENERAL RULES AND IDEAS

Why do people write prose? Certainly such a question has a built-in counter: As opposed to writing what, poetry? One possible answer is that the person is a poor poet. The requirements and restrictions of the various genres make different demands upon a writer; most writers find their niche and stay there, secure in their private "comfort zone." Shakespeare did not write essays; Hemingway did not write poetry. If either did venture outside of his literary domain, the world took little note.

Students are sometimes confused as to what exactly is prose. Basically, prose is **not** poetry. Prose is what we write and speak most of the time in our everyday intercourse: unmetered, unrhymed language. Which is not to say that prose does not have its own rhythms—language, whether written or spoken, has cadence and balance. And certainly prose can have instances of rhyme or assonance, alliteration or onomatopoeia. Language is, after all, **phonic.**

Furthermore, **prose** may be either **fiction** or **non-fiction**. A novel (like a short story) is fiction; an autobiography is non-fiction. While a novel (or short story) may have autobiographical elements, an autobiography is presumed to be entirely factual. Essays are usually described in other terms: expository, argumentative, persuasive, critical, narrative. Essays may have elements of either fiction or non-fiction, but are generally classed as a separate subgenre.

Satire, properly speaking, is not a genre at all, but rather a **mode**, elements of which can be found in any category of literature—from poetry and drama to novels and essays. Satire is a manifestation of authorial attitude (tone) and purpose. Our discussion of satire will be limited to its use in prose.

But we have not addressed the initial question: "Why do people write prose?" The answer depends, in part, on the writer's intent. If he wishes to tell a rather long story, filled with many characters and subplots, interlaced with motifs, symbols, and themes, with time and space to develop interrelationships and to present descriptive passages, the writer generally chooses the novel as his medium. If he believes he can present his story more compactly and less complexly, he may choose the novella or the short story.

These subgenres require from the reader a different kind of involvement than does the essay. The essay, rather than presenting a story from which the reader may discern meaning through the skillful analysis of character, plot, symbol, and language, presents a relatively straightforward account of the writer's opinion(s) on an endless array of topics. Depending upon the type of essay, the reader may become informed (expository), provoked (argumentative), persuaded, enlightened (critical), or, in the case of the narrative essay, better acquainted with the writer who wishes to illustrate a point with his story, whether it is autobiographical or fictitious.

Encountering satire in prose selections demands that the reader be sensitive to the nuances of language and form, that he detect the double-edged sword of irony, and that he correctly assess both the writer's tone and his purpose.

Readers of prose, like readers of poetry, seek aesthetic pleasure, entertainment, and knowledge, not necessarily in that order. Fiction offers worlds—real and imagined—in which characters and ideas, events and language, interact in ways familiar and unfamiliar. As readers, we take delight in the wisdom we fancy we have acquired from a novel or short story. Non-fiction offers viewpoints which we may find comforting or horrifying, amusing or sobering, presented by the author rather than by his once-removed persona. Thus, we are tempted to believe that somehow the truths presented in non-fiction are more "real" than the truths revealed by fiction. But we must resist! **Truth** is not "genre-specific."

Reading prose for the AP exam is really no different from reading prose for your own purposes, except for the time constraints, of course! Becoming a competent reader is a result of practicing certain skills. Probably most important is acquiring a broad reading base. Read widely; read eclectically; read actively; read avidly. The idea is not that you might stumble onto a familiar prose selection on the AP exam and have an edge in writing about it; the idea is that your familiarity with many authors and works gives you a framework upon which to build your understanding of **whatever** prose selection you encounter on the AP exam. So read, read, read!

A second strategy for success in reading prose for the AP exam is to read the selection you will be writing about **carefully**. The temptation to skim it, or—if you think you recognize it—to begin writing at once, is understandable because of the time limit you will work against. But failure to read carefully—and **reread**—the selection may prevent your doing a thorough analysis.

Third, as you **reread** the selection, mark it up! Note major thesis statements; transitions; repeated key words, phrases, and ideas; words which signal shifts, contrasts, contradictions; punctuation or formatting which signals important ideas or concepts; parallel structures. Look for connotative language, various types of sensory imagery, possible symbols.

Finally, weigh the total effect of the selection; try to assess the writer's purpose, his attitude toward his subject matter (tone), his intended audience, the effectiveness of his style and techniques. Ask yourself, "How well did he do what he seemed to be trying to do?"

Of course, the amount of time and effort you expend on those four areas will depend in part on what the question asks you about the selection. And that is the other major area where strategy is crucial. **Read, reread, analyze, and mark up the question!** No matter how much you know about the selection, and no matter how eloquently you write about it, if you do not write "on topic," your essay will be marked down. You **must** answer the question! Look for key words, such as **contrast, compare, analyze, explain, narrator, attitude, tone, mood, language, imagery, style, diction, narrative structure, specific detail**. A clear understanding of such literary terms is extremely important as you write for the AP exam.

Most essay questions will contain the directive, **show how**; it is imperative that you not simply assert that the selection has certain characteristics, or that it has a certain tone. You are required to give specific and ample support for your assertion, or specific examples of **how** the writer achieves the effect the question states is present. Make sure you understand what it is you are asked to **compare** or **contrast**; is it the **shift** in tone within the selection, or is it the **difference** in tone between one selection and another? Are you asked to provide examples of a certain type of imagery, or to show how the writer's style contributes to **mood** in the selection?

It is a good idea to jot down at least a few key ideas or topics you want to cover in your essay before you begin to write. A full-fledged outline is not necessary, but a sense of direction is extremely helpful. Make sure that your outline or "map" covers the items mandated by the question. Deciding on the order in which to discuss them, unless specified in the question format, is your option.

Many students have been trained to begin a composition with a clever opening paragraph which contains a three-part thesis statement, each part of which will occupy a subsequent paragraph, followed by a fifth and final paragraph. Readers for the AP essay exams urge students to dispense with this "inverted funnel" opening paragraph, opting for a clear thesis statement which will direct and structure the essay. Regard the elements of your thesis statement—regardless of their number—as sections or "chunks" of your essay, rather than as single paragraphs. There is nothing magic or sacred about the number three! Let the number of idea units dictate the paragraphs, rather than a predetermined number of paragraphs dictate the idea units in your thesis statement.

Don't let "writer's block" on the introductory paragraph stop you from answering the question. If you can't seem to find the words to begin, leave enough lines for a paragraph and get to the ideas and elements you wish to discuss. Come back to paragraph one later; if nothing else, simply write your thesis sentence down in the blank space. Usually the thesis sentence for AP essays is built right into the exam question; that's why it is so important to read the question carefully.

Specific examples from the selection are required in most essays on prose, and are advisable in all cases. It is not necessary to quote entire passages; use ellipses (…) to indicate that you are excerpting from the work. Be sure to put all quoted material in quotation marks, or underline terms to indicate italics. If the selection has line numbers, use those to locate pertinent quoted material for the reader. Try to contextualize any quotes skillfully; make them fit within the flow of your own prose as you demonstrate your thesis.

When you have discussed the required items and have supported your thesis to the best of your ability, conclude your essay briefly and gracefully by reminding the reader of your original thesis—but do not merely restate it verbatim. And resist the urge to praise the writer—especially if he/she is well-known—as "magnificent" or "one of the most outstanding authors of all time." Focus on the selection and your analysis of it—then quit.

Sometimes students write marginal notes to the AP graders, either to explain or to amuse. The graders regard such marginalia as inappropriate and discourage students from including them. Explanations of subject matter should be incorporated into the essay itself; explanations of format and/or paragraph or sentence order can be demonstrated by neatly drawn arrows. In fact, all corrections—including major revisions or rewriting—can be indicated simply and neatly by arrows or numbers. Graders indicate that such evidence of revision is an indication that the essay was a "process of thought," which is what good writing should be.

READING NOVELS

Most literary handbooks will define a novel as an extended fictional prose narrative, derived from the Italian *novella*, meaning "tale, piece of news." The term "novelle," meaning short tales, was applied to works such as Boccaccio's *Decameron*, a collection of stories which had an impact on later works such as Chaucer's *Canterbury Tales*. In most European countries, the word for **novel** is **roman**, short for **romance**, which was applied to longer verse narratives (Malory's *Morte d'Arthur*), which were later written in prose. Early romances were associated with "legendary, imaginative, and poetic material"—tales "of the long ago or the far away or the imaginatively improbable"; novels, on the other hand, were felt to be "bound by the facts of the actual world and the laws of probability" (*A Handbook to Literature*, C. Hugh Holman, p. 354).

The novel has, over some 600 years, developed into many special forms which are classified by subject matter: detective novel, psychological novel, historical novel, regional novel, picaresque novel, Gothic novel, stream-of-consciousness novel, epistolary novel, and so on. These terms, of course, are not exhaustive nor mutually exclusive. Furthermore, depending on the conventions of the author's time period, his style, and his outlook on life, his *mode* may be termed **realism, romanticism, impressionism, expressionism, naturalism,** or **neo-classicism** (Holman, p. 359).

Our earlier description of a novel ("...a rather long story, filled with many characters and subplots, interlaced with motifs, symbols, and themes, with time and space to develop interrelationships and to present descriptive passages") is satisfactory for our purposes here. The works generally included on AP essay exams are those which have stood the test of time in significance, literary merit, and reader popularity. New works are incorporated into the canon as students begin to use them in their essays, which is a reflection of what works are being taught in AP classes. And teachers begin to teach those works which are included frequently among the choices on the essay questions. So the process is circular, but the standards remain high for inclusion.

A casual survey of recent years' exams reveals that the following works are frequently offered for discussion: (American) *The Grapes of Wrath, Catch-22, Light in August, Invisible Man, Native Son, Ethan Frome, The Scarlet Letter, The Great Gatsby, Billy Budd, Huckleberry Finn, Moby Dick*; (British) *Portrait of the Artist as a Young Man, Great Expectations, Jude the Obscure, Moll Flanders, Wuthering Heights, Jane Eyre, David Copperfield, Lord Jim.* Other less traditional novels that AP teachers report using successfully include *Emma, Heart of Darkness, Siddhartha, Watership Down, Passage to India,* and *Cry, the Beloved Country.* Some of the leading multi-ethnic novels and novels by women which have been integrated into AP English Literature and Composition curricula include *The Woman Warrior: Memoirs of a Childhood Among Ghosts* (Kingston), *Jasmine* (Mukherjee), *Things Fall Apart* (Achebe), *Their Eyes Were Watching God* (Hurston) and *Song of Solomon* (Morrison).

What these novels have in common is, as we noted earlier, their significance and relevance to the human condition, as well as their merit as literary works. They have something to say, and they say it well. Much "popular" literature today is formulaic—the endless series of romance novels by various publishers, the sequels *ad infinitum* of sword-and-sorcery novels, and Western novels by a genuine cowboy. But popularity alone is not the measure for significance nor for merit. Telling a story whose plot is probable yet refreshingly unpredictable is an art. Characters who seem real and familiar, yet unique and individual, are the creations of skilled writers.

Analyzing novels is a bit like asking the journalist's five questions: what? who? why? where? and how? The **what?** is the story, the narrative, the plot and subplots. Most students are familiar with Freytag's Pyramid, originally designed to describe the structure of a five-act drama but now widely used to analyze fiction as well. The stages generally specified are **introduction** or **exposition**, **complication**, **rising action**, **climax**, **falling action**, and **denouement** or **conclusion**. As the novel's events are charted, the "change which structures the story" should emerge. There are many events in a long narrative; generally, however, only one set of events constitutes the "real" or "significant" story.

However, subplots often parallel or serve as counterpoints to the main plot line, serving to enhance the central story. Minor characters sometimes have essentially the same conflicts and goals as the major characters, but the consequences of the outcome seem less important. Sometimes the parallels involve reversals of characters and situations, creating similar yet distinct differences in the outcomes. Nevertheless, seeing the parallels makes understanding the major plot line less difficult.

Sometimes an author divides the novel into chapters—named or unnamed, perhaps just numbered. Or he might divide the novel into "books" or "parts," with chapters as subsections. Readers should take their cue from these divisions; the author must have had some reason for them. Take note of what happens in each larger section, as well as within the smaller chapters. Whose progress is being followed? What event or occurrence is being foreshadowed or prepared for? What causal or other relationships are there between sections and events? Some writers, such as Steinbeck in *The Grapes of Wrath*, use intercalary chapters, alternating between the "real" story (the Joads) and peripheral or parallel stories (the Okies and migrants in general). Look for the pattern of such organization; try to see the interrelationships of these alternating chapters.

Of course, plots cannot happen in isolation from characters, the **who?** element of a story. Not only are there major and minor characters to consider; we need to note whether the various characters are **static** or **dynamic**. Static characters do not change in significant ways—that is, in ways which relate to the story which is structuring the novel. A character may die, i.e., change from alive to dead, and still be static, unless his death is central to the narrative. For instance, in Golding's *Lord of the Flies*, the boy with the mulberry birthmark apparently dies in a fire early in the novel. Momentous as any person's death is, this boy's death is not what the novel is about. However, when Simon is killed, and later Piggy, the narrative is directly impacted because the reason for their deaths is central to the novel's theme regarding man's innate evil. A dynamic character may change only slightly in his attitudes, but those changes may be the very ones upon which the narrative rests. For instance, Siddhartha begins as a very pure and devout Hindu but is unfulfilled spiritually. He eventually does achieve spiritual contentment, but his change is more a matter of degree than of substance. He is not an evil man who attains salvation, nor a pious man who becomes corrupt. It is the process of his search, the stages in his pilgrimage, which structure the novel *Siddhartha*.

We describe major characters or "actors" in novels as **protagonists** or **antagonists**. Built into those two terms is the Greek word **agon**, meaning "struggle." The *pro*tagonist, from the Greek "proto," meaning "primary or chief," is therefore the "primary struggler." The *ant(i)*agonist struggles **against** someone or something. The possible conflicts are usually cited as man against himself, man against man, man against society, man against nature. Sometimes more than one of these conflicts appears in a story, but usually one is dominant and serves as the structuring device.

A character can be referred to as **stock**, meaning that he exists because the plot demands it. For instance, a Western with a gunman who robs the bank will require a number of **stock** characters: the banker's lovely daughter, the tough but kindhearted barmaid, the cowardly white-shirted citizen who sells out the hero to save his own skin, and the young freckle-faced lad who shoots the bad guy from a second-story hotel window.

Or a character can be a **stereotype**, without individuating characteristics. For instance, a sheriff in a small Southern town; a football player who is all brawn; a librarian clucking over her prized books; the cruel commandant of a POW camp.

Characters often serve as **foils** for other characters, enabling us to see one or more of them better. A classic example is Tom Sawyer, the Romantic foil for Huck Finn's Realism. Or, in Lee's *To Kill a Mockingbird*, Scout as the naive observer of events that her brother Jem, four years older, comes to understand from the perspective of the adult world.

Sometimes characters are **allegorical**, standing for qualities or concepts rather than for actual personages. For instance, Jim Casey (initials "J. C.") in *The Grapes of Wrath* is often regarded as a Christ figure, pure and self-sacrificing in his aims for the migrant workers. Or Kamala, Siddhartha's teacher in the art of love, whose name comes from the tree whose bark is used as a purgative; she purges him of his ascetic ways on his road to self-hood and spiritual fulfillment.

Other characters are fully three-dimensional, "rounded," "mimetic" of humans in all their virtue, vice, hope, despair, strength and weakness. This verisimilitude aids the author in creating characters who are credible and plausible, without being dully predictable and mundane.

The interplay of plot and characters determines in large part the **theme** of a work, the **why?**. First of all, we must distinguish between a mere topic and a genuine theme or thesis; and then between a theme and contributing *motifs*. A **topic** is a phrase, such as "man's inhumanity to man"; or "the fickle nature of fate." A **theme**, however, turns a phrase into a statement: "Man's inhumanity to man is barely concealed by 'civilization'." Or "Man is a helpless pawn, at the mercy of fickle fate." Many writers may deal with the same topic, such as the complex nature of true love; but their themes may vary widely, from "True love will always win out in the end" to "Not even true love can survive the cruel ironies of fate."

To illustrate the relationship between plot, character, and theme, let's examine two familiar fairy tales. In "The Ugly Duckling," the structuring story line is "Once upon a time there was an ugly duckling, who in turn became a beautiful swan." In this case, the duckling did nothing to merit either his ugliness nor his eventual transformation; but he did not curse fate. He only wept and waited, lonely and outcast. And when he became beautiful, he did not gloat; he eagerly joined the other members of his flock, who greatly admired him. Theme: "Good things come to him who waits," or "Life is unfair—you don't get what you deserve, nor deserve what you get"? What happens to the theme if the ugly duckling remains an ugly duckling: "Some guys just never get a break"?

Especially rewarding to examine for the interdependence of plot and theme is "Cinderella": "Once upon a time, a lovely, sweet-natured young girl was forced to labor and serve her ugly and ungrateful stepmother and two stepsisters. But thanks to her fairy godmother, Cinderella and the Prince marry, and live happily ever after."

We could change events (plot elements) at any point, but let's take the penultimate scene where the Prince's men come to the door with the single glass slipper. Cinderella has been shut away so that she is not present when the other women in the house try on the slipper. Suppose that the stepmother or either of the two stepsisters tries on the slipper—and it fits! Cinderella is in the back room doing the laundry, and her family waltzes out the door to the palace and she doesn't even get an invitation to the wedding. And imagine the Prince's dismay when the ugly, one-slippered lady lifts her wedding veil for the consummating kiss! Theme: "There is no justice in the world, for those of low or high station"; or "Virtue is not its own reward"?

Or let's say that during the slipper-test scene, the stepsisters, stepmother, and finally Cinderella all try on the shoe, but to no avail. And then in sashays the

Fairy Godmother, who gives them all a knowing smirk, puts out her slipper-sized foot and cackles hysterically, like the mechanical witch in the penny arcade. Theme: "You can't trust anybody these days"; or, a favorite statement of theme, "Appearances can be deceiving." The link between plot and theme is very strong, indeed.

Skilled writers often employ **motifs** to help unify their works. A motif is a detail or element of the story which is repeated throughout, and which may even become symbolic. Television shows are ready examples of the use of motifs. A medical show, with many scenes alternately set in the hospital waiting room and operating room, uses elements such as the pacing, anxious parent or loved one, the gradually filling ashtray, the large wall clock whose hands melt from one hour to another. And in the operating room, the half-masked surgeon whose brow is frequently mopped by the nurse; the gloved hand open-palmed to receive scalpel, sponge, and so on; the various oscilloscopes giving read-outs of the patient's very fragile condition; the expanding and collapsing bladder manifesting that the patient is indeed breathing; and, again, the wall clock, assuring us that this procedure is taking forever. These are all **motifs**, details which in concert help convince the reader that this story occurs in a hospital, and that the mood is pretty tense, that the medical team is doing all it can, and that Mom and Dad will be there when Junior or Sissy wakes up.

But motifs can become symbolic. The oscilloscope line quits blipping, levels out, and gives off the ominous hum. And the doctor's gloved hand sets down the scalpel and shuts off the oscilloscope. In the waiting room, Dad crushes the empty cigarette pack; Mom quits pacing and sinks into the sofa. The door to the waiting room swings shut silently behind the retreating doctor. All these elements signal "It's over, finished."

This example is very crude and mechanical, but motifs in the hands of a skillful writer are valuable devices. And in isolation, and often magnified, a single motif can become a controlling image with great significance. For instance, Emma Bovary's shoes signify her obsession with material things; and when her delicate slippers become soiled as she crosses the dewy grass to meet her lover, we sense the impurity of her act as well as its futility. Or when wise Piggy, in *Lord of the Flies,* is reduced to one lens in his specs, and finally to no specs at all, we see the loss of insight and wisdom on the island, and chaos follows.

Setting is the **where?** element of the story. But setting is also the **when?** element: time of day, time of year, time period or year; it is the dramatic moment, the precise intersection of time and space when this story is being told. Setting is also the atmosphere: positive or negative ambiance, calm, chaotic, Gothic, Romantic. The question for the reader to answer is whether the setting is ultimately essential to the plot/theme, or whether it is incidental; i.e., could this story/theme have been told successfully in another time and/or place? For instance, could the theme in *Lord of the Flies* be made manifest if the boys were not on an island?

Could they have been isolated in some other place? Does it matter whether the "war" that they are fleeing is WWII or WWIII or some other conflict, in terms of the theme?

It is hoped that the student will see that the four elements of plot, character, theme, and setting are intertwined and, to a great extent, interdependent. A work must really be read as a whole, rather than dissected and analyzed in discrete segments.

The final question, **how?**, relates to an author's style. Style involves language (word choice), syntax (word order, sentence type and length), the balance between narration and dialogue, the choice of narrative voice (first person participant, third person with limited omniscience), use of descriptive passages, and other aspects of the actual words on the page which are basically irrelevant to the first four elements (plot, character, theme, and setting). Stylistic differences are fairly easy to spot among such diverse writers as Jane Austen, whose style is—to today's reader—very formal and mannered; Mark Twain, whose style is very casual and colloquial; William Faulkner, whose prose often spins on without punctuation or paragraphs far longer than the reader can hold either the thought or his breath; and Ernest Hemingway, whose dense but spare, pared-down style has earned the epithet, "Less is more."

The AP Exam never asks for specific information about a novel, such as "What was Emma Bovary's husband's first name?" The essay questions on novels are generally of two types: those which give the student a brief excerpt from a specific work (which may or may not be identified) and ask for a stylistic analysis of some sort; or those which pose a general question or problem and ask the student to focus on one or more novels in order to discuss the question. In the first instance, having read the novel may help the student analyze the style, tone, or other related elements of the excerpt; but the student's understanding of those elements is more important than his familiarity with the novel. In the second instance, the student's familiarity with many novels will certainly give him more options as he formulates his answer to the general question. But since this type of question *always* allows the student to select "a work of comparable literary merit," the student is free to go outside the list provided on the exam and use a work with which he feels more comfortable. The problem, of course, is that the student's choice may not lend itself as well to the essay question as those works suggested on the exam.

A typical AP essay exam question begins with a broad concept—such as the nature of good and evil, the manipulation of time, the struggle for power or domination of one group over another, and so on. Students are then asked to select a work and discuss the concept as it appears in or applies to the work, with special attention to some particular aspect—such as the author's attitude toward the opposing forces of good and evil; the effect of the manipulation of time on the reader's understanding of the characters, theme, or other aspect of the novel;

or the means by which one group attempts to exert and achieve control over the other, and how that relates to theme.

Let's use the following as a sample question in order to explore possible essay responses: "Many works use major images as emblems or symbols of a **character's** virtue, vice, or the transformation from one to the other. In a well-organized essay, discuss how the author employs this technique of characterization, and show how the images relate to the central theme of the work."

Assuming that the student feels comfortable with several of the titles offered as options, let's say that he narrows his choice to *Heart of Darkness*. He must deal with three aspects of the question: the emblems or images; the author's use of these emblems to develop his characters; and the relationship of the emblems to the novel's central theme. In *Heart of Darkness*, he might identify these three items as emblematic: the oil sketch Kurtz painted of the draped, blindfolded woman holding the torch against the darkness; the dirty, dog-eared, "ciphered," white-stitched book on seamanship Marlow finds and returns to the Russian; and Kurtz's report on "The Suppression of Savage Customs."

With the painting, Conrad gives the reader insight into the character not only of Kurtz, but of the British colonialists as well. Numerous quotes throughout the book depict the role of the white ivory traders as "beacons of light" and "emissaries of light" and "bringing light to the dark heart" of Africa. The woman in the painting is carrying a torch through the darkness, like the British colonialists. But her blindfold renders her torch useless, and suggests further that the British are "blind" at their own task, that there is a certain futility in their efforts and purpose.

The Russian's book on seamanship by "Towser? Towsen?" is another emblem of the futility of the British effort, and, by extension, of Kurtz's mission. The book, first of all, is found on land, not at sea. It is useless on the serpentine Congo River. It has, however, been used so much that it has literally fallen apart and been stitched back together—to what end? And the marginalia which Marlow assumes to be code renders the Russian's notations useless to Marlow, just as the book itself is useless as a guide to "doing things right."

And Kurtz's report, which ostensibly is a guide to the British control and salvation of the savages, is marred by Kurtz's scrawled postscript, "Exterminate all the brutes!" thus presenting yet a third emblem of the futility of the British attempts to bring "light" to the "heart of darkness."

These three emblems, presented by the student as characterizing the British ivory traders as blindly endeavoring to achieve the impossible, presume that the novel's theme is broadly set at a level above the individual characters—notably Kurtz. These emblems suggest this novel is about the smugly "civilized" British who insist on imposing their values and lifestyle on people who do not want or need them. The theme relates to the blindness of those who believe their way is the best way, the only way.

But suppose the student thinks the theme more closely relates to individuals than to nations, that the novel is the psychological or spiritual journey of one man—Kurtz? The images or emblems he selects in this case will probably differ. He might well select the image of Kurtz's Intended as Marlow meets her in London, the dappled Harlequin (Russian) Marlow encounters at the Inner Station, and the "magnificent" black savage woman who lives with Kurtz in the jungle.

Although Marlow does not meet the Intended until the very end of the story, she represents Kurtz as he was before he left "civilization," when he still had high ideals and noble "intentions." Dressed in mourning black, she is described as greeting Marlow in a room which grows darker as they speak, until finally only her white forehead glows out of the blackness surrounding them. She is unaware of Kurtz's transformation over the years he has been away from her; she believes him still to be the remarkable and wonderful man he was when he was part of her present world. The room's darkness ironically betokens the blindness and evil of the "civilized" world Kurtz left behind, while her glowing brow suggests the "inextinguishable light of belief and love."

When Marlow meets the Russian, he notes the play of dark and light across the man's face, as well as the colorful mismatched patchwork of the "Harlequin's" clothing. The Russian clearly adores Kurtz, although he acknowledges that atrocities have occurred—even that he himself had been threatened by this man who had "taught [him]... things." Acknowledging the fact that the natives had fired on Marlow's boat as it approached Kurtz's landing, the Russian beckoned them ashore, saying, " It's all right... Come along." The Russian, as emblematic image, represents a perception of Kurtz in transition, aware of Kurtz's flaws, but non-judgmental; Kurtz's remarkable personality still tilts the balance in Kurtz's favor.

Kurtz's black mistress represents the view of Kurtz as totally corrupted by the darkness of the world he has adopted and refused to leave. She is described as "a wild and gorgeous apparition of a woman." Her jewelry and rich adornment suggest the materialism which Kurtz has come to embrace, as opposed to the well-intentioned idealism suggested by the Intended's starkly plain attire. Unflinching in her confrontation with Marlow as representative of the world outside which threatens to steal Kurtz from her, she stretches out her arms after the retreating boat—an image echoed by the other two characters, suggesting their similar devotion to Kurtz, albeit three very different versions of this remarkable man. The shifting lens, from the Intended to the Harlequin to the Mistress, reveals Kurtz's gradual descent into "the horror."

Yet another possible strategy for answering this same question could focus on the use of black and white imagery to characterize various personages in the novel; certainly the major thrust of the second sample answer (above) could be retained, but with the focus altered ever so slightly to emphasize the ironic interplay of black/evil, white/good. The whites in the novel, including the Intended, come to represent a hypocritical and corrupt society, based upon falsehood and deceit. The blacks, including the mistress, represent a society which embodies truth, sincerity, loyalty, and, above all, restraint. Again, the Harlequin straddles the two worlds, without the will or the ability to choose, as Kurtz did.

Given the broad nature of the question, and the range of novels available for application, the student really has a wonderful opportunity to demonstrate his understanding of fiction and his ability to articulate and defend a thesis. And that is what the AP essay exam sets out to verify.

READING SHORT STORIES

The modern short story differs from earlier short fiction such as the parable, fable, and tale, in its emphasis on character development through scenes rather than summary: through *showing* rather than *telling*. Gaining popularity in the 19th century, the short story generally was realistic, presenting detailed accounts of the lives of middle-class personages. This tendency toward realism dictates that the plot be grounded in *probability*, with causality fully in operation. Furthermore, the characters are human with recognizable human motivations, both social and psychological. Setting—time and place—is realistic rather than fantastic. And, as Poe stipulated, the elements of plot, character, setting, style, point of view, and theme all work toward a single *unified* effect.

However, some modern writers have stretched these boundaries and have mixed in elements of nonrealism—such as the supernatural and the fantastic—sometimes switching back and forth between realism and nonrealism, confusing the reader who is expecting conventional fiction. Barth's "Lost in the Funhouse" and Allen's "The Kugelmass Episode" are two stories which are not, strictly speaking, *realistic*. However, if the reader will approach and accept this type of story on its own terms, he will be better able to understand and appreciate them fully.

Unlike the novel, which has time and space to develop characters and interrelationships, the short story must rely on flashes of insight and revelation to develop plot and characters. The "slice of life" in a short story is of necessity much narrower than that in a novel; the time span is much shorter, the focus much tighter. To attempt anything like the panoramic canvas available to the novelist would be to view fireworks through a soda straw: occasionally pretty, but ultimately not very satisfying or enlightening.

The elements of the short story are those of the novel, discussed earlier. However, because of the compression of time and concentration of effect, probably the short story writer's most important decision is **point of view**. A narrator may be *objective*, presenting information without bias or comment. Hemingway frequently uses the objective *third-person* narrator, presenting scenes almost dramatically, i.e., with a great deal of dialogue and very little narrative, none of which directly reveals the thoughts or feelings of the characters. The third-person narrator may, however, be less objective in his presentation, directly revealing the thoughts and feelings, of one or more of the characters, as Chopin does in "The Story of an Hour." We say that such a narrator is fully or partially *omniscient*, depending on how complete his knowledge is of the characters' psychological and emotional makeup. The least objective narrator is the *first-person* narrator, who presents information from the perspective of a single character who is a participant in the action. Such a narrative choice allows the author to present the discrepancies between the writer's/reader's perceptions and those of the narrator.

One reason the choice of narrator, the point of view from which to tell the story, is immensely important in a short story is that the narrator reveals character and event in ways which affect our understanding of theme. For instance, in Faulkner's "A Rose for Emily," the unnamed narrator who seems to be a townsperson recounts the story out of chronological order, juxtaposing events whose causality and significance are uncertain. The narrator withholds information which would explain events being presented, letting the reader puzzle over Emily Grierson's motivations, a device common in detective fiction. In fact, the narrator presents contradictory information, making the reader alternately pity and resent the spinster. When we examine the imagery and conclude that Miss Emily and her house represent the decay and decadence of the Old South which resisted the invasion of "progress" from the North, we see the importance of setting and symbol in relation to theme.

Similarly, in Mansfield's "Bliss," the abundant description of setting creates the controlling image of the lovely pear tree. But this symbol of fecundity becomes ironic when Bertha Young belatedly feels sincere and overwhelming desire for her husband. The third-person narrator's omniscience is limited to Bertha's thoughts and feelings; otherwise we would have seen her husband's infidelity with Miss Fulton.

In O'Connor's "Good Country People," the narrator is broadly omniscient, but the reader is still taken by surprise at the cruelty of the Bible salesman who seduces Joy-Hulga. That he steals her artificial leg is perhaps poetic justice, since she (with her numerous degrees) had fully intended to seduce him ("just good country people"). The story's title, the characters' names—Hopewell, Freeman, Joy; the salesman's professed Christianity, the Bibles hollowed out to hold whiskey and condoms, add to the irony of Mrs. Freeman's final comment on the young man: "Some can't be that simple... I know I never could."

The *initiation story* frequently employs the first-person narrator. To demonstrate the subtle differences which can occur in stories which ostensibly have the same point of view and general theme, let's look at three: "A Christmas Memory" (Capote), "Araby" (Joyce), and "A & P" (Updike).

Early in "A Christmas Memory," Capote's narrator identifies himself:

> The person to whom she is speaking is myself. I am seven; she is sixty-something. We are cousins, very distant ones, and we have lived together—well, as long as I can remember. Other people inhabit the house, relatives; and though they have power over us, and frequently make us cry, we are not, on the whole, too much aware of them. We are each other's best friend. She calls me Buddy, in memory of a boy who was formerly her best friend. The other Buddy died in the 1880's, when she was still a child. She is still a child.

Buddy and his cousin, who is called only "my friend," save their meager earnings throughout the year in order to make fruitcakes at Christmas to give mainly to "persons we've met maybe once, perhaps not at all... Like President Roosevelt.... Or Abner Packer, the driver of the six o'clock bus from Mobile, who exchanges waves with us everyday...." Their gifts to one another each year are always handmade, often duplicates of the year before, like the kites they present on what was to be their last Christmas together.

Away at boarding school, when Buddy receives word of his friend's death, it "merely confirms a piece of news some secret vein had already received, severing from me an irreplaceable part of myself, letting it loose like a kite on a broken string. That is why, walking across a school campus on this particular December morning, I keep searching the sky. As if I expected to see, rather like hearts, a lost pair of kites hurrying toward heaven."

Buddy's characterizations of his friend are also self-revelatory. He and she are peers, equals, despite their vast age difference. They are both totally unselfish, joying in the simple activities mandated by their economic circumstances. They are both "children."

The story is told in present tense, making the memories from the first paragraphs seem as "real" and immediate as those from many years later. And Buddy's responses from the early years ("Well, I'm disappointed. Who wouldn't be? With socks, a Sunday school shirt, some handkerchiefs, a hand-me-down sweater and a year's subscription to a religious magazine for children. *The Little Shepherd*. It makes me boil. It really does.") are as true to his seven-year-old's perspective, as are those when he, much older, has left home ("I have a new home too. But it doesn't count. Home is where my friend is, and there I never go.").

The youthful narrator in "A & P" also uses present tense, but not consistently, which gives his narrative a very colloquial, even unschooled flavor. Like Buddy, Sammy identifies himself in the opening paragraph: "In walks these three girls in nothing but bathing suits. I'm in the third checkout slot, with my back to the door, so I don't see them until they're over by the bread." And later, "Stokesie's married, with two babies chalked up on his fuselage already, but as far as I can tell that's the only difference. He's twenty-two, and I was nineteen this April." The girls incur the wrath of the store manager, who scolds them for their inappropriate dress. And Sammy, in his adolescent idealism, quits on the spot; although he realizes that he does not want to "do this" to his parents, he tells us "... it seems to me that once you begin a gesture it's fatal not to go through with it." But his *beau geste* is ill-spent: "I look around for my girls, but they're gone, of course.... I could see Lengel in my place in the slot, checking the sheep through. His face was dark gray and his back stiff, as if he'd just had an injection of iron, and my stomach kind of fell as I felt how hard the world was going to be to me hereafter."

Like Buddy, Sammy tells his story from a perch not too distant from the events he recounts. Both narrators still feel the immediacy of their rites of passage very strongly. Buddy, however, reveals himself to be a more admirable character, perhaps because his story occurs mainly when he is seven—children tend not to be reckless in the way that Sammy is. Sammy was performing for an audience, doing things he knew would cause pain to himself and his family, for the sake of those three girls who never gave him the slightest encouragement and whom he would probably never even see again.

In "Araby," the unnamed narrator tells of a boyhood crush he had on the older sister of one of his chums: "I thought little of the future. I did not know whether I would ever speak to her or not or, if I spoke to her, how I could tell her of my confused adoration. But my body was like a harp and her words and gestures were like fingers running upon the wires." She asks the boy if he is going to Araby, a "splendid bazaar," and reveals that she cannot. He promises to go himself and bring her something. But his uncle's late homecoming delays the boy's excursion until the bazaar is nearly closed for the night, and he is unable to find an appropriate gift. Forlornly, "I turned away slowly and walked down the middle of the bazaar…. Gazing up into the darkness I saw myself as a creature driven and derided by vanity; and my eyes burned with anguish and anger." This narrator is recounting his story from much further away than either Buddy or Sammy tells his own. The narrator of "Araby" has the perspective of an adult, looking back at a very important event in his boyhood. His "voice" reflects wisdom born of experience. The incident was very painful then; but its memory, while poignant, is no longer devastating. Like Sammy, this narrator sees the dichotomy between his adolescent idealism and the mundane reality of "romance." However, the difference is in the narrator's ability to turn the light on himself; Sammy is still so close to the incident that he very likely would whip off his checker's apron again if the girls returned to the A & P. The "Araby" narrator has "mellowed," and can see the futility—and the necessity—of adolescent love.

Here, then, is a possible exam question dealing with point of view in the short story, drawing on the similarities and differences we have noted among the three foregoing works: "Using two or more stories, show how the narrator reveals his own values, virtues, and vices as well as those of the other characters in the story." This question might draw more on "A Christmas Memory" and especially "A & P" than on "Araby," if the student emphasized vices more than *virtues*. However, the broad scope of the question would allow, and even encourage, details from all three stories from the three perspectives suggested.

Another possible question: "Using two or more stories, compare and contrast the ways in which the narrator's relationships with other characters have an impact on the theme of the story." The student would need first to discuss the narrator's point of view in each story, then to deal with the characters with whom the narrator interacts (in this case, all female), and finally to state each story's theme, noting how the theme depends upon the narrator's actions and insights.

The student might do well to work with "A Christmas Memory" and "Araby," both of which have narrators who have looked back with maturity on intense relationships, albeit relationships of two very different kinds (friendship, romantic love). However, the student might prefer to deal with "A & P" and "Araby," both of which deal with romantic love with distant or "unattainable" females, but whose narrators behave very differently. Sammy's *beau geste* is costly, and he looks ahead to the day when he will pay the price of his recklessness. The boy in "Araby" could not control the circumstances of his visit to the bazaar, so he is not to blame for his failure to achieve his quest. But his disillusionment is very similar to Sammy's. The major difference is that the "Araby" narrator is looking *backward* on his lesson; Sammy is looking *ahead*.

Answering AP exam questions on short stories is much the same as addressing questions on novels. Sometimes, however, a section of a story is presented in the objective section; the student must answer multiple-choice items which require close reading for such elements as tone, style, atmosphere, and inference. Knowing the story beforehand may help the student, but the ability to analyze is the major component of this type of exam item.

In the essay portion, the student is likely to meet two kinds of questions: 1) an excerpt from one or more stories, which he is asked to discuss from a particular viewpoint (such as style, characterization, etc.); and 2) an open-ended essay question which allows the student to select, either from a list or from his own reading, one or more short stories with which to support a particular thesis.

Typical questions of the second sort might include the following: "Compare and contrast the treatment of **X** in any two short stories" (**X** could be human relationships, time, women, the generation gap); "Discuss how the author uses setting to enhance theme"; "Show how the author uses irony to reveal character"; "Many stories lead to a final revelation; use a story as an example to show how the author's withholding information influences our understanding of the story"; "Some authors employ physical movement—home, away, back home, or a temporary isolation as a symbol of spiritual, emotional, or psychological growth or development. Select a short story and show how the author has used a journey or other physical movement to represent such growth."

Many collections of short stories organize works by theme (war, initiation), by element (plot, setting, character), by approach (realism, romanticism), or by some other principle. The student can learn much by reading short stories by "category," noting similarities and differences. A broad reading background is, as we have noted before, excellent preparation for the AP Literature exam.

READING ESSAYS

Essays fall into four rough categories: **speculative**, **argumentative**, **narrative**, and **expository**. Depending on the writer's purpose, his essay will fit more or less into one or these groupings.

The **speculative** essay is so named because, as its Latin root suggests, it *looks* at ideas; explores them rather than explains them. While the speculative essay may be said to be *meditative*, it often makes one or more points. But the thesis may not be as obvious or clear-cut as that in an expository or argumentative essay. The writer deals with ideas in an associative manner, playing with ideas in a looser structure than he would in an expository or argumentative essay. This "flow" may even produce *intercalary* paragraphs, which present alternately a narrative of sorts and thoughtful responses to the events being recounted, as in White's "The Ring of Time."

The purposes of the **argumentative** essay, on the other hand, are always clear: to present a point and provide evidence, which may be factual or anecdotal, and to support it. The structure is usually very formal, as in a debate, with counterpositions and counterarguments. Whatever the organizational pattern, the writer's intent in an argumentative essay is to persuade his reader of the validity of some claim, as Bacon does in "Of Love."

Narrative and **expository** essays have elements of both the speculative and argumentative modes. The narrative essay may recount an incident or a series of incidents and is almost always autobiographical, in order to make a point, as in Orwell's "Shooting an Elephant." The informality of the storytelling makes the narrative essay less insistent than the argumentative essay, but more directed than the speculative essay.

Students are probably most familiar with the **expository** essay, the primary purpose of which is to explain and clarify ideas. While the expository essay may have narrative elements, that aspect is minor and subservient to that of explanation. Furthermore, while nearly all essays have some element of persuasion, argumentation is incidental in the expository essay. In any event, the four categories—speculative, argumentative, narrative, and expository—are neither exhaustive nor mutually exclusive.

As non-fiction, essays have a different set of elements from novels and short stories: **voice**, **style**, **structure**, and **thought**.

Voice in non-fiction is similar to the narrator's tone in fiction; but the major difference is in who is "speaking." In fiction, the author is not the speaker—the **narrator** is the speaker. Students sometimes have difficulty with this distinction, but it is necessary if we are to preserve the integrity of the fictive "story." In an essay, however, the author speaks directly to the reader, even if he is presenting ideas which he may not actually espouse personally—as in a satire. This direct-ness creates the writer's **tone**, his attitude toward his subject.

Style in non-fiction derives from the same elements as style in fiction: word choice, syntax, balance between dialogue and narration, voice, use of descrip-tion—those things specifically related to words on the page. Generally speaking, an argumentative essay will be written in a more formal style than will a narrative essay, and a meditative essay will be less formal than an expository essay. But such generalizations are only descriptive, not prescriptive.

Structure and **thought**, the final elements of essays, are so intertwined as to be inextricable. In our discussion of the interdependence of plot and theme, we must be aware that to change the structure of an essay will alter its meaning. For instance, in White's "The Ring of Time," to abandon the *intercalary* paragraph organization, separating the paragraphs which narrate the scenes with the young circus rider from those which reflect on the circularity and linearity of time, would alter our understanding of the essay's thesis. Writers signal structural shifts with alterations in focus, as well as with visual clues (spacing), verbal clues—(*but, therefore, however*), or shifts in the kind of information being pre-sented (personal, scientific, etc).

Thought is perhaps the single element which most distinguishes non-fiction from fiction. The essayist chooses his form not to tell a story but to present an idea. Whether he chooses the speculative, narrative, argumentative, or expository format, the essayist has something on his mind that he wants to convey to his readers. And it is this idea which we are after when we analyze his essay.

Often anthologized is Orwell's "Shooting an Elephant," a narrative essay re-counting the writer's (presumably) experience in Burma as an officer of the British law that ruled the poverty-ridden people of a small town. Orwell begins with two paragraphs which explain that, as a white European authority figure, he was subjected to taunts and abuse by the natives. Ironically, he sympathized with the Burmese and harbored fairly strong anti-British feelings, regarding the im-perialists as the oppressors rather than the saviors. He tells us that he felt caught, trapped between his position of authority which he himself resented, and the hatred of those he was required to oversee.

The body of the essay—some eleven paragraphs—relates the incident with an otherwise tame elephant gone "must" which had brought chaos and destruction to the village. Only occasionally does Orwell interrupt the narrative to reveal his reactions directly, but his descriptions of the Burmese are sympathetically drawn. The language is heavily connotative, revealing the helplessness of the villagers against both the elephant and the miserable circumstances of their lives.

Orwell recounts how, having sent for an elephant gun, he found that he was compelled to shoot the animal, even though its destruction was by now unwarranted and even ill-advised, given the value of the elephant to the village. But the people expected it, demanded it; the white man realized that he did not have dominion over these people of color after all. They were in charge, not he.

To make matters worse, Orwell bungles the "murder" of the beast, which takes half an hour to die in great agony. And in the aftermath of discussions of the rightness or wrongness of his action, Orwell wonders if anyone realizes he killed the elephant only to save face. It is the final sentence of the final paragraph which directly reveals the author's feelings, although he has made numerous indirect references to them throughout the essay. Coupled with the opening paragraphs, this conclusion presents British imperialism of the period in a very negative light: "the unable doing the unnecessary to the ungrateful."

Having discovered Orwell's main idea, we must look at the other elements (voice, style, structure) to see *how* he communicates it to the reader. The voice of the first-person narrative is fairly formal, yet remarkably candid, using connotation to color our perception of the events. Orwell's narrative has many complex sentences, with vivid descriptive phrases in series, drawing our eye along the landscape and through the crowds as he ponders his next move. Structurally, the essay first presents a premise about British imperialism, then moves to a gripping account of the officer's reluctant shooting of the elephant; and ends with an admission of his own culpability as an agent of the institution he detests. Orwell frequently signals shifts between his role as officer and his responses as a humane personage with *but*, or with dashes to set off his responses to the events he is recounting.

The AP exam is more likely to present part or all of an essay, and then ask either objective (multiple-choice) questions about it or ask the student to write an essay on some aspect of the essay, such as style or language. The major difference between questions on essays and those on novels or short stories is that the essay (or part of it) will actually be in front of the student as he answers the items.

If "Shooting an Elephant" were presented on the AP exam, a logical essay topic would be: "Show how the language reveals the discrepancy between the writer's official role and his personal feelings." Or perhaps, depending on what portion of the essay were excerpted, "Show how the attitudes of the Burmese people are revealed by the writer's description of their actions, and demonstrate how those attitudes lead to the writer's final statement."

Sometimes the AP exam will present portions of two essays and ask the students to compare and/or contrast them with regard to some specific element. For instance, Dillard's "Living Like Weasels" uses her confrontation with a weasel as a springboard to a Thoreau-like meditation on "how to live." Toth, in "In Search of Quiet Places" explores the same idea. In White's essay "The Ring of Time," he asserts that time, while circular, is also linear, altering those touched by it: "… but she was too young to know that time does not really move in a circle at all." However, in another of White's essays, "Once More to the Lake," he seems to assert that "there had been no years" between his boyhood at the lake and that of his son: "I began to sustain the illusion that he was I, and therefore, by simple transposition, that I was my father.... I seemed to be living a dual existence.... Everywhere we went I had trouble making out which was I, the one walking at my side, the one walking in my pants." And Toth, in "Birthday Balloons," explores the pain and futility of trying to relive one's childhood through one's children: "Fragile and evanescent, [birthday balloons] will also remind me that celebrations do not last, so we must catch what pleasures we can as they waft by. Finally, I will try not to fill them so full with [my daughter's] and my hopes that they burst before everyone can take one home."

The AP essay exam could conceivably take any work listed above and ask the student to discuss how the writer's attitude toward *time* is revealed; to compare/contrast the attitudes toward time in any pair of essays; to look at the writers' use of language in any pair of essays and discuss the resulting *voices*. The most important thing, as always, is to read and reread the question carefully; the next most important thing is to read and reread the work(s) to be discussed. Try to find the *thought* which the writer means to communicate; then analyze for *voice*, *style*, and *structure*.

READING SATIRE

Satire, is a *mode* which may be employed by writers of various genres: poetry, drama, fiction, non-fiction. It is more a perspective than a product.

Satire mainly exposes and ridicules, derides and denounces vice, folly, evil, stupidity, as these qualities manifest themselves in persons, groups of persons, ideas, institutions, customs, or beliefs. While the satirist has many techniques at his disposal, there are basically only two types of satire: gentle or harsh, depending on the author's intent, his audience, and his methods.

The terms *romanticism*, *realism*, and *naturalism* can help us understand the role of *satire*. Romanticism sees the world idealistically, as perfectible if not perfect. Realism sees the world as it is, with healthy doses of both good and bad. Naturalism sees the world as imperfect, with evil often triumphing over good. The satirist is closer to the naturalist than he is to the romantic or realist, for both the satirist and the naturalist focus on what is wrong with the world, intending to expose the foibles of man and his society. The difference between them lies in their techniques. The naturalist is very direct and does not necessarily employ humor; the satirist is more subtle, and does.

For instance, people plagued with overpopulation and starvation is not, on first glance, material for humor. Many works have treated such conditions with sensitivity, bringing attention to the plight of the world's unfortunate. Steinbeck's *Grapes of Wrath* is such a work. However, Swift's "A Modest Proposal" takes essentially the same circumstances and holds them up for our amused examination. How does the satirist make an un-funny topic humorous? And why would he do so?

The satirist's techniques—his weapons—include **irony**, **parody**, **reversal** or **inversion**, **hyperbole**, **understatement**, **sarcasm**, **wit**, **invective**. By exaggerating characteristics, by saying the opposite of what he means, by using his cleverness to make cutting or even cruel remarks at the expense of his subject, the writer of satire can call the reader's attention to those things he believes are repulsive, despicable, or destructive.

Whether he uses more harsh (Juvenalian) or more gentle (Horatian) satire depends upon the writer's attitude and intent. Is he merely flaunting his clever intellect, playing with words for our amusement or to inflate his own sense of superiority? Is he probing the psychological motivations for the foolish or destructive actions of some person(s)? Is he determined to waken an unenlightened or apathetic audience, moving its members to thought or action? Are the flaws which the satirist is pointing out truly destructive or evil, or are they the faults we would all recognize in ourselves if we glanced in the mirror, not admirable but not really harmful to ourselves or society? Is the author amused, sympathetic, objective, irritated, scornful, bitter, pessimistic, mocking? The reader needs to identify the satirist's purpose and tone. Its subtlety sometimes makes satire a difficult mode to detect and to understand.

Irony is perhaps the satirist's most powerful weapon. The basis of irony is inversion or reversal, doing or saying the opposite or the unexpected. Shakespeare's famous sonnet beginning "My mistress' eyes are nothing like the sun..." is an ironic tribute to the speaker's beloved, who, he finally declares is "as rare/As any she belied with false compare." At the same time, Shakespeare is poking fun at the sonnet form as it was used by his contemporaries—himself included—to extol the virtues of their ladies. By selecting a woman who, by his own description, is physically unattractive in every way imaginable, and using the conventions of the love sonnet to present her many flaws, he has inverted the sonnet tradition. And then by asserting that she compares favorably with any of the other ladies whose poet-lovers have lied about their virtues, he presents us with the unexpected twist. Thus, he satirizes both the love sonnet form and its subject by using irony.

Other notable poetic satires include Koch's "Variations on a Theme by William Carlos Williams," in which he parodies Williams "This is Just to Say." Koch focuses on the simplicity and directness of Williams' imagery and makes the form and ideas seem foolish and trivial. In "Boom!," Nemerov takes issue with a pastor's assertion that modern technology has resulted in a concomitant rise in religious activities and spiritual values. Nemerov catalogues the instant, disposable, and extravagant aspects of Americans' lifestyles, which result in "pray as you go... pilgrims" for whom religion is another convenience, commercial rather than spiritual.

Satire in drama is also common; Wilde's "The Importance of Being Earnest" is wonderfully funny in its constant word play (notably on the name *Ernest*) and its relentless ridiculing of the superficiality which Wilde saw as characteristic of British gentry. Barrie's "The Admirable Crichton" has a similar theme, with the added assertion that it is the "lower" or servant class which is truly superior—again, the ironic reversal so common in satire. Both of these plays are mild in their ridicule; the authors do not expect or desire any change in society or in the viewer. The satire is gentle; the satirists are amused, or perhaps bemused at the society whose foibles they expose.

Classic novels which employ satire include Swift's *Gulliver's Travels* and Voltaire's *Candide*, both of which fairly vigorously attack aspects of the religions, governments, and prevailing intellectual beliefs of their respective societies. A modern novel which uses satire is Heller's *Catch-22*, which is basically an attack on war and the government's bureaucratic bungling of men and materiel, specifically in WWII. But by extension, Heller is also viewing with contempt the unmotivated, illogical, capricious behavior of all institutions which operate by that basic law: "catch-22." Like Swift and Voltaire, Heller is angry. And although his work, like the other two, has humor and wit, exaggeration and irony, his purpose is more than intellectual entertainment for his readers. Heller hopes for reform.

Heller's attack is frontal, his assault direct. Swift had to couch his tale in a fantastic setting with imaginary creatures in order to present his views with impunity. The audience, as well as the times, also affect the satirist's work. If the audience is hostile, the writer must veil his theme; if the audience is indifferent, he must jolt them with bitter and reviling language if he desires change. If he does not fear reprisals, the satirist may take any tone he pleases.

We can see satire in operation in two adaptations of the Biblical story of King Solomon, who settled the dispute between two mothers regarding an infant: Cut the baby in two and divide it between you, he told them. The rightful mother protested, and was promptly awarded the child. The story is meant to attest to the King's wisdom and understanding of parental love, in this case.

However, Twain's Huck Finn has some difficulty persuading runaway slave Jim that Solomon was wise. Jim insists that Solomon, having fathered "'bout five million chillen," was "waseful.... *He* as soon chop a chile in two as a cat. Dey's plenty mo'. A chile er two, mo' er less, warn't no consekens to Solermun, dad fetch him!" Twain is ridiculing not only Jim's ingenuousness, as he does throughout the novel; he is also deflating time-honored beliefs about the Bible and its traditional heroes, as he earlier does with the account of Moses and the "bulrushers." While Twain's tone is fairly mild, his intent shows through as serious; Twain was disgusted with traditional Christianity and its hypocritical followers, as we see later in *Huck Finn* when young Buck Grangerford is murdered in the feud with the Shepherdsons: "I wished I hadn't ever come ashore that night to see such things."

A second satiric variation on the Solomon theme appears in Asprin's *Myth Adventures*, in the volume *Hit or Myth*. Skeebe, the narrator, realizes that he, as King pro-tem, must render a decision regarding the ownership of a cat. Hoping to inspire them to compromise, he decrees that they divide the cat between them: "Instead they thanked me for my wisdom, shook hands, and left smiling, presumably to carve up their cat." He concludes that many of the citizens of this realm "don't have both oars in the water," a conclusion very like Huck's: "I never see such a nigger. If he got a notion in his head once, there warn't no getting it out again." The citizens' unthinking acceptance of the infallibility of authority is as laughable as Jim's out-of-hand rejection of Solomon's wisdom because no wise man would "want to live in the mids' er sich a blim-blammin' all de time" as would prevail in the harem with the King's "million wives."

Questions on the AP exam regarding satire may appear in the objective sections over specific excerpts, but more often they appear as essay topics dealing with sections of poetry, fiction, or non-fiction. Students are asked to *show how* the author uses satire to enhance his theme, or to *show how* the author's rhetorical devices help convey the satiric tone, or to deduce the author's intended audience, judging from the satiric tone of the work. In any case, the student's ability to perceive that the writer is using satire and to identify his techniques and evaluate their effectiveness is the basis of AP exam items on satire.

Let's look at an excerpt from a Wodehouse essay, "Do Thrillers Need Heroines?" in which the author argues that females do not contribute to the plot of thrillers and only cause problems for the villains, who seem unable to dispatch the heroines with anything like intelligence and efficiency properly.

"For, though beautiful, with large grey eyes and hair the colour of ripe corn, the heroine of the thriller is almost never a very intelligent girl. Indeed, it would scarcely be overstating it to say that her mentality is that of a cockroach—and not an ordinary cockroach, at that, but one which has been dropped on its head as a baby. She may have escaped death a dozen times. She may know perfectly well that the notorious Blackbird Gang is after her to secure the papers. The police may have warned her on no account to stir outside her house. But when a messenger calls at half-past two in the morning with an unsigned note saying 'Come at once,' she just snatches her hat and goes. The messenger is a one-eyed Chinaman with a pock-marked face and an evil grin, so she trusts him immediately and, having accompanied him to the closed car with steel shutters over the windows, bowls off in it to the ruined cottage in the swamp. And when the hero, at great risk and inconvenience to himself, comes to rescue her, she will have nothing to do with him because she has been told by a mulatto with half a nose that it was he who murdered her brother Jim." (*The English Tradition, Non-fiction*, MacMillan, 1968, p. 404).

The question: "Discuss the techniques by which the author reveals his tone and purpose in this excerpt from 'Do Thrillers Need Heroines?'" The student should note the author's use of exaggeration ("... her mentality is that of a cockroach... which has been dropped on its head as a baby"), ironic reversal ("... so she trusts him immediately...."), parody ("... a one-eyed Chinaman with a pock-marked face and an evil grin,... a mulatto with half a nose..."), understatement ("... the heroine of the thriller is almost never a very intelligent girl"), and sarcasm ("... she will have nothing to do with him because she has been told... that it was he who murdered her brother Jim").

The writer's tone is mock-serious; while the issue in and of itself is not very important or profound, Wodehouse does have a point about the apparent stupidity of heroines with "large grey eyes and hair the colour of ripe corn." He is being clever and witty for our entertainment; he is ridiculing the institution of detective fiction and its characters with no expectation that anything will come of his revelations. Judging from the excerpt only, the student would conclude that Wodehouse's answer to the question posed in his title is a resounding "No!"

Only the final sentence of the paragraph hints at the author's later point, that the hero is "a broken reed" who has "let us down too often, and forfeited our confidence" (p. 405). The fact that the heroine "will have nothing to do with him" suggests that he will be ineffectual in his task, her rescue. The student cannot guess that later Wodehouse will in fact assert that "the best way of disposing of a girl with hair the colour of ripe corn is to hit the hair as hard as possible with a bit of gas-pipe" (p. 407). However, he laments, villains must be schooled in purging thrillers of heroines, although they seem to do fine against members of their own sex.

Thus, the excerpt gives a false rendering of the essay's totality. The student, however, should stick to the section provided, which reveals a gently mocking attitude toward the typical heroines in thrillers.

Being alert for irony, sarcasm, parody, inversions, hyperbole, and the other techniques of satire will help the student understand the writer's tone and intent. Satire is a very sophisticated literary device, most often directed at pointing out the difference between the way things are and how they ought to be. The satirist depends upon our ability to see the humor in the weaknesses which he reveals in those things we cherish.

CHAPTER 2

POETRY

Opening a book to study for an examination is perhaps the worst occasion on which to read poetry, or about poetry, because above all, poetry should be enjoyed; it is definitely "reading for pleasure." This last phrase seems to have developed recently to describe the reading we do other than for information or for study. Perhaps you personally would not choose poetry as pleasure reading because of the bad name poetry has received over the years. Some students regard the "old" poetry such as Donne's or Shelley's as effete (for "wimps" and "nerds" only, in current language), or modern poetry as too difficult or weird. It is hard to imagine that poetry was the "current language" for students growing up in the Elizabethan or Romantic eras. Whereas in our world information can be retrieved in a nanosecond, in those worlds time was plentiful to sit down, clear the mind and let poetry take over. Very often the meaning of a poem does not come across in a nanosecond and for the modern student this proves very frustrating. Sometimes it takes years for a poem to take on meaning—the reader simply knows that the poem sounds good and it provokes an emotional response that cannot be explained. With time, more emotional experience, more reading of similar experiences, more life, the reader comes to a meaning of that poem that satisfies for the time being. In a few more years that poem may take on a whole new meaning.

This is all very well for reading for pleasure but you are now called upon, in your present experience, to learn poetry for an important examination. Perhaps the first step in the learning process is to answer the question, "Why do people write poetry?" An easy answer is that they wish to convey an experience, an emotion, an insight, or an observation in a startling or satisfying way, one that remains in the memory for years. But why not use a straightforward sentence or paragraph? Why wrap up that valuable insight in fancy words, rhyme, paradox, meter, allusion, symbolism and all the other seeming mumbo-jumbo that explicators of poetry use? Why not just come right out and say it like "normal people" do? An easy answer to these questions is that poetry is not a vehicle for conveying meaning alone. Gerard Manley Hopkins, one of the great innovators of rhythm in poetry, claimed that poetry should be "heard for its own sake and interest even over and above its interest or meaning." Poetry provides intellectual stimulus of course, one of the best ways of studying a poem is to consider it a jigsaw puzzle presented to you whole, an integral work of art, which can be taken apart piece by piece (word by word), analyzed scientifically, labelled, and put back together again into a whole, and then the meaning is complete. But people write poetry to convey more than meaning.

T.S. Eliot maintained that the meaning of the poem existed purely to distract us "while the poem did its work." One interpretation of a poem's "work" is that it changes us in some way. We see the world in a new way because of the way the poet has seen it and told us about it. Maybe one of the reasons people write poetry is to encourage us to *see* things in the first place. Simple things like daffodils take on a whole new aspect when we read the way Wordsworth saw them. Why did Wordsworth write that poem? His sister had written an excellent account of the scene in her journal. Wordsworth not only evokes nature as we have never seen it before, alive, joyous, exuberant, he shows nature's healing powers, its restorative quality as the scene flashes "upon that inward eye/Which is the bliss of solitude." Bent over your books studying, how many times has a similar quality of nature's power in the memory come to you? Maybe for you a summer beach scene rather than daffodils by the lake is more meaningful, but the poet captures a moment that we have all experienced. The poet's magic is to make that moment new again.

If poets enhance our power of sight they also awaken the other senses as powerfully. We can hear Emily Dickinson's snake in the repeated "s" sound of the lines:

His notice sudden is—
The Grass divides as with a Comb—
A spotted shaft is seen—

and because of the very present sense of sound, we experience the indrawn gasp of breath of fear when the snake appears. We can touch the little chimney sweep's hair "that curled like a lamb's back" in William Blake's poetry and because of that tactile sense we are even more shocked to read that the child's hair is all shaved off so that the soot will not spoil its whiteness. We can smell the poison gas as Wilfred Owen's soldiers fumble with their gas masks; we can taste the blood gurgling in the poisoned lungs.

Poets write, then, to awaken the senses. They have crucial ideas but the words they use are often more important than the meaning. More important still than ideas and sense awakening is the poet's appeal to the emotions. And it is precisely this area that disturbs a number of students. Our modern society tends to block out emotions—we need reviews to tell us if we enjoyed a film, a critic's praise to see if a play or novel is worth our time. We hesitate to laugh at something in case it is not the "in" thing to do. We certainly do not cry—at least in front of others. Poets write to overcome that blocking (very often it is their own blocking of emotion they seek to alleviate), but that is not to say that poetry immediately sets us laughing, crying, loving, hating. The important fact about the emotional release in poetry is that poets help us explore our own emotions, sometimes by shocking us, sometimes by drawing attention to balance and pattern, sometimes by cautioning us to move carefully in this inner world.

Poets tell us nothing really new. They tell us old truths about human emotions that we begin to restructure anew, to reread our experiences in light of theirs, to reevaluate our world view. Whereas a car manual helps us understand the workings of a particular vehicle, a poem helps us understand the inner workings of human beings. Poets frequently write to help their emotional life—the writing then becomes cathartic, purging or cleansing the inner life, feeding that part of us that separates us from the animal. Many poets might paraphrase Byron, who claimed that he had to write or go mad. Writer and reader of poetry enter into a collusion, each helping the other to find significance in the human world, to find safety in a seemingly alien world.

This last point brings any reader of poetry to ask the next question: Why read poetry? One might contend that a good drama, novel or short story might provide the same emotional experience. But a poem is much more accessible. Apart from the fact that poems are shorter than other genres, there is a unique directness to them which hinges purely on language. Poets can say in one or two lines what may take novelists and playwrights entire works to express. For example, Keats' lines—

Beauty is truth, truth beauty,—that is all
Ye know on earth, and all ye need to know—

studied, pondered, open to each reader's interpretations, linger in the memory with more emphasis than George Eliot's *Middlemarch*, or Ibsen's *The Wild Duck*, which endeavor to make the same point.

In your reading of poems remember that poetry is perhaps the oldest art and yet surrounds us without our even realizing it. Listeners thrilled to Homer's poetry; tribes chanted invocations to their gods; today we listen to pop-song lyrics and find ourselves, sometimes despite ourselves, repeating certain rhythmic lines. Advertisements we chuckle over or say we hate have a way of repeating themselves as we use the catchy phrase or snappy repetition. Both lyricists and advertisers cleverly use language, playing on the reader's/listener's/watcher's ability to pick up on a repeated sound or engaging rhythm or inner rhyme. Think of a time as a child when you thoroughly enjoyed poetry: nursery rhymes, ball-game rhythms, jump-rope patterns. Probably you had no idea of the meaning of the words ("Little Miss Muffet sat on a tuffet..." a tuffet?!) but you responded to the sound, the pattern. As adults we read poetry for that sense of sound and pattern. With more experience at reading poetry there is an added sense of pleasure as techniques are recognized: alliteration, onomatopoeia; forms of poetry become obvious—the sonnet, the rondelle (all of which and more will be dealt with later). Even greater enjoyment comes from watching a poet's development, tracing themes and ideas, analyzing maturity in growth of imagery, use of rhythm.

To the novice reader of poetry, a poem can speak to the reader at a particular time and become an experience in itself. A freshman's experience after her mother's death exemplifies this. Shortly after the death, the student found Elizabeth Jenning's poem "Happy Families." Using the familiar names of the cards, Mrs. Beef and Master Bun, the poet describes how strangers try to help the family carry on their lives normally although one of the "happy family" is "missing." The card game continues although no one wants it to. At the end the players go back to their individual rooms and give way to their individual grief. The student described the relief at knowing that someone else had obviously experienced her situation where everyone in the family was putting up a front, strangers were being very kind, and a general emptiness prevailed because of that one missing family member. The poem satisfied. The student saw death through another's eyes; the experience was almost the same, yet helped the reader to reevaluate, to view a universal human response to grief as well as encourage her to deal with her own.

On reading a poem the brain works on several different levels: it responds to the sounds; it responds to the words themselves and their connotations; it responds to the emotions; it responds to the insights or learning of the world being revealed. For such a process poetry is a very good training ground—a boot camp—for learning how to read literature in general. All the other genres have elements of poetry within them. Learn to read poetry well and you will be a more accomplished reader, even of car manuals! Perhaps the best response to reading poetry comes from a poet herself, Emily Dickinson, who claimed that reading a book of poetry made her feel "as if the top of [her] head were taken off!"

Before such a process happens to you, here are some tips for reading poetry before and during the examination.

Before the exam

1) Make a list of poets and poems you remember; analyze poems you liked, disliked, loved, hated, and were indifferent to. Find the poems. Reread them and for each one analyze your *feelings*, first of all, about the poetry itself. Have your feelings changed? Now what do you like or hate? Then paraphrase the *meaning* of each poem. Notice how the "magic" goes from the poem, i.e., "To Daffodils:" the poet sees many daffodils by the side of a lake and then thinks how the sight of them later comforts him.

2) Choose a poem at random from an anthology or one mentioned in this introduction. Read it a couple of times, preferably aloud, because the speaking voice will automatically grasp the rhythm and that will help the meaning. Do not become bogged-down in individual word connotation or the meaning of the poem—let the poetry do its "work" on you; absorb the poem as a whole jigsaw puzzle.

3) Now take the puzzle apart. Look carefully at the title. Sometimes a straightforward title helps you focus. Sometimes a playful title helps you get an angle on the meaning. "Happy Families," of course, is an ironic title because the family playing the card game of that name is not happy.

4) Look carefully at the punctuation. Does the sense of a line carry from one to

another? Does a particular mark of punctuation strike you as odd? Ask why that mark was used.

5) Look carefully at the words. Try to find the meaning of words with which you are not familiar within the context. Familiar words may be used differently; analyze why a particular use is chosen. If, having tapped into your memory bank of vocabulary, you are still at a loss, go to a dictionary. Once you have the *denotation* of the word, start wondering about the *connotation*. Put yourself in the poet's position and think why that word was used.

6) Look carefully at all the techniques being used. You will gain these as you progress through this section and through the test preparation. As soon as you come across a new idea—"caesura" perhaps—learn the word, see how it applies to poetry, where it is used. Be on the lookout for it in other poetry. Ask yourself questions such as why the poet used alliteration here; why the rhythm changes there; why the poet uses a sonnet form and which sonnet form is in use. Forcing yourself to ask the WHY questions, and answering them, will train the brain to read more perceptively. Poetry is not accidental; poets are deliberate people; they do things for specific reasons. Your task under a learning situation is to discover WHY.

7) Look carefully at the speaker. Is the poet using another persona? Who is that persona? What is revealed about the speaker? Why use that particular voice?

8) Start putting all the pieces of the puzzle together. The rhythm helps the meaning. The word choice helps the imagery. The imagery adds to the meaning. Paraphrase the meaning. Ask yourself simple questions: What is the poet saying? How can I relate to what is being said? What does this poet mean to me? What does this poem contribute to human experience?

9) Find time to read about the great names in poetry. Locate people within time areas and analyze what those times entailed. For example, the Elizabethans saw a contest between secular love and love of God. The Romantics (Wordsworth, Coleridge, Keats, Shelley, Byron) loved nature and saw God within nature. The Victorians (Tennyson, Blake) saw nature as a threat to mankind and God, being replaced by the profit cash-nexus of the Industrial Age. The moderns (T.S. Eliot, Pound, Yeats) see God as dead and man as hollow, unwanted and unsafe in an alien world. The Post-Moderns see life as "an accident," a comic/cosmic joke, fragmented, purposeless—often their topics will be political: apartheid, abortion, unjust imprisonment.

10) Write a poem of your own. Choose a particular style; use the sonnet form; parody a famous poem; express yourself in free verse on a crucial, personal aspect of your life. Then analyze your own poetry with the above ideas.

During the exam

You will have established a routine for reading poetry, but now you are under pressure, must work quickly, and will have no access to a dictionary. You cannot read aloud but you can:

1) Internalize the reading—hear the reading in your head. Read through the poem two or three times following the absorbing procedure.

2) If the title and poet are supplied, analyze the title as before and determine the era of the poetry. Often this pushes you toward the meaning.

3) Look carefully at the questions which should enable you to be able to "tap into" your learning process. Answer the ones that are immediately clear to you: form, technique, language perhaps.

4) Go back for another reading for those questions that challenge you—theme or meaning perhaps—analyze the speaker or the voice at work— paraphrase the meaning—ask the simple question "What is the poet saying?"

5) If a question asks you about a specific line, metaphor, opening or closing lines, highlight or underline them to force your awareness of each crucial word. Internalize another reading emphasizing the highlighted area—analyze again the options you have for your answers.

6) Do not waste time on an answer that eludes you. Move onto another section and let the poetry do its "work." Very often the brain will continue working on the problem on another level of consciousness. When you go back to the difficult question, it may well become clear.

7) If you still are not sure of the answer, choose the option that you *feel* is the closest to correct.

Go home, relax, forget about the examination—read your favorite poem!

VERSE and METER

As children reading or learning poetry in school, we referred to each section of a poem as a verse. We complained we had ten verses to learn for homework. In fact the word **verse** strictly refers to a line of poetry, perhaps from the original Latin word "versus": a row or a line, and the notion of turning, "vertere," to turn or move to a new idea. In modern use we refer to poetry often as "verse" with the connotation of rhyme, rhythm and meter but we still recognize verse because of the positioning of lines on the page, the breaking of lines that distinguish verse from prose.

The verses we learned for homework are in fact known as **stanzas:** a grouping of lines with a metrical order and often a repeated rhyme which we know as the **rhyme scheme.** Such a scheme is shown by letters to show the repeating sounds. Byron's "Stanzas" will help you recall the word, see the use of a definite rhyme and how to mark it:

"Stanzas"

(When a man hath no freedom to fight for at home)

When a man hath no freedom to fight for at home,	*a*
Let him combat for that of his neighbors;	*b*
Let him think of the glories of Greece and of Rome,	*a*
And get knocked on the head for his labors.	*b*
To do good to mankind is the chivalrous plan,	*c*
And is always as nobly requited;	*d*
Then battle for freedom wherever you can,	*c*
And, if not shot or hanged, you'll get knighted.	*d*

The rhyme scheme is simple: *abab*—we shall be dealing with much more complicated schemes—and your first question should be "Why such a simple, almost sing-song rhyme?" The simplicity reinforces the **tone** of the poem: sarcastic, cryptic, cynical. There is almost a sneer behind the words "And get knocked on his head for his labors." It is as if the poet sets out to give a lecture or at least a homily along the lines of: "Neither a lender nor a borrower be," but then undercuts the seriousness. The **irony** of the poem rests in the fact that Byron joined a freedom fighting group in Greece and died, not gloriously, but of a fever. We shall return to this poem for further discussion.

Certain types of rhyme are worth learning. The most common is the **end rhyme**, which has the rhyming word at the end of the line, bringing the line to a definite stop but setting up for a rhyming word in another line later on, as in "Stanzas": home... Rome, a perfect rhyme. **Internal rhyme** includes at least one rhyming word within the line, often for the purpose of speeding the rhythm or making it linger. Look at the effect of Byron's internal rhymes mixed with half-rhymes: "combat... for that"; "Can/And... hanged" slowing the rhythm, making the reader dwell on the harsh long "a" sound, prolonging the sneer which almost becomes a snarl of anger. **Slant rhyme**, sometimes referred to as half, off, near or approximate rhyme, often jolts a reader who expects a perfect rhyme; poets thus use such a rhyme to express disappointment or a deliberate let-down. **Masculine rhyme** uses one-syllable words or stresses the final syllable of polysyllabic words, giving the feeling of strength and impact. **Feminine rhyme** uses a rhyme of two or more syllables, the stress not falling upon the last syllable, giving a feeling of softness and lightness, one can see that these terms for rhyme were written in a less enlightened age! The terms themselves for the rhymes are less important than realizing or at least appreciating the effects of the rhymes.

If the lines from "Stanzas" had been unrhymed and varying in metrical pattern, the verse would have been termed **free**, or to use the French term, *"Vers libre,"* not to be confused with **blank verse**, which is also unrhymed but has a strict rhythm. The Elizabethan poets Wyatt and Surrey introduced blank verse, which Shakespeare uses to such good effect in his plays, and later, Milton in the great English epic, *Paradise Lost*. Free verse has become associated with "modern" poetry, often adding to its so-called obscurity because without rhyme and rhythm, poets often resort to complicated syntactical patterns, repeated phrases, awkward cadences and parallelism. Robert Frost preferred not to use it because, as he put it, "Writing free verse is like playing tennis with the net down," suggesting that free verse is easier than rhymed and metrical. However, if you have ever tried writing such verse, you will know the problems. (Perhaps a good exercise after your learning about meter is to write some "free" verse.) T.S. Eliot, who uses the form most effectively in "The Journey of the Magi," claimed that no *"vers"* is *"libre"* for the poet who wanted to do a good job.

Such a claim for the artistry and hard work behind a poem introduces perhaps the most difficult of the skills for a poet to practice and a reader to learn: meter. This time the Greeks provide the meaning of the word from *"metron,"* meaning measure. **Meter** simply means the pattern or measure of stressed or accented words within a line of verse. When studying meter a student should note where stresses fall on syllables—that is why reading aloud is so important, because it catches the natural rhythm of the speaking voice—and if an absence of stressed syllables occurs there is always an explanation why. We "expect" stressed and unstressed syllables because that is what we use in everyday speech. We may stress one syllable over another for a certain effect, often using the definite article "THE well known author..." or the preposition "Get OUT of here!" Usually, however, we use a rising and falling rhythm, known as **iambic rhythm**. A line of poetry that alternates stressed and unstressed syllables is said to have **iambic meter**. A line of poetry with ten syllables of rising and falling stresses is known as **iambic pentameter**, best used by Shakespeare and Milton in their blank verse. The basic measuring unit in a line of poetry is called a **foot**. An **iambic foot** has one unstressed syllable followed by a stressed marked by ◡ ╱. Pentameter means "five-measure." Therefore **iambic pentameter** has five groups of two syllables, or ten beats, to the line. Read aloud the second and fourth, sixth and eighth lines

"Stanzas," tapping the beat on your desk or your palm, and the ten beat becomes obvious. Read again with the stresses unstressed and stressed (or soft and loud, short or long, depending on what terminology works for you) and the iambic foot becomes clear.

Tapping out the other alternate lines in this poem, you will not find ten beats but twelve. The term for this line is **hexameter**, or six feet, rather than five. Other line-length names worth learning are:

monometer	one foot	**dimeter**	two feet
trimeter	three feet	**tetrameter**	four feet
heptameter	seven feet	**octameter**	eight feet

Other foot names worth learning are:

the **anapest** marked $\cup\ \cup\ /$, the most famous anapestic line being:
$$\cup\ \cup\ /\ \ \cup\ \cup\ \ \ /\ \cup\ \ \ \cup\ \ /\ \ \cup\ \ \ \cup\ \ \ /$$
"Twas the night before Christmas, when all through the house…"

the **trochee**, marked $/\ \cup$, the most memorable trochaic line being:
$$/\ \cup\ /\ \cup\ /\ \ \cup\ \ /\ \cup$$
"Double double toil and trouble…"

the **dactyl** marked $/\ \cup\ \cup$, the most often quoted dactylic line being:
$$/\ \ \cup\ \cup\ /\ \cup\ \cup$$
"Take her up tenderly…"

Old English poetry employs a meter known as **accentual meter**, with four stresses to the line without attention to the unstressed syllables. Contemporary poets tend not to use it, but one of the greatest innovators in rhythm and meter, Gerard Manley Hopkins, used it as the "base line" for his counterpointed "Sprung Rhythm." Living in the 19th century, Hopkins produced poetry that even today strikes the reader as "modern," in that the rhymes and rhythms often jar the ear, providing stressed syllables where we expect unstressed and vice versa. The rhythm was measured by feet of from one to four syllables, and any number of unstressed syllables. Underneath the rhythm we hear the "regular" rhythm we are used to in speech, and an intriguing counterpoint develops. One stanza from "The Caged Skylark" will show the method at work (later in the Essay Questions you will have a chance to study the entire poem):

As a dare-gale skylark scanted in a dull cage
Man's mounting spirit in his bone-house, mean house, dwells—
That bird beyond the remembering his free fells;
This in drudgery, day-labouring-out life's age.

The stress on "That" and "This" works particularly well to draw attention to the two captives: the skylark and Man. The accentual meter in the second line reinforces the wretchedness of the human condition. No reader could possibly read that line quickly, nor fail to put the full length of the syllable on "dwells." The dash further stresses the length and the low pitch of the last word. The essay question will deal with alliteration and figurative language, for which Hopkins is also noted as an innovator.

If at first the terms for meter are new and strange, remember that what is most important is not that you mindlessly memorize the terminology but are able to recognize the meter and analyze why the poet has used it in the particular context of the poem. For example, Shakespeare did not want the lyrical fall and rise of the iamb for his witches around the cauldron, so he employs the much more unusual trochee to suggest the gloom and mystery of the heath in "Macbeth." Many poets will "mix and match" their meter and your task as a student of poetry is to analyze why. Perhaps the poet sets up the regular greeting card meter, rising and falling rhythm, regular end-stopped rhyme. If the poet abruptly changes that pattern, there is a reason. If the poet subtly moves from a disruptive meter into a smooth one, then analyze what is going on in the meaning. If the poet is doing "a good job" as T.S. Eliot suggested, then the rhyme, rhythm and meter should all work together in harmony to make the poem an integral whole. Answer the test essay questions to practice the points in this section and the integrity of a poem as a single unit will become clearer.

FIGURATIVE LANGUAGE and POETIC DEVICES

It will be becoming ever more obvious that a poem is not created from mere inspiration. No doubt the initial movement for a poem has something of divine intervention: the ancients talked of being visited by the Muse of Poetry; James Joyce coined the word "epiphany" for the clear moment of power of conception in literature, but then the poet sets to, working at the expression to make it the best it can be.

Perhaps what most distinguishes poetry from any other genre is the use of figurative language—figures of speech—used through the ages to convey the poet's own particular world-view in a unique way. Words have **connotation** and **denotation, figurative** and **literal** meanings. We can look in the dictionary for denotation and literal meaning, but figurative language works its own peculiar magic, tapping into shared experiences within the psyche. A simple example involves the word "home." If we free-associated for awhile among a group of twenty students we would find a number of connotations for the word, depending on the way home was for us in our experiences: comforting, scary, lonely, dark, creepy, safety, haven, hell.... However, the denotation is quite straightforward: a house or apartment or dwelling that provides shelter for an individual or family. Poets include in their skill various figures of speech to "plug into" the reader's experiences, to prompt the reader to say "I would have never thought of it in those terms but now I see!"

The most important of these skills is perhaps the **metaphor**, which compares two unlike things, feelings, objects, and the **simile**. Metaphors are more difficult to find than **similes**, which also compare two dissimilar things but always use the words "as if" (for a clause) or "like" (for a word or phrase). Metaphors suggest the comparison, the meaning is implicit. An easy way to distinguish between the two is the simple example of the camel. **Metaphor:** the camel is the ship of the desert. **Simile**: a camel is like a ship in the desert. Both conjure up the camel's almost sliding across the desert, storing up its water as a ship must do for survival for its passengers, and the notion of the vastness of the desert parallels the sea. The metaphor somehow crystallizes the image. Metaphors can be *extended* so that an entire poem consists of a metaphor (see Shakespeare's "Sonnet xviii" in the essay questions) or unfortunately they can be *mixed*. The latter rarely happens in poetry unless the poet is deliberately playing with his readers and provoking humor. Watch for them in your own writing however, odd statements such as "The roots of my ambition needed dental work," or "The forests fed me in my quest for peace."

Start thinking of how many times you use similes in your own writing or speech. The secret is, as Isaac Babel once said, that similes must be "as precise as a slide rule and as natural as the smell of dill." The precision and naturalness coming together perfectly often set up an equation of comparison. A student once wrote "I felt torn apart by my loyalty to my mother and grandmother, like the turkey wishbone at Thanksgiving." We have all experienced divided loyalties. Using the graphic wishbone-tearing idea, something we have all done at Thanksgiving or have seen done lets us more easily relate to the student's experience. Another student wrote of his friends waiting for the gym class to begin "like so many captive gazelles." Again the visual point of comparison is important but also the sense of freedom in the idea of gazelle, the speed, the grace; juxtaposing that freedom with the word "captive" is a master stroke that makes a simile striking.

The same student went on to an *extended simile* to state precisely and naturally his feelings upon going into a fistfight: "I was like the kid whose parents were killed by the crooked sheriff, waiting for high noon and the showdown that would pit a scared kid with his father's rusty old pistol against the gleaming steel of a matched pair, nestled in the black folds of the sheriff's holsters. I knew there was no way out. Surrounded by friends, I marched out into the brilliant sun, heading for the back fields of the playground, desperately trying to polish the rusty old gun." Although this student was writing in prose, his use of figurative language is poetic. He plugs into readers' movie experience with the central idea of the showdown at high noon, an **allusion** (see later) that involves the reader on the same plane as the writer. The notion of the black holster extends the allusion of the old cowboy films where the "baddies" wore black hats and rode black horses. The use of the word "nestled" provokes some interesting connotations of something soft and sweet like a kitten nestling into something. But then the gun is an implement of destruction and death; maybe "nestles" takes on the connotation of how a snake might curl in the sun at the base of a tree. The metaphor then ends with the child going out into the sun. The "rusty gun" in context of the essay was in fact the outmoded ideas and morals his father and old books had inculcated in him. All in all a very clever use of figurative language in prose. If the same concept had been pursued in poetry, the metaphor would have moved more speedily, more subtly—a poet cannot waste words—and of course would have employed line breaks, rhythm and meter.

Personification is a much easier area than metaphor to detect in poetry. Usually the object that is being personified—referred to as a human with the personal pronoun sometimes, or possessing human attributes—is capitalized, as in this stanza from Thomas Gray's "Ode on a Distant Prospect of Eton College" (to be discussed in full later):

> Ambition this shall tempt to rise,
> Then whirl the wretch from high,
> To bitter Scorn a sacrifice,
> And grinning Infamy.
> The stings of Falsehood those shall try,
> And hard Unkindness' altered eye,
> That mocks the tear it forced to flow;
> And keen Remorse with blood defiled,
> And moody Madness laughing wild
> Amid severest woe.

As the poet watches the young Eton boys, he envisions what the years have to offer them, and the qualities he sees he gives human status. Thus Ambition is not only capable of tempting, an amoral act, but also of "whirling," a physical act. Scorn is bitter, Infamy grinning, and so on. Coleridge employs a more visual personification in "The Ancient Mariner," for the sun whom he describes as:

> ...the Sun (was) flecked with bars
> (Heaven's Mother send us grace!)
> As if through a dungeon-grate he peered
> With broad and burning face.

More so than with Gray's more formal personification, Coleridge's supplies an image that is precise—we can see the prisoner behind the bars, and what's more this particular prisoner has a broad and burning face... of course because he is the sun! The personification brings us that flash of recognition when we can say "Yes, I see that!"

The word **image** brings us to another important aspect of figurative language. Not a figure of speech in itself, the image plays a large role in poetry because the reader is expected to **imag**ine what the poet is evoking, through the senses. The image can be **literal**, wherein the reader has little adjustment to make to see or touch or taste the image; a **figurative image** demands more from readers, almost as if they have to be inside the poet's imagination to understand the image. Very often this is where students of poetry, modern poetry particularly, find the greatest problems because the poetry of **imagism**, a term coined by Ezra Pound, is often intensely personal, delving into the mind of the poet for the comparison and connection with past memories that many readers cannot possibly share. Such an image is referred to as *free*, open to many interpretations. This concept suits the post-modern poet who feels that life is fragmented, open to multi-interpretations— there is no fixed order. Poets of the Elizabethan and Romantic eras saw the world as whole, steady, *fixed*, exactly the word used for their type of images. Readers of this poetry usually share the same response to the imagery. For example, the second stanza of Keats' "Ode to a Nightingale" sets up the taste imagery of a

draught of vintage that hath been
Cooled a long age in the deep-delvéd earth,
Tasting of Flora and the country green,
Dance, and Provençal song, and sunburnt mirth!
O for a beaker of the warm South,
Full of the true, the blushful Hippocrene,
With beaded bubbles winking at the brim,
And purple-stainéd mouth;

Even though Flora and Hippocrene are not names we are readily familiar with, the image of the cool wine, the taste, the look, the feeling evoked of the South and warmth, all come rushing into our minds as we enter the poet's imagination and find images in common.

Blake's imagery in "London" works in a similar way but as readers we have to probe a little harder, especially for the last line of the last stanza:

But, most thro' midnight streets I hear
How the youthful Harlot's curse
Blasts the new-born Infant's tear,
And blights with plagues the Marriage hearse.

You will have a chance at working on this poem in entirety later, but notice how the "Marriage hearse" immediately sets up a double image. Marriage we associate with happiness and joy; hearse we associate with death and sorrow. The image is troubling. We go back to the previous lines. The harlot curses her (?) new-born—the curse of venereal disease—that child marries and carries the disease to marriage? Or the young man consorting with the harlot passes on the disease to his marriage partner? Marriage then becomes death? The image is intriguing and open to interpretation.

Image in figurative language inevitably leads to **symbol**. When an object, an image, a feeling, takes on larger meaning outside of itself, then a poet is employing a symbol, something which stands for something greater. Because mankind has used symbols for so long many have become **stock** or **conventional**: the rose standing for love; the flag standing for patriotism, love of one's country (thus the controversy over flag-burning today); the color yellow standing for corruption (hence Gatsby's Daisy Buchanan—the white-dressed virginal lady with the center core of carelessness); the bird for freedom; the sea for eternity; the cross for suffering and sacrifice. If you are not versed in the Christian tradition it might be useful to read its symbols because the older poetry dwells on the church and the trials of loving God and loving Woman—the latter also has become a symbol deteriorating over the ages from Eve to the Madonna to Whore.

If the symbol is not conventional then it may carry with it many interpretations, depending on the reader's insight. Some students "get carried away" with symbolism, seeing more in the words than the poets do! If the poet is "doing a good job" the poetry will steer you in the "right" direction of symbolism. Sometimes we are unable to say what "stands for" what, but simply that the symbol evokes a mood; it suggests an idea to you that is difficult to explain. The best way to approach symbolism is to understand a literal meaning first and then shift the focus, as with a different camera lens, and see if the poet is saying something even more meaningful. Blake again supplies an interesting example. In his poem "The Chimney Sweeper" he describes the young child's dream of being locked up in "coffins of black." Literally of course coffins are brown wood, the color of mourning is black. Shift the focus then to the young child chimney sweeper, so young he can barely lisp the street cry "Sweep" so it comes out "'weep! 'weep! 'weep! 'weep!" (a symbolic line in itself). Your reading of the Industrial Age's cruelty to children who were exploited as cheap, plentiful, and an expendable labor force will perhaps have taught you that children were used as chimney brushes—literally thrust up the thin black chimneys of Victorian houses and factories, where very often they became trapped, suffocated, sometimes burned to death if fires were set by unknowing owners. Now the black coffins stand for the black-with-soot chimneys the little children had to sweep, chimneys which sometimes became their coffins. The realization of the symbol brings a certain horror to the poem. In the dream an Angel releases the children who then run down "a green plain leaping, laughing.../And wash in a river, and shine in the sun." The action is of course symbolic in that in real life the children's movements were restricted, living in monstrous cities where green plains would be enjoyed only by the rich, and totally limited by the size of the chimneys. They were always black with soot. They rarely saw the sun, never mind shone in it! Again the symbolism adds something to the poem. In many students there have been reactions of tears and anger when they *see* the symbolism behind such simple lines. This poem stands good discussion which we will turn to later.

The idea of reading about the Industrial Age brings us to an important part of figurative language, briefly mentioned before: **allusion**. Poets tap into previous areas of experience to relate their insights, to draw their readers into shared experiences. Remember how the student writer alluded to old cowboy movies, the classic "High Noon." Poets will refer to history, myth, other older poems, plays, music, heroes, famous people. Allusion is becoming more and more difficult for the modern student because reading is becoming more and more a lost art. Core courses in schools have become hotbeds of controversy about what students should know. Fortunately modern poets are shifting their allusions so that contemporary readers can appreciate and join in with their background of knowledge. However, be aware that for the examination in poetry it will be useful to have a working knowledge of, at least a passing acquaintance with, "oldness." Think of areas of history that were landmarks: the burning of Catharge; Hannibal's elephants; Caesar's greatness; Alexander the Great; the first World War and its carnage of young men; the Second World War and the Holocaust. Think of the great Greek and Roman myths: the giving of fire to the world; the entrance of sin world; the labyrinth; the names associated with certain myths: Daedalus, Hercules, the Medusa. You may never have a question on the areas you read but your background for well-rounded college study will already be formulated.

If we now return to more specific figures of speech and other poetic devices, you may feel you can immediately get to grips with these rather than read for background! Alphabetical order may help in your studying:

Alliteration: the repetition of consonants at the beginning of words that are next door to each other or close by. The Hopkins' stanza quoted earlier provides some fine examples: "skylark scanted"; "Man's mounting... mean house"; "free fells"; "drudgery, day-labouring-out life's age." Always try to understand the reason for the alliteration. Does it speed or slow the rhythm? Is it there for emphasis? What does the poet want you to focus on?

Apostrophe: the direct address of someone or something that is not present. Many odes begin this way. Keats' "Ode on a Grecian Urn" for example: "Thou still unravished bride of quietness," and "Ode to Psyche": "O Goddess! hear these tuneless numbers."

Assonance: the repetition of vowel sounds usually internally rather than initially. "Her goodly eyes like sapphires shining bright." Here the poet, Spenser, wants the entire focus on the blue eyes, the crispness, and the light.

Bathos: deliberate anticlimax to make a definite point or draw attention to a falseness. The most famous example is from Pope's "Rape of the Lock": "Here thou, great Anna! whom three realms obey, /Dost sometimes counsel take—and sometimes tea."

The humor in the bathos is the fact that Anna is the Queen of England—she holds meetings in the room Pope describes but also indulges in the venerable English custom of afternoon tea. The fact that tea should rhyme with obey doubles the humor as the elongated vowel of the upper-class laconic English social group is also mocked.

Caesura: the pause, marked by punctuation (/) or not within the line. Sometimes the caesura (sometimes spelled cesura) comes at an unexpected point in the rhythm and gives the reader pause for thought.

Conceits: very elaborate comparisons between unlikely objects. The metaphysical poets such as John Donne were criticized for "yoking" together outrageous terms, describing lovers in terms of instruments, or death in terms of battle.

Consonance: similar to slant rhyme—the repetition of consonant sounds without the vowel sound repeated. Hopkins again frequently uses this as in "Pied Beauty": "All things counter, original, spare, strange;... adazzle, dim."

Diction: the word for word choice. Is the poet using formal or informal language? Does the poetry hinge on slang or a dialect? If so what is the purpose? Are the words "highfalutin" or low-brow? As always, the diction needs examining and questions like these answering.

Enjambment: the running-on of one line of poetry into another. Usually the end of lines are rhymed so there is an end-stop. In more modern poetry, without rhyme, often run-on lines occur to give a speedier flow, the sound of the speaking voice or a conversational tone.

Hyperbole: refers to large overstatement often used to draw attention to a mark of beauty or a virtue or an action that the poet disagrees with. Donne's instruction to the woman he is trying to seduce not to kill the flea, by contrasting her reluctance with "a marriage" of blood within a flea, reinforces the hyperbole used throughout the poem (for study later):

> Oh stay, three lives in one flea spare,
> Where we almost, yea, more than married are.

The example is also good for an unexpected caesura for emphasis at the second pause.

Irony: plays an important role in voice or tone, inferring a discrepancy between what is said and what is meant. A famous example (also in a later section for study) is Shelley's "Ozymandias," which tells of the great ruler who thought that he and his name would last forever, but the traveller describes the huge statue in ruins with the inscription speaking truer than the ruler intended: "My name is Ozymandias, king of kings: /Look on my works, ye Mighty, and despair!"

Metonymy: the name for something closely related to it which then takes on a larger meaning. "You can't fight City Hall" has taken on the meaning of fighting against an entire bureaucracy. "You can't go home again" suggests that you can never emotionally return to your roots.

Onomatopoeia: a device in which the word captures the sound. In many poems the words are those in general use: the whiz of fireworks; the crashing of waves on the shore; the booming of water in a underground sea-cave. However, poets like Keats use the device to superb effect in, for example, " To Autumn," when he describes the gleaner sitting by the cider press watching the last "oozings hours by hours"… one can hear the last minute drops squeezed from the apples.

Oxymoron: a form of paradox in which contradictory words are used next to each other: "painful pleasure," "sweet sorrow."

Paradox: a situation or action or feeling that appears to be contradictory but on inspection turns out to be true or at least make sense. "The pen is mightier than the sword" at first glance is a contradiction of reality. One can hardly die by being stabbed by a pen... but in the larger world view the words of men, the signing of death warrants, the written issuing of commands to the gas chambers have killed. Or reason has prevailed by men writing out their grievances and as a result lives have been saved. Paradox always opens up the doors of thinking.

Pun: a play on words often for humorous or sarcastic effect. The Elizabethans were very fond of them; many of Shakespeare's comedies come from punning. Much of Donne's sexual taunting involves the use of the pun.

Sarcasm: when verbal irony is too harsh it moves into the sarcastic realm. It is the "lowest form of wit" of course but can be used to good effect in the tone of a poem. Browning's dramatic monologues make excellent use of the device.

Synecdoche: when a part of an object is used to represent the entire thing or vice versa. When we ask someone to give us a hand we would be horrified if they cut off the hand, what we want is the person's help, from all of the body!

Syntax: the ordering of words into a particular pattern. If a poet shifts words from the usual word order you know you are dealing with an older style of poetry (Shakespeare, Milton) or a poet who wants to shift emphasis onto a particular word.

Tone: the voice or attitude of the speaker. Remember that the voice need not be that of the poet's. He or she may be adopting a particular tone for a purpose. Your task is to analyze if the tone is angry, sad, conversational, abrupt, wheedling, cynical, affected, satiric, etc. Is the poet including you in a cozy way by using "you," or is he accusing "you" of what he is criticizing? Is the poet keeping you at a distance with coldness and third person pronouns. If so, why? The most intriguing of voices is Browning's in his **dramatic monologues**: poems that address another person who remains silent. Browning brought this type of poetry to an art. Look in the sample questions for an opportunity to learn about tone from a master. Think of all the variations of voices and attitudes and be prepared to meet them in poetry.

TYPES OF POETRY

Having begun to grasp that poetry contains a great deal more than initially meets the eye, you should now start thinking about the various types of poetry. Of course, when reading for pleasure, it is not vital to recognize that the poem in hand is a sonnet or a villanelle, but for the exam you may well be asked to determine what sort of poem is under scrutiny. Certainly in discussing a poem it is also useful to know what "breed" you are dealing with because the form may dictate certain areas of rhyme or meter and may enhance the meaning.

The pattern or design of a poem is known as **form**, and even the strangest, most experimental poetry will have some type of form to it. Allen Ginsberg's "A Supermarket in California" caused a stir because it didn't read like poetry, but on the page there is a certain form to it. Some poets even try to match the shape of the poem to the subject. See George Herbert's "Easter Wings" in the later section for study, and find in anthologies John Hollander's "Swan and Shadow," and Dorthi Charles' "Concrete Cat." Such visual poems are not just fun to look at and read but the form adds to the subject and helps the reader appreciate the poet's worldview. **Closed form** will be immediately recognizable because lines can be counted, shape determined. The poet must keep to the recognized form, in number of lines, rhyme scheme, and/or meter. **Open form** developed from "vers libre," a name some poets objected to as it suggested that there was little skill or craft behind the poem; simply creativity, as the name suggests, gives a freedom of pattern to the poet.

The most easily recognized closed form of poetry is the **sonnet**, sometimes referred to as a **fixed form**. The sonnet always has fourteen lines but there are two types of sonnets, the Petrarchan or Italian, and the Shakespearean or English. The word sonnet in fact comes from the Italian word "sonnetto" meaning a "little song," and Petrarch, the 14th century Italian poet, took the form to its peak with his sonnets to his loved one Laura. This woman died before he could even declare his love, and such poignant, unrequited love became the theme for many Elizabethan sonnets. As a young man might telephone a young woman for a date in today's society, the Elizabethan would send a sonnet. The Petrarchan sonnet is organized into two groups: eight lines and six: the **octave** and the **sestet**. Usually the rhyme scheme is is abbaabba-cdecde, but the sestet can vary in its pattern. The octave may set up a problem or a proposition, and then the answer or resolution follows in the sestet after a turn or a shift. The Shakespearean sonnet organizes the lines into three groups of four lines: **quatrains** and a **couplet**: two rhyming lines. The rhyming scheme is always abab cdcd efef gg, and the turn or shift can happen at one of three places or leave the resolution or a "twist in the tail" at the end. The two sonnets in the study section will help you not only recognize the two forms but also realize what utter skill is involved in writing them. A student once wrote an English sonnet to her old car taken to the wrecker's yard—much more difficult to write than she anticipated. You might try a similar exercise!

Couplet, mentioned earlier, leads us to a closed form of poetry that is very useful for the poet. It is a two-line stanza that usually rhymes with an end rhyme. If the couplet is firmly end-stopped and written in iambic pentameter it is known as an **heroic couplet,** after the use was made of it in the English translations of the great classical or heroic epics such as *The Iliad* and *The Odyssey.* Alexander Pope became a master of the heroic couplet, sometimes varying to the twelve-syllable line from the old French poetry on Alexander the Great. The line became known as the **Alexandrine.** Pope gained fame first as a translator of the epics and then went on to write **mock-heroic** poems like "The Rape of the Lock," written totally in heroic couplets which never become monotonous, as a succession of regularly stepped-out couplets can, because he varied the place of the caesura and masterfully employed enjambment.

Rarely in an exam will you be presented with an **epic** because part of the definition of the word is vastness of size and range. However, you may be confronted with an excerpt and will need to recognize the structure. The translation will usually be in couplets, the meter regular with equal line lengths, because originally these poems were sung aloud or chanted to the beat of drums. Because of their oral quality, repetition plays an important part, so that if the bard, or singer, forgot the line, the audience, who had heard the stories many times before, could help him out. The subject deals with great deeds of heroes: Odysseus (Ulysses), Hector, and Aeneus, their adventures and their trials; the theme will be of human grief or pride, divided loyalties—but all "writ large." The one great English epic, *Paradise Lost* is written by Milton and deals with the story of Adam and Eve and the Fall. Adam thus becomes the great hero. The huge battle scenes of *The Iliad* are emulated in the War of the Heavens when Satan and his crew were expelled into Hell; the divided loyalties occur when Adam must choose between obedience to God and love for his wife.

On much simpler lines are the **ballads**, sometimes the earliest poems we learn as children. Folk or popular ballads were first sung as early as the 15th century and then handed down through generations until finally written down. Usually the ballads are anonymous and simple in theme, having been composed by working folk who originally could not read or write. The stories—a ballad is a story in a song—revolve around love and hate and lust and murder, often rejected lovers, knights, and the supernatural. As with the epic, and for the same reason, repetition plays a strong part in the ballad and often a repeated refrain holds the entire poem together. The form gave rise to the **ballad stanza**, four lines rhyming abcb with lines 1 and 3 having 8 syllables and lines 2 and 4 having 6. Poets who later wrote what are known as **literary ballads** kept the same pattern. Read Coleridge's "Ancient Mariner" and all the elements of the ballad come together as he reconstructs the old folk story but writes it in a very closed form.

The earlier poetry dealt with narrative. The "father of English poetry," Geoffrey Chaucer, told stories within a story for the great *Canterbury Tales*. The Elizabethans turned to love and the humanistic battle between love of the world and love of God. Wordsworth and Coleridge marked a turning point by not only using "the language of men" in poetry but also by moving away from the narrative poem to the **lyric**. The word comes again from the Greek, meaning a story told with the poet playing upon a lyre. Wordsworth moves from story to emotion, often "emotion recollected in tranquillity" as we saw in "Daffodils." Although sometimes a listener is inferred, very often the poet seems to be musing aloud.

Part of the lyric "family" is the **elegy**, a lament for someone's death or the passing of a love or concept. The most famous is Thomas Gray's "Elegy Written in a Country Churchyard," which mourns not only the passing of individuals but of a past age and the wasted potential within every human being, no matter how humble. Often **ode** and elegy become synonymous, but an ode, also part of the lyric family, is usually longer, dealing with more profound areas of human life than simply death. Keats' odes are perhaps the most famous and most beloved in English poetry.

More specialized types of poetry need mentioning so that you may recognize and be able to explicate how the structure of the poem enhances the meaning or theme. For example the **villanelle**: a Courtly Love poem structure from medieval times, built on five three-line stanzas known as **tercets**, with the rhyme scheme aba, followed by a four-line stanza, a **quatrain** which ends the poem abaa. As if this were not pattern and order enough, the poem's first line appears again as the last line of the 2nd and 4th tercets; *and* the third line appears again in the last line of the 3rd and 5th tercets; *and* these two lines appear again as rhyming lines at the end of the poem! The most famous and arguably the best villanelle—as some of the older ones can be so stiff in their pattern as to render the meaning inconsequential—is Dylan Thomas' "Do not go gentle into that good night." The poem stands on its own with a magisterial meaning of mankind raging against death, but when one appreciates the structure also, the rage is even more emphatic because it is so controlled. It is a poem well worth seeking out to read for pleasure. In James Joyce's *A Portrait of the Artist as a Young Man*, writing a villanelle on an empty cigarette packet turns the young boy, Stephen Daedalus, dreaming of being an artist, into a poet—a "real" artist.

Said to be the most difficult of all closed forms is the **sestina**, also French, sung by medieval troubadours, a "song of sixes." The poet presents six six-line stanzas, with six end-words in a certain order, then repeats those six repeated words in any order in a closing tercet. Find Elizabeth Bishop's "Sestina" or W.H. Auden's "Hearing of Harvests Rotting in the Valleys" and the idea of six images running through the poet's head and being skillfully repeated comes across very clearly. You might even try working out a sestina for yourself.

Perhaps at this stage an **epigram** might be more to your liking and time scale because it is short, even abrupt, a little cynical and always to the point. The cynical Alexander Pope mastered the epigram, as did Oscar Wilde centuries later. Perhaps at some stage we have all written **doggerel**, rhyming poetry that becomes horribly distorted to fit the rhymes, not through skill but the opposite. In contrast **limericks** are very skilled: five lines using the anapest meter with the rhyme scheme: aabba. Unfortunately they can deteriorate into types such as "There was a young lady from....," but in artful hands such as Shakespeare's (see Ophelia's mad song in *Hamlet*: "And will he not come again?") and Edward Lear's, limericks display fine poetry. Finally, if you are trying to learn all the different types of closed-form poetry, you might try an **aubade**—originally a song or piece of music sung or played at dawn—a poem written to the dawn or about lovers at dawn—the very time when poetic creation is extremely high!

Although the name might suggest open-form, **blank verse** is in fact closed-form poetry. As we saw earlier, lines written in blank verse are unrhymed and in iambic pentameter. Open-form poets can arrange words on the page in any order, not confined by any rhyme pattern or meter. Often it seems as if words have spilled onto the page at random with a direct address to the readers, as if the poets are cornering them in their room, or simply chatting over the kitchen table. The lines break at any point—the dash darts in and out—the poets are talking to the audience with all the "natural" breaks that the speaking voice will demonstrate. Open-form poets can employ rhyme, but sometimes it seems as if the rhyme has slipped into the poem quite easily—there is no wrenching of the word "to make it rhyme." Very often there is more internal rhyme as poets play with words, often giving the sensation they are thinking aloud. Open-form poetry is usually thought of as "modern," at least post-World War I, but the use of space on the page, the direct address of the voice and the use of the dash clearly marks Emily Dickinson as an open-form poet, though she lived from 1830 to 1886. The examples in the poems for study will show the main difference between poets of the 19th century and their point of view, and those of the 20th century who seem to relish the open-form to express the muti-faceted world with its paradoxes and confusions that everyone can relate to and, ironically, when reading about them, come to terms with and, in a strange way, enjoy.

In the following poems, suggestions are made for how to answer an essay question centering on one specific poem or excerpts from poems. Bear in mind that there are many ways for a student to answer the questions—above all be true to your own interpretation, keeping of course an open mind, avoiding any judgmental opinions—but there are always certain elements that must be covered. Never be tempted to give an opinion on the worth of the poem, whether you thought it "good" or "bad." Rarely will you be asked for an opinion so keep to a certain guideline in your answers, being as unjudgmental as you can. Tackle the essay questions by yourself first, then check your answer against the suggested answer.

SAMPLE ESSAY AND POSSIBLE ANSWERS

1) Read the following poem carefully. Discuss whether the poem is open or closed-form poetry, drawing attention to the poetry itself to prove your point. Does the "creature" have any symbolic quality? What do you interpret as the meaning of the poem?

THE HEART

In the desert
I saw a creature, naked, bestial,
Who, squatting upon the ground,
Held his heart in his hands,
And ate of it.
I said, "Is it good, friend?"
"It is bitter—bitter," he answered;
"But I like it
Because it is bitter,
And because it is my heart."

—Stephen Crane (1871-1900)

2) Read the following poem carefully and explain the difference between the English and the Italian sonnet, showing into which category this poem fits. Discuss the theme of the sonnet, pointing out any striking areas in the poetry and what they contribute to the poem as a whole.

SONNET 116

Let me not to the marriage of true minds
  Admit impediments. Love is not love
Which alters when it alteration finds,
  Or bends with the remover to remove.
O, no! it is an ever-fixèd mark,
  That looks on tempests and is never shaken;
It is the star to every wandering bark,
  Whose worth's unknown, although his height be taken.
Love's not Time's fool, though rosy lips and cheeks
  Within his bending sickle's compass come;
Love alters not with his brief hours and weeks,
  But bears it out even to the edge of doom
    If this be error, and upon me proved,
    I never writ, nor no man ever loved.

—William Shakespeare (1564-1616)

3) Scan the following poem carefully (scanning means measuring the length of the line, determining the kind and number of feet in it). Analyze the tone of the poem showing how the meter adds to the tone. What effect does the repetition

have in the second stanza? Comment on the imagery in stanza three. Discuss the imagery in the last stanza.

LONDON

I wander through each chartered street,
Near where the chartered Thames does flow,
And mark in every face I meet
Marks of weakness, marks of woe.

In every cry of every man,
In every infant's cry of fear,
In every voice, in every ban,
The mind-forged manacles I hear.

How the chimney-sweeper's cry
Every black'ning church appalls;
And the hapless soldier's sigh
Runs in blood down palace walls.

But most through midnight streets I hear
How the youthful harlot's curse
Blasts the new-born infant's tear,
And blights with plagues the marriage hearse.

—William Blake (1757-1827)

4) Read the following poem carefully and discuss the setting, speaker, tone and meaning. What does the speaker's companion do in the third stanza? How does the speaker use this action to his advantage?

THE FLEA

Mark but this flea, and mark in this
How little that which thou deny'st me is;
It sucked me first, and now sucks thee,
And in this flea our two bloods mingled be;
Thou know'st that this cannot be said
A sin, nor shame, nor loss of maidenhead,
  Yet this enjoys before it woo,
  And pampered swells with one blood made of two,
  And this, alas, is more than we would do.

Oh stay, three lives in one flea spare,
Where we almost, yea, more than married are.
This flea is you and I, and this
Our marriage bed, and marriage temple is;

Though parents grudge, and you, we're met
And cloistered in these living walls of jet.
  Though use make you apt to kill me,
  Let not to that, self-murder added be,
  And sacrilege, three sins in killing three.

Cruel and sudden, hast thou since
Purpled thy nail in blood of innocence?
Wherein could this flea guilty be,
Except in that drop it sucked from thee?
Yet thou triumph'st, and say'st that thou
Find'st not thyself, nor me, the weaker now;
  'Tis true; then learn how false, fears be;
  Just so much honor, when thou yield'st to me,
  Will waste, as this flea's death took life from thee.

—John Donne (1572-1631)

5) Read the following poem carefully, determining whether the poem is in open or closed form. Pick out and discuss any areas (word choice, unusual images of the poem that strike you as crucial to the meaning, which perhaps might be seen on two levels.

BECAUSE I COULD NOT STOP FOR DEATH (1863)

Because I could not stop for Death-
He kindly stopped for me-
The Carriage held but just Ourselves-
And Immortality.

We slowly drove-He knew no haste
And I had put away
My labor and my leisure too,
For His Civility-

We passed the School, where Children strove
At Recess-in the Ring-
We passed the Fields of Gazing Grain-
We passed the Setting Sun-

Or rather-He passed Us-
The Dews drew quivering and chill-
For only Gossamer, my Gown-
My Tippet-only Tulle-

We paused before a House that seemed
A Swelling of the Ground-
The Roof was scarcely visible-
The Cornice-in the Ground-

Since then-'tis Centuries-and yet
Feels shorter than the Day
I first surmised the Horses' Heads
Were toward Eternity-

—Emily Dickinson (1830-1886)

QUESTIONS TO WORK ON ALONE

1) Read the following elegy carefully, bearing in mind it was written by an eighteen-year-old boy a few days before he was hanged, drawn, and quartered for his part in a conspiracy against Elizabeth the First. Explain what an elegy is by showing how this one is constructed. What is the tone of the speaker? What does knowing the background of the poet do for you as a reader? Should we always be provided with background material? Reread "Stanzas" by Byron quoted earlier. Comment on whether knowing how Byron died made any difference to your interpretation of the poem.

ELEGY

My prime of youth is but a frost of cares,
　My feast of joy is but a dish of pain,
My crop of corn is but a field of tares,
　And all my good is but vain hope of gain;
　　The day is past, and yet I saw no sun,
　　And now I live, and now my life is done.

My tale was heard and yet it was not told,
　My fruit is fallen and yet my leaves are green,
My youth is spent and yet I am not old,
　I saw the world and yet I was not seen;
　　My thread is cut and yet it is not spun,
　　And now I live, and now my life is done.

I sought my death and found it in my womb,
　I looked for life and saw it was a shade,
I trod the earth and knew it was my tomb,
　And now I die, and now I was but made;
　　My glass is full, and now my glass is run,
　　And now I live, and now my life is done.

—Chidiock Tichborne, d. 1586

2) Look carefully at and read the visual poem. How does the form suit the subject? Does the look of the poem enhance the meaning or confuse it?

EASTER WINGS

Lord, who createdst man in wealth and store,
Though foolishly he lost the same,
Decaying more and more
Till he became
Most poor;
With thee
Oh, let me rise
As larks, harmoniously,
And sing this day thy victories;
Then shall the fall further the flight in me.

My tender age in sorrow did begin;
And still with sicknesses and shame
Thou didst so punish sin,
That I became
Most thin.
With thee
Let me combine,
And feel this day thy victory;
For if I imp my wing on thine,
Affliction shall advance the flight in me.

—George Herbert (1593-1633)

3) Read the following poem carefully and explain who the speaker is and what form of poetry this is. What is the irony involved in the last two lines?

OZYMANDIAS

I met a traveller from an antique land
Who said: Two vast and trunkless legs of stone
Stand in the desert... Near them, on the sand,
Half sunk, a shattered visage lies, whose frown,
And wrinkled lip, and sneer of cold command,
Tell that its sculptor well those passions read
Which yet survive, stamped on these lifeless things,
The hand that mocked them, and the heart that fed:
And on the pedestal these words appear:
'My name is Ozymandias, king of kings:
Look on my works, ye Mighty, and despair!'
Nothing beside remains. Round the decay
Of that colossal wreck, boundless and bare
The lone and level sands stretch far away.

—Percy Bysshe Shelley (1792-1822)

4) Read the following poem carefully. What is the main poetic device used here? Explain the term "bone-house, mean house" and the meaning of the last stanza.

THE CAGED SKYLARK

As a dare-gale skylark scanted in a dull cage
  Man's mounting spirit in his bone-house, mean house, dwells-
  That bird beyond the remembering his free fells;
This in drudgery, day-labouring-out life's age.

Though aloft on turf or perch or poor low stage,
  Both sing sómetimes the sweetest, sweetest spells,
  Yet both droop deadly sometimes in their cells
Or wring their barriers in bursts of fear or rage.

Not that the sweet-fowl, song-fowl, needs no rest-
Why, hear him, hear him babble and drop down to
  his nest,
  But his own nest, wild nest, no prison.

Man's spirit will be flesh-bound when found at best,
But uncumbered: meadow-down is not distressed
  For a rainbow footing it nor he for his bónes rísen.

—Gerard Manley Hopkins (1844-1889)

5) Read the following excerpt from Gray's ode quoted earlier. Describe the tone of the speaker and explain what he feels. Explain the two figures of speech at work in the last two lines of the first stanza. What effect does personification have in the last stanza?

ODE ON A DISTANT PROSPECT OF ETON COLLEGE

  Ye distant spires, ye antique towers,
That crown the watery glade,
Where grateful Science still adores
Her Henry's holy shade;
And ye that from the stately brow
Of Windsor's heights the expanse below
Of grove, of lawn, of mead survey,
Whose turf, whose shade, whose flowers among
Wanders the hoary Thames along
His silver-winding way.

Ah, happy hills, ah, pleasing shade,
Ah, fields beloved in vain,
Where once my careless childhood strayed,
A stranger yet to pain!
I feel the gales, that from ye blow,
A momentary bliss bestow,
As waving fresh their gladsome wing,
My weary soul they seem to soothe,
And, redolent of joy and youth,
To breathe a second spring.

Say, Father Thames, for thou hast seen
Full many a sprightly race
Disporting on thy margent green
The paths of pleasure trace,
Who foremost now delight to cleave
With pliant arm thy glassy wave?
The captive linnet which enthrall?
What idle progeny succeed
To chase the rolling circle's speed,
Or urge the flying ball?

While some on earnest business bent
Their murmuring labours ply
'Gainst graver hours, that bring constraint
To sweeten liberty:
Some bold adventurers disdain
The limits of their little reign,
And unknown regions dare descry:
Still as they run they look behind,
They hear a voice in every wind,
And snatch a fearful joy.

Gay hope is theirs by fancy fed,
Less pleasing when possessed;
The tear forgot as soon as shed,
The sunshine of the breast:
Theirs buxom health of rosy hue,
Wild wit, invention ever-new,
And lively cheer of vigour born;
The thoughtless day, the easy night,
The spirits pure, the slumbers light,
That fly the approach of morn.

Alas, regardless of their doom,
The little victims play!
No sense have they of ills to come,

Nor care beyond today:
Yet see how all around 'em wait
The ministers of human fate,
And black Misfortune's baleful train!
Ah, show them where in ambush stand
To seize their prey the murtherous band!
Ah, tell them, they are men!

    These shall the fury Passions tear,
The vultures of the mind,
Disdainful Anger, pallid Fear,
And Shame that skulks behind;
Or pining Love shall waste their youth,
Or Jealousy with rankling tooth,
That inly gnaws the secret heart,
And Envy wan, and faded Care,
Grim-visaged comfortless Despair,
And Sorrow's piercing dart.

—Thomas Gray (1716-1771)

6) Read the following poem carefully. Explain who the speaker is and the meaning of Tom's dream. Explain the use of the word "your" in the first stanza and "want" in stanza 5 and how these words fit into the general meaning of the poem. Drawing attention to figures of speech, meter and rhyme, show how the poet gives a wider meaning to the poem. What effect does the last line have on you?

THE CHIMNEY SWEEPER

When my mother died I was very young,
And my father sold me while yet my tongue
Could scarcely cry "weep! 'weep! 'weep! 'weep!"
So your chimneys I sweep, and in soot I sleep

There's little Tom Dacre, who cried when his head,
That curled like a lamb's back, was shaved: so I said
"Hush, Tom! never mind it, for when your head's bare
You know that the soot cannot spoil your white hair."

And so he was quiet, and that very night,
As Tom was a-sleeping, he had such a sight!
That thousands of sweepers, Dick, Joe, Ned, and Jack,
Were all of them locked up in coffins of black.

And by came an Angel who had a bright key,
And he opened the coffins and set them all free;
Then down a green plain leaping, laughing, they run,
And wash in a river, and shine in the sun.

Then naked and white, all their bags left behind,
They rise upon clouds and sport in the wind;
And the Angel told Tom, if he'd be a good boy,
He'd have God for his father, and never want joy.

And so Tom awoke; and we rose in the dark,
And got with our bags and our brushes to work.
Though the morning was cold, Tom was happy and warm;
So if all do their duty they need not fear harm.

—William Blake (1757-1827)

7) Discuss the following poem carefully, explaining what form of poetry it is, how the poet makes the reader aware of the listener, and how the speaker reveals his true colors. Pay particular attention to the last two lines.

MY LAST DUCHESS

That's my last Duchess painted on the wall,
Looking as if she were alive. I call
That piece a wonder, now: Frà Pandolf's hands
Worked busily a day, and there she stands.
Will't please you sit and look at her ? I said
'Frà Pandolf' by design, for never read
Strangers like you that pictured countenance,
The depth and passion of its earnest glance,
But to myself they turned (since none puts by
The curtain I have drawn for you, but I)
And seemed as they would ask me, if they durst,
How such a glance came there; so, not the first
Are you to turn and ask thus. Sir, 't was not
Her husband's presence only, called that spot

Of joy into the Duchess' cheek: perhaps
Frà Pandolf chanced to say 'Her mantle laps
Over my lady's wrist too much,' or 'Paint
Must never hope to reproduce the faint
Half-flush that dies along her throat:' such stuff
Was courtesy, she thought, and cause enough
For calling up that spot of joy. She had

A heart—how shall I say ?—too soon made glad,
Too easily impressed; she liked whate'er
She looked on, and her looks went everywhere.
Sir, 't was all one! My favour at her breast,
The dropping of the daylight in the West,
The bough of cherries some officious fool
Broke in the orchard for her, the white mule
She rode with round the terrace—all and each
Would draw from her alike the approving speech,
Or blush, at least. She thanked men,—good! but thanked
Somehow—I know not how—as if she ranked
My gift of a nine-hundred-years-old name
With anybody's gift. Who'd stoop to blame
This sort of triffing? Even had you skill
In speech—(which I have not)—to make your will
Quite clear to such an one, and say, 'Just this
Or that in you disgusts me; here you miss,
Or there exceed the mark'—and if she let
Herself be lessoned so, nor plainly set
Her wits to yours, forsooth, and made excuse,
—E'en then would be some stooping; and I choose
Never to stoop. Oh sir, she smiled, no doubt,
Whene'er I passed her; but who passed without
Much the same smile? This grew; I gave commands;
Then all smiles stopped together. There she stands
As if alive. Will't please you rise? We'll meet
The company below, then. I repeat,
The Count your master's known munificence
Is ample warrant that no just pretence
Of mine for dowry will be disallowed;
Though his fair daughter's self, as I avowed
At starting, is my object. Nay, we'll go
Together down, sir. Notice Neptune, though,
Taming a sea-horse, thought a rarity,
Which Claus of Innsbruck cast in bronze for me!

—Robert Browning (1812-1889)

SUGGESTED SAMPLE ANSWERS

l) The poem is written in open-form poetry demonstrated by the fact there is no set rhyme pattern or rhythm. The expression could have been written in prose and still have the same meaning but not the same impact. The composition of the words on the page draws attention to the horror of the scene. The frequent use of the comma in the first stanza makes the reader pause at each idea, stressing the importance of "creature, naked, bestial." The line breaks give the impression that the poet is pondering an actual scene he once saw, relaying the scene to listeners rather than readers. The enjambment of the first line into the second suggests a the smooth flow of a conversation, as if we have just entered an ongoing discussion. Similarly, the enjambment between lines eight and nine accentuates the down-to-earth statement of the creature, making something that is gruesome seem perfectly reasonable. The repetition of the word "bitter" with the dash in line seven works as an emphatic point—the reader must pause and stress the words.

The creature might be the symbol of 20th century existentialism, whereby one creates one's own essence of being, but that explanation does not totally explain the horrifying picture the creature makes, nor why it should be in the desert. The poet may be making an allusion to Yeats' creature which slouches its way to Bethlehem, in which case the creature might symbolize an antichrist, a turning away from the external word to an inner obsession, an element in modern living that is inexplicable evil, but evil that feeds upon itself to engender itself.

The meaning of the poem might be that everyone has the right to live his or her life in a chosen way simply because it is that person's life. To others it may appear that the person is wasting his life, leading it in an antisocial way, which is destructive if not downright suicidal, but in the existential thinking the essence of life is made by the person who owns it: "it is my heart" and I shall do what I please with it. In a modern interpretation one could cite the example of young teenagers wasting their time on drugs and alcohol because although it is a "bitter" way in other people's point of view, it is their life and they can do what they like with it. Overall the poem suggests that life in modern times has a nightmarish quality, and as we hunt for meaning in the poem's imagery, it might be underlining the fact that there is no meaning to life but it is bitter and we had better get on with living.

COMMENTS: The poem is very much open to interpretation, but start immediately analyzing the form and that will help you come to your own interpretation. Avoid words such as "horrible" or "scary"; try to elevate the communication of your fear: I think you would agree the image is horrifying. If you have the William Butler Yeats' poem "The Second Coming" in your reading background, then you will see connections. Remember that poets very often allude to other works in literature; remember the more reading you do the more you will pick up on allusions which can only aid in your answer.

2) This sonnet is English or Shakespearean because it has the set rhyme pattern of three quatrains and a rhyming couplet: abab cdcd efef gg. The last rhyming couplet has the shift or turn or twist at the end, a signature of the English sonnet. The meter is iambic pentameter, another indicator of the English sonnet. The Italian or Petrarchan sonnet usually has the same meter but the rhyme scheme falls into an octave and a sestet: the former having a set rhyme scheme abbaabba and the sestet any order, usually cdecde. The Italian sonnet would set up a proposal or thought in the octave then the shift would come and the sestet would answer the proposal or resolve the thought.

Most of the early sonnets dealt with love as this one does. The poet suggests that if two people really love one another, the love is not just physical and alters as soon as the physical body changes or is removed; but a mind-love—there should be no obstacles put in the way of such a love. Love should be constant even in times of difficulty or "tempests." It should be like a star that guides the mariner home in a ship whose worth may not be known but whose dimension is. Love should not change because Time alters the people who love, nor should it alter through the short span of time on earth, when people are presented with adversity, but live eternally. The shift in the meaning comes in the couplet, suggesting if the poet is not right about any of the above then he has never written anything, and obviously he is an accomplished poet, nor has any man ever loved, and of course part of the human condition is to love and fall in love.

The most striking areas are the metaphor of the star and boat and the personification of Time. The poet writes in a time when navigation by the stars and the loss of boats were real concerns for everyone. The audience would have great interest in and could relate to this metaphor. Time was often seen as an old man with a scythe or sickle ("he" is still depicted like this in modern-day New Year's cards!) cutting a swathe through youth, shown by rosy cheeks of health. Again the audience would relate to the devices and "see" the point of the images. The tone of the sonnet is another striking area in that the pace is lively and "no-nonsense" even if it does deal with a "soft" subject. The enjambment between lines 1 and 2, 2 and 3, and 9 and 10 give a speedy reading to the poem, and the last couplet states the point in a challenging, engaging way that no one could possibly refute.

COMMENTS: Get straight to the point about the rhyme scheme and meter and the meaning will come as you work on the lines. Underline the points of meaning—paraphrase them in rough before you write. Pull out all the devices you have learned and then apply them to the poetry, asking yourself, "Why use these particular images?"

3) The tone of the poem starts as if the speaker is a casual observer of the streets of London. As he walks, however, the tone becomes grimmer and more depressed until at the end it explodes into anger. The meter is based on seven- or eight-syllable lines with the stresses falling in irregular places at the end with the anger expressed with "Blasts" "new-born," and "blights," the alliteration adding

to the stress length and making the words erupt as one reads. The regular rhyme suggests the speaker's feet walking in a regular pattern, footsteps echoing as he walks.

The repetition in the second stanza stresses the fact that all the city dwellers are suffering under this society's cruelty. It serves to build to the frightening image in the last line of the stanza when the repeated "every" now takes on the regular beat of a hammer on an anvil forging the manacles. The image is frightening because it suggests on a deeper level that we are all in chains, and the worst type of manacles are those we forge for ourselves, the captivity we make for our own minds.

In stanza three, the darkness of the vision is carried out through the image of the sweeps, children, having to clean the blackened-by-industry churches—on a deeper level again the notion of England's strongest institutions becoming blackened or spoiled by industry. The soldier's sighs suggest the waste of wars, sending young men to their deaths for useless causes. The alliteration of the "s" sound conjures the sound of the sighs and helps the graphic quality of the blood running down palace walls—the palace suggesting the imperialism that this society was founded upon.

The last stanza bursts with anger as the speaker deals with the plight of young girls who often took to prostitution to survive—their own survival as well as their families'. The new-born child's disease or blight would be syphilis. The word "blight" suggests a spreading mold, as if on flowers or plants. The disease was spread through prostitution and often children would develop symptoms of blindness and insanity years later. The "child" could refer to the girl's newborn. who would perpetuate the disease, or to a young man who has consorted with prostitutes, married "respectably" and passed on the disease, which will turn his marriage into a tragedy.

COMMENTS: Whatever interpretation, you need to stress the anger the speaker feels at a society that allows this type of vicious circle of despair and poverty to continue. You might want to deal with the meaning first and then the poetic devices, but make sure you mention the relevant points of meter, alliteration, etc., and how the poem works as a whole.

4) The poem is an early example of a dramatic monologue in which the speaker addresses a listener who does not speak, but we are aware of its presence and what the listener is doing. The speaker, a male, addresses a woman, in what must be termed a witty seduction scene. The setting must be somewhere intimate enough that they can speak of such matters as courtship and sexual intercourse before marriage. The woman is obviously a virgin and the man an experienced wooer. He wants to convince the woman that losing her virginity is of no consequence, rather like that of the flea losing its life. The poem is built on the conceit of the flea being like the woman and then being like the couple. The Elizabethans would have found this conceit brilliantly witty and intelligent.

The speaker dives straight into the conversation so that the reader feels part of the scene in progress. Because the flea has sucked blood from both of them, the speaker believes that this mingling of their blood symbolizes their marriage, at least in a physical sense, and tries to persuade the woman that there has been no loss: no shame, no loss of honor. The enjambment of the lines makes the poetry fast moving and conversational. The caesuras coming at unexpected places, line 9 is a good example, break the rhythm and again give the poem a natural speaking tone.

When the woman moves to kill the flea the speaker stops her because the flea represents their union; although parents might begrudge the union, as does the woman, their bodies, their blood, have joined. If she kills the flea she commits murder of the flea, the speaker and herself, which is suicide—all sins, so she commits three sins in one. Between stanzas 2 and 3 the woman does kill the flea and the speaker turns her delight that she has felt no loss to his advantage: just as she finds herself unchanged by the death of the flea so will she find herself unchanged by yielding to the speaker—no loss of honor. He tries to allay her fears with a witty turn to the event. The "pat" tone of the speaker, almost a glib tone, makes the poetry race along and the argument very convincing.

COMMENTS: With a poem as complex as this it is perhaps best to take the meaning line by line, commenting on the language as you go along. You could comment on language first, the rhythm and rhyme, and then tackle the meaning.

5) Although the poem has rhyme, both end-stopped: me/Immortality/Civility; and half-rhyme: chill/tulle, there is no constant fixed pattern. Nor is there is a set meter: the dashes breaking the meter and the line count at unusual places. The form, then, is open. The tone comes across as breathless; the speaker is relaying an experience she has had as if reliving it in its original intensity. The poem, though open, may be referred to as an allegory: a spiritual meaning hidden beneath physical or concrete terminology.

The ironic tone is crucial at the beginning because it links with the turn toward optimism at the end. The speaker is not ready for this "gentleman caller" but he nevertheless calls on her. Death is personified as courtly and kind and the speaker, a woman, has to put away her day-by-day life and go with him, matching his courtesy. The game the children are playing—ironically they strive at playing it, not really enjoying it—is "Ring a Ring of Roses"—a game that simulated death in the time of the great plagues in Europe. All falling down at the end suggested the massive amounts of dead. Of course the children do not appreciate the gloom of the game but the game is a crucial part of the poem's theme: the inevitability of death—even these children will die.

The weather growing colder suggests that death is drawing closer for the woman; the gossamer cape of thin material suggests already the funeral shroud. The carriage then stops in front of the place which will house the woman: her tomb. If the poem had ended here the overall feeling would have been fear of death and sadness. But the last stanza suggests that the above "story" was a vision of what death is about. The event happened a long time ago and yet seems like yesterday, again suggesting inevitability, that at some point in time someone dies. The last line gives a firm assertion of belief in the afterlife. The horses drawing the carriage were faced toward Eternity, the concept of the Christian tradition of the eternal life.

COMMENTS: Your interpretation of the ending might be more along the lines of fearing the eternity the horses face toward. If so, bring out from the poetry what areas will back you up: the tone of gloom perhaps, or the coldness. Whatever your interpretation of meaning, be sure to deal with the dashes and the rhyme, showing the examiners you know the elements of poetry involved.

CHAPTER 3

DRAMA AND THEATER

The Glass Menagerie by Tennessee Williams begins when one of its four characters, Tom, steps into the downstage light and addresses the audience directly as though he were the chorus from a much earlier play. "I have tricks in my pocket, I have things up my sleeve," says Tom. "But I am the opposite of a stage magician. He gives you illusion that has the appearance of truth. I give you truth in the pleasant disguise of illusion."

To sit among the audience and watch a skillful production of *The Glass Menagerie* is to visit Tom's paradoxical world of theater, a magic place in which known imposters and stagecraft trickery create a spectacle which we know is illusion but somehow recognize as truth. Theater, as a performed event, combines the talents and skills of numerous artists and craftspersons, but before the spectacle must come the playwright's work, the pages of words designating what the audience sees and hears. These words, the written script separate from the theatrical performance of them, is what we call *drama*, and the words give the spectacle its significance because without them the illusion has neither frame nor content. Truth requires boundaries and substance. When Shakespeare's Hamlet advises actors just before their performance, he places careful emphasis on the importance of the words, cautioning the players to speak them "trippingly on the tongue." If all actions are not suited to the words, Hamlet adds, the performance will fail because the collaborative purpose combining the dramatist's literary art and the actors' performing art "is to hold as 'twere the mirror up to Nature."

Although drama is literature written to be performed, it closely resembles the other genres. In fact, both poetry and prose also can be performed; but as captivating as these public readings sometimes are, only performed drama best creates the immediate living "illusion as truth" Tom promises. Like fiction and narrative poetry, drama tells a tale—that is, it has plot, characters, and setting—but the author's voice is distant, heard only through the stage directions and perhaps some supplementary notes. With rare exceptions, dialogue dominates the script. Some drama is poetry, such as the works of Shakespeare and Molière, and all plays resemble poems as abstractions because both forms are highly condensed, figurative expressions. Even in Henrik Ibsen's social realism, the dramatic action is metaphorical.

A scene set inside a house, for instance, requires a room with only three walls. No audience complains, just as no movie audience feels betrayed by film characters' appearing ridiculously large. Without a thought, audiences employ what Samuel Taylor Coleridge called "a willing suspension of disbelief"; in other words, they know that the images before them are not real but rather representations, reflections in the mirror of which Hamlet speaks, not the real world ("Nature").

A play contains conflict which can be enacted immediately on the stage without any alterations in the written word. **Enacted** means performed by an actor or actors free to use the entire stage and such theatrical devices as sets, costumes, makeup, special lighting, and props for support. This differs from the oral interpretation of prose or poetry. No matter how animated, the public reader is not acting. This is the primary distinction between drama and other literary forms. Their most obvious similarity is that any form of literature is a linguistic expression. There is, however, one other feature shared by all kinds of narratives: the pulsating energy which pushes the action along is generated by human imperfection. We speak of tragic characters as having "flaws," but the same is true about comic characters as well. Indeed, nothing is more boring either on a stage or in a written text than a consistently flawless personality, because such characters can never be congruent with the real people of our everyday experiences. The most fundamental human truth is human frailty.

Although it can be argued that a play, like a musical composition, must be performed to be realized, the script's linguistic foundation always gives the work potential as a literary experience. Moreover, there is never a "definitive" interpretation. The script, in a sense, remains unfinished because it never stops inviting new variations, and among those invited to participate are individual readers whose imaginations should not be discounted. For example, when *Death of a Salesman* was originally produced, Lee J. Cobb played Willy Loman. Aside from the character's age, Dustin Hoffman's Willy in the revival forty years later bore hardly any physical resemblance to Cobb's. Yet both portrayals "worked." The same could be said about the Willys created by the minds of the play's countless readers. Quite capable of composing its own visions and sounds, the human imagination is the original mirror, the place where all human truths evolve from perceived data.

Hamlet's mirror and Tom's truthful illusions are figures of speech echoing drama's earliest great critic, Aristotle, who believed art should create a **mimesis**, the Greek word for "imitation." For centuries this "mimetic theory" has asserted that a successful imitation is one which reproduces natural objects and actions in as realistic portrayal as possible. Later, this notion of imitation adopted what has been called the "expressive theory," a variation allowing the artist a freer, more individual stylized approach. A drama by Ibsen, for example, attempts to capture experience as unadorned raw sense, the way it normally appears to be. This is realistic imitation. As 20th century drama moved toward examinations of people's inner consciousness as universal representations of some greater human predicament, new expressive styles emerged. The diversity in the works of Eugene O'Neill, Samuel Beckett, and Harold Pinter illustrate how dramatists' imitations can disrupt our sense of the familiar as their plays become more personally expressive. But the theater of Aristotle's time was hardly "realistic" in today's objective sense. Instead, it was highly stylized and full of conventions derived from theater's ritualistic origins. The same is true of medieval morality plays and the rigid formality of Japanese Kabuki theater, yet these differ greatly from each other and from ancient Greek and Roman dramas. In other words, imitating "what's out there" requires only that the form be consistent with itself, and any form is permissible.

PLOT STRUCTURE

As with other narrative types, a play's **plot** is its sequence of events, its organized collection of incidents. At one time it was thought that all the actions within a play should be contained within a single twenty-four hour period. Few lengthy plays have plots which cover only the period of time enacted on the stage. Most plays condense and edit time much as novels do. Decades can be reduced to two hours. Included in the plot is the **exposition**, the revealing of whatever information we need in order to understand the impending conflict. This exposed material should provide us with a sense of place and time (**setting**), the central participants, important prior incidents, and the play's overall mood. In some plays such as Shakespeare's, the exposition comes quickly. Notice, for instance, the opening scenes in *Macbeth, Hamlet,* and *Romeo and Juliet*: not one presents us with a central character, yet each—with its witches or king's ghost or street brawl—clearly establishes an essential tension heralding the main conflict to come. These initial expositions attack the audience immediately and are followed by subsequent events in chronological order. Sophocles' *Oedipus Rex* works somewhat differently, presenting the central character late in the myth from which the play is taken. The exposition must establish what has come previously, even for an audience familiar with the story, before the plot can advance. Like Shakespeare, Sophocles must start his exposition at the beginning, but he takes a longer (though not tedious) time revealing the essential facts. Arthur Miller, in his *Death of a Salesman,* continuously interrupts the central action with dislocated expositions from earlier times as though the past were always in the present. He carefully establishes character, place, mood, and conflict throughout the earliest scenes; however, whatever present he places on stage is always caught in a tension between the audience's anticipation of the future and its suspicions of the past. The plots in plays like *Oedipus Rex* and *Death of a Salesman* tend not to attack us head-on but rather to surround us and gradually close in, the circle made tighter by each deliberately released clue to a mysterious past.

Conflict requires two opposing forces. We see, for instance, how King Lear's irresponsible abdication and conceited anger are countered by Goneril and Regan's duplicity and lusts for power. We also see how Creon's excessive means for restoring order in Thebes is met by Antigone's allegiance to personal conscience. Fairly soon in a play we must experience some incident that incites the fundamental conflict when placed against some previously presented incident or situation. In most plays the conflict's abrasive conditions continuously chafe and even lacerate each other. The play's tempo might provide some interruptions or variations in the pace; nevertheless, conflicts generate the actions which make the characters' worlds worse before they can get better. Any plot featuring only repetitious altercations, however, would soon become tiresome. Potentially, anything can happen in a conflict. The **complication** is whatever presents an element capable of altering the action's direction. Perhaps some new information is discovered or a previously conceived scheme fails, creating a reversal of what had been expected. The plot is not a series of similar events but rather a compilation of related events leading to a culmination, a **crisis**.

In retrospect we should be able to accept a drama's progression of actions leading to the crisis as inevitable. After the crisis comes the **resolution** (or **denouement**), which gives the play its concluding boundary. This does not mean that the play should offer us solutions for whatever human issues it raises. Rather, the playwright's obligation is to make the experience he presents to us seem filled within its own perimeters. George Bernard Shaw felt he had met this obligation when he ended *Pygamalion* with his two principal characters, Higgins and Eliza, utterly incapable of voicing any romantic affection for each other; and the resolution in Ibsen's *A Doll's House* outraged audiences a hundred years ago and still disturbs some people today, even though it concludes the play with believable consequences.

Terms such as **exposition, complication, crisis,** and **resolution,** though helpful in identifying the conflict's currents and directions, at best only artificially define how a plot is molded. If the play provides unity in its revelations, these seams are barely noticeable. Moreover, any successful creative composition clearly shows that the artist accomplished much more than merely plugging components together to create a finished work. There are no rules which all playwrights must follow, except the central precept that the play's unified assortment of actions be complete and contained within itself. *Antigone*, for instance, depicts the third phase of Sophocles' Oedipus trilogy, although it was actually written and performed before *Oedipus Rex* and *Oedipus at Colonus*. And although a modern reader might require some background information before starting, *Antigone* gives a cohesive dramatic impact independent from the other two plays.

CHARACTER

Essential to the plot's success are the characters who participate in it. Midpoint in *Hamlet* when Elsinore Castle is visited by the traveling theater company, the prince joyously welcomes the players, but his mood quickly returns to bitter depression shortly after he asks one actor to recite a dramatic passage in which the speaker recalls the fall of Troy and particularly Queen Hecuba's response to her husband's brutal murder. The player, caught by the speech's emotional power, becomes distraught and cannot finish. Left alone on stage, Hamlet compares the theatrical world created by the player with Hamlet's "real" world and asks: "What's Hecuba to him, or he to Hecuba,/ That he should weep for her!" Under ordinary circumstances Hamlet's anxiety would not overshadow his Renaissance sensibilities, because he knows well that fictional characters always possess the potential to move us. As though by instinct, we know the same. We read narratives and go to the theater precisely because we want to be shocked, delighted, thrilled, saddened, titillated, or invigorated by "a dream of passion." Even though some characters are more complex and interesting than others, they come in countless types as the playwright's delegates to our imaginations and as the imitations of reality seeking our response.

Antigone begins with two characters, Antigone and Ismene, on stage. They initiate the exposition through their individual reactions to a previous event, King Creon's edict following the battle in which Thebes defeated an invading army. Creon has proclaimed Eteocles and the others who recently died defending Thebes as heroes worthy of the highest burial honors; in addition, Creon has forbidden anyone, on penalty of death, from burying Poloneices and the others who fell attacking the city. Since Antigone, Ismene, Polyneices, and Eteocles are the children of Oedipus and Iocaste, the late king and queen, conflict over Creon's law seems imminent. These first two characters establish this inevitability. They also reveal much about themselves as individuals.

ANTIGONE:... now you must prove what you are:
A true sister, or a traitor to your family.

ISMENE: Antigone, are you mad! What could I possibly do?

ANTIGONE: You must decide whether you will help me or not.

ISMENE: I do not understand you. Help you in what?

ANTIGONE: Ismene, I am going to bury him. Will you come?

ISMENE: Bury him! You have just said the new law forbids it.

ANTIGONE: He is my brother. And he is your brother, too.

ISMENE: But think of the danger! Think what Creon will do!

ANTIGONE: Creon is not strong enough to stand in my way.

ISMENE: Ah sister!
Oedipus died, everyone hating him
For what his own search brought to light, his eyes
Ripped out by his own hand; and Iocaste died,
His mother and wife at once: she twisted the cords
That strangled her life; and our two brothers died,
Each killed by the other's sword. And we are left:
But oh, Antigone,
Think how much more terrible than these
Our own death would be if we should go against Creon
And do what he has forbidden! We are only women,
We cannot fight with men, Antigone!
The law is strong, we must give in to the law

In this thing, and in worse. I beg the Dead
To forgive me, but I am helpless: I must yield
To those in authority. And I think it is dangerous business
To be always meddling.

ANTIGONE: If that is what you think,
I should not want you, even if you asked to come.
You have made your choice, you can be what you want to be.
But I will bury him; and if I must die,
I say that this crime is holy: I shall lie down
With him in death, and I shall be as dear
To him as he to me.
It is the dead,
Not the living, who make the longest demands:
We die for ever...
You may do as you like,
Since apparently, the laws of the gods mean nothing to you.

ISMENE: They mean a great deal to me; but I have no strength
To break laws that were made for the public good.

ANTIGONE: That must be your excuse, I suppose. But as for me,
I will bury the brother I love.

ISMENE: Antigone, I am so afraid for you!

ANTIGONE: You need not be:
You have yourself to consider, after all.

ISMENE: But no one must hear of this, you must tell no one!
I will keep it a secret, I promise!

ANTIGONE: Oh tell it! Tell everyone!
Think how they'll hate you when it all comes out
If they learn that you knew about it all the time!

ISMENE: So fiery! You should be cold with fear.

ANTIGONE: Perhaps. But I am doing only what I must.

ISMENE: But can you do it? I say that you cannot.

ANTIGONE: Very well: when my strength gives out, I shall do no more.

ISMENE: Impossible things should not be tried at all.

ANTIGONE: Go away, Ismene:
I shall be hating you soon, and the dead will too,
For your words are hateful. Leave me my foolish plan:
I am not afraid of the danger; if it means death,
It will not be the worst of deaths—death without honor.

ISMENE: Go then, if you feel that you must.
You are unwise,
But a loyal friend to those who love you.

[Exit into the Palace. ANTIONE goes off...]

READING THE PLAY

All we know about Antigone and Ismene in this scene comes from what they say; therefore, we read their spoken words carefully. However, we must also remain attentive to dramatic characters, propensity for not revealing all they know and feel about a given issue, and often characters do not recognize all the implications in what they say. We might be helped by what one says about the other, yet these observations are not necessarily accurate or sincere. Even though the previous scene contains fewer abiguities than some others in dramatic literature, we would be oversimplifying to say the conflict here is between one character who is "right" and another who is "wrong." Antigone comes out challenging, determined and unafraid, whereas Ismene immediately reacts fearfully. Antigone brims with the self-assured power of righteousness while Ismene expresses vulnerability. Yet Antigone's boast that "Creon is not strong enough to stand in my way" suggests a rash temperament. We might admire her courage, but we question her judgment. Meanwhile, Ismene can evoke our sympathies with her burden of family woes, at least until she confesses her helplessness and begs the Dead to forgive her, at which point we realize her objections stem from cowardice and not conscience.

Although we might remain unsettled by Antigone's single-mindedness, we soon find ourselves sharing her disdain for Ismene's trepidation, particularly when Ismene rationalizes her position as the more responsible and labels unauthorized intervention in royal decisions as "meddling" against the "public good." Soon, as we realize the issue here demands moral conscience, we measure Ismene far short of what is required. Quickly though, Ismene is partly redeemed by her obvious concern for Antigone's well-being: "I am so afraid for you." Unaffected, Antigone retorts with sarcasm and threats, but her demeanor never becomes so impetuously caustic that we dismiss her as a conceited adolescent. In fact, we are touched by her integrity and devotion, seeing no pretensions when she says: "I am not afraid of the danger: if it means death,/It will not be the worst of deaths—death without honor." Ismene's intimation that loyalty and love are unwise counters Antigone's idealism enough to make us suspect that the stark, cruel world of human imperfection will not tolerate Antigone's solitary rebellion, no matter how selfless her motivation. At the same time we wonder how long Ismene could remain neutral if Antigone were to clash with Creon.

What immediately strikes us about Antigone and Ismene is that each possesses a sense of self, a conscious awareness about her existence and her connection with forces greater than herself. This is why we can identify with them. It may not always feel reassuring, yet we too can define our existence by saying "I am, and I am not alone." As social creatures, a condition about which they have had no choice, both Antigone and Ismene have senses of self which are touched by their identification with others: each belongs to a family, and each belongs to a civil state. Indeed, much of the play's conflict focuses on which identification should be stronger. Another connection influences them as well—the unbreakable tie to truth. This truth, or ultimate reality, will vary from play to play, and not all characters ever realize it is there, and few will define it the same way. Still, the universe which characters inhabit has definition, even if the resolution suggests a great human absurdity in our insufficient capacity to grasp this definition or, worse, asserts the only definition is the absence of an ultimate reality. With Antigone, we see how her sense of self cannot be severed from its bonds to family obligations and certain moral principles.

Characters with a sense of self and an identity framed by social connections and unmitigated truths dwell in all good narratives. As readers we wander within these connecting perimeters, following the plot and sensing a commentary about life in general. This commentary, the theme, places us within the mirror's image along with the characters and their actions. We look and see ourselves. The characters' universe is ours, the playwright would have us believe, for a while at least. If his art succeeds, we do believe him. But reading literary art is no passive experience; it requires active work. And since playwrights seldom help us decide *how* characters say what they do or interrupt to explain *why* they say what they do, what personal voice he gives through stage directions deserves special attention, because playwrights never tell as much as novelists; instead they show. Our reading should focus on the tone of the dialogue as much as on the information in what is said. Prior to the 19th century, dramatists relied heavily on poetic diction to define their characters. Later playwrights provided stage directions which detail stage activities and modify dialogue. Modern writers usually give precise descriptions for the set and costume design and even prescribe particular background music. But no matter when a play was written or what its expressive style is, our role as readers and audience is to make judgments about characters in action, just as we make judgments about Antigone and Ismene the first time we see them. We should strive to be "fooled" by the truthful illusion by activating our sensitivities to human imperfections and the potential conflicts such flaws can generate. And, finally, as we peer into the playwright's mirror, we seek among the populated reflections shadows of ourselves.

TYPES OF PLAYS

When Polonius presents the traveling players to Hamlet, he reads from the theater company's license, which identifies them as

> The best actors in the world, either for tragedy, comedy, history, pastoral, pastoral-comical, historical-pastoral, tragical-historical, tragical-comical-historical-pastoral, scene individable or poem unlimited...

Shakespeare's sense of humor runs through this speech which sounds like a parody of the license granted Shakespeare's own company by James I, authorizing "the Arte and faculty of playing Comedies, Tragedies, histories, Enterludes, moralls, pastoralls, Stageplaies and Such others..." for the king's subjects and himself. The joke is on those who think all plays somehow can be categorized according to preconceived definitions, as though playwrights follow literary recipes. The notion is not entirely ridiculous, to be sure, since audiences and readers can easily tell a serious play from a humorous one, and a play labeled "tragedy" or "comedy" will generate certain valid expectations from us all, regardless of whether we have read a word by Aristotle or any other literary critic. Still, if beginning playwrights had to choose between writing according to some rigid strictures designating the likes of a "tragical-comical-historical-pastoral" or writing a play unrestricted by such rules (a "poem unlimited"), they would probably choose the latter.

All plays contain thought—its accumulated themes, arguments, and overall meaning of the action—together with a mood or tone, and we tend to categorize dramatic thought into three clusters: the serious, the comic, and the seriocomic. These distinctions echo the primitive rites from which theater evolved, religious observances usually tied to seasonal cycles. In the course of a year numerous situations could arise which would initiate dramatic, communal prayers of supplication or thanksgiving. Indeed, for humanity to see its fate held by the will of a god is to see the intricate unity of flesh and spirit, a paradox ripe for representation as dramatic conflict. And if winter's chill brings the pangs of tragedy and summer's warmth the delight of comedy, the year becomes a metaphor for the overall human condition, which contains both. Thus, in our attempts to interpret life's complexities, it is tempting to place the art forms representing it in precise, fixed designations. From this can come critical practices which ascertain how well a work imitates life by how well it adheres to its designated form. Of course, such a critical system's rigidity would limit the range of possible human experiences expressed on stage to a narrow few, but then the range could be made elastic enough to provide for possible variations and combinations. Like the old Ptolomaic theories which held the earth as the center of the universe, these precepts could work for a while. After a few centuries, though, it would become clear that there is a better way of explaining what a play's form should be—not so much fixed as organic. In other words, we should think of a play as similar to a plant's growing and taking shape according to its own design. This analogy works well because the plant is not a mechanical device constructed from a predetermined plan, yet every plant is a species and as such contains qualities which identify it with others. So just as Shakespeare could ridicule overly precise definitions for dramatic art, he could still write dramas which he clearly identified as tragedies, comedies, or histories, even though he would freely mix two or more of these together in the same play. For the purpose of understanding some of the different perspectives available to the playwright's examining eye, we will look at plays from different periods which follow the three main designations Shakespeare used, followed by a fourth which is indicative of modern American drama. A knowledge of *The Importance of Being Earnest*, *Othello*, *A Man for All Seasons*, and *Death of a Salesman* will be helpful.

Comedy

The primary aim of comedy is to amuse us with a happy ending, although comedies can vary according to the attitudes they project, which can be broadly identified as either **high** or **low**, terms having nothing to do with an evaluation of the play's merit. Generally, the amusement found in comedy comes from an eventual victory over threats or ill fortune. Much of the dialogue and plot development might be laughable, yet a play need not be funny to be comic. **Farce** is low comedy intended to make us laugh by means of a series of exaggerated, unlikely situations that depend less on plot and character than on gross absurdities, sight gags, and coarse dialogue. The "higher" a comedy goes, the more natural the characters seem and the less boisterous their behavior. The plots become more sustained, and the dialogue shows more weighty thought. As with all dramas, comedies are about things that go wrong. Accordingly, comedies create deviations from accepted normalcy, presenting incongruities which we might or might not see as harmless. If these incongruities make us judgmental about the involved characters and events, the play takes on the features of **satire**, a rather high comic form implying that humanity and human institutions are in need of reform. If the action triggers our sympathy for the characters, we feel even less protected from the incongruities as the play tilts more in the direction of **tragi-comedy**. In other words, the action determines a figurative distance between the audience and the play. Such factors as characters' personalities and the plot's predictability influence this distance. The farther away we sit, the more protected we feel and usually the funnier the play becomes. Closer proximity to believability in the script draws us nearer to the conflict, making us feel more involved in the action and less safe in its presence. It is a rare play that can freely manipulate its audience back and forth along this plane and still maintain its unity. Shakespeare's *The Merchant of Venice* is one example.

A more consistent play is Oscar Wilde's *The Importance of Being Earnest*, which opened in 1895. In the following scene, Lady Bracknell questions Jack Worthing, who has just announced that Lady Bracknell's daughter, Gwendolyn, has agreed to marry him. Being satisfied with Jack's answers concerning his income and finding his upper-class idleness and careless ignorance about world affairs an asset, she queries him about his family background. In grave tones, the embarrassed Jack reveals his mysterious lineage. His late guardian, Thomas Cardew—"an old gentleman of a very charitable and kindly disposition"—had found the baby Jack in an abandoned handbag.

LADY BRACKNELL: A hand-bag?

JACK: (very seriously): Yes, Lady Bracknell. I was in a hand-bag—a somewhat large, black leather hand- bag, with handles to it—an ordinary hand-bag in fact.

LADY BRACKNELL: In what locality did this Mr. James, or Thomas, Cardew come across this ordinary hand-bag?

JACK: In the cloak-room at Victoria Station. It was given him in mistake for his own.

LADY BRACKNELL: The cloak-room at Victoria Station?

JACK: Yes. The Brighton line.

LADY BRACKNELL: The line is immaterial, Mr. Worthing. I confess I feel somewhat bewildered by what you have just told me. To be born, or at any rate bred, in a hand-bag, whether it had handles or not, seems to me to display a contempt for the ordinary decencies of family life that reminds one of the worst excesses of the French Revolution. And I presume you know what that unfortunate movement led to? As for the particular locality in which the hand-bag was found, a cloak-room at a railway station might serve to conceal a social indiscretion—has probably, indeed, been used for that purpose before now—but it could hardly be regarded as an assured basis for recognized position in good society.

JACK: May I ask you then what would you advise me to do? I need hardly say I would do anything in the world to ensure Gwendolyn's happiness.

LADY BRACKNELL: I would strongly advise you, Mr. Worthing, to try and acquire some relations as soon as possible, and to make a definite effort to produce at any rate one parent, of either sex, before the season is over.

JACK: Well, I don't see how I could possibly manage to do that. I can produce the hand-bag at any moment. It is in my dressing-room at home. I really think that should satisfy you, Lady Bracknell.

LADY BRACKNELL: Me, sir! What has it to do with me? You can hardly imagine that I and Lord Bracknell would dream of allowing our only daughter—a girl brought up with the utmost care—to marry into a cloak-room, and form an alliance with a parcel. Good morning, Mr. Worthing!

(LADY BRACKNELL sweeps out in majestic indignation.)

This dialogue between Lady Bracknell and Jack is typical of what runs throughout the entire play. It is full of exaggerations, in both the situation being discussed and the manner in which the characters, particularly Lady Bracknell, express their reactions to the situation. Under other circumstances a foundling would not be the focus of a comedy, but we are relieved from any concern for the child since the adult Jack is obviously secure, healthy, and, with one exception, carefree. Moreover, we laugh when Lady Bracknell exaggerates Jack's heritage by comparing it with the excesses of the French Revolution. On the other hand, at the core of their discussion is the deeply ingrained and oppressive notion of English class consciousness, a mentality so flawed it almost begs to be satirized. Could there be more there than light, witty entertainment?

COMEDY ESSAY QUESTION

One critic has stated that we find humor not in the subject matter presented to us but in how the subject matter is presented. Explain what this means an how it applies to *The Importance of Being Earnest*.

Sample Answer #1

The Importance of Being Earnest has a subject matter filled with dramatic potential. With its examples of deception, mysterious pasts, impersonations, loves lost and regained, and formidable obstacles, the possibilities for humorous situations are great; however, it is equally possible that there would be nothing funny in the play at all. Certain factors in the play's presentation keep it continuously comic: improbable situations, the absence of any important issues, one-dimensional characters, and witty dialogue.

The improbability of the incidents keeps the play isolated from the real world rather than reflective of it. Comic devices such as plot reversals, mistaken identities, and the presence of a blocking figure like Lady Bracknell provide conventional comic ingredients. Jack Worthing's fabrication of a brother named Ernest is complicated by Cecily's infatuation with this roguish character whom she has never met. Furthermore, Jack lies to Gwendolyn that Earnest is his name. Algernon pretends to be Jack's brother to win Cecily, who like Gwendolyn insists her future husband's name should be Ernest. Further complicating this most unlikely situation is Lady Bracknell's opposition to Gwendolyn's marrying Jack and the confrontation between Cecily and Gwendolyn in which each proclaims to be engaged to Ernest Worthing. When the prim governess, Miss Prism, reveals her personal secret, everyone discovers that Jack is indeed an Ernest with a brother, who turns out to be Algernon. Jack's found heritage eliminates Lady Bracknell's opposition, making way for a happy conclusion for all the lovers, including Miss Prism and Dr. Chasuble.

No great issues are at stake in this plot; consequently, the play's tension remains only tight enough to maintain a continuity of action, never any great suspense over the characters' fates. Moreover, the characters are subservient to the plot. All are amusing and likeable within their self-contained social environment. The play's real substance is Wilde's witty dialogue filled with farcical pronouncements and ironic epigrams. The fluffy, harmless world Wilde creates, reinforced by the characters' self-serving but unoffending values, gives the play a unique logic of its own that stays safely removed from any significant realities. The clever revelations of character and incident make us enjoy this play not for its content but for its execution.

Sample Answer #2

The subject matter in *The Importance of Being Earnest* focuses on an outlandish plot with affable and amusing characters involved in actions which lead to no harsh consequences. This seemingly trivial subject matter is successfully presented to create an amusing entertainment; however, within the comic world Wilde creates there is also an element of satire showing the Victorian upper class as a generally ridiculous lot. In addition, *The Importance of Being Earnest* reveals how the comic tone in a play's subject matter can vary depending on how the characters and events are revealed.

The play's satirical element possesses none of the abrasive or didactic punches found in the works of Molière or Shaw; indeed, Wilde's satire is comparatively gentle. Nonetheless, the plot moves with the fortunes and misfortunes of two upper-class dandies, who like the others in their class appear utterly useless and wasteful. Lady Bracknell consistently espouses her belief that laziness, mindlessness, and snobbery are virtues when practiced by members of her class. The two female prizes, Cecily and Gwendolyn, are as childish as their male pursuers in their understanding of marriage. In fact, because all the characters are caricatures, they lack the capacity to see in others anything worthy of intelligent appreciation. This shallowness in their characterizations serves two purposes. Just as there is duplicity in Jack's and Algernon's pretending to be Ernest (earnest), there is a more subtle duplicity in the play's perspectives. The characters and their environment are isolated from the real world's serious issues, a quality which keeps the play initially segregated within the work of art, but eventually the play reveals its own double life which ridicules the upper class for its self-absorbed obsessions. Thus the very quality which makes the play a social comedy also makes it satirical. Wilde's dialogue, marked by witty comic twists spoken in solemn tones, produces the irony which reveals all that is hypocritical and frivolous in the privileged class's moral pretensions. The plot's contrivances and the dialogue's amusing reversals produce a self-contained world which the audience can easily accept while simultaneously sensing the play's satire of an affluent class characterized by individuals forever defined by their overblown attention to their narrow, trivial prejudices.

Practice Essay Question

In some plays a central character's conceptions of himself and his world are filled with illusions. Through the course of the play, the character continues to perpetuate these misconceptions successfully or he sees them destroyed. Choose a comedy in which encounters with illusions are the core of the play's actions and explain why in this play the conflict is comic.

Tragedy

The term "tragedy" when used to define a play has historically meant something very precise, not simply a drama which ends with unfortunate consequences. This definition originated with Aristotle, who insisted that the play be an imitation of complex actions which should arouse an emotional response combining fear and pity. Aristotle believed that only a certain kind of plot could generate such a powerful reaction. Comedy, as we have seen, shows us a progression from adversity to prosperity. Tragedy must show the reverse; moreover, this progression must be experienced by a certain kind of character, says Aristotle, someone whom we can designate as the **tragic hero**. This central figure must be basically good and noble: "good" because we will not be aroused to fear and pity over the misfortunes of a villain, and "noble" both by social position and moral stature because the fall to misfortune would not otherwise be great enough for tragic impact. These virtues do not make the tragic hero perfect, however, for he must also possess **hamartia**—a tragic flaw—the frailty which leads him to make an error in judgment which initiates the reversal in his fortunes, causing his death or the death of others or both. These dire consequences become the hero's **catastrophe**. The most common tragic flaw is **hubris**, an excessive pride that adversely influences the protagonist's judgment.

Often the catastrophic consequences involve an entire nation because the tragic hero's social rank carries great responsibilities. Witnessing these events produces the emotional reaction Aristotle believed the audience should experience, the **catharsis**. Although tragedy must arouse our pity for the tragic hero as he endures his catastrophe and must frighten us as we witness the consequences of a flawed behavior which anyone could exhibit, there must also be a purgation, "a cleansing," of these emotions which should leave the audience feeling not depressed but relieved and almost elated. The assumption is that while the tragic hero endures a crushing reversal, somehow he is not thoroughly defeated as he gains new stature though suffering and the knowledge that comes with suffering. Classical tragedy insists that the universe is ordered. If truth or universal law is ignored, the results are devastating, causing the audience to react emotionally; simultaneously, the tragic results prove the existence of truth, thereby reassuring our faith that existence is sensible.

Sophocles' plays give us some of the clearest examples of Aristotle's definition of tragedy. Shakespeare's tragedies are more varied and more modern in their complexities. *Othello* is one of Shakespeare's most innovative and troublesome extensions of tragedy's boundaries. The title character commands the Venetian army and soon becomes acting governor of Cyprus. He is also a Moor, a dark-skinned African whose secret marriage to the beautiful Desdemona has infuriated her father, a wealthy and influential Venetian, whose anger reveals a racist element in Venice which Othello tries to ignore. Iago hates Othello for granting a promotion to Cassio which Iago believes should rightfully be his. With unrelenting determination and malicious deception, Iago attempts to persuade Othello that Desdemona has committed adultery with Cassio. The following excerpt catches Iago in the early stages of his successful manipulation:

IAGO: In Venice they [wives] do let heaven see pranks
They dare not show their husbands; their best conscience
Is not to leave 't undone, but keep 't unknown.

OTHELLO: Dost thou say so?

IAGO: She did deceive her father, marrying you;
And when she seem'd to shake and fear your looks,
She lov'd them most.

OTHELLO: And so she did.

IAGO: Why, go to, then;
She that so young could give out such a seeming,
To see her father's eyes up close as oak,
He thought 'twas witchcraft; but I am much to blame;
I humbly do beseech you of your pardon
For too much loving you.

OTHELLO: I am bound to thee for ever.

IAGO: I see, this hath a little dash'd your spirits.

OTHELLO: Not a jot, not a jot.

IAGO: I' faith, I fear it has.
I hope you will consider what is spoke
Comes from my love. But I do see you're mov'd;
I am to pray you not to strain my speech
To grosser issues nor to larger reach
Than to suspicion.

OTHELLO: I will not.

IAGO: Should you do so, my lord,
My speech should fall into such vile success
As my thoughts aim not at. Cassio's my worthy friend—
My lord, I see you're mov'd.

OTHELLO: No, not much mov'd:
I do not think but Desdemona's honest.

IAGO: Long live she so! and long live you to think so!

OTHELLO: And yet, how nature erring from itself,—

IAGO: Ay, there's the point: as, to be bold with you,
Not to affect many proposed matches
Of her own clime, complexion, and degree,
Whereto, we see, in all things nature tends;
Foh! one may smell in such, a will most rank,
Foul disproportion, thoughts unnatural.
But pardon me; I do not in position
Distinctly speak of her, though I may fear
Her will, recoiling to her better judgment,
May fall to match you with her country forms
And happily repent.

OTHELLO: Farewell, farewell:
If more thou dost perceive, let me know more;
Set on thy wife to observe. Leave me, Iago.

IAGO: My lord, I take my leave. (Going)

OTHELLO: Why did I marry? This honest creature, doubtless,
Sees and knows more, much more, than he unfolds.

Notice that Iago speaks much more than Othello. This is typical of their conversations, as though Iago were the superior of the two. Dramatically, for Iago's machinations to compel our interests we must perceive in Othello tragic proportions, both in his strengths and weaknesses; otherwise, *Othello* would slip into a malevolent tale about a rogue and his dupe. Much of the tension in this scene emanates from Othello's reluctance either to accept Iago's innuendos immediately or to dismiss them. This confusion places him on the rack of doubt, a torture made more severe because he questions his own desirability as a husband. Consequently, since Iago is not the "honest creature" he appears to be and Othello is unwilling to confront openly his own self-doubts, Iago becomes the dominant personality—a situation which a flawless Othello would never tolerate.

TRAGEDY ESSAY QUESTION

One critic has defined the tragedy in *Othello* as partly the victory of Iago's reason over Othello's instinct and passion. To what extent is this an accurate summary of the play's tragic action?

Sample Answer #1

We know from the high regard for Othello held by nearly all Venetians and from the demeanor he presents in Act I that Othello possesses the virtues and social station which should classify him as good and noble. He calmly prevents sword play when accosted by the furious Brabantio, and his speeches before the Senate show his tenderness and capacity for eloquent expression. At the end of the play, however, he obliquely refers to himself as a "malignant Turk" and kills himself. Unlike some other tragic figures, particularly Hamlet, Othello gives no evidence of having a great, reflective mind. Rather, he thinks like a child, at least when he is excited by a stimulus as volatile as sexual jealousy which for him quickly becomes explosive passion. In his unsophisticated way he clings to the simplicities of war and a general faith in others as his intellectual guidelines, a condition which makes him easily manipulated by the diabolical and vengeful Iago.

Beneath Othello's quiet dignity lies a well of uncertainty about himself as a husband for one as young and beautiful as Desdemona. Doubts about his age, race, and inexperience in anything other than military adventures make him vulnerable. Iago's motives have no reasonable basis, but Iago's guile, a perverted reason, gives him a powerful advantage over Othello's tendency toward emotional extremes, which we first see when Othello overreacts by stripping Cassio of his rank. There is a kind of innocence to Othello—a purity in his standards of decency, adherence to duty, and depth of love—which makes him great. The irony in the play's racial imagery is in this simple purity, matched by Desdemona's uncalculating love and loyalty to her husband, and in Iago's blackening of this innocence so beautifully shared by husband and wife. Thus, Othello's tragic flaw is "Of one that lov'd not wisely, but too well," causing him to be corrupted because his instincts and passion lack the controlling discipline that reason could apply, and because Iago could so adeptly manifest his malevolent desires in cold, purposeful scheming. In fact, even after all is revealed to him in Act V, Othello remains slightly befuddled. Still "perplex'd in the extreme," his emotional turmoil and sense of military justice motivate his self-destruction.

Sample Answer #2

To say the tragic action in *Othello* is released when Iago's deceitful reason is pitted against Othello's instinct and passion is to miss the fundamental catastrophic force in the play. It is true that Othello's errors in judgment set in motion a series of events resulting in his death and Desdemona's, and that Iago's chicanery leads Othello to his faulty thinking; however, what makes the play so compelling is the absence of any pure reason whatsoever.

The world of *Othello* is chaotic, a place where a dropped handkerchief can cause disaster. With only a few interruptions of tranquility, all the actions are propelled by misfortune and mental anarchy. When the punishments Iago devises are placed against their provocations, his villainy becomes inhuman, not simply because it lacks any trace of conscience but because it lacks any sense. He drives himself to destroy virtues which he maintains do not exist. We should not confuse his devilish determination and cleverness with reason. Fear more than anything else motivates Othello, an emotion he can easily crush when he confronts physical threats but not when faced with doubts about his sexual desirability. All his distorted notions about Desdemona's virtue are really projections of this maddening terror, and it is madness, not passion, that spurs him on in an arena of conflict for which he is utterly unprepared and reduces his otherwise noble proportions to tragic folly. How unconvincing he sounds when he says he murders her to save her from betraying more men, weeping while he strangles.

Othello is a tragedy played out in a disordered universe. Although Iago has remarkable success getting Othello, Roderigo, Cassio, and Emilia to do what he wants, he is not the controlling influence in the play. Disturbing us more than Iago's skill, the absence of order frightens us as though a greater, more mysterious malice were at work providing just enough chance encounters to advance Iago's illusions and to deprive Othello of a moment's more lucid thought. Othello's "Who can control his fate?" is no cowardly attempt to deflect blame. At a horrible price, human order has a flickering triumph through Desdemona's dying words of love and Othello's dying kiss, but no Venetian justice can repair the damage already done. His own executioner, Othello embraces once again the hero's code that ultimately the individual must accept the responsibility for his own actions, as he submits to the paradoxical cosmos that makes his sentence both necessary and unfair.

Practice Essay Question

Below is Emily Dickinson's poem "Crumbling is not an Instant's Act." Write an essay in which you explain how the poem's content and theme apply to a particular tragedy's content and theme.

> Crumbling is not an instant's Act,
> A fundamental pause
> Dilapidation's processes
> Are organized Decays.
>
> 'Tis first a Cobweb on the Soul,
> A Cuticle of Dust,
> A borer in the Axis
> An Elemental Rust—
>
> Ruin is formal—Devil's work,
> Consecutive and slow—
> Fail in an instant, no man did
> Slipping—is Crash's law.

HISTORY

The playwright's raw data can spring from any source. A passion play, for instance, is a dramatic adaptation of the Crucifixion as told in the gospels. A history play is a dramatic perspective of some event or series of events identified with recognized historical figures. Television docudramas are the most recent examples. Among the earliest histories were the chronicle plays which flourished during Shakespeare's time and often relied on *Chronicles* by Raphael Holinshed, first published in 1577. Holinshed's volumes and similar books by others glorified English history and were very popular throughout the Tudor period, especially following the defeat of the Spanish Armada. Similarly, Shakespeare's *Henry V* and *Henry VIII* emphasize national and religious chauvinism in their treatments of kings who, from a more objective historical perspective appear less than nobly motivated. These plays resemble romantic comedies with each one's protagonist defeating some adversary and establishing national harmony through royal marriage. *King Lear* and *Macbeth*, on the other hand, movingly demonstrate Shakespeare's skill at turning historical figures into tragic heroes.

Ever since the 16th century history plays have seldom risen above the level of patriotic whitewash and political propaganda. Of course there are notable exceptions to this trend: Robert Bolt's *A Man for All Seasons* is one. The title character, Sir Thomas More, is beheaded at the play's conclusion, following his refusal to condone Henry VIII's break from the Roman Catholic Church and the king's establishment of the Church of England with the monarch as its head. Henry wants More to condone these actions because the Pope will not grant Henry a divorce from Queen Catherine so that he can marry Anne Boleyn, who the king believes will bear him the male heir he desperately wants. The central issue for us is not whether More's theology is valid but whether any person of conscience can act freely in a world dominated by others far less principled. In Henry's only scene he arrives at Sir Thomas' house hoping his Lord Chancellor will not disappoint him:

[music in background]

HENRY: Son after son she's borne me, Thomas, all dead at birth, or dead within a month; I never saw the hand of God so clear in anything... I have a daughter, she's a good child, a well-set child—But I have no son. (He flares up) It is my bounden duty to put away the Queen, and all the Popes back to St. Peter shall not come between me and my duty! How is it that you cannot see? Everybody else does.

MORE: (Eagerly) Then why does Your Grace need my poor support?

HENRY: Because you are honest. What's more to the purpose, you're known to be honest... There are those like Norfolk who follow me because I wear the crown, and there are those like Master Cromwell who follow me because they are jackals with sharp teeth and I am their lion, and there is a mass that follow me because it follows anything that moves—and there is you.

MORE: I am sick to think how much I must displease Your Grace.

HENRY: No, Thomas, I respect your sincerity. Respect? Oh, man, it's water in the desert... How did you like our music? That air they played, it had a certain—well, tell me what you thought of it.

MORE: (Relieved at this turn; smiling) Could it have been Your Grace's own?

HENRY: (Smiles back) Discovered! Now I'll never know your true opinion. And that's irksome, Thomas, for we artists, though we love praise, yet we love truth better.

MORE: (Mildly) Then I will tell Your Grace truly what I thought of it.

HENRY: (A little disconcerted) Speak then.

MORE: To me it seemed—delightful.

HENRY: Thomas—I chose the right man for Chancellor.

MORE: I must in fairness add that my taste in music is reputably deplorable.

(From *A Man for All Seasons* by Robert Bolt. Copyright © 1960, 1962 by Robert Bolt. Reprinted by permission of Random House Inc.)

To what extent Henry and More discussed the king's divorce and its subsequent events nobody knows, let alone what was actually said, although we can be certain they spoke an English distinctively different from the language in the play. Bolt's imagination, funnelled through the dramatist's obligation to tell an interesting story, presides over the historical data and dictates the play's projections of More, Henry, and the other participants. Thus, we do not have "history"; instead we have a dramatic perception of history shaped, altered, and adorned by Robert Bolt, writing about 16th century figures from a 1960 vantage point. But as the scene above shows, the characters' personalities are not simple reductions of what historical giants should be. Henry struts a royal self-assurance noticeably colored by vanity and frustration; yet although he lacks More's wit and intelligence, the king clearly is no fool. Likewise, as troubled as More is by the controversy before him, he projects a formidable power of his own. *A Man for All Seasons* succeeds dramatically because Bolt provides only enough historical verisimilitude to present a context for the characters' development while he allows the resultant thematic implications to touch all times, all seasons. When we read any history play, we should search for similar implications; otherwise, the work can never become more than a theatrical précis with a narrow, didactic focus.

HISTORY PLAY ESSAY QUESTION

An often repeated conflict in literature is one which places a character between opposing duties. How is this conflict present in *A Man for All Seasons and* what conclusions should we reach about how it is resolved?

Sample Answer #1

A Man for All Seasons dramatizes the conflict that arises when a pious man of conscience must act on the Biblical dictate "to render unto Caesar the things that are Caesar's and render unto God the things that are God's." For More, the differentiation between the two is never in doubt, even though his decision makes his earthly situation progressively worse: his social status and wealth are deprived him, he loses friends, he is imprisoned, he must endure his family's sufferings and their misreading of why he takes his stand, he sees unscrupulous men like Cromwell and Rich increase their power, he grieves for his country which seemingly forsakes him, and he dies a traitor's death.

More struggles longer with these consequences than with the decision that brings them on. Throughout the play, he refuses opportunities to change his fate, by either acquiescing to Henry's demands or throwing in to England's rival, Catholic Spain, as Chapuys urges him. Moreover, he never seeks solace in the fanatical self-righteousness Roper displays. He clings to his conscience because he cannot separate it from himself, and he clings to the law, believing an innocent Englishman will always be safe from execution if he knows the law's intricacies. Only this second faith deserts him. The same villains who would override church law are quite capable of devising a temporal law to suit their needs.

Motivated by conscience and guided by wisdom, he never commits a tragic hero's errors, although his fate is similar. We see a good man brought to ruin by the doings of others whose numbers include more than the high-ranking schemers. The Common Man, though an engaging figure, believes only heroes and fools follow their own courses regardless of prevailing winds, and he consciously chooses to be neither. Bolt succeeds in making us recognize More as a hero, one who is overpowered by forces of expediency, self-service, narrow interest, and hypocrisy, but not defeated by them. All other characters appear puny beside him.

Sample Answer #2

Up to the Act of Succession, More has maintained his balance of duties harmoniously, thinking he can serve God by serving justice as prescribed by English law. More's well-known success causes Henry to elevate him to Wolsey's office as Lord Chancellor when Wolsey dies, a move filled with foreboding since More differs greatly from the worldly Cardinal. The decision to side with the church rather than his king is the prelude to his deeper conflict, which is whether he can abandon his lawyer-like reliance on human reason and give himself over completely to blind faith.

One would think that under ordinary circumstances More's success would continue. but the ordinary human circumstances which govern the play's actions are inherently disruptive because they flow from dark, emotional impulses. Henry's masculine self-image requires that he control his own fate by siring an unquestionable successor who would guarantee a kind of Tudor immortality. There is more self-service than national concern at the root of this, especially when placed with Henry's lustful infatuation with Anne Boleyn. Complementing Henry's desires is Cromwell's cynical passion for self-promotion, a characteristic also displayed by Wolsey, Rich, Chapuys, and to a less ambitious degree by the Common Man, a fellow whose intuitive sense is superior to Norfolk's and at times more perceptive than More's. No fool, More has always recognized humanity's tendency for callous self-interest, an awareness which draws him to the law as though it were the stockade of human reason, restricting the dark human potentials and thus the common force all must obey because without it all would be in danger. What More must learn is the degree to which human reason can be a slave to the worst impulses governing human behavior. He painfully discovers human reason cannot save him while he still heroically refuses to renounce his decision.

More is then left with only his faith, a "super reason" which no one else truly understands. Although he is aware of the pain and confusion his actions have caused those he loves, he also disdains the martyr's glory Roper finds so attractive, because More finds no solace in anything inconsistent with the super reason his conscience dictates. Throughout much of the play More clings to life, but at the end he gladly goes to his God as he leaves the world of moral chaos abetted by misused intellects. Having discovered the impotence of human reason to curtail human corruption, he dies a courageous and devout but world-weary hero.

Practice Essay Question

A good history play removes historical figures from the one-dimensional definitions usually assigned to them and instead places these figures in a context that allows their full humanity to be revealed. Choose a history play that successfully presents a historical personage as a fuller character and explain the variety of human features he or she demonstrates.

MODERN DRAMA

From the 1870's to the present, the theater has participated in the artistic movements reflecting accumulated theories of science, social science, and philosophy which attempt to define reality and the means we use to discern it. First caught in a pendulum of opposing views, modern drama eventually synthesized these perspectives into new forms, familiar in some ways and boldly original in others. Henrik Ibsen's plays began the modern era with their emphasis on **realism,** a seeking of truth through direct observation using the five senses. As objectively depicted, contemporary life received a closer scrutiny than ever before, showing everyday people in everyday situations. Before Ibsen, theatrical sets were limited, with rare exceptions, to castles and country estates. After Ibsen the farmhouse and city tenement were suitable for the stage. Ibsen's work influenced many others, and from realism came two main variations. The first, **naturalism,** strove to push realism towards a direct transformation of life on stage, a "slice of life" showing how the scientific principles of heredity and environment have shaped society, especially in depicting the plights of the lower classes. The second variation, **expressionism,** moved in a different direction and actually denied realism's premise that the real world could be objectively perceived; instead—influenced by Sigmund Freud's theories about human behavior's hidden, subconscious motivations and by other modernist trends in the arts, such as James Joyce's fiction and Picasso's paintings—expressionism imitated a disconnected dream-like world filled with psychological images at odds with the tangible world surrounding it. While naturalism attempts to imitate life directly, expressionism is abstract and often relies on symbols.

A modern play can employ any number of elements found in the spectrum between these extremes as well as suggest divergent philosophical views about whether humanity has the power to change its condition or whether any of its ideas about the universe are verifiable. Moreover, no work of art is necessarily confined within a particular school of thought. It is quite possible that seemingly incongruent forms can appear in the same play and work well. *The Glass Menagerie*, *A Man for All Seasons*, and *Death of a Salesman* feature characters and dialogue indicative of realistic drama, but the sets described in the stage directions are expressionistic, offering either framed outlines of places or distorted representations. Conventions from classical drama are also available to the playwright. As previously noted, Tom acts as a Greek chorus as well as an important character in his play; the same is true of the Common Man, whose identity changes from scene to scene. Playwrights Eugene Ionesco and Harold Pinter have created characters speaking and behaving in extraordinary ways while occupying sets which are typically realistic. In short, anything is possible in modern drama, a quality which is wholly compatible with the diversity and unpredictability of 20th century human experiences.

In a sense all good drama is modern. No label about a play's origin or form can adequately describe its content. Establishing the people, places, and thought within the play is crucial to our understanding. For the characters to interest us we must perceive the issues that affect their lives, and eventually we will discover why the characters' personalities and backgrounds, together with their social situations, inevitably converge with these issues and create conflicts. We must also stay aware of drama's kinship with lyric poetry's subjective mood and tone, a quality dominating all plays regardless of the form. *Death of a Salesman* challenges the classical definitions of tragedy by giving us a modern American, Willy Loman, who is indeed a "low man," a person of little social importance and limited moral fiber. His delusionary values have brought him at age sixty-four to failure and despair, yet more than ever he clings to his dreams and painted memories for solace and hope. Late one night, after Willy has returned from an aborted sales trip, his rambling conversation with his wife Linda returns to the topic which haunts him the most, his son Biff.

WILLY: Biff is a lazy bum!

LINDA: They're sleeping. Get something to eat. Go on down.

WILLY: Why did he come home? I would like to know what brought him home.

LINDA: I don't know. I think he's still lost, Willy. I think he's very lost.

WILLY: Biff Loman is lost. In the greatest country in the world a young man with such—personal attractiveness, gets lost. And such a hard worker. There's one thing about Biff—he's not lazy.

LINDA: Never.

WILLY (with pity and resolve): I'll see him in the morning; I'll have a nice talk with him. I'll get him a job selling. He could be big in no time. My God! Remember how they used to follow him around in high school? When he smiled at one of them their faces lit up. When he walked down the street... (He loses himself in reminiscences.)

LINDA (trying to bring him out of it): Willy, dear, I got a new kind of American-type cheese today. It's whipped.

WILLY: Why do you get American cheese when you know I like Swiss?

LINDA: I just thought you'd like a change—

WILLY: I don't want change! I want Swiss cheese. Why am I always being contradicted?

LINDA (with a covering laugh): I just thought it would be a surprise.

WILLY: Why don't you open a window in here, for God's sake?

LINDA (with infinite patience): They're all open dear.

WILLY: The way they boxed us in here. Bricks and windows, windows and bricks.

LINDA: We should have bought the land next door.

WILLY: The street is lined with cars. There's not a breath of fresh air in the neighborhood. The grass don't grow any more, you can't raise a carrot in the backyard. They should've had a law against apartment houses. Remember those two beautiful elms out there? When I and Biff hung the swing between them?

LINDA: Yeah, like a million miles from the city.

WILLY: They should've arrested the builder for cutting those down. They massacred the neighborhood. (Lost) More and more I think of those days, Linda. This time of year it was lilac and wisteria. And then the peonies would come out, and the daffodils. What fragrance in this room!

LINDA: Well, after all, people had to move somewhere.

WILLY: No, there's more people now.

LINDA: I don't think there's more people. I think—

WILLY: There's more people! That's what ruining this country! Population is getting out of control. The competition is maddening! Smell the stink from that apartment house! And another on the other side... How can they whip cheese?

In Arthur Miller's stage directions for *Death of a Salesman*, the Loman house is outlined by simple framing with various floors represented by short elevated platforms. Outside the house the towering shapes of the city angle inward presenting the crowded oppressiveness Willy complains about. First performed in 1949, the play continues to make a powerful commentary on modern American life. We see Willy as more desperate than angry about his condition, which he defines in ways as contradictory as his assessments of Biff. In his suffocating world so nebulously delineated, Willy gropes for peace while hiding from truth; and although his woes are uniquely American in some ways, they touch broader, more universal human problems as well.

MODERN DRAMA ESSAY QUESTION

Very often a distinguished literary work is structured from events either mental or psychological as some character or characters experience a change in consciousness. These internal events can become as important as the external conflict and contribute significantly to the suspense and climax. In what ways is *Death of a Salesman* indicative of this kind of literature?

Sample Answer #1

Willy Loman's struggle evolves from his corruption by modern commercialism which causes an inner dissonance that eventually overwhelms him. Because his environment dictates shoddy values of self-aggrandizement, Willy both consciously and unconsciously does the same, in the process losing touch with any permanent values to support him. Willy dwells in two worlds: the first is the objectively real, external and present; the second is subjectively real, internal and past. The objective world presents immediate problems. Two involve other characters—his son, Biff, and his boss, Howard—and Willy's traumatic experiences with both. The others are defined quantitatively by money and time—his unpaid bills, his deteriorating house, and his age. In varying ways these problems are connected to the modern business ethics which have both victimized Willy and made him a dedicated believer. He is caught in the system's contradictory standards about a person's worth. On one hand it upholds an individual's character and accomplishment while on the other it focuses on one's material rewards as the most meaningful measure of personal value. This contradiction gets settled in Willy's consciousness by his confusing merchandise and personality. As long as his reveries and pipe dreams in the past sustain him, he can hide from the recognition of how he has cheapened himself. He escapes total self-recognition by deciding to die after having concluded he has ceased to be marketable.

In a world where the refrigerator with the biggest advertisement is automatically deemed the best, Willy strives to be a "big shot." Symbolically, he gives his sons a punching bag to prepare them for the business world, privately knowing he bears a failed contender's scars and bruises. He yearns to emulate his brother Ben, who in Willy's mind takes on mythic proportions in his white-suited embodiment of business success and rugged individualism, a champion in both the boardroom and the jungle. Finding security in his delusions, Willy despises change, especially the change in Biff from the adoring football hero to the seemingly shiftless, bitter antagonist. To Willy this transformation sneers at him, mocking his need to be well-liked. Still trapped by the notion that a person is a commodity that can be transferred into money, his last sale is his own life. The twenty-thousand dollar "commission," he thinks, can then be transferred into success for Biff. This transaction is the closest Willy's internal quest to love and be loved comes to realization. Willy is so tainted by commercial values that his change in consciousness is too slight to save him.

Sample Answer #2

As Charley states at the end of *A Death of a Salesman*, Willy Loman "was a happy man with a batch of cement." For reasons only vaguely explained in the play, Willy chooses a career in selling rather than in working with his hands and consequently never finds lasting happiness. Perhaps his older brother's example of self-determination and financial success influenced his thinking, particularly since Willy hardly knew his father, the other male model, whose life as an itinerant craftsman is the one which Biff in his own way will choose to follow. The other model in Willy's life is Dave Singleman, the singular example of the fulfillment that comes from being well-liked. Of these three only Ben appears on stage, but mostly as a personified ideal, a fleeting inaccessible energy always hurrying off to some new triumph. Willy pompously refers to his father as someone "better than a carpenter," but the father's real identity comes indirectly through the mournful flute music in the background as a haunting representation of Willy's innermost longings for a simple life filled with fresh air and sunshine and the satisfaction of having something in the ground. Biff accurately defines Willy's hamartia as the failure to achieve self-knowledge, in Willy's case the failure to embrace his love and talent for a particular kind of labor and accomplishment.

Willy's problems stem not from big city business values. Charley and Bernard clearly demonstrate how honest fulfillment can be gained in that environment because they realistically apply themselves in endeavors which they find satisfying, and neither pretends knowledge or skill in subjects outside his range. Posing and pretending that his choices and visions are correct, Willy is indeed the "phony" Biff calls him, a soul-piercing label for one who desperately wants to be liked. What makes Willy redeemable in our eyes is his guilt; but just as he has lost control of his life he loses control of his guilt, and it consumes him, driving him to suicide which he rationalizes as the noble sacrifice that will reconcile him with the son he thinks he has failed. If Willy cannot know himself, he can not really know anything. He does not understand selling; his genuine affection for Linda gets tangled in betrayal and unwarranted irritability; and he never really understands his responsibilities to his sons, making one a conceited, aimless wanderer and the other an even more simple-minded, self-centered version of Willy. Thus, Willy's struggles with his eternal world are doomed, weighted by his failure to establish a valid sense of self. While Happy eagerly accepts the business world's challenges as though they were his father's bequest, Biff accepts the necessity of self-knowledge and thus liberates himself from the mire of guilt and delusion which blinded and suffocated Willy.

Practice Essay Question

The 20th century has been labeled "The Age of Anxiety." Choose a modern play and explain what implications about contemporary times are reflected in the physiological disquietudes characters experience.

CHAPTER 4

WRITING AN ESSAY

WHY PEOPLE WRITE ESSAYS

By definition, an essay is a structured, creative, written composition dealing with a specific subject from a more or less personal point of view. People write essays because it gives them an opportunity to analyze ideas, situations and people and to preserve them indefinitely. Not only does it ensure permanence of ideas, but it also ensures a degree of permanence for the author. In addition, writing essays also provides personal benefits for the writer. It is a way for the writer to understand more clearly ideas and concepts. It is a way for the writer to participate in the world by sharing his feelings. It is a way for the writer to sharpen thinking and organizational skills. It is also a way for the writer to enjoy the personal thrill and satisfaction of effectively communicating his own personal ideas and feelings on paper. An essay is a reflection of the author since it presents ideas, insights, emotions and attitudes that he alone possesses. His personality colors and shines through the finished product.

TIPS ON WRITING ESSAYS FOR THE AP EXAM

Thinking

Before initiating your response to an essay question, you must carefully think through the question, considering all issues to be discussed, and all possible responses to the question. Answering questions such as the following will help you to focus on the task at hand:

1. Will the response require a comparison/contrast?/an analysis of one or more of the elements of fiction and/or poetry—plot, theme, character, point of view, symbolism, setting, imagery, figurative language, tone, musical devices, rhythm and meter, pattern, structure, a major idea, or diction?

2. Does the question dictate that your response be expository or argumentative?

3. Will the response require discussion of specific details from the work cited?

4. Will the response require a discussion of cause and effect?

A clear understanding of the question will help you to determine the scope and extent of your essay.

Planning

Once you have firmly established the task at hand, the next step is to plan an appropriate approach. Developing the thesis statement is foremost in the planning stage. This statement identifies the central idea of your essay and should clearly state your attitude about the subject. It will also dictate the basic content and developmental process of your essay. A thesis statement such as: "Blood is an important image in *Macbeth*" suggests that the content will involve identifying specific references to blood in the play and discussing their importance. Because this statement is so important to shaping the essay, you should try out several ways of phrasing it to be assured of its effectiveness in your writing of the essay. Once you have developed an effective thesis statement, you should briefly outline the body of your essay, including such details, examples, illustrations which are necessary to prove your thesis statement. A simple list of ideas is usually sufficient, since the writing section is timed and will not permit extensive outlines. Your outline will serve as the skeleton of your essay and will help to keep you on track as you write. Note the following list of ideas:

1. Macbeth seees blood on dagger

2. Duncan's blood spilled

3. Duncan's blood on Macbeth's hands

4. Macbeth steeped in blood

5. Lady Macbeth, sleepwalking, tries to wash blood from hands

During this stage you will also determine your pattern of organization—chronologically, in order of importance, etc.

Composing

This is the actual writing of the essay. Using your outline as a guide, you should expand your ideas until they grow and your essay takes shape. Do not allow the outline to become restrictive. New ideas may emerge as you write. Feel free to include them if they are supportive of your thesis and improve your essay.

In terms of structure, consider three parts for the essay: introduction, body and conclusion. The introduction should include your thesis statement. The body should be the actual proving of your thesis and the conclusion should sum up your ideas and signal that you have finished.

Polishing

Finally, read your essay carefully. You may add, delete, rearrange, substitute and make any other changes that improve your presentation. This step also includes proofreading for errors in punctuation, spelling and usage. No matter how effectively you have developed the content of your essay, errors in mechanics and usage will detract from the finished product.

Style

Style is you. It is what you say and how you say it. As you write, consider these three elements that make up style: (1) grammar and punctuation, (2) use of language, and (3) elements of interesting writing.

Grammar and Punctuation

Since your essay will be formal, you should strive to avoid common errors in grammar and usage. Effective sentence structure is vital to the effectiveness of your essay. You should avoid the following common errors in sentence structure:

1. Sentence fragment—a group of words not stating a complete thought.

   Example: Going to school early

   Corrected: Going to school early, Kim was able to spend extra time in the library.

2. Run-on sentences—two sentences written as one.

   Example: I enjoyed reading Shakespeare's plays they were exciting.

   Corrected: I enjoyed reading Shakespeare's plays. They were exciting.

3. Comma splice—two sentences separated by a comma.

   Example: Our class completed several research projects on poetry, we then shared our findings with each other.

   Corrected: Our class completed several research projects on poetry. We then shared our findings with each other.

In addition to structure, some attention should be given to sentence variety. Varying sentence structure adds interest and eliminates boredom in the content of the essay. Variety can be achieved in a number of ways. Consider the fact that there are three basic stuctures of English sentences:

1. Simple sentence—contains one subject and one verb, either of which may be plural.

   Example: Students and teachers participated in the Fun Day activities.

2. Compound—contains two independent clauses joined by a coordinating conjunction.

   Example: The teachers won the basketball game and the students won the soccer game.

3. Complex—contains one independent clause and one or more depedent clauses.

   Example: When the day was over, we were completely exhausted.

A paragraph containing all or any of the three would be dull and monotonous. Effective writing contains sentences employing a combination of the three structures.

Another way to eliminate monotony and add variety and emphasis is by sentence combining. Combine short choppy sentences by:

1. Inserting a participial phrase

    Example: The poems were written by students. The poems were published in the school newspaper.

    Improved: The poems, written by students, were published in the school newspaper.

2. Using appositives or appositive phrases

    Example: John contributed many articles to the school newspaper. He was the editor.

    Improved: John, the editor, contributed many articles to the school newspaper.

3. Combining simple sentences into a compound sentence

    Example: The students wrote all of the articles. The advisor proofread them.

    Improved: The students wrote all of the articles, but the advisor proofread them.

4. Using an adjective clause

    Example: The photographer was an outstanding staff member. He received many awards.

    Improved: The photographer who received many awards was an outstanding staff memeber.

5. Using an adverb clause

    Example: Bob was named sports editor. He became an avid sports fan.

    Improved: After Bob was named sports editor, he became an avid sports fan.

6. Using a noun clause

    Example: The staff members thought that they could not complete their assignments. This was a foolish idea.

    Improved: The staff members had the foolish idea that they could not complete their assignments.

Variety in sentence structure is an indication of maturity and sophistication in style.

Another important element of style is appropriate usage. The following guide will help in eliminating some common problems in usage:

1. accept–to give, to take

    except–but

    Did she *accept* the invitation?

    Mary worked every day *except* Sunday.

2. affect–(verb) to influence

    effect–(noun) the result of an action

    The mayor's speech did not *affect* the audience.

    The *effects* of the wind can be devastating.

3. allusion–reference to something

    illusion–mistaken idea

    Her essay contained many biblical *allusions*.

    Did Macbeth's *illusions* cause him to commit murder?

4. all right–always two words

    It is *all right* to dream.

5. and, etc.–etc. means "and the rest." Should not be preceded by "and" because "et" means "and".

6. beside–at the side of

    besides–in addition to

    She sat quietly *beside* her older sister.

    Besides calculus, James enrolled in physics.

7. between–with two elements

    among–with two or more elements

    They had to choose *between* Sylvia and Diane.

    From *among* blue, green and red, they chose red.

8. could of–often used carelessly for "could have."

9. done–not the past tense of "do"; always needs a helping verb

    They *have done* their chores.

10. don't–a contraction of do not; should not be used with a singular noun or the third person of singular pronouns.

    They don't worry about changing the decisions.

11. different from–use before a noun or pronoun

    different than–before some clauses/phrases

    Cars are *different from* buses.

    Driving in Atlanta is *different than* it is in Boston.

12. farther–refers to physical distance

    further–usually refers to time or degree

    Sam drove *farther* than Tim.

    There will be no *further* discussion of the issue.

13. fewer–before a plural noun

    less–before a singular noun

    Last year there were *fewer girls* in the class.

    We had *less time* in class today.

14. good–(adjective) used to modify nouns and pronouns

    well–(usually an adverb) used to modify verbs

    She did a *good job* of organizing the files.

    The ensemble *sang well*.

15. hisself, theirselves–mistakenly used for himself, themselves.

16. irregardless–double negative mistakenly used for regardless.

17. lay–means to "put" or "place"

    lie–means to "rest" or "recline"

    *Lay th*e book on the desk.

    Please *lie* down if you are ill.

18. off of–the "of" is unnecessary

    He fell *off* the roof.

19. reason is because–Because means "for the reason that." The expression is repetitive. Use either "the reason is" or "because."

20. sit–means to place oneself in a sitting position; does not take an object

    set–means to "place" or "put"

Sit wherever you find a seat.

The schedule has already been *set*.

Other common errors that you should avoid are:

1. Subject–verb agreement–A singular subject takes a singular verb; a plural subject takes a plural verb.

   The *soloist sings* at all of the group's performances.

   The *students sing* their school song each morning.

2. Incorrect pronoun reference–A personal pronoun must agree with its antecedent in number.

   If a *person* looks carefully *he* can usually find some hidden talent.

Another important element of style is punctuation. Appropriate punctuation helps to make your meanings clear to the reader. It also helps to present your ideas in a logical, coherent fashion. The following rules of punctuation should help you in writing your essay.

The Comma

1. To separate items in series (except first and last items)

   Example: Susan read novels by Steinbeck, Hemingway, and Faulkner.

2. Before and, but, or, nor, for and yet, when they join independent clauses

   Example: Susan started reading *Lord of the Flies,* but she did not finish.

3. To set off non-essential clauses and participial phrases

   Example: The novels, written by renowned authors, required close reading.

4. After specific introductory elements

   a. After yes and no when they introduce the sentence.

   Example: Yes, Susan got an "A" on her reading assignment.

   b. After an introductory participial phrase

   Example: Beaming with pride, she happily accepted the award.

   c. After an introductory prepositional phrase

   Example: After completing the basic course, Susan enrolled in an advanced course.

   d. After an introductory subordinate clause

   Example: Because Susan wanted to become a writer, she took as many English courses as she could.

5. To set off expressions that interrupt the sentence

   a. appositives and appositive phrases

   Example: Susan, an honor student, will enroll in college in the fall.

   b. words in direct address

   Example: "Susan, did you discuss your plans with the counselor?"

   c. parenthetical expressions

   Example: She will, of course, accept the advice of her parents, too.

The Colon

1. Before a list of items, especially after expressions such as "as follows" and "the following."

   Example: Most student lockers contained the following items: books, a jacket, a comb, and a mirror.

2. Between independent clauses, when the second explains or restates the idea in the first.

   Example: They refused to give up: they were fighters.

3. Before a long, formal statement or quotation.

   Example: The Constitution of the United States begins:

We the people, in order to form a more perfect union, establish justice and secure domestic tranquility, provide for the common defense, promote the general welfare and secure the blessings of liberty, to ourselves and our prosperity, do ordain and establish this Constitution for the United States of America.

The Semicolon

1. Between independent clauses not joined by and, but, or, nor, for, yet, so

   Example: Hawthorne is a favorite of high school students; they usually read several of his works.

2. Between main clauses joined by conjunctive adverbs such as however, therefore, nevertheless, moreover, furthermore, and consequently, or by such expressions as for example, for instance, or that is.

   Example: The assembly was long and boring; consequently, many students went to sleep.

3. To separate clauses joined by a coordinating conjunction when there are commas within the clauses

   Example: Not only students, but parents, faculty, and community leaders sang, danced and played games at the school fair; and all the winners received prizes, certificates and trophies for their efforts.

Quotation Marks

1. To enclose a direct quotation

   Example: The principal said, "All students report to the auditorium at first period."

2. To enclose titles of chapter, articles, short stories, poems, songs, and other parts of books and periodicals.

   Example: The students had to read Frost's "The Road Not Taken" and "Stopping By Woods On a Snowy Evening" over the weekend.

3. To enclose slang words, technical terms and other expressions that are unusual in standard English.

   Example: Mary's new dazzling outfit was "bad."

Hyphen

1. To divide a word at the end of a line

2. With compound numbers from twenty-one to ninety-nine and with fractions used as adjective

3. With prefixes ex-, self-, all-, and with all prefixes before a proper noun or proper adjective.

Dash

1. To indicate an abrupt break in thought or to set off interrupting or additional material

   Example: No one—as I remember—expected John to win the presidency.

Parentheses

1. To enclose incidental explanatory matter that is added to a sentence but is not considered of major importance.

   Example: The novels (see page 5) should be read by the end of the semester.

Use of Language

All effective writing is the direct result of the effective use of words. Appropriate words and the interplay among them can make the difference between a successful essay and an unsuccessful one. You should choose words that make your meaning clear, your paper interesting and lively and create the total impression that you choose to achieve. Remember, first, to use standard English in your essay. In addition, give special attention to the following elements that can detract from the essay:

Wordiness

More does not necessarily mean better. Avoid the inclination to pad your essay by including unnecessary words and repetitions.

Example: During the hours in the morning before noon, there is a variety of radio programs of different kinds to which you can listen to.

Improved: In the morning, there is a variety of radio programs.

Example: The drive over to Cross Village follows and winds along the top of a great, huge bluff above the lake.

Improved: The drive to Cross Village winds along the top of a huge bluff above the lake.

Be concise in your selection of words.

Clichés

A cliché is an expression that has been used so often that it has lost its effectiveness. Professional writers occasionally use clichés, but it is generally better to avoid using them. It is far more impressive to create a fresh comparison or description to convey your meaning. Try your hand by creating an original substitution for the following clichés:

1. cold as ice _____

2. blind as a bat _____

3. to miss the boat _____

4. sings like a bird _____

ELEMENTS OF INTERESTING WRITING

Interesting writing is like an interesting person; certain characteristics stand out and make it both appealing and memorable. Here are four elements of writing which create interest:

Honesty–refers to your ability to be sincere in what you are trying to express, to be straightforward and fair in your judgments. Your essay should be free of hypocrisy. Avoid the tendency to include off-the-subject fillers and nonsensical and illogical padding. The reader can quickly spot such hypocrisy.

Emotions–Your attitude and feelings are basic to creating interest in your essay. The reader must be convinced that you have an interest in people and that you care about what happens to them. Revealing your attitude clearly establishes a bond of intimacy between you and the reader and also helps to create interest.

Originality–Your essay represents you. It employs your own unique judgments and standards. Just so, your ideas should express you, not someone else.

The interesting writer takes familiar things and looks at them from a new angle. He puts them together in new combinations creating a lively, original, fresh approach.

ORGANIZATION

A. PURPOSE and MAIN IDEA—Your essay must have a definite purpose. You must determine the purpose based upon the question. Your purpose will influence both the content and the language you select to express it. Since most of the questions usually require either exposition or argumentation, your purpose will usually be (1) to explain or (2) to persuade.

The main idea will, of course be clearly identified in your thesis statement. Then, if your purpose is to explain you should carefully select specific details necessary to sufficiently develop your thesis statement. If, on the other hand your purpose is to persuade, you should select reasons, evidence or opinions necessary to develop your argument.

B. OUTLINES—Most writers begin with some type of plan for writing. This plan may range from a simple jot list (see page 97) to a formal outline. In either case, it is a useful tool for classifying and arranging your ideas. It will help you to indicate the order of the details and will indicate where paragraph divisions will begin. The outline becomes the pattern for your essay.

A formal outline may be either a topic outline or a sentence outline. Do not mix the two styles; use either one or the other Although the sentence outline is clearer because it gives more details, the topic outline should be adequate for the writing that you will be doing. For either a series of Roman numerals, capital letters Arabic numerals and lower case letters is used to designate divisions in a formal outline. Example:

I. _____

   A. _____

      1. _____

      2. _____

   B. _____

      1. _____

         a. _____

         b. _____

      2. _____

II. _____

  A. _____

    1. _____

    2. _____

      a. _____

        (1.) _____

        (2.) _____

      b. _____

    3. _____

  B. _____

    1. _____

    2. _____

  C. _____

    1. _____

    2. _____

    3. _____

General Rules for Outlining

1. Use a period after each letter or numeral.

2. If you divide a topic or subtopic, the result must be at least two topics or subtopics. A topic cannot be divided into fewer than two parts. You may have any number above two.

3. The subdivisions added together should equal the main topic.

4. Divisions should not overlap.

5. Capitalize the first word in each item. Other words should not be capitalized unless they are proper nouns and/or proper adjectives.

6. No period should appear after a topic, but a period should follow each sentence.

7. Indent each subtopic four or five spaces beyond its main topic so that all letters or numbers of the same kind will come directly under each other in a vertical line.

8. Main topics should be parallel in form and subtopics under the same topic should be parallel. If the first topic is a list on nouns the others should be nouns. If the first is a phrase the others should also be phrases. Subtopics need not be parallel with main topics. Example:

Unparallel Structure

A.How to answer questions

B. Writing the essay

Parallel Structure

A. How to answer questions

B. How to write the essay

         or

A. Answering the questions

B. Writing the essay

9. Do not include the terms Introduction, Body and Conclusion in the outline. These are merely organizational units for the author.

Sample Outline

Thesis Statement: Good physical conditioning can be achieved by following several simple rules.

I. Appropriate diet

   A. Regular meals

   B. Between meals

II. Exercise

   A. Walking

   B. Running

III. Regular physical check-ups

   A. Women

      1. Under thirty

      2. Over thirty

   B. Men

TOPIC SENTENCES

The topic sentence is to the paragraph what the thesis statement is to the essay. It tells the reader what you're going to talk about. It has a specific subject and is neither too broad nor too narrow. It also establishes the author's attitude and gives the reader a sense of the direction in which the writer is going.

Although it may occur in the middle or at the the the end of the paragraph, it usually occurs at the beginning of the paragraph. Placing it at the beginning of the paragraph is advantageous for the writer in that it helps him keep clearly in mind the main idea to be developed. An effective topic sentence also arouses the reader's interest. Main ideas from your outline should be used to develop topic sentence, for each paragraph (see the samples above).

Example:

An appropriate diet is an essential element in achieving adequate physical conditioning. Eating regular meals is a necessary step. Those meals should include sufficient amounts of food from the major food groups: milk, meat, vegetable-fruit, bread-cereals. From these groups the body receives the proteins, carbohydrates, fats, fiber, vitamins, and minerals needed for sustenance. Eating regular meals should eliminate the need for between meal snacks. If, however, a snack is necessary it should come from the vegetable-fruit group. Although a balanced diet taken in moderation cannot guarantee good physical health, it is an essential component.

ELEMENTS OF A WELL ORGANIZED ESSAY

A well organized essay has several characteristics: it is unified, coherent, has smooth transitions, and maintains consistent tone.

Unity

Unity simply means that you must stay on the subject. The subject will be dictated, of course, by the essay question. Your response will be guided by your thesis statement, outline, and your topic sentences. Using concrete details, examples, and reasons related to the topic sentence will ensure unity in your essay.

Coherence

Sentences are coherent when they are logically and clearly related to each other. Coherence is achieved by linking ideas and sentences together by means of pronouns, references to ideas previously mentioned, and transitional expressions.

Transitional devices makes specific logical connections between ideas and keep the thought of a paragraph flowing smoothly from sentence to sentence. Transitional expressions or words may be grouped according to the kinds of ideas they express.

Linking similar ideas

again	for example	likewise
also	for instance	moreover
and	further	nor
another	furthermore	of course
besides	in addition	similarly
equally important	in like manner	too

Linking dissimilar/contradictory ideas

although	however	otherwise
and yet	in spite of	provided that
as if	instead	still
but	nevertheless	yet
conversely	on the contrary	
even if	on the other hand	

Indicating cause, purpose, or result

as	for	so
as a result	for this reason	then
because	hence	therefore
consequently	since	thus

Indicating time or position

above	before	meanwhile
across	beyond	next
afterward	eventually	presently
around	finally	second
at once	first	thereafter
at the present time	here	thereupon

Indicating an example or summary

as a result	in any event	in short
as I have said	in brief	on the whole
for example	in conclusion	to sum up
for instance	in fact	
in any case	in other words	

A second means is to arrange ideas in a clear and logical order that the reader can easily follow. You should choose chronological (the order in which events happen in time), spatial (the order of position) or order of importance depending upon you purpose.

Consistency of tone

A writer's tone results from (1) his attitude toward his subject and his attitude toward his reader. You may love your subject, despise it, revere it, laugh at or even seem detached from it. You may wish to shock the reader, outrage him, play upon his prejudices, amuse him, or merely inform him in the briefest and most efficient way possible. You must, however, be consistent and maintain that tone throughout your essay. If there is a need to change, some explanation should offered to the reader.

The following is a sample of a well written essay based upon a prose passage.

First impressions are as important in literature as they are in "real" life. The following passage is the opening chapter of Ernest Hemingway's *The Sun Also Rises*, a memoir of life in 1920 Paris by Jake Barnes. Write an essay in which you describe the "impression" you are given of Robert Cohn by Jake and, consequently, the "impression" you are given of Jake by Hemingway. What does Jake try to do as a writer to make you feel a certain way about Cohn? What does Hemingway do as a writer to make you feel a certain way about Jake? Be sure to use specific examples from the passage.

Robert Cohn was once middleweight boxing champion of Princeton. Do not think that I am very much impressed by that as a boxing title, but it meant a lot to Cohn. He cared nothing for boxing, in fact he disliked it, but he learned it painfully and thoroughly to counteract the feeling of inferiority and shyness he had felt on being treated as a Jew at Princeton. There was a certain inner comfort in knowing he could knock down anyone who was snooty to him, although being very shy and a thoroughly nice boy, he never fought except in the gym. He was Spider Kelly's star pupil. Spider Kelly taught all his young gentlemen to box like featherweights, no matter whether they weighed one hundred and five or two hundred and five pounds. But it seemed to fit Cohn. He was really very fast. He was so good that Spider promptly overmatched him and got his nose permanently flattened. This increased Cohn's distaste for boxing, but it gave him a certain satisfaction of some strange sort, and it certainly improved his nose. In his last year at Princeton he read too much and took to wearing spectacles. I never met any one of his class who remembered him. They didn't even remember that he was middleweight boxing champion.

I mistrust all frank and simple people, especially when their stories hold together, and I always had a suspicion that Robert Cohn had never been middleweight boxing champion, and that perhaps a horse had stepped on his face, or that maybe his mother had been frightened or had seen something, or that he had, maybe, bumped into something as a young child, but I finally had somebody verify the story from Spider Kelly. Spider Kelly not only remembered Cohn. He had often wondered what had become of him.

Robert Cohn was a member, through his father, of one of the richest Jewish families in New York, and through his mother of one of the oldest. At the military school where he prepped for Princeton, and played a very good end on the football team, no one had made him race-conscious. No one had ever made him feel he was a Jew, and hence any different from anybody else, until he went to Princeton. He was a nice boy, a friendly boy, and very shy, and it made him bitter. He took it out in boxing, and he came out of Princeton with painful self-consciousness and the flattened nose, and was married to the first girl who was nice to him. He was married five years, had three children, lost most of the fifty thousand dollars his father left him, the balance of the estate going to his mother, hardened into a rather unattractive mold under domestic unhappiness with a rich wife; and just when he made up his mind to leave his wife she left him and went off with a miniature-painter. As he had been thinking for months about leaving his wife and had not done it because it would be too cruel to deprive her of himself, her departure was a very healthful shock.

The divorce was arranged and Robert Cohn went out to the Coast. In California he fell among literary people and, as he still had a little of the fifty thousand left, in a short time he was backing a review of the Arts. The review commenced publication in Carmel, California, and finished in Provincetown, Massachusetts. By that time Cohn, who had been regarded purely as an angel, and whose name had appeared on the editorial page merely as a member of the advisory board, had become the sole editor. It was his money and he discovered he liked the authority of editing. He was sorry when the magazine became too expensive and he had to give it up.

By that time, though, he had other things to worry about. He had been taken in hand by a lady who hoped to rise with the magazine. She was very forceful, and Cohn never had a chance of not being taken in hand. Also he was sure that he loved her. When this lady saw that the magazine was not going to rise, she became a little disgusted with Cohn and decided that she might as well get what there was to get while there was still something available, so she urged that they go to Europe, where Cohn could write. They came to Europe, where the lady had been educated, and stayed three years. During these three years, the first spent in travel, the last two in Paris, Robert Cohn had two friends, Braddocks and myself. Braddocks was his literary friend. I was his tennis friend.

The lady who had him, her name was Frances, found toward the end of the second year that her looks were going, and her attitude toward Robert changed from one of careless possession and exploitation to the absolute determination that he should marry her. During this time Robert's mother had settled an allowance on him, about three hundred dollars a month. During two years and a half I do not believe that Robert Cohn looked at another woman. He was fairly happy, except that, like many people living in Europe, he would rather have been in America, and he had discovered writing. He wrote a novel, and it was not really such a bad novel as the critics later called it, although it was a very poor novel. He read many books, played bridge, played tennis, and boxed at a local gymnasium.

One role of the narrator in a work of fiction is to relate to the reader the events which comprise the story. Jake Barnes, however, does more than this: he charges his words with great bitterness and sarcasm, lacing the "facts" of Cohn's life with apparent anger and resentment.

Jake begins by telling us a fact (Cohn was once the middleweight boxing champion of Princeton) but quickly dismisses it with, "Do not think that I am very impressed by that as a boxing title, but it meant a lot to Cohn." This is typical of Jake's off-the-cuff style of belittling his subject who (according to Jake) was foolish enough to think that his boxing title was some sort of achievement. Jake feels he is qualified to psychoanalyze him by "explaining" to us that Cohn was so insecure that he participated in a sport he disliked just to "counteract his feeling[s] of inferiority." Here we see Jake "reading" a fact and "interpreting" it through the lens of his own opinions. He mocks Cohn's boxing ability ("He was so good that Spider Kelly promptly overmatched him and got his nose permanently flattened") and popularity by saying that he "never met anyone of his class who remembered him" as if he (Jake) had met everyone in Cohn's class and was therefore qualified to make such a statement. The finishing touch of the attack is when Jake says that for a while he didn't even believe Cohn, until he had someone "verify" the story from Spider Kelly. Jake must really hate Cohn to go through such pains to discredit him!

Cohn's relationships with women also come under attack. Again psychoanalyzing him in a quick and cursory manner, he says Cohn "married the first girl who was nice to him," as if he was too stupid or naive to "understand" women. Jake tells us that Cohn's thoughts of divorce never left his mind, "because it would [have been] too cruel to deprive her of himself," as if he was as arrogant as his biographer. He dismisses a girl whom Cohn was "sure that he loved" as a gold-digger that Cohn was too blind to recognize as such. He describes her as "very forceful," and states that Cohn "never had a chance at not being taken in hand," as if he was a spineless stuffed dummy with no say in anything. Again we see Jake presenting facts and coloring them with his own opinions and prejudices.

As he did with his boxing title, Jake mocks Cohn's career as a writer. Early in the passage he states that Cohn "read too much" and that in California he "fell among literary people," which oddly sounds like a line from the Bible ("He fell among thieves and murderers"). He plainly states that Cohn's review started in Carmel, California and ended in Provincetown, Massachusetts, the implication being that due to lack of support ("he was the sole editor") his review was a failure. He describes Cohn in Paris as "happy" except for the fact that he had "discovered writing." He presents Cohn's novel in a condescending manner, telling us that it was not as bad as the critics said (after all, what do *they* know about literature?), "although it was a very poor novel." He is as thorough in the defamation of Cohn as a writer as he is of Cohn as a boxer and a husband.

Hemingway's role in all of this is to present his narrator as a bitter, cynical, and arrogant person, and perhaps to warn his audience that the opinions expressed by his narrator are not necessarily his own. He has Jake take cheap shots at Cohn (his Jewishness never made him feel "any different from anybody else" until college) and assumes you will agree ("Do not think that I am very much impressed..."). Hemingway also has Jake defame Cohn in a great hurry and with great urgency, as if Jake was the insecure one who needed the audience on "his side." What happened between these two men is, presumably, the subject of the novel, and by beginning it this way, Hemingway heightens his readers' curiosity.

The essay is a good one chiefly due to its thoroughness. The detailed analyses of Cohn as a boxer, husband, and writer are both insightful and accurate. The writer of the essay let the structure of the passage dictate the structure of the essay, i.e., the essay progresses at the same speed and order of events as the passage. This is a sensible way to write an analytical essay, for it keeps the writer from jumping around from topic to topic and, when done well, ends up as a sort of "critical rewrite" of the passage. The writer was able to make general statements ("Jake is arrogant") backed up with proof ("He feels he knows more about literature than critics," etc.). The writer also shows a great deal of insight into both the "big issues" (what does the fact that Jake had someone verify Cohn's story suggest?) to the "smaller ones" (what is the tone of the phrase "he fell among literary people?"). Lastly, the writer is able to clearly differentiate between Jake and Hemingway (a common mistake made by young readers is mistaking the author for the narrator). The writer seems aware of Hemingway's presence in the passage and comments thoughtfully on Hemingway's intentions (Why is Jake so urgent? Why make this the first chapter?). Overall, the essay is on-target and patient; the writer left no stone unturned, and in a timed essay test where you must display your ability to read insightfully, it is better to flip every rock you can and worry about the snakes later.

THE ADVANCED PLACEMENT EXAMINATION IN

English Literature & Composition

TEST 1

1. (A) (B) (C) (D) (E)
2. (A) (B) (C) (D) (E)
3. (A) (B) (C) (D) (E)
4. (A) (B) (C) (D) (E)
5. (A) (B) (C) (D) (E)
6. (A) (B) (C) (D) (E)
7. (A) (B) (C) (D) (E)
8. (A) (B) (C) (D) (E)
9. (A) (B) (C) (D) (E)
10. (A) (B) (C) (D) (E)
11. (A) (B) (C) (D) (E)
12. (A) (B) (C) (D) (E)
13. (A) (B) (C) (D) (E)
14. (A) (B) (C) (D) (E)
15. (A) (B) (C) (D) (E)
16. (A) (B) (C) (D) (E)
17. (A) (B) (C) (D) (E)
18. (A) (B) (C) (D) (E)
19. (A) (B) (C) (D) (E)
20. (A) (B) (C) (D) (E)

21. (A) (B) (C) (D) (E)
22. (A) (B) (C) (D) (E)
23. (A) (B) (C) (D) (E)
24. (A) (B) (C) (D) (E)
25. (A) (B) (C) (D) (E)
26. (A) (B) (C) (D) (E)
27. (A) (B) (C) (D) (E)
28. (A) (B) (C) (D) (E)
29. (A) (B) (C) (D) (E)
30. (A) (B) (C) (D) (E)
31. (A) (B) (C) (D) (E)
32. (A) (B) (C) (D) (E)
33. (A) (B) (C) (D) (E)
34. (A) (B) (C) (D) (E)
35. (A) (B) (C) (D) (E)
36. (A) (B) (C) (D) (E)
37. (A) (B) (C) (D) (E)
38. (A) (B) (C) (D) (E)
39. (A) (B) (C) (D) (E)
40. (A) (B) (C) (D) (E)

41. (A) (B) (C) (D) (E)
42. (A) (B) (C) (D) (E)
43. (A) (B) (C) (D) (E)
44. (A) (B) (C) (D) (E)
45. (A) (B) (C) (D) (E)
46. (A) (B) (C) (D) (E)
47. (A) (B) (C) (D) (E)
48. (A) (B) (C) (D) (E)
49. (A) (B) (C) (D) (E)
50. (A) (B) (C) (D) (E)
51. (A) (B) (C) (D) (E)
52. (A) (B) (C) (D) (E)
53. (A) (B) (C) (D) (E)
54. (A) (B) (C) (D) (E)
55. (A) (B) (C) (D) (E)
56. (A) (B) (C) (D) (E)
57. (A) (B) (C) (D) (E)
58. (A) (B) (C) (D) (E)
59. (A) (B) (C) (D) (E)
60. (A) (B) (C) (D) (E)

This test is also on CD-ROM in our special interactive AP English Literature & Composition TEST*ware*®. It is highly recommended that you take this exam on computer first. You will then have the additional study features and benefits of enforced timed conditions, individual diagnostic analysis, and instant scoring. See page ix for guidance on how to get the most out of our AP English Literature & Composition book and software.

AP EXAMINATION IN ENGLISH LITERATURE AND COMPOSITION

TEST 1
Section 1

TIME: 60 Minutes
60 Questions

DIRECTIONS: This test consists of selections from literary works and questions on their content, form, and style. After reading each passage or poem, choose the best answer to each question and blacken the corresponding space on the answer sheet.

NOTE: Pay particular attention to the requirement of questions that contain the words NOT, LEAST, or EXCEPT.

QUESTIONS 1–15. Read the following passage carefully before you choose your answers.

My daddy's face is a study. Winter moves into it and presides there. His eyes become a cliff of snow threatening to avalanche; his eyebrows bend like black limbs of leafless trees. His skin takes on the pale, cheerless yellow of winter sun; for a jaw he has the edges of a snowbound field
5   dotted with stubble; his high forehead is the frozen sweep of the Erie, hiding currents of gelid thoughts that eddy in darkness. Wolf killer turned hawk fighter, he worked night and day to keep one from the door and the other from under the windowsills. A Vulcan guarding the flames, he gives us instructions about which doors to keep closed or opened for proper
10 distribution of heat, lays kindling by, discusses qualities of coal, and teaches us how to rake, feed, and bank the fire. And he will not unrazor his lips until spring.

Winter tightened our heads with a band of cold and melted our eyes. We put pepper in the feet of our stockings, Vaseline on our faces, and
15 stared through dark icebox mornings at four stewed prunes, slippery lumps of oatmeal, and cocoa with a roof of skin.

But mostly we waited for spring, when there could be gardens.

By the time this winter had stiffened itself into a hateful knot that nothing could loosen, something did loosen it, or rather someone. A
20 someone who splintered the knot into silver threads that tangled us, netted us, made us long for the dull chafe of the previous boredom.

This disrupter of seasons was a new girl in school named Maureen Peal. A high-yellow dream child with long brown hair braided into two lynch ropes that hung down her back. She was rich, at least by our
25 standards, as rich as the richest of the white girls, swaddled in comfort and care. The quality of her clothes threatened to derange Frieda and me. Patent-leather shoes with buckles, a cheaper version of which we got only at Easter and which had disintegrated by the end of May. Fluffy sweaters the color of lemon drops tucked into skirts with pleats so orderly they
30 astounded us. Brightly colored knee socks with white borders, a brown velvet coat trimmed in white rabbit fur, and a matching muff. There was a hint of spring in her sloe green eyes, something summery in her complexion, and a rich autumn ripeness in her walk.

She enchanted the entire school. When teachers called on her, they
35 smiled encouragingly. Black boys didn't trip her in the halls; white girls didn't suck their teeth when she was assigned to be their work partners; black girls stepped aside when she wanted to use the sink in the girls' toilet, and their eyes genuflected under sliding lids. She never had to search for anybody to eat with in the cafeteria — they flocked to the table
40 of her choice, where she opened fastidious lunches, shaming our jelly-stained bread with egg-salad sandwiches cut into four dainty squares, pink-frosted cupcakes, stocks of celery and carrots, proud, dark apples. She even bought and liked white milk.

Frieda and I were bemused, irritated, and fascinated by her. We
45 looked hard for flaws to restore our equilibrium, but had to be content at first with uglying up her name, changing Maureen Peal to Meringue Pie. Later a minor epiphany was ours when we discovered that she had a dog tooth — a charming one to be sure — but a dog tooth nevertheless. And when we found out she had been born with six fingers on each hand and
50 that there was a little bump where each extra one had been removed, we smiled. They were small triumphs, but we took what we could get — snickering behind her back and calling her Six-finger-dog-tooth-meringue-pie. But we had to do it alone, for none of the other girls would cooperate with our hostility. They adored her.

From THE BLUEST EYE *by Toni Morrison. Copyright © 1970 by Toni Morrison.*
Reprinted by permission of Henry Holt and Company, Inc.

1. It can be inferred from the opening paragraph that

    (A)   the narrator's father was a cold and unloving man

    (B)   the house was besieged by wild animals in the winter

    (C)   the narrator's father was strange and alien to his children

    (D)   the narrator's father fought hunger and cold unceasingly

    (E)   the narrator's father was an accomplished hunter

2. The sentence "My daddy's face is a study" (line 1) is best interpreted to mean that his face

    (A)   reflects the formal learning he has acquired

    (B)   reflects the quiet of a study room

    (C)   is an expressive landscape

    (D)   is expressive of his extensive experiences in life

    (E)   is worthy of attention

3. The phrase "will not unrazor his lips until spring" (lines 11–12) evokes his

    (A)   determination to win the battle for survival

    (B)   refusal to shave

    (C)   decision not to shave until spring comes

    (D)   preoccupation with his appearance

    (E)   stern, hostile attitude toward the family

4. The phrase "proud, dark apples" (line 42) presents an example of

    (A)   ambiguity   (D)   dramatic irony

    (B)   metaphor   (E)   simile

    (C)   personification

5. The narrator and Frieda resent Maureen primarily for

    (A)   her braided long brown hair

    (B)   her newness to the school

(C)   the fact that she was a dream child

(D)   the fact that she wore the same patent leather shoes they did

(E)   the expensive quality of her clothes

6.   The image of a "hateful knot" (line 18) is a reference to

(A)   the poverty of their home

(B)   the unspent anger of their father

(C)   the boredom of school

(D)   the unyielding cold weather

(E)   their cold, stiffened muscles

7.   In context, which of the following best defines the meaning of the phrase "minor epiphany" (line 47)

(A)   an unimportant social transgression

(B)   a small religious experience

(C)   a canine resemblance

(D)   an enlightening and gratifying realization

(E)   the small imperfections of nature

8.   In context, the phrase "dull chafe" (line 21) is best interpreted to mean

(A)   the rubbing of winter garments

(B)   the discomfort of wearing the same old clothes

(C)   the slow passage of time

(D)   the absence of new people in their lives

(E)   the unvaried rituals of winter life

9.   The description of the school's reactions to Maureen (lines 34 – 43) serves primarily to

(A)   provide a contrast to the father's earlier description

(B)   illustrate the narrator's jealousy

(C)   summarize Maureen's character

(D)   emphasize everyone's blindness to Maureen's true nature

(E)   demonstrate the subtlety of her conquests

10. According to the narrator, the discoveries and hostilities described in lines 45–53 served to

    (A) depict Maureen as a social misfit

    (B) arouse the superstitious side of their classmates

    (C) produce widespread laughter among the students

    (D) unite them with their classmates against Maureen

    (E) lessen their own sense of inferiority

11. In line 20, the "silver threads that tangled us" most likely refer to

    (A) the icy tracings that winter left on their windows

    (B) the net of poverty that envelopes them all

    (C) the finery of Maureen's clothing

    (D) the narrator and Frieda's plot to discredit Maureen

    (E) itching threads of winter garments that chafe them

12. Which of the following best describes the narrator at the end of the passage?

    (A) She has proven that Maureen is unworthy of friendship

    (B) She envies and admires Maureen

    (C) She feels confident about herself

    (D) She relishes her major victories over Maureen

    (E) She remains bitter about Maureen's superior wealth

13. The tone of paragraph six (line 34 – 43) is best described as

    (A) feigned outrage   (D) forced anger

    (B) shocked disbelief   (E) exaggerated sympathy

    (C) ironic glee

14. The phrase "splintered the knot into silver threads" (line 20) is

    (A) a simile   (D) onomatoepia

    (B) dramatic irony   (E) personification

    (C) a mixed metaphor

15. All of the following represent figurative language EXCEPT

    (A) "the color of lemon drops" (line 29)

    (B) "a band of cold" (line 13)

    (C) "currents of gelid thoughts" (line 6)

    (D) "their eyes genuflected" (line 38)

    (E) "a roof of skin" (line 16)

QUESTIONS 16–32. Read the following poem carefully before you choose your answers.

> Unnumbered suppliants crowd Preferment's gate,
> Athirst for wealth, and burning to be great;
> Delusive Fortune hears the incessant call,
> They mount, they shine, evaporate, and fall.
> 5 On every stage the foes of peace attend,
> Hate dogs their flight, and Insult mocks their end.
> Love ends with hope, the sinking statesman's door
> Pours in the morning worshiper no more;
> For growing names the weekly scribbler lies,
> 10 To growing wealth the dedicator flies;
> From every room descends the painted face,
> That hung the bright palladium¹ of the place;
> And smoked in kitchens, or in auctions sold,
> To better features yields the frame of gold;
> 15 For now no more we trace in every line
> Heroic worth, benevolence divine:
> The form distorted justifies the fall,
> And Detestation rids the indignant wall.
>   But will not Britain hear the last appeal,
> 20 Sign her foes' doom, or guard her favorites' zeal?
> Through Freedom's sons no more remonstrance rings,
> Degrading nobles and controlling kings;
> Our supple tribes repress their patriot throats,
> And ask no questions but the price of votes,
> 25 With weekly libels and septennial ale.²
> Their wish is full to riot and to rail.
>   In full-blown dignity, see Wolsey stand,
> Law in his voice, and fortune in his hand:
> To him the church, the realm, their powers consign,

30 Through him the rays of regal bounty shine;
    Turned by his nod the stream of honor flows,
    His smile alone security bestows:
    Still to new heights his restless wishes tower,
    Claim leads to claim, and power advances power;
35 Till conquest unresisted ceased to please,
    And rights submitted, left him none to seize.
    At length his sovereign frowns—the train of state
    Mark the keen glance, and watch the sign to hate.
    Where'er he turns, he meets a stranger's eye,
40 His suppliants scorn him, and his followers fly;
    At once is lost the price of awful state,
    The golden canopy, the glittering plate,
    The regal palace, the luxurious board,
    The liveried army, and the menial lord.
45 With age, with cares, with maladies oppressed,
    He seeks the refuge of monastic rest.
    Grief aids disease, remembered folly stings,
    And his last sighs reproach the faith of kings.
        Speak thou, whose thoughts at humble peace repine,
50 Shall Wolsey's wealth, with Wolsey's end be thine?
    Or liv'st thou now, with safer pride content,
    The wisest justice on the banks of Trent?
    For why did Wolsey, near the steeps of fate,
    On weak foundations raise the enormous weight?
55 Why but to sink beneath misfortune's blow,
    With louder ruin to the gulfs below?

1. Sacred object having the power to preserve a city or state.
2. Ale given away by candidates during parliamentary elections which are held every seven years.

From "The Vanity of Human Wishes," by Samuel Johnson

16. In line 1–4, the desire for fame is seen chiefly as

  (A) everyone's birthright

  (B) the right of a select few

  (C) motivated by an urge to improve society

  (D) a disappearing phenomenon

  (E) a universal aspiration

17. In line 5, the phrase "the foes of peace" refers to

     (A) the enemies of the realm

     (B) "Delusive Fortune"

     (C) poverty, envy and disease

     (D) plots to overthrow the government

     (E) worries that plague celebrities

18. According to the speaker, "The morning worshiper" (line 8), "the weekly
     scribbler" (line 9), and "the dedicator" (line 10) lack all of the following
     EXCEPT

     (A) compassion   (D) insensitivity

     (B) piety   (E) honor

     (C) loyalty

19. The main point about those described in lines 5–18 is that

     (A) they are abandoned when fortune frowns on them

     (B) they become deeply religious because of their success

     (C) they are remembered long after they are gone

     (D) they form friendships that last a lifetime

     (E) they are sorely missed when gone

20. In lines 19–26, the speaker regards the integrity of his countrymen as

     (A) politically unblemished

     (B) sound for their opposition to abuses by the nobility

     (C) evident in their condemnation of their country's foes

     (D) best expressed in their raillery for justice

     (E) non-existent or up for sale

21. The man Wolsey pictured in lines 27–36 is best described as which of the
     following?

     (A) Wealthy and benevolent

     (B) Authoritative and feared

(C)   Revered and humble

(D)   Prominent and respected

(E)   Spiritual and congenial

22.   The man Wolsey described in lines 27–36 is pictured chiefly in his role as

(A)   Church dignitary

(B)   Influential banker

(C)   Government minister

(D)   Kind benefactor

(E)   Loyal patriot

23.   The change referred to in lines 37–40 is described as one from

(A)   Innocence to corruption

(B)   Wealth to poverty

(C)   Eminence to commonality

(D)   Wickedness to contriteness

(E)   Favor to disfavor

24.   In line 30, the phrase "rays of regal bounty" is best taken to mean which of the following?

(A)   Kingly generosity

(B)   August blessings

(C)   Majestic boons

(D)   Grand favors

(E)   Haughty condescension

25.   Lines 37–38 suggest that the members of the king's court

(A)   follow the king's lead in their treatment of Wolsey

(B)   take note of the sharp look on Wolsey's face

(C)   fear the signs that Wolsey hates them

(D)   avoid Wolsey's superior scowl

(E)   parade themselves before Wolsey's penetrating stare

26.   The relationship between lines 1–4 and lines 27–40 is best described by which of the following?

(A)   Lines 1–4 present a description; lines 27–40 present a contrasting description

(B)   Lines 1–4 establish a thesis; lines 27–40 illustrate it

(C)   Lines 1–4 present an observation; lines 27–40 contradict it

(D)   Lines 1–4 present a poetic image; lines 27–40 present a contrasting image

(E)   Lines 1–4 present a moral dilemma; lines 27–40 solve it

27.   Beginning with line 49, the speaker does which of the following

(A)   concludes the development of his opening image

(B)   solves the moral dilemma he has presented

(C)   admonishes the reader to take heed of Wolsey's fate

(D)   dismisses an objection to his argument

(E)   furnishes evidence for a counter argument

28.   According to the speaker, Wolsey's rise to high office served to

(A)   inspire love and admiration among his followers

(B)   achieve "conquest unresisted" over the enemies of church and state

(C)   prove the value of the clergy to the state

(D)   bring him to greater grief when misfortune struck

(E)   render his situation unique and beyond imitation

29.   According to the speaker, those who achieve wealth and fame can expect to experience all of the following EXCEPT

(A)   the praise of the press

(B)   the love and admiration of subordinates

(C)   having their portraits studied for distinguished traits

(D)   visitations from those seeking favors

(E)   being forgotten when they fall from office

30.   According to the speaker, the common people are

(A)   innocent of wrongdoing

(B)   simply bystanders to history

(C)   victims of their own greed

(D)   guardians of freedom

(E)   the moral backbone of the country

31.   This excerpt is written in which of the following?

(A)   Ballad meter   (D)   Terza rima

(B)   Imabic dimeter   (E)   Heroic couplets

(C)   Blank verse

32.   In line 41, the words "awful state" refer to

(A)   the impoverished realm

(B)   the misrule that marked the king's reign

(C)   the luxurious life Wolsey enjoyed

(D)   the immoral condition of the kingdom

(E)   Wolsey's downcast state

QUESTIONS 33–45. Read the following passage carefully before you choose your answers.

Meditation XVII
Nunc Lento Sonitu dicunt, morieris.
Now this bell tolling softly for another, says to me, Thou must die.

Perchance he for whom this bell tolls may be so ill as that he knows not it tolls for him; and perchance I may think myself so much better than I am, as that they who are about me and see my state may have caused it to toll for me, and I know not that. The church is catholic, universal, so are all
5   her actions; all that she does belongs to all. When she baptizes a child, that action concerns me; for that child is thereby connected to that body which is my head too, and ingrafted into that body whereof I am a member. And when she buries a man, that action concerns me: all mankind is of one author and is one volume; when one man dies, one chapter is not torn out
10 of the book, but translated into a better language; and every chapter must be so translated. God employs several translators; some pieces are translated by age, some by sickness, some by war, some by justice; but God's hand is in every translation, and his hand shall bind up all our scattered leaves again for that library where every book shall lie open to one
15 another. As therefore the bell that rings to a sermon calls not upon the

preacher only, but upon the congregation to come, so this bell calls us all; but how much more me, who am brought so near the door by this sickness … The bell doth toll for him that thinks it doth; and though it intermit again, yet from that minute that the occasion wrought upon him, he is
20 united to God. Who casts not up his eye to the sun when it rises? but who takes off his eye from a comet when that breaks out? Who bends not his ear to any bell which upon any occasion rings? but who can remove it from that bell which is passing a piece of himself out of this world? No man is an island, entire of itself; every man is a piece of continent, a part of
25 the main. If a clod be washed away by the sea, Europe is the less, as well as if a promontory were, as well as if a manor of thy friend's or of thine own were. Any man's death diminishes me because I am involved in mankind, and therefore never send to know for whom the bell tolls, it tolls for thee. Neither can we call this a begging of misery or a borrowing of misery, as
30 though we were not miserable enough of ourselves but must fetch in more from the next house, in taking upon us the misery of our neighbors. Truly it were an excusable covetousness if we did; for affliction is a treasure, and scarce any man hath enough of it. No man hath affliction enough that is not matured and ripened by it and made fit for God by that affliction….
35 Tribulation is treasure in the nature of it, but it is not current money in the use of it, except we get nearer and nearer our home, heaven, by it. Another man may be sick too, and sick to death, and this affliction may lie in his bowels as gold in a mine and be of no use to him; but this bell that tells me of his affliction digs out and applies that gold to me, if by his consideration
40 of another's danger I take mine own into contemplation and so secure myself by making my recourse to my God, who is our only security.

—*John Donne*

33.   The passage contains all of the following rhetorical devices EXCEPT

    (A)   metaphor   (D)   apostrophic speech

    (B)   repetition   (E)   parallel syntax

    (C)   contrast

34.   It can be inferred from the passage that the speaker would agree with which of the following statements about another person's suffering and death?

    (A)   Reforming in that we think about our own death

    (B)   Important in that we avoid catching the same disease

    (C)   Aggravating in that the bell distracts us from our work

(D)   Unproductive in that dying yields nothing but suffering

(E)   Gladdening in that we have avoided death once again

35.   In the last sentence of the passage the speaker uses language that might best describe a

(A)   poisoning

(B)   smelting process

(C)   financial transaction

(D)   recovery from an illness

(E)   mining operation

36.   It is most likely that the speaker thinks himself so much better than he is (lines 2–3) in order to

(A)   acknowledge his moral superiority over the dying

(B)   luxuriate in life and health while another awaits death

(C)   contradict the idea that his own death is imminent

(D)   remind himself of his own shortcomings

(E)   hide the seriousness of his illness from himself

37.   The speaker gives metaphorical significance to which of the following?

I.   a chapter

II.   an island

III. a comet

IV.   a library

(A)   I and II only

(B)   II and III only

(C)   I, II, and III only

(D)   I, II, and IV only

(E)   I, III, and IV only

38.   The comparison in lines 8–10 of "mankind" to a "volume" suggests that death is all of the following EXCEPT

(A)   inevitable

(B)   pervasive

(C)   dynamic

(D)   isolating

(E)   transcending

39.   Lines 36–39 suggest that salvation will be achieved through

(A)   incessant prayer

(B)   "excusable covetousness"

(C)   trying ordeals

(D)   "borrowing of misery"

(E)   the misery of our neighbors

40.   The clause "but who can ... world" (lines 22–23) supports the speaker's proposition that individuals are

(A)   unable to resist looking at the sun

(B)   unable to ignore a bell

(C)   all spiritually interconnected

(D)   unaware of land lost to the sea

(E)   unable to ignore the sight of a comet

41.   In context, "that" in line 4 refers to

(A)   "they ... have caused it to toll" (lines 2–3)

(B)   "who are about me" (line 3)

(C)   "he knows not it tolls for him" (line 1)

(D)   "church is catholic" (line 5)

(E)   "so much better than I am" (line 3)

42.   A more conventional placement for "scarce" in line 33 would be

(A)   rarely   (D)   infrequently

(B)   hardly   (E)   little

(C)   seldom

43.   "Tribulation ... by it," (lines 35–36) appears to be a contradictory statement because

(A)   one can not buy the way into heaven

(B)   suffering alone will not open the gates of heaven

(C)   earthly treasures can not be taken into the afterlife

(D)   the currency of heaven is prayer

(E)   accepted affliction opens the gates of heaven

44. At the conclusion the speaker knows that

    (A) others die and so can he

    (B) each of us approaches death alone

    (C) others die so that he could be spared

    (D) treasures should all be spent before we die

    (E) the nearer death the nearer despair

45. Which of the following seems LEAST compatible with the speaker's philosophy?

    (A) The spiritual body of the church

    (B) Salvation is preordained

    (C) Purification through suffering

    (D) The afterlife

    (E) The family of man

QUESTIONS 46–60. Read the following poem carefully before you choose your answers.

The Garden

How vainly men themselves amaze,
To win the palm, the oak, or bays,
And their uncessant labors see
Crowned from some single herb or tree
5 Whose short and narrow-vergèd shade
Does prudently their toils upbraid,
While all the flowers and trees do close
To weave the garlands of repose!

Fair Quiet, have I found thee here,
10 And Innocence, thy sister dear?
Mistaken long, I sought you then
In busy companies of men.
Your sacred plants, if here below,
Only among the plants will grow;
15 Society is all but rude
To this delicious solitude.

No white nor red was ever seen
So amorous as this lovely green.
Fond lovers, cruel as their flame,
20   Cut in these trees their mistress' name.
Little, alas! they know or heed,
How far these beauties hers exceed!
Fair trees! wheres'e'r your barks I wound
No name shall but your own be found.

25   When we have run our passion's heat,
Love hither makes his best retreat.
The gods, that mortal beauty chase,
Still in a tree did end their race;
Apollo hunted Daphne so,
30   Only that she might laurel grow;
And Pan did after Syrinx speed,
Not as a nymph, but for a reed.

What wondrous life in this I lead!
Ripe apples drop about my head;
35   The luscious clusters of the vine
Upon my mouth do crush their wine;
The nectarine, and curious peach,
Into my hands themselves do reach;
Stumbling on melons, as I pass,
40   Ensnared with flowers, I fall on grass.

Meanwhile the mind, from pleasure less,
Withdraws into its happiness;—
The mind, that ocean where each kind
Does straight its own resemblance find;
45   Yet it creates, transcending these,
Far other worlds, and other seas,
Annihilating all that's made
To a green thought in a green shade.

Here at the fountain's sliding foot,
50   Or at some fruit-tree's mossy root,
Casting the body's vest aside,
My soul into the boughs does glide:
There, like a bird, it sits and sings,
Then whets and combs its silver wings,

55   And, till prepared for longer flight,
Waves in its plumes the various light.

Such was that happy garden-state,
While man there walked without a mate
After a place so pure and sweet.
60   What other help could yet be meet!
But 't was beyond a mortal's share
To wander solitary there:
Two paradises 't were in one,
To live in paradise alone.

65   How well the skilful gardener drew
Of flowers, and herbs, this dial new;
Where, from above, the milder sun
Does through a fragrant zodiac run,
And, as it works, th' industrious bee
70   Computes its time as well as we!
How could such sweet and wholesome hours
Be reckoned but with herbs and flowers?

by Andrew Marvell

46.   In the first stanza of the poem, the speaker seeks to convey a feeling of

    (A)   uneasiness   (D)   contentedness

    (B)   light-heartedness   (E)   bitterness

    (C)   passiveness

47.   In context "rude" (line 15) suggests that the people

    (A)   spurn solitude

    (B)   behave unmannerly towards solitude

    (C)   are primitive

    (D)   take advantage of those seeking solitude

    (E)   appreciate solitude

48.   The speaker gives metaphoric significance to which of the following?

    I.   the ocean   III.   the laurel

    II.   the oak   IV.   a reed

(A)   I and II only   (D)   I, II, and IV only

(B)   III and IV only   (E)   I, II, III, and IV

(C)   I, II, and III only

49.   Lines 13 and 14 ("Your ... grow") are best understood to mean which of the following?

(A)   the sacred trusts that bind men grow best in solitude

(B)   the art of horticulture is one of civilization's sacred gifts

(C)   the soul grows best when planted among the best of society

(D)   Innocence and Quiet are nurtured best amidst nature

(E)   sacred plants can be grown only where other plants already grow

50.   In lines 42–46, the mind is compared to

(A)   a mirror   (D)   the seas

(B)   other worlds   (E)   green shade

(C)   an ocean

51.   Which of the following occurs because the mind "withdraws into its happiness" (line 42)?

(A)   "other worlds" of insects are discovered among the plants

(B)   the "green thought" of a new idea emerges

(C)   "other seas" of waving grass are appreciated

(D)   "pleasure less" actions of society are contemplated

(E)   the mind finds "its own resemblance" in green nature

52.   The speaker's description of the garden emphasizes that it offers all of the following delights EXCEPT that of

(A)   taste   (D)   intellect

(B)   spirit   (E)   fellowship

(C)   sound

53.   The lines 7–8, ("While all the flowers ... repose") suggest that

(A)   flowers and leaves make a more suitable victory garland

(B)   nature's shade is effortlessly available

(C)   nature closes ranks against the victor

(D)   crowns of herb and tree quickly fade into repose

(E)   nature celebrates the victor by weaving his victory garland

54.   In line 6, "prudently" functions as an adverb modifying which of the following?

(A)   "upbraid" (line 6)   (D)   "to weave" (line 8)

(B)   "toils" (line 6)   (E)   "shade" (line 5)

(C)   "close" (line 7)

55.   In lines 51–56, the speaker compares

(A)   his soul to his vest

(B)   his body to his vest

(C)   his soul to boughs

(D)   the boughs to his vest

(E)   his vest to feathers

56.   In the poem, the garden is, for the speaker, a source of all of the following EXCEPT

(A)   rejuvenation   (D)   inspiration

(B)   beauty   (E)   pleasure

(C)   censure

57.   Lines 65–72 can best be described as a

(A)   counter statement to the argument of the poem

(B)   simile for the relationship between the garden and the bees

(C)   digression from the subject of the poem

(D)   metaphor of time's passage in the garden

(E)   change from description to philosophizing

58. In the eighth stanza of the poem, the speaker implies that the first and best "happy garden-state"

    (A) still awaits us as our earthly heritage

    (B) was marred by the absence of a mate

    (C) was a place both "pure and sweet"

    (D) was undeserved by man

    (E) was marred by the presence of a mate

59. It can be inferred that the speaker's attitude toward women is one of

    (A) respect   (D) adoration

    (B) disapproval   (E) hatred

    (C) amusement

60. The poem is an example of which of the following verse forms?

    (A) Free verse   (D) Dactylic hexameter

    (B) Iambic tetrameter (E) Terza rima

    (C) Ballad meter

Section 2

TIME: 2 Hours
3 Essay Questions

QUESTION 1. *(Suggested time — 40 minutes. This question counts one-third of the total essay-section score.)* In the selection below, Joseph Conrad describes a boat trip up the Congo River and the psychological and physical effects that trip has on the narrator. Read the passage carefully. Then write an essay in which you describe the psychological stresses and the physical demands that the narrator endured. Use specific references to the text to show how Conrad's diction, syntax, and use of detail served to convey those demands.

      Going up the river was like travelling back to the earliest beginnings of the world, when vegetation rioted on the earth and the big trees were kings. An empty stream, a great silence, an impenetrable forest. The air was warm, thick, heavy, sluggish. There was no joy in the brilliance of sun-
5 shine. The long stretches of the waterway ran on, deserted, into the gloom of overshadowed distances. On silvery sandbanks hippos and alligators sunned themselves side by side. The broadening waters flowed through a mob of wooded islands; you lost your way on that river as you would in a desert, and butted all day long against shoals, trying to find the channel, till
10 you thought yourself bewitched and cut off forever from everything you had known once — somewhere — far away — in another existence perhaps. There were moments when one's past came back to one, as it will sometimes when you have not a moment to spare to yourself; but it came in the shape of an unrestful and noisy dream, remembered with wonder
15 amongst the overwhelming realities of this strange world of plants, and water, and silence. And this stillness of life did not in the least resemble a peace. It was the stillness of an implacable force brooding over an inscru- table intention. It looked at you with a vengeful aspect. I got used to it afterwards; I did not see it any more; I had no time. I had to keep guessing
20 at the channel; I had to discern, mostly by inspiration, the signs of hidden banks; I watched for sunken stones; I was learning to clap my teeth smartly before my heart flew out, when I shaved by a fluke some infernal sly old snag that would have ripped the life out of the tin-pot steamboat and drowned all the pilgrims; I had to keep a look-out for the signs of dead
25 wood we could cut up in the night for next day's steaming. When you have to attend to things of that sort, to the mere incidents of the surface, the reality — the reality, I tell you — fades. The inner truth is hidden —

luckily, luckily. But I felt it all the same; I felt often its mysterious stillness watching me at my monkey tricks....

From Heart of Darkness *— Joseph Conrad.*

QUESTION 2. *(Suggested time — 40 minutes. This question counts one-third of the total essay-section score.)* These poems present portraits of women by two poets; however, the two poets approach their portraits very differently. In a well-organized essay, distinguish between the attitudes of the poets towards their lovers and the techniques each uses to express his attitude. Support your statement with specific references to the texts.

YE TRADEFULL MERCHANTS
Ye tradefull merchants, that with weary toyle,
Do seeke most pretious things to make your gain,
And both the Indias of their treasures spoile,
What needeth you to seeke so farre in vaine?
For loe! my love doth in her selfe containe
All this worlds riches that may farre be found:
If saphyres, loe! her eies be saphyres plaine;
If rubies, loe! hir lips be rubies sound;
If pearles, hir teeth be pearls, both pure and round;
If yvorie, her forhead yvorie weene;
If gold, her locks are finest gold on ground;
If silver, her faire hands are silver sheene:
    But that which fairest is but few behold,
    Her mind, adornd with vertues manifold.

Edmund Spenser

130
My mistress' eyes are nothing like the sun;
Coral is far more red than her lips' red;
If snow be white, why then her breasts are dun;
If hairs be wires, black wires grow on her head.
I have seen roses damasked, red and white,
But no such roses see I in her cheeks;
And in some perfumes is there more delight
Than in the breath that from my mistress reeks.
I love to hear her speak, yet well I know
That music hath a far more pleasing sound;

I grant I never saw a goddess go;
My mistress, when she walks, treads on the ground.
And yet, by heaven, I think my love as rare
As any she belied with false compare.

William Shakespeare

QUESTION 3. *(Suggested time — 40 minutes. This question counts one-third of the total essay-section score.)* Some novels and plays portray the consequences that occur when individuals pursue their own personal good at the expense of the common good of the group or society. Choose such a novel or play, and write a well-organized essay that explains how the interests of a character or group of characters conflict with the common good and produces dire consequences for another group or society. Avoid plot summary.

You may choose one of the works listed below or another of comparable quality that is appropriate for the question. Do not write about a film or television program.

The Crucible	*Hard Times*
Adventures of Huckleberry Finn	*The Scarlet Letter*
Heart of Darkness	*The Little Foxes*
The Once and Future King	*Animal Farm*
Ethan Frome	*Raisin in the Sun*
Richard III	*Hamlet*
A Long Day's Journey into Night	*Macbeth*
An Ememy of the People	*The Jungle*
Nineteen Eighty-Four	*Catch-22*
All My Sons	*King Lear*

TEST 1

ANSWER KEY

1.	(D)	16.	(E)	31.	(E)	46.	(B)
2.	(C)	17.	(E)	32.	(C)	47.	(A)
3.	(A)	18.	(D)	33.	(D)	48.	(C)
4.	(C)	19.	(A)	34.	(A)	49.	(D)
5.	(E)	20.	(E)	35.	(E)	50.	(C)
6.	(D)	21.	(B)	36.	(E)	51.	(B)
7.	(D)	22.	(C)	37.	(D)	52.	(E)
8.	(E)	23.	(E)	38.	(D)	53.	(B)
9.	(B)	24.	(A)	39.	(C)	54.	(A)
10.	(E)	25.	(A)	40.	(C)	55.	(B)
11.	(C)	26.	(B)	41.	(A)	56.	(C)
12.	(B)	27.	(C)	42.	(B)	57.	(D)
13.	(B)	28.	(D)	43.	(E)	58.	(E)
14.	(C)	29.	(B)	44.	(A)	59.	(B)
15.	(A)	30.	(C)	45.	(B)	60.	(B)

DETAILED EXPLANATIONS OF ANSWERS

TEST 1

Section 1

1. **(D)** Answer (A) is wrong. Although he is described in wintery terms, he is never accused of harshness or indifference. His devotion to keeping them warm displays his love. Answers (B) and (E) are wrong because they stem from a misreading of the figurative expressions "wolf killer," and "hawk fighter," i.e., one who battles the wolf of hunger and the winds of winter. Answer (C) is wrong because it stems from a misreading of "Vulcan" to mean alien rather than the Roman god of fire and metalworking. Answer (D) is correct and is supported by lines 8–11.

2. **(C)** Answer (A) is wrong because it is based on a misreading of the word "study" to mean the acquisition of learning. Answer (B) is wrong because it interprets "study" to mean a room. Answer (C) is correct because "study" in this context means a description or portrait. Answer (D) is incorrect because the paragraph does not reveal anything about his experiences in life other than his actions to protect his family from the cold. Answer (E) is wrong because it arises from a misreading of the word "study" to mean "apply the mind," which it does not in this context.

3. **(A)** Answer (A) is correct because he will not relax or open up until the threat of winter disappears completely. Answers (B) and (C) are wrong because "unrazor" in this context does not have anything to do with shaving. Answer (D) is wrong because it implies that "unrazor" has a literal instead of a figurative meaning in this context, which it does not have. Answer (E) is wrong because it is unsupported by the paragraph. He does not scold, but instructs the family on how to keep the house warm.

4. **(C)** Answer (A) is wrong because ambiguity implies confusion about the meaning of the words. There is no confusion in this phrase. Answer (B) is wrong because there is no comparison being made between the apple and some other object. Answer (C) is correct because pride is a human quality not shared by

136

inanimate objects like apples. Answer (D) is wrong because dramatic irony is a statement made by a character that ironically describes the character's fate later in the story. Answer (E) is wrong because there is no comparison utilizing "like" or "as" in this phrase.

5.   **(E)**   Answer (A) is wrong because although the word "lynch" is used to describe her braids, it is not the source of their dislike. Answer (B) is wrong because Maureen's newness is only mentioned and does not come in for further critical comment. Answer (C) is wrong because the girls do not resent her looks. Answer (D) is wrong because she did not wear the same shoes. She wore much better shoes to school. Answer (E) is correct and is supported by line 27.

6.   **(D)**   Answer (A) is wrong because the passage only implies their poverty and does not pass judgment on it. Answer (B) is wrong because nowhere in the passage is there any mention of the father's anger. Answer (C) is wrong because the passage makes no mention of being bored with school. They are bored with winter, not school. Answer (D) is the correct answer because the unyielding cold weather has tightened around them like a knot. Answer (E) is wrong because the passage states that the winter "stiffens," not their muscles.

7.   **(D)**   Answer (A) is wrong because the discovery of the "dog tooth" represents a physical blemish not a social one. Answer (B) is wrong because it stems from a misreading of the "epiphany" as having a religious meaning here, which it does not. Answers (C) and (E) are wrong because "epiphany" has nothing to do with discovering resemblances, canine or otherwise, or small imperfections of nature. Answer (D) is correct. They are both enlightened and gratified to discover a physical flaw in Maureen's beauty.

8.   **(E)**   Answers (A) and (B) are wrong because they stem from a literal reading of the word "chafe" when it is meant metaphorically. Answer (C) is wrong. The days are slow because the activities are dull; not vice versa. Answer (D) is wrong because although Maureen was new, more importantly she was rich. Answer (E) is correct because the first two paragraphs include descriptions of winter life that rub them the same way day after day.

9.   **(B)**   Answer (A) is wrong because the narrator does not link the two descriptive passages in this fashion. Answer (B) is correct because every action described by the narrator points toward the special treatment given to Maureen and not to her. Answer (C) is wrong because there is nothing substantial about her character presented here. Answer (D) is wrong because Maureen's real nature is never revealed. Answer (E) is wrong because there does not appear to be a plan behind Maureen's actions.

10. **(E)**   Answer (A) is wrong because Maureen remains popular in spite of the discoveries. Answer (B) is wrong because Maureen's six fingers apparently meant little to the other girls. Answers (C) and (D) are contradicted by lines 53–54 of the text. Answer (E) is correct and is supported by lines 45–46.

11. **(C)**   Answer (A) is wrong because the "silver threads" do not represent the ice that clouds the windows. Answer (B) is wrong because they are caught up in a net of jealousy not poverty. Answer (C) is correct because Maureen's clothing upsets the girls most of all in that it makes them conscious of their own dull clothes. Answer (D) is incorrect because "silver threads" is too picturesque a phrase for something as mean as their plots against Maureen. Answer (E) is incorrect because there is no mention of garments that itch and chafe them.

12. **(B)**   Answer (A) is incorrect because the other girls refuse to join in the plots against Maureen. Answer (B) is correct because it is supported by lines 44-45. Answer (C) is wrong because the narrator's need to put down Maureen comes from her lack of self-confidence. Answer (D) is wrong because in line 51 the narrator admits that her triumphs are small. Answer (E) is wrong because lines 44–45 contradict it.

13. **(B)**   Feigned outrage (A) is wrong because the many courtesies extended to Maureen do anger the narrator but there is nothing feigned about it. Answer (B) is correct because the narrator is shocked into disbelief by the fact that Maureen escapes all the indignities other black girls encountered in school. Answer (C) is wrong because there is no glee or joy expressed in the lines. Answer (D) is wrong because the narrator is angry. To her the issues are genuine and there is no need to force her emotions. Answer (E) is wrong because the narrator expresses no sympathy for Maureen's treatment in these lines. Indeed, there is nothing to sympathize about since everyone goes out of their way to accommodate Maureen.

14. **(C)**   Answer (A) is wrong through the absence of "like" or "as." Answer (B) is wrong because dramatic irony involves a statement made by a character that ironically describes the character's fate later in the story. Answer (C) is correct because a knot is not splintered like a piece of wood but unraveled or slit with a knife. Answer (D) is wrong because the words do not contain or imitate the sound they make. Answer (E) is wrong because the knot is not imbued with human qualities.

15. **(A)**   Answer (A) is the exception. It describes a particular shade of yellow and makes no comparison. Answers (B), (C) and (E) are metaphors comparing one thing to another thing. Answer (D) is a personification.

16. **(E)**   Most individuals desire fame but it is not labeled a birthright (A) in the poem. The "unnumbered suppliants" in line 1 contradict the idea that it is a right of a select few (B). Like Wolsey, individuals are motivated toward fame and fortune for strictly personal reasons, the least of which is a desire to improve society (C). The words "unnumbered" and "incessant" do not support the idea that this is a disappearing phenomenon (D). However, the words "unnumbered" and "the incessant call" both suggest that it is a universal aspiration (E).

17. **(E)**   Only a misreading of the word "foes" can make them the enemies of the realm (A), or poverty, envy and disease (C). These are the foes of domestic peace which is not the meaning of "peace" in this passage. "Delusive Fortune" (B) is not the antecedent of "foes." Neither do the "foes" reside within the government and plot its overthrow (D). The correct answer is (E) in that the meaning of "peace" in this line is the tranquility of life that is shattered by the many worries that come to plague a celebrity.

18. **(D)**   By abandoning the former celebrity when hard times struck, the "worshipper," "scribbler" and "dedicator" show a lack of compassion (A), loyalty (C) and honor (E). Choice (B) is wrong because it stems from a misreading of the word "worshiper," which in the context of the poem means those who come to offer flattery in return for favors. Choice (D) is correct because the behavior of these individuals demonstrates "insensitivity."

19. **(A)**   The correct answer is (A) because of the selfish interests of those who attend them, i.e., the "worshiper," "scribbler" and "dedicator." Their success does not make them (B), as that is not the meaning of "worshiper" in this context. Answers (C), (D), and (E) are wrong because the actions described in each contradicts the meaning of the lines, which essentially catalogue how the "worshiper" and others abandon them.

20. **(E)**   The speaker charges his countrymen with selling their votes, hence (A) is wrong. They used to be watchful of abuses by the nobility, but are no longer (B). There is no condemnation of their country's foes (C), and neither do they "rail" for justice (D). Rather they "riot and rail" for pure devilment. Answer (E) is correct because the portrait is that of men who lack integrity and sell their votes for a drink of ale.

21. **(B)**   Although Wolsey possessed wealth "fortune in his hand" (A), there is no indication in the poem that he dispensed it with benevolence. Though he was respected, the idea of him being revered (C) is undermined by line 40, and humility is contradicted by line 33. He was prominent (D), but the poem does not support respected. Line 24 ties him to the church, but Johnson's portrait does not suggest

that he had a spiritual dimension (E). The smile in line 32 is that of the Cheshire cat rather than an expression of a congenial nature. Therefore, (B) is the best answer because it is supported by the phrase "Law in his voice," his smile that bestows security, and line 36.

22. **(C)**   Although Cardinal Wolsey was a church dignitary (A), Johnson does not mention his title in the poem. While Wolsey dispensed "regal bounty" he was neither a banker (B) nor kind benefactor (D) as is evident in lines 35 and 36. Choice (E) can be supported only by a misreading of lines 23–26. Choice (C) is the best answer because it is supported by details like "Law in his voice," and his role as a source of "regal bounty."

23. **(E)**   Nothing in the lines suggest Wolsey was innocent (A). That he was wealthy is evident, but his downfall was not to poverty (B). The same can be said of eminence and commonality (C). Wickedness is implied in many lines, but there is no indication of contriteness (D). The change that is described is one from favor to disfavor (E) in the eyes of his king.

24. **(A)**   Choice (A) is correct because Wolsey is described as the conduit for kingly generosity, which was certainly more substantial than mere august blessings (B), but less fairy-taled than majestic boons (C) and grand favors (D). Haughty (E) is an inaccurate reading of the word "regal" in the context of the line.

25. **(A)**   Answer (A) is correct, because line 38 states that they observe the king's "keen glance" and await his signal that it is safe to hate Wolsey. Answer (B) is wrong because the "keen glance" does not appear on Wolsey's face, nor do they at that point care whether Wolsey hates them or not (C). Only a misreading of line 37 can place the scowl on Wolsey's face (D). The word "train" means those that follow the king; it does not mean that they parade themselves before Wolsey (E).

26. **(B)**   The two sets of lines in question here present thesis and illustration (B). While the first set of lines describes the course fate lays out for those who seek inordinate worldly fame and power, the second set of lines do not contradict it in any sense (A) and (C). An image can be found in "Preferment's gate," but the second set of lines do not contrast with it (D). Choice (E) is wrong because no dilemma is posed in the first set of lines, and Wolsey's fate does not serve as a solution but as a warning.

27. **(C)**   The opening image "Preferment's gate" is not mentioned in these lines (A). No moral dilemma has been presented in the earlier lines (B), but rather an example in the form of Wolsey and his fate. Thus, the correct answer is (C) because this is the speaker's intention in describing Wolsey in the first place.

Answers (D) and (E) are wrong because the lines neither dismiss an objection nor furnish evidence for a counter argument.

28. **(D)** Lines 32-36 catalogue a series of actions that cannot inspire love and admiration (A). "Conquest unresisted" (B) was achieved by Wolsey over those who opposed him, not over the enemies of the church and state. There is nothing in this portrait of Wolsey to suggest that he was waging a campaign to prove the value of the clergy to the state. Lines 49–52 are an admonition to the reader not to imitate Wolsey's example; therefore, answer (E) is wrong. Lines 55–56, on the other hand, state that Wolsey's great rise was solely for the purpose of making his fall all the more painful when it came. Answer (D) is correct.

29. **(B)** The press "scribbler" always lauds (A) those who are influential. When that person arrives at the top, it is common to have a portrait painted which is praised by those seeking to flatter the individual in hope of favors (C). Line 8 describes the cessation of daily visits of those seeking favors (D). Lines 6–10 describes how the ambitious are quickly forgotten when they fall upon hard times (E). Answer (B) is correct, according to the speaker, because the selfish behavior of those on the rise and the selfish motives of those who serve them do not provide a suitable atmosphere for the development of love and admiration.

30. **(C)** The common people are not innocent of blame (A), because they no longer safeguard liberty (line 21). Neither are they onlookers (B), in that their votes are for sale (line 24), which makes them victims of their own greed (C). Their role as guardians of liberty (D) is denied by line 21. Answers (D) and (E) are wrong because they contradict the accusations made in lines 21–26.

31. **(E)** Ballad meter alternates three and four stresses in the lines, the lines of this poem have five (A). The line uses Iambic feet, but Dimeter means only two stresses per line (B). These lines rhyme and blank verse does not (C). Terza rima (D) is a three-line stanza which is not evident in this sample. Answer (E) is correct because every two lines of a couplet rhyme.

32. **(C)** A misreading of "state" as meaning a political unit renders answer (A) wrong. A misreading of "awful" as meaning mismanagement by the king renders answer (B) wrong. The same can be said for answer (D). "Awful" in this context does not mean rotten or bad. Neither does it mean frightful or dreadful which would lead to the selection of answer (E). "Awful" in this context means inspiring awe, thus answer (C) is correct. The luxury of Wolsey's life did inspire awe.

33. **(D)** Answer (A) is incorrect because the phrase "affliction is a treasure" is a metaphor. Answer (B) is incorrect because the speaker repeats the phrase "the bell

tolls" through out the passage. Answer (C) is incorrect because lines 33–34 contain contrasting statements. Answer (D) is correct because nowhere in the passage does the speaker address someone not present or a personified idea or object. Answer (E) is incorrect. Line 12 uses parallel syntax when it states, "some by sickness, some by war, some by justice."

34. **(A)** Answer (A) is correct because the speaker believes that we can use another's death to prepare ourselves for our own encounter with our Maker. Answer (B) is wrong because the passage is concerned with preserving our soul not our physical body. Answer (C) is incorrect because the speaker maintains that the tolling of the death bell reminds us of our own mortality and serves to motivate our own moral reform. Answer (D) is incorrect because the speaker believes we can use suffering (tribulation) to earn our entrance to a heavenly afterlife. Answer (E) is incorrect because the speaker believes that death is unavoidable and we should be prepared for it.

35. **(E)** Poisoning (A) and financial transaction (C) are wrong because the gold in the man's bowels is figurative and not actual. Smelting metal (B) is wrong because the processing of this figurative gold is done by examining one's life and not by any manufacturing process. Recovery from illness (D) is wrong because the person is "sick to death" meaning he/she dies. Mining operation (E) is correct because the stranger's affliction and death can become as gold to the speaker if the speaker does some serious thinking about reforming his own moral state before death approaches him.

36. **(E)** Answer (A) is wrong because the context suggests that the speaker may be as seriously ill as the dying man but unaware of it. Answer (B) is wrong because the speaker does not express satisfaction with himself and he is ill, himself (line 17). Answer (C) is incorrect because the opening implies that others may be seeing things more accurately than he is. Answer (D) is incorrect because it is contrary to the sense of the lines 2–3. Answer (E) is correct because the speaker implies that the true state of his physical and moral health may be too upsetting to acknowledge.

37. **(D)** The chapter (I) stands for the life of a person. An island (II) stands for the isolation of individuals from each other. A comet (III) in the context of the passage is a natural phenomenon and has no figurative meaning. A library (IV) stands for heaven or that gathering place where all the dead will be open to one another. The correct answer is (D) because it is the only answer that includes all of the metaphorical expressions.

38. **(D)** Inevitable (A) is wrong because the speaker wants the reader to con-

template the meaning of the bell because our own deaths may also be imminent. Pervasive (B) is wrong because the universality of death is one of the givens in this passage. Dynamic (C) is wrong because death comes through several means: age, sickness, war, and justice. Isolating (D) is correct because the experience is universal and lines 13–15 present an image of the departed gathered together and open to each other as books in a library Transcending (E) is wrong because line 10 implies that death is a "translation" into a better language or state.

39. **(C)** Answer (A) is wrong because the emphasis of the lines in question is on the cleansing power of affliction and not on achieving salvation through prayer. Answer (B) is wrong because the phrase "excusable covetousness" describes the act of borrowing misery, but this in itself is not sufficient to achieve salvation. Answer (C) is correct because the speaker maintains that tribulation matures, humbles and even ripens us for heaven. Answer (D) is wrong because the speaker states that our concern for others may be viewed as a borrowing of misery, but he does not state that such borrowing is the way to salvation. Answer (E) is wrong because the speaker believes that the misery of our neighbors can save them, but it is our own tribulations and how we react to them that will bring salvation for ourselves.

40. **(C)** Answers (A), (B) and (E) are wrong. These three statements are examples supporting the sentence in lines 31–33, not vice versa. Answer (D) is wrong because it is based on a misreading of the figurative passage. Answer (C) is correct because it serves to introduce the idea "No man is an island" that immediately follows it.

41. **(A)** Answer (A) is correct because the speaker, unaware of his true condition, is not sure if his friends have ordered the bell tolled for him. Answer (B) is wrong because it implies mistakenly that the speaker does not know who is around his sick bed. Answer (C) is wrong because the issue here is what the speaker knows or does not know and not what the other person knows or not. Answer (D) is wrong because antecedents to words always appear before the word, not after it. Answer (E) is incorrect because the speaker sets this situation up as a possible condition that masks his true situation, which is what "that" refers to in the sentence.

42. **(B)** Answers (A) and (C) are wrong because adverbs do not modify nouns. Answer (B) is correct because it conveys the idea that few individuals have enough affliction. Answer (E) is wrong because "little" would act as a noun that indicates how much man "hath" of affliction, when the intention of the lines is to convey how few "men" have enough affliction in their lives.

43. **(E)** Answers (A) and (C) are wrong because they misread the connotations of "treasure" and "current money" literally, when they are being used figuratively. Answer (B) is wrong because it implies that only suffering will open the gates of heaven, when the speaker means that suffering only when it is used properly will accomplish the task. Answer (D) is wrong because the passage does not make this assertion at all. Answer (E) is correct because most individuals believe "affliction" or suffering is worthless, but the speaker maintains that acceptance of affliction converts physically bad experience into a spiritually valuable one.

44. **(A)** Answer (A) is correct and is supported by the last lines of the passage. Answer (B) is wrong because it contradicts the speaker's insistence on the unity of humanity. Answer (C) is wrong because it is not supported by the text and because the speaker knows that his death will occur no matter how many others die. Answer (D) is wrong because it misreads the treasures as real when they are meant figuratively and spiritually. Answer (E) is wrong because hope and not dispair is the by-product of making one's peace with one's Maker.

45. **(B)** Answer (A) is wrong because it is referred to by the speaker in lines 6–8. Answer (B) is correct because the speaker maintains that we must make recourse with God. If we do we are saved; if we do not we do not enter heaven. There is nothing preordained about the process. Answer (C) is wrong because the speaker gives his support for the process. Answer (D) is wrong because the speaker states his belief in the afterlife in lines 10–11. Answer (E) is wrong because this idea serves as one of the central arguments of the passage as expressed in lines 36–37.

46. **(B)** The stanza describes a questionable human pursuit; however, it does not convey anything remotely ominous, so uneasiness (A) is wrong. Lightheartedness (B) is conveyed by the playful flow of the single sentence that makes up the stanza and by the exclamation point that punctuates the end of the sentence. If the speaker were passive (C) about the state of humanity, there would be no exclamation point at the end of the stanza. Contentedness is not supported by the connotations of words like "vainly" and "uncessant labors" which imply that the speaker views the actions he describes in the stanza as foolish. The stanza does not bitterly (E) attack humanity's weaknesses, but rather it is a plea for a slower, more contemplative life.

47. **(A)** In context, "rude" means that society rejects solitude in favor of companionship and activity (A). It does not mean that people behave unmannerly towards solitude, because this reading of "rude" misinterprets the word to mean that individuals are ill-treated, which is not supported by the context. (C) is a misreading of "rude" to mean ill-fashioned which is unsupported by context.

Answer (D) is wrong because the line conveys the idea of rejection and not that of victimization. Answer (E) completely contradicts the meaning of the line and thus is wrong.

48. **(C)** The "ocean" (I) stands for the victor's accomplishments, as does the "oak" (II) and the "laurel" (III). On the other hand, the "reed" (IV) has no metaphorical significance. In context, it is the thing from which Pan fashions his pipe. The correct answer is, therefore, (C) because it is the only answer that includes all the correct choices without including the incorrect one (IV).

49. **(D)** The word "Your" in line 13 does not refer to men (A), but to "Fair Quiet" and "Innocence." Answer (B) is wrong because horticulture is the deliberate cultivation of plants, which is contrary to the unplanned aspect of nature favored by the speaker. Answer (C) is wrong because it is based on a misreading of "plants" to mean soul. Answer (E) offers a too literal reading of the line and fails to recognize that the phrase "sacred plants" is a metaphor for the peaceful and innocent solitude found in nature. Answer (D) correctly paraphrases the meaning of the lines in question.

50. **(C)** Answer (A) is wrong because it arises from a misreading of "resemblance find" to in some way mean Mirror. Answers (B) and (D) are wrong because the speaker goes on to state that other worlds and seas are what the mind is capable of creating in solitude. Answer (C) is correct because the comparison is accomplished by a juxtapositioning of the words "mind" and "ocean". Answer (E) is wrong because the phrase describes nature and not the mind.

51. **(B)** The "other worlds" (A) and the "other seas" (C) are imaginary and not real like the world of insects and the seas of grass. Answer (B) is correct because the mind in solitude amidst nature produces new or "green" ideas. Answer (D) is wrong because the phrase "from pleasure less" means from pleasure of a lesser degree and not "without pleasure" as the phrase might mean if "pleasure" and "less" were joined in one word. Answer (E) is wrong because the mind does not find its resemblance but recognizes resemblances between thoughts and objects, etc.

52. **(E)** Answer (E) is correct because it is contradicted by stanzas 2 and 8. Taste (A) is found in stanza 5, delights of the spirit (B) in stanza 7, auditory delights (C) in stanza 2, and intellectual (D) in stanza six.

53. **(B)** Answer (A) is wrong because flowers and leaves weave a garland of "repose" or rest, not victory. Answer (B) is correct because the facetious sense of the first six lines of the stanza 1 is that men seek the "narrow verged shade" of the

victory garland worn about the head when they could have the restful shade of nature with no effort at all. Answer (C) is a misreading of the word "close" in line 7. Answer (D) is wrong because it incorrectly links lines 4 and 8. Answer (E) is wrong because it attributes to nature the weaving of victory garlands, when the poet is stating that nature weaves a pleasant shade for rest that is available to all.

54. **(A)**   Answer (A) is correct because in context "prudently" does modify the verb "upbraid." Answer (B) is wrong because "toils" is a noun and not a verb in this context. Answer (C) is wrong because although "close" is a verb in this context, it is not modified by "prudently." Neither is the infinitive "To weave" (D). Answer (E) is wrong because "shade" is a noun and not a verb in this context.

55. **(B)**   Answer (B) is correct because the vest is a metaphor for the body. Answer (A) is wrong because it is contrary to the meaning of the lines. The speaker would not cast his soul aside. The liberated soul alights on the boughs (C); it does not become them. Neither are the boughs a metaphor for his vest (D). Finally, the speaker does not draw an analogy between his body and that of a bird's body (E). His liberated soul behaves like a bird, but his body does not share in the experience.

56. **(C)**   Answer (C) is correct because the garden, as the speaker describes it, possesses no seemingly negative aspects. Censure is a reprimand for some mistake and is thus negative. The garden rejuvenates (A) in stanza 7, is a source of beauty (B) in lines 21–22, inspiring (D) in stanza 6, and provides pleasure in stanza 5.

57. **(D)**   Answer (D) is correct, because the lines in question set up a metaphor of the sun dial to mark time's passage in the garden. Answer (A) is wrong because the final stanza does not contradict the basic argument of the poem; rather it leaves us with a description that emphasizes that the garden is a place of solitude and rest. Answer (B) is not correct, because the garden and the bee are not being compared. The bee marks the passing of time just as the visitor to the garden can mark the passing of time by observing the shifting shadows in the garden. Answer (C) is not correct because the final stanza of a poem, and this poem in particular, is not a logical place to digress from the main argument of the poem. Answer (E) is incorrect because the previous stanza philosphizes, while this stanza gives the reader a concluding image.

58. **(E)**   Answer (A) is not correct because the phrase "happy garden-state" does not mean our earthly heritage but refers to the biblical garden-state of Eden. Answer (B) is contradicted by line 60 which states that a mate was unnecessary. Answer (C) is incorrect because the poem explicitly states that the garden was "pure and sweet". The question asks what the speaker implies. Answer (D) is

incorrect because the speaker makes no judgment on humanity's moral worthiness of the Garden of Eden. Answer (E) is correct because lines 61–64 imply that solitude was one paradise too many for humanity to enjoy.

59. **(B)** If a mate was unnecessary in the Garden of Eden, then the reader can infer that the speaker disapproved (B) of women. Answer (A) is not correct because he finds women unnecessary and the inspirers of lovers to carve their ladies' initials into the bark of trees in stanza 3. Answer (C) is not correct because the speaker does not express amusement toward women anywhere in the poem. Answer (D) is incorrect because lines 21–22 proclaim nature to be more beautiful than women, and stanza 8 argues that they were unnecessary to Eden. Answer (E) is not correct because it is an extreme emotion not supported by the poem.

60. **(B)** In free verse (A) the lines are of uneven length whereas the lines of this poem are of equal length and rhyme. The lines of this poem are composed of four iambic feet, thus answer (B} is correct. The poem is not written in ballad meter (C) because all the lines have four accented syllables and ballad meter alternates lines with four accents with lines with three. Answer (D) is incorrect because the basic foot of the poem is iambic not dactylic and the lines have four accents instead of six. Terza rima (E) consists of three-line stanzas; this poem has eight-line stanzas.

Section 2

Essay 1

Joseph Conrad's description of the trip up the Congo River is a description of a journey into a world overwhelmingly foreign and all-consuming.

The change in setting, "like travelling back to the earliest beginning of the world," placed the narrator in a setting unlike anything he had ever seen before. According to the narrator, "vegetation rioted" and large trees were "kings," as they were long ago. Even the bright sunlight conveyed "no joy," as the lonely waterway "ran on, deserted, into the gloom of overshadowed distances."

The problem of determining the correct river course was unnerving. The narrator said of this journey that, "you lost your way on that river as you would in a desert." The task was so confusing and demanding that it was like finding "yourself bewitched and cut off forever from everything you had known once — somewhere — far away — in another existence perhaps." This shows how psychologically isolated he had become from his past. He explained that when he did remember his past, it came to him in "the shape of an unrestful and noisy dream" because the past had been overwhelmed by the realities of his "strange world of plants, and water, and silence." This silence did not represent "peace" to the narrator; rather it was like "an implacable force brooding over an inscrutable intention." What it might do to him was unstoppable and beyond comprehension.

The narrator becomes totally absorbed in he task of navigating the river. Conrad uses a series of short sentences beginning with the word "I" to emphasize the narrator's total preoccupation with the job. "I" looked for channels, watched for sunken rocks, driftwood, and other such hazards. "When you have to attend to things of that sort, to the mere incidents of the surface," the narrator explained, "the reality — the reality, I tell you — fades. The inner truth is hidden — luckily, luckily." In spite of this, the narrator still felt the "mysterious stillness watching (him) at (his) monkey tricks."

The psychological stresses on the narrator grow in the early stages of the trip, but later on they are nullified by the physical stresses that he experiences.

Essay 1 — Comments

This essay accurately identifies the various elements of the river journey that exert psychological and physical demands on the narrator. It begins with a discussion of the overwhelming sense of dislocation he experienced, and supports this observation with appropriate evidence from the text. Next, it links his mental state with the impossible task of finding his way up stream. The aimless nature of the journey, the growing sense of isolation from his past, and the alien environment of the jungle merge into the narrator's growing sense of paranoia. The essay concludes with the insight that it was the narrator's devotion to task which saved his sanity.

The essay gives clear evidence that the writer understood Conrad's passage and addressed the two aspects of the question. In addition to an accurate content, it cites appropriate examples of Conrad's use of diction, syntax and detail to achieve his effect. The essay is well organized; its paragraphs develop logically. While it is not without flaws, it demonstrates that the writer is in clear command of a wide range of writing skills. The writer is able to express ideas accurately, clearly and effectively.

Essay 2

Edmund Spenser and William Shakespeare express contrasting views of their lovers. They do, however, use similar styles to describe their women. Both compare their woman to objects which are usually symbolic of an aspect of a woman's beauty. Spenser does this in a positive way; Shakespeare does it in a negative way.

In "Ye Tradefull Merchants" Spenser gives his lover's beauty the highest praises when he compares her to the riches which merchants travel so far to "make their gain." He asks these merchants, "What needeth you to seek so farre in vaine?" and then advises them that "For loe, my love doth in herselfe contain all this worlds riches that may farre be found." Spenser then goes on to compare his lover to gems and precious articles: her eyes to sapphires, her lips to rubies, her teeth to pearls, and so on. Finally, he caps his flattery of her beauty by paying tribute to her mind. "But that which fairest is but few behold/ Her mind, adorned with vertues manifold." Spenser says that not only is his woman physically attractive, but she is mentally attractive, too.

The second sonnet, by William Shakespeare, is much different. Like Spenser, Shakespeare uses comparisons to describe his lover, but his description does not flatter her beauty as Spenser's does. Rather, his comparisons tell the reader exactly what her beauty is not like. The result is not a description of a physically attractive person whatsoever. Her eyes are not like the sun; coral is redder than her lips. "I have seen roses… but no such roses see I in her cheeks." The most damaging line to his mistress's beauty is his observation about "the breath that from my mistress reeks." This is not exactly a description fit for a valentine, but by combining honesty with love Shakespeare does say that he loves her.

His intent becomes evident in the final two lines of the sonnet. "And yet, by heaven, I think my love as rare,/ As any she belied with false compare." He loves her, but he refuses to describe her with artificial comparisons that cannot possibly be true.

Both poets use comparisons to describe their lovers. Spenser strings together a list of impossible ones. Shakespeare, perhaps out of disgust for such dishonesty, elects to describe his love with less flattering ones. One thing that is sure, both men love their lovers for their minds as well as their bodies.

Essay 2 — Comments

This well-written essay exhibits an accurate and perceptive analysis of the two sonnets by Spenser and Shakespeare. It reveals a clear understanding of the two poems and accurately identifies them as sonnets. The writer deals effectively with the attitudes of the poets and the markedly different portraits they produce. The flattering tone of Spenser's poem is nicely contrasted to the unflattering realism of Shakespeare's sonnet. It avoids the mistake of asserting that Shakespeare's lover was unattractive, and correctly interprets his realism as a reaction to the artificial comparisons used by poets like Spenser. The essay contains appropriate examples of the main elements of each portrait such as diction and choice of detail. It does this while demonstrating an effective command of sentence structure, diction and logical organization. In short, the writer displays the ability to use a wide range of elements found in effective writing.

Essay 3

Charles Dickens in *Hard Times* tells the story of the Gradgrind family and their life in the city of Coketown. One of the main characters of the novel, young Tom Gradgrind, pursues his own personal good at the expense of the common good of his family and a man named Stephen Blackpool.

Tom Gradgrind is a very selfish and unhappy man. In order to get a job at Bounderby's bank, Tom asks his sister Louisa to marry Bounderby. He is an older man whom she does not love. Later, she comes to despise him. Once in the bank, Tom lies, cheats and swindles. He uses and manipulates his sister's feelings for his own benefit, because he is, unfortunately, the only person she loves. She gives him money to pay off his gambling debts, and she even lies to her father for him.

Tom's selfish need for more and more money leads him to frame a kind and honest worker, named Stephen Blackpool, for a robbery which Tom committed himself. Much later, when the truth about Tom's action become known, Tom has the nerve to expect his father to help him escape capture by the authorities.

Tom Gradgrind's pursuit of money produces many dire consequences for those he uses to satisfy his selfish wants. When Louisa ends her loveless marraige to Bounderby, the rest of her days unhappily pass without love of husband or child. Tom's father violates his own conscience and beliefs in order to help his son escape prosecution for his crime. Tom's selfishness injures Stephen Blackpool worst of all. The man loses his good name and the respect of his fellow workers. When Stephen makes an effort to clear his name, he suffers a fatal fall into an abandoned mine shaft.

Tom Gradgrind, through the efforts of his father and sister, is able to escape the country. Gradually, he learns to hate his estrangement from his sister and father. Louisa, he admits, is the person he loves most on this earth. Finally, he dies of a fever contracted on his journey home to them. He pursued his own personal good at the expense of his family and Stephen. His actions produced dire consequences for these people. His own selfishness even cost him his life.

Essay 3 — Comments

This essay accurately explains how Tom Gradgrind selfishly pursued his own personal good at the expense of others. It sketches the nature of Tom's selfish acts without resorting to lengthy plot summary. The corrupt nature of his selfishness is accurately portrayed: gambling, robbery, malicious duplicity, and fugitive flight from prosecution. In addition it describes his sister's misdirected devotion, his father's humiliation, and Blackpool's unlucky fate. The overall discussion reveals a thorough acquaintance with the characters and details of the story, and utilizes only those aspects of the story that apply to the question. The essay displays a general fluency and an ability to focus on the question and to convey in an organized way a number of accurate observations about the novel.

THE ADVANCED PLACEMENT EXAMINATION IN

English Literature & Composition

TEST 2

1. Ⓐ Ⓑ Ⓒ Ⓓ Ⓔ
2. Ⓐ Ⓑ Ⓒ Ⓓ Ⓔ
3. Ⓐ Ⓑ Ⓒ Ⓓ Ⓔ
4. Ⓐ Ⓑ Ⓒ Ⓓ Ⓔ
5. Ⓐ Ⓑ Ⓒ Ⓓ Ⓔ
6. Ⓐ Ⓑ Ⓒ Ⓓ Ⓔ
7. Ⓐ Ⓑ Ⓒ Ⓓ Ⓔ
8. Ⓐ Ⓑ Ⓒ Ⓓ Ⓔ
9. Ⓐ Ⓑ Ⓒ Ⓓ Ⓔ
10. Ⓐ Ⓑ Ⓒ Ⓓ Ⓔ
11. Ⓐ Ⓑ Ⓒ Ⓓ Ⓔ
12. Ⓐ Ⓑ Ⓒ Ⓓ Ⓔ
13. Ⓐ Ⓑ Ⓒ Ⓓ Ⓔ
14. Ⓐ Ⓑ Ⓒ Ⓓ Ⓔ
15. Ⓐ Ⓑ Ⓒ Ⓓ Ⓔ
16. Ⓐ Ⓑ Ⓒ Ⓓ Ⓔ
17. Ⓐ Ⓑ Ⓒ Ⓓ Ⓔ
18. Ⓐ Ⓑ Ⓒ Ⓓ Ⓔ
19. Ⓐ Ⓑ Ⓒ Ⓓ Ⓔ
20. Ⓐ Ⓑ Ⓒ Ⓓ Ⓔ

21. Ⓐ Ⓑ Ⓒ Ⓓ Ⓔ
22. Ⓐ Ⓑ Ⓒ Ⓓ Ⓔ
23. Ⓐ Ⓑ Ⓒ Ⓓ Ⓔ
24. Ⓐ Ⓑ Ⓒ Ⓓ Ⓔ
25. Ⓐ Ⓑ Ⓒ Ⓓ Ⓔ
26. Ⓐ Ⓑ Ⓒ Ⓓ Ⓔ
27. Ⓐ Ⓑ Ⓒ Ⓓ Ⓔ
28. Ⓐ Ⓑ Ⓒ Ⓓ Ⓔ
29. Ⓐ Ⓑ Ⓒ Ⓓ Ⓔ
30. Ⓐ Ⓑ Ⓒ Ⓓ Ⓔ
31. Ⓐ Ⓑ Ⓒ Ⓓ Ⓔ
32. Ⓐ Ⓑ Ⓒ Ⓓ Ⓔ
33. Ⓐ Ⓑ Ⓒ Ⓓ Ⓔ
34. Ⓐ Ⓑ Ⓒ Ⓓ Ⓔ
35. Ⓐ Ⓑ Ⓒ Ⓓ Ⓔ
36. Ⓐ Ⓑ Ⓒ Ⓓ Ⓔ
37. Ⓐ Ⓑ Ⓒ Ⓓ Ⓔ
38. Ⓐ Ⓑ Ⓒ Ⓓ Ⓔ
39. Ⓐ Ⓑ Ⓒ Ⓓ Ⓔ
40. Ⓐ Ⓑ Ⓒ Ⓓ Ⓔ

41. Ⓐ Ⓑ Ⓒ Ⓓ Ⓔ
42. Ⓐ Ⓑ Ⓒ Ⓓ Ⓔ
43. Ⓐ Ⓑ Ⓒ Ⓓ Ⓔ
44. Ⓐ Ⓑ Ⓒ Ⓓ Ⓔ
45. Ⓐ Ⓑ Ⓒ Ⓓ Ⓔ
46. Ⓐ Ⓑ Ⓒ Ⓓ Ⓔ
47. Ⓐ Ⓑ Ⓒ Ⓓ Ⓔ
48. Ⓐ Ⓑ Ⓒ Ⓓ Ⓔ
49. Ⓐ Ⓑ Ⓒ Ⓓ Ⓔ
50. Ⓐ Ⓑ Ⓒ Ⓓ Ⓔ
51. Ⓐ Ⓑ Ⓒ Ⓓ Ⓔ
52. Ⓐ Ⓑ Ⓒ Ⓓ Ⓔ
53. Ⓐ Ⓑ Ⓒ Ⓓ Ⓔ
54. Ⓐ Ⓑ Ⓒ Ⓓ Ⓔ
55. Ⓐ Ⓑ Ⓒ Ⓓ Ⓔ
56. Ⓐ Ⓑ Ⓒ Ⓓ Ⓔ
57. Ⓐ Ⓑ Ⓒ Ⓓ Ⓔ
58. Ⓐ Ⓑ Ⓒ Ⓓ Ⓔ
59. Ⓐ Ⓑ Ⓒ Ⓓ Ⓔ
60. Ⓐ Ⓑ Ⓒ Ⓓ Ⓔ

AP EXAMINATION IN ENGLISH LITERATURE AND COMPOSITION

TEST 2
Section 1

TIME: 60 Minutes
        60 Questions

DIRECTIONS: *This test consists of selections from literary works and questions on their content, form, and style. After reading each passage or poem, choose the best answer to each question and blacken the corresponding space on the answer sheet.*

NOTE: Pay particular attention to the requirement of questions that contain the words NOT, LEAST, or EXCEPT.

<u>QUESTIONS 1–15</u> are based on the following poem. Read the poem carefully before choosing your answers.

> As virtuous men pass mildly away,
>> And whisper to their souls to go,
> Whilst some of their sad friends do say
>> The breath goes now, and some say, No;
>
> 5   So let us melt, and make no noise,
>> No tear-floods, nor sigh-tempests move,
> 'Twere profanation of our joys
>> To tell the laity our love.
>
> Moving of th' earth brings harms and fears,
> 10   Men reckon what it did and meant;

But trepidation of the spheres,
　　Though greater far, is innocent.[1]

Dull sublunary lovers' love
　　(Whose soul is sense) cannot admit
15　Absence, because it doth remove
　　Those things which elemented it.

But we by a love so much refined
　　That our selves know not what it is,
Inter-assuréd of the mind,
20　　Care less, eyes, lips, and hands to miss.

Our two souls therefore, which are one,
　　Though I must go, endure not yet
A breach, but an expansion,
　　Like gold to airy thinness beat.

25　If they be two, they are two so
　　As stiff twin compasses are two;
Thy soul, the fixed foot, makes no show
　　To move, but doth, if th' other do.

And though it in the center sit,
30　　Yet when the other far doth roam,
It leans and hearkens after it,
　　And grows erect, as that comes home.

Such wilt thou be to me, who must
　　Like th' other foot, obliquely run;
35　Thy firmness makes my circle just,
　　And makes me end where I begun.

1.　I.e., earthquakes are thought to threaten evil consequences, but the variations of the spheres from true circularity, though they involve greater motions, are not considered sinister. "Trepidation of the spheres" (literally, "shuddering") was an additional arbitrary motion of the eighth sphere, introduced into the Ptolemaic system about the year 950 to account for certain celestial phenomena which were really due to the wobbling of the earth on its axis.

"A Valediction: Forbidding Mourning," by John Donne.

1. In line 16, "it" refers to

   (A) absence

   (B) soul

   (C) love

   (D) sublunary lovers

   (E) sense

2. The speaker is addressing

   (A) a loved one from whom he is going to be temporarily parted

   (B) a parent from whom he seeks advice

   (C) a loved one who is seriously ill

   (D) his mistress, who does not sufficiently appreciate him

   (E) a virtuous friend who is on his deathbed

3. The speaker says he wants their behavior at parting to resemble

   (A) that of sad friends who watch a loved one die

   (B) an earthquake

   (C) a band of gold that breaks

   (D) the deaths of virtuous men

   (E) that of sublunary lovers

4. The speaker says that the deaths of virtuous men

   (A) cause great weeping and sighing among their friends

   (B) should not be a cause of sorrow because their virtue assures them of heavenly rewards

   (C) can never be explained in rational terms, but must be accepted on the basis of religious faith

   (D) cannot be understood by the profane masses who only value pleasure

   (E) are so quiet that their friends cannot determine the exact moment of death

5. Which of the following best expresses the idea in lines 7 and 8?

   (A) It would cheapen our love to make a public display of it.

   (B) Our love is sacred, not profane.

(C) We should not keep our love a secret because we need not be ashamed of it.

(D) Our love should set an example for the less fortunate.

(E) If others knew of our love, they would be jealous.

6. In the third stanza, the speaker indirectly suggests that their behavior at parting can most appropriately be compared to

(A) moving of the earth

(B) men who analyze movements of the earth

(C) men who are harmed by movements of the earth

(D) trepidation of the spheres

(E) innocent men

7. Sublunary lovers cannot bear to be parted because

(A) they cannot sustain their love if they cannot communicate by talking

(B) uncertainty about being reunited undermines their love

(C) absence removes the physical attributes that constitute their love

(D) behavioral patterns are interrupted and are difficult to reestablish

(E) their souls are separated

8. "Eyes, lips, and hands" (line 20)

(A) are part of the refined love referred to in line 17

(B) are examples of the "things" mentioned in line 16

(C) are attributes that the speaker values more than gold

(D) are examples of things the speaker will miss

(E) constitute the "soul" of the speaker's love

9. The two lovers' souls are like "gold to airy thinness beat" (line 24) in that they

(A) are made up of both gold and air

(B) can last as long as gold lasts

(C) are both beautiful and brittle

(D)   can endure as much abuse as gold can endure

(E)   stretch to cover distance but do not break or separate

10.   In the last three stanzas the comparison of the lovers' two souls to compasses is an example of

(A)   a conceit   (D)   pathetic fallacy

(B)   a paradox   (E)   hyperbole

(C)   personification

11.   In the last three stanzas the soul of the speaker's beloved is compared to

(A)   stiff twin compasses

(B)   the fixed foot of a compass

(C)   the traveling foot of a compass

(D)   a firm circle

(E)   a moving circle

12.   In line 31, the first "it" refers to the

(A)   speaker's soul   (D)   beloved's love

(B)   beloved's soul   (E)   twin compass feet

(C)   speaker's love

13.   In line 32, "that" refers to

(A)   "they" (line 25)   (D)   "it" (line 29)

(B)   "the fixed foot" (line 27)   (E)   "thou" (line 33)

(C)   "the other" (line 28)

14.   The last two lines of the poem literally refer to drawing a perfect circle; metaphorically, they refer to the

(A)   speaker's need to see other women

(B)   speaker's unfaithfulness being caused by his beloved's domineering tendencies

(C)   speaker's guilt in having left his beloved

(D)   speaker's desire for a clean break

(E)   beloved's faithfulness causing the speaker to come home

15. The speaker's tone or state of mind can best be described as

    (A) sarcastic   (D) serious

    (B) comic   (E) near desperation

    (C) gently ironic

QUESTIONS 16–30 are based on the following poem. Read the poem carefully before choosing your answers.

> It little profits that an idle king,
> By this still hearth, among these barren crags,
> Matched with an aged wife, I mete and dole
> Unequal laws unto a savage race,
> 5   That hoard, and sleep, and feed, and know not me.
> I cannot rest from travel: I will drink
> Life to the lees: all times I have enjoyed
> Greatly, have suffered greatly, both with those
> That loved me, and alone; on shore, and when
> 10   Through scudding drifts the rainy Hyades[1]
> Vexed the dim sea: I am become a name;
> For always roaming with a hungry heart
> Much have I seen and known; cities of men
> And manners, climates, councils. governments,
> 15   Myself not least. but honored of them all;
> And drunk delight of battle with my peers,
> Far on the ringing plains of windy Troy.
> I am part of all that I have met;
> Yet all experience is an arch wherethrough
> 20   Gleams that untraveled world whose margin fades
> Forever and forever when I move.
> How dull it is to pause, to make an end,
> To rust unburnished, not to shine in use!
> As though to breathe were life! Life piled on life
> 25   Were all too little, and of one to me
> Little remains: but every hour is saved
> From that eternal silence, something more,
> A bringer of new things; and vile it were
> For some three suns to store and hoard myself,
> 30   And this gray spirit yearning in desire
> To follow knowledge like a sinking star,
> Beyond the utmost bound of human thought.

This is my son, mine own Telemachus,
To whom I leave the scepter and the isle—
35 Well-loved of me, discerning to fulfill
This labor, by slow prudence to make mild
A rugged people, and through soft degrees
Subdue them to the useful and the good.
Most blameless is he, centered in the sphere
40 Of common duties, decent not to fail
In offices of tenderness, and pay
Meet adoration to my household gods,
When I am gone. He works his work. I mine.
There lies the port; the vessel puffs her sail:
45 There gloom the dark, broad seas, My mariners,
Souls that have toiled, and wrought, and thought with me—
That ever with a frolic welcome took
The thunder and the sunshine, and opposed
Free hearts, free foreheads—you and I are old;
50 Old age hath yet his honor and his toil;
Death closes all: but something ere the end,
Some work of noble note, may yet be done,
Not unbecoming men that strove with gods.
The lights begin to twinkle from the rocks:
55 The long day wanes: the slow moon climbs: the deep
Moans round with many voices. Come, my friends,
'Tis not too late to seek a newer world.
Push off, and sitting well in order smite
The sounding furrows; for my purpose holds
60 To sail beyond the sunset, and the baths
Of all the western stars, until I die.
It may be that the gulfs will wash us down:
It may be we shall touch the Happy Isles,
And see the great Achilles, whom we knew.
65 Though much is taken, much abides; and though
We are not now that strength which in old days
Moved earth and heaven; that which we are, we are;
One equal temper of heroic hearts,
Made weak by time and fate, but strong in will
70 To strive, to seek, to find, and not to yield.

1. *rainy Hyades* (hī´ e dēz´), constellation of stars whose appearance brought rainy weather.

From "Ulysses," by Alfred Lord Tennyson

16. This poem is an example of a(n)

    (A) ode

    (B) elegy

    (C) sonnet

    (D) dramatic monologue

    (E) ballad

17. The speaker is

    (A) a boy

    (B) a young man

    (C) middle-aged

    (D) elderly

    (E) speaking from the grave

18. The poem is addressed primarily to

    (A) Ulysses' mariners

    (B) Telemachus

    (C) Ulysses' wife

    (D) Ithaca's "savage race"

    (E) the gods

19. The "idle king" in line 1 refers to

    (A) Ulysses' father

    (B) the speaker

    (C) Telemachus

    (D) the man who ruled Ithaca in Ulysses' absence

    (E) King Priam of Troy

20. The speaker's past experiences have

    (A) led to spiritual disillusionment

    (B) taught him to value safety more than family

    (C) increased his love of home and family

    (D) made him feel isolated from other men

    (E) fed his desire for additional adventure

21. Ulysses regards the majority of his subjects as

    (A) friends

    (B) timid

    (C) uncivilized

    (D) morally good

    (E) effete

22. The poem depicts Telemachus as

    (A)   a loving and dutiful son, but tainted by ambition

    (B)   a hypocrite who pretends to be loyal while secretly desiring Ulysses' throne

    (C)   a hard worker who sometimes lacks prudence

    (D)   virtuous and well-meaning, but somewhat hot-tempered

    (E)   a competent administrator, but an unexciting man

23. The speaker's greatest "flaw" is probably his

    (A)   complacency   (D)   anti-intellectualism

    (B)   indecisiveness   (E)   avarice

    (C)   pride

24. Ulysses implicitly suggests that Telemachus is better suited to rule Ithaca than he because Telemachus possesses to a greater degree all of the following qualities EXCEPT

    (A)   patience   (D)   imagination

    (B)   piety   (E)   prudence

    (C)   gentleness

25. The image of experience as an arch (line 19) suggests that

    (A)   Ulysses has not profited from experience

    (B)   wisdom is unattainable

    (C)   restlessness undermines man's happiness

    (D)   man quickly forgets the past

    (E)   Ulysses' quest is never-ending

26. Ulysses seeks further adventures for all of the following reasons EXCEPT to

    (A)   gain additional knowledge

    (B)   conquer additional lands for his kingdom

    (C)   test further his will

    (D)   discover new worlds

    (E)   have additional experience for its own sake

27. By "I am become a name" (line 11), the speaker means that he

    (A) is aware that death is near

    (B) is greatly admired in Ithaca

    (C) cannot be happy unless he becomes famous

    (D) is known and respected in many lands

    (E) is afraid that people know his reputation, but not him

28. In line 25, "one" refers to

    (A) ambition   (D) experience

    (B) time   (E) friendship

    (C) strength

29. "That" in "that which we are, we are" (line 67) might best be described as

    (A) arrogant   (D) hot-tempered

    (B) physically strong (E) intimidated

    (C) determined

30. The speaker regards time chiefly as

    (A) threatening and destructive

    (B) something that all men can control

    (C) friendly, because it ends man's suffering

    (D) irrelevant to his personal desires and circumstances

    (E) a neutral force in man's life

QUESTIONS 31–45 are based on the following passage. Read the passage carefully before choosing your answers.

And the agreement of the law of nature in this our ground with the laws and constitutions of God and man already alleged will by two similitudes easily appear. The king towards his people is rightly compared to a father of children, and to a head of a body composed of divers
5 members. For as fathers the good princes and magistrates of the people of God acknowledged themselves to their subjects. And for all other well-ruled commonwealths, the style of *Pater patriae* (father of his country) was ever and is commonly used to kings. And the proper office of a king

towards his subjects agrees very well with the office of the head towards
10 the body and all members thereof. For from the head, being the seat of
judgment, proceedeth the care and foresight of guiding and preventing all
evil that may come to the body or any part thereof. The head cares for the
body, so doth the king for his people. As the discourse and direction flows
from the head, and the execution according thereunto belongs to the rest of
15 the members, every one according to their office: so is it betwixt a wise
prince and his people. As the judgment coming from the head may not
only employ the members, every one in their own office, as long as they
are able for it; but likewise in case any of them affected with any infirmity
must care and provide for their remedy, in case it be curable, and if
20 otherwise gar[1] cut them off for fear of infecting the rest: even so is it
betwixt the prince and his people. And as there is ever hope of curing any
diseased member by the direction of the head, as long as it is whole; but by
the contrary, if it be troubled, all the members are partakers of that pain, so
is it betwixt the prince and his people.
25   And now first of the father's part (whose natural love to his children I
described in the first part of this my discourse, speaking of the duty that
kings owe to their subjects), consider, I pray you, what duty his children
owe to him, and whether upon any pretext whatever it will not be thought
monstrous and unnatural for his sons to rise up against him, to control him
30 at their appetite, and when they think good to slay him, or to cut him off,
and adopt to themselves any other they please in his room. Or can any
pretense of wickedness or rigor on his part be a just excuse for his children
to put hand into him? And although we see by the course of nature
that love useth to descend more than to ascend, in case it were true that the
35 father hated and wronged the children never so much, will any man
endued with the least sponk[2] of reason think it lawful for them to meet him
with the line? Yea, suppose the father were furiously following his sons
with a drawn sword, is it lawful for them to turn and strike again, or make
any resistance but by flight? I think surely if there were no more but the
40 example of brute beasts and unreasonable creatures, it may serve well
enough to qualify and prove this my argument. We read often the piety
that the storks have to their old and decayed parents: and generally we
know that there are many sorts of beasts and fowls that with violence and
many bloody strokes will beat and banish their young ones from them,
45 how soon they perceive them to be able to fend themselves; but we never
read nor heard of any resistance on their part, except among the vipers;
which proves such persons as ought to be reasonable creatures, and yet
unnaturally follow this example, to be endued with their viperous nature.
      And for the similitude of the head and the body, it may very well fall
50 out that the head will be forced to gar cut off some rotten member (as I

have already said) to keep the rest of the body in integrity: but what state the body can be in, if the head for any infirmity that can fall to it be cut off, I leave it to the reader's judgment.

So as (to conclude this part) if the children may upon any pretext that
55 can be imagined lawfully rise up against their father, cut him off, and choose any other whom they please in his room; and if the body for the weal of it may for an infirmity that may be in the head strike it off, then I cannot deny that the people may rebel, control and displace, or cut off their king, at their own pleasure, and upon respects moving them. * * *

1. Have someone (a Scots locution).
2. Spunk, spark.

From The True Law of Modern Monarchies *by King James I*

31. In line 15, "members" can best be understood literally to mean

     (A) members of Parliament

     (B) landowners or nobles

     (C) sons

     (D) parts of the body

     (E) public servants

32. Which of the following can substitute for "otherwise" in line 20 without changing the meaning?

     (A) someone

     (B) these diseased members

     (C) incurable

     (D) not withstanding that

     (E) they refuse

33. In the second paragraph, the author uses vipers

     (A) as examples of creatures that are ruled by reason rather than loyalty

     (B) to reenforce his contention that nature supports his argument

     (C) as one in a series of examples proving man's superiority to nature

     (D) as exceptions to a general behavioral pattern in nature

     (E) to argue that man must defend his self-interest

34. The controlling metaphor in the second paragraph compares

    (A) the king to a father

    (B) princes to sons

    (C) government to nature

    (D) commoners to beasts

    (E) nature to reason

35. The controlling metaphor in the third paragraph compares

    (A) the head to the body

    (B) the king's subjects to a body

    (C) revolution to disease

    (D) the king to a body

    (E) treason to decay

36. In line 57, "weal" can best be understood to mean

    (A) pity   (D) political power

    (B) difficulty   (E) remainder

    (C) well-being

37. Which of the following statements best describes the relationships among the first three paragraphs?

    (A) Each is centered around separate but related metaphors.

    (B) The first introduces two analogies; the second elaborates on one of them, and the third elaborates on the other.

    (C) All three deal with a single analogy that is introduced in the first paragraph and developed further in the second and third paragraphs.

    (D) The first is based on an analogy; the second and third paragraphs introduce a second analogy that is separate from but related to the first.

    (E) The first paragraph argues from analogy; the second and third do not rely on metaphor or analogy.

38. Which of the following statements best describes the organization of the first three paragraphs?

    (A) The first presents a general argument and the next two provide historical examples.

    (B) The first presents the author's chief argument and the next two present alternative points of view.

    (C) Paragraphs one and three are parts of the same argument, while paragraph two is a digression.

    (D) All three are part of the same argument.

    (E) Paragraph one presents one of the author's two main arguments; paragraphs two and three present the other.

39. With which of the following statements would the author of the passage most likely agree?

    (A) Government depends on the consent of the governed.

    (B) Kings can be legally challenged only when they act irrationally.

    (C) The king can do whatever he pleases, and nobody can rebel against him.

    (D) Revolutions are justified when the majority of the ruler's subjects believe there is adequate reason to depose him.

    (E) The king must carefully balance concern for public good with self-interest.

40. The author uses the "law of nature" primarily to support his argument concerning

    (A) right of succession   (D) laws of inheritance

    (B) imprisonment   (E) obedience

    (C) religious faith

41. The reasoning process in the first three paragraphs can best be classified as

    (A) argument by analogy

    (B) inductive logic

    (C) thesis-antithesis-synthesis

    (D) deductive logic

    (E) a series of "If x, then y" propositions

42. This essay can best be classified as which of the following types?

    (A) Celebratory   (D) Personal

    (B) Persuasive   (E) Informal

    (C) Descriptive

43. The reasoning process in the last paragraph can best be classified as

    (A) argument by analogy

    (B) inductive logic

    (C) thesis-antithesis-synthesis

    (D) deductive logic

    (E) an "If x, then y" proposition

44. The excerpt most likely expresses the point of view of

    (A) a monarch who believes in the divine right of kings

    (B) a prince who wishes to overthrow his father

    (C) members of a Senate or Parliament

    (D) an objective legal scholar

    (E) workers in a socialist state

45. In the last line of the excerpt, "respects" can best be understood to mean

    (A) esteem   (D) respectfulness

    (B) benefits   (E) considerations

    (C) pleasures

QUESTIONS 46–60 are based on the following passage. Read the passage carefully before choosing your answers.

Besides the neutral expression that she wore when she was alone, Mrs. Freeman had two others, forward and reverse, that she used for all her human dealings. Her forward expression was steady and driving like the advance of a heavy truck. Her eyes never swerved to left or right but
5 turned as the story turned as if they followed a yellow line down the center of it. She seldom used the other expression because it was not often necessary for her to retract a statement, but when she did, her face came to a complete stop, there was an almost imperceptible movement of her black

eyes, during which they seemed to be receding, and then the observer
10 would see that Mrs. Freeman, though she might stand there as real as
several grain sacks thrown on top of each other, was no longer there in
spirit. As for getting anything across to her when this was the case, Mrs.
Hopewell had given it up. She might talk her head off. Mrs. Freeman
could never be brought to admit herself wrong on any point. She would
15 stand there and if she could be brought to say anything, it was something
like, "Well, I wouldn't of said it was and I wouldn't of said it wasn't," or
letting her gaze range over the top kitchen shelf where there was an
assortment of dusty bottles, she might remark, "I see you ain't ate many of
them figs you put up last summer."
20   They carried on their most important business in the kitchen at breakfast. Every morning Mrs. Hopewell got up at seven o'clock and lit her gas
heater and Joy's. Joy was her daughter, a large blonde girl who had an
artificial leg....
      It was hard for Mrs. Hopewell to realize that her child was thirty-two
25 now and that for more than twenty years she had had only one leg. She
thought of her still as a child because it tore her heart to think instead of the
poor stout girl in her thirties who had never danced a step or had any
normal good times. Her name was really Joy but as soon as she was
twenty-one and away from home, she had had it legally changed. Mrs.
30 Hopewell was certain that she had thought and thought until she had hit
upon the ugliest name in any language. Then she had gone and had the
beautiful name, Joy, changed without telling her mother until after she had
done it. Her legal name was Hulga.... She considered the name her
personal affair. She had arrived at it first purely on the basis of its ugly
35 sound and then the full genius of its fitness had struck her. She had a vision
of the name working like the ugly sweating Vulcan[1] who stayed in the
furnace and to whom, presumably, the goddess had to come when called.
She saw it as the name of her highest creative act. One of her major
triumphs was that her mother had not been able to turn her dust into Joy,
40 but the greater one was that she had been able to turn it herself into
Hulga....
      When Hulga stumped into the kitchen in the morning (she could walk
without making the awful noise but she made it — Mrs. Hopewell was
certain because it was ugly-sounding), she glanced at them and did not
45 speak. Mrs. Hopewell would be in her red kimono with her hair tied
around her head in rags. She would be sitting at the table, finishing her
breakfast and Mrs. Freeman would be hanging by her elbow outward
from the refrigerator, looking down at the table. Hulga always put her eggs
on the stove to boil and then stood over them with her arms folded, and
50 Mrs. Hopewell would look at her — a kind of indirect gaze divided
between her and Mrs. Freeman — and would think that if she would only
keep herself up a little, she wouldn't be so bad looking. There was nothing

wrong with her face that a pleasant expression wouldn't help. Mrs. Hopewell
said that people who looked on the bright side of things would be beautiful
55   even if they were not.

Whenever she looked at Joy this way, she could not help but feel that
it would have been better if the child had not taken the Ph.D. It had
certainly not brought her out any and now that she had it, there was no
more excuse for her to go to school again. Mrs. Hopewell thought it was
60   nice for girls to go to school to have a good time but Joy had "gone
through." Anyhow, she would not have been strong enough to go again.
The doctors had told Mrs. Hopewell that with the best of care, she might
see forty-five. She had a weak heart. Joy had made it plain that if it had not
been for this condition, she would be far from these red hills and good
65   country people. She would be in a university lecturing to people who
knew what she was talking about. And Mrs. Hopewell could very well
picture her there, looking like a scarecrow and lecturing to more of the
same. Here she went about all day in a six-year-old skirt and a yellow
sweat shirt with a faded cowboy on a horse embossed on it. She thought
70   this was funny; Mrs. Hopewell thought it was idiotic and showed simply
that she was still a child. She was brilliant but she didn't have a grain of
sense. It seemed to Mrs. Hopewell that every year she grew less like other
people and more like herself—bloated, rude, and squint-eyed. And she
said such strange things! To her own mother she had said—without
75   warning, without excuse, standing up in the middle of a meal with her face
purple and her mouth half full — "Woman! do you ever look inside? Do
you ever look inside and see what you are not? God!" she had cried
sinking down again and staring at her plate, "Malebranche was right: we
are not our own light. We are not our own light!" Mrs. Hopewell had no
80   idea to this day what brought that on. She had only made the remark,
hoping Joy would take it in, that a smile never hurt anyone.

The girl had taken the Ph.D. in philosophy and this left Mrs. Hopewell
at a complete loss. You could say, "My daughter is a nurse," or "My
daughter is a school teacher," or even, "My daughter is a chemical
85   engineer." You could not say, "My daughter is a philosopher." That was
something that had ended with the Greeks and Romans. All day Joy sat on
her neck in a deep chair, reading. Sometimes she went for walks but she
didn't like dogs or cats or birds or flowers or nature or nice young men.
She looked at nice young men as if she could smell their stupidity.

1.   In Roman mythology, the lame blacksmith to the gods and husband of Venus, goddess
of love.

46. The basic metaphor used to describe Mrs. Freeman in the first paragraph involves

   (A) farming
   (B) operating a vehicle
   (C) cooking and other domestic chores
   (D) changes of season
   (E) hunting

47. The images used to describe Mrs. Freeman in the first paragraph chiefly suggest she is

   (A) refined
   (B) intellectual
   (C) reliable
   (D) earth-bound
   (E) religious

48. In lines 1–8, the narrator describes Mrs. Freeman's presence through the use of

   (A) simile
   (B) invective
   (C) paradox
   (D) hyperbole
   (E) symbolism

49. Judging from paragraph one, Mrs. Freeman might best be described as

   (A) polite
   (B) indecisive
   (C) lacking self-assurance
   (D) reticent
   (E) stubborn

50. The kind of narration used in this excerpt is

   (A) first-person
   (B) objective
   (C) unreliable third-person
   (D) stream of consciousness
   (E) omniscient

51. Joy's attitude toward Mrs. Hopewell and Mrs. Freeman can best be described as one of

   (A) pity
   (B) envy
   (C) contempt
   (D) curiosity
   (E) admiration

52. All of the following accurately describe Mrs. Hopewell EXCEPT

    (A) anti-intellectual   (D) naively optimistic

    (B) introspective   (E) self-assured

    (C) conventional

53. It can be inferred from the passage that Mrs. Hopewell is distressed chiefly by Hulga's

    (A) laziness   (D) lack of intellectual curiosity

    (B) rudeness   (E) conventionality

    (C) abnormality

54. Mrs. Hopewell's explanation of Joy's name change

    (A) is completely incorrect

    (B) is partially correct but does not fully account for the complexity of Joy's motives

    (C) reflects her tendency always to believe the best about others

    (D) fully and accurately explains the reasons for Joy's act

    (E) indicates her desire to manipulate or control her daughter

55. Which of the following statements about Joy's "highest creative act" (line 38) is most accurate?

    (A) Hulga reduces her mother to the status of Vulcan, the lame black-smith.

    (B) Hulga sees herself as a perverse goddess of love after changing her name.

    (C) Hulga had not fully considered the extent of the damage to others that would result from her name change.

    (D) It is an essentially spiteful act designed to turn her mother's dust to ugliness.

    (E) It is an act that frees her from the control of her mother and the other good country people she despises.

56. In context, "more like herself" (lines 72–73) can best be understood to mean more

(A) like Mrs. Hopewell

(D) like country people

(B) idiosyncratic

(E) like university people

(C) childish

57. Joy's outburst (lines 66–79) probably resulted from

(A) anger at Mrs. Freeman's interference in their lives

(B) pain from her artificial leg

(C) annoyance at Mrs. Hopewell's mindless platitudes

(D) stress from worrying about her heart condition

(E) resentment at not being a lecturer in a university

58. It can be inferred from the excerpt that Mrs. Hopewell regards a university education chiefly as

(A) an opportunity to socialize

(B) a waste of hard-earned money

(C) crucial to any liberated woman's development

(D) appropriate only to the upper classes

(E) something she resents not having received

59. To Mrs. Hopewell, Hulga's Ph.D. in philosophy is

(A) something that makes her superior to other people in the area

(B) more exalted than a Ph.D. in a more "useful" discipline

(C) the chief source of her admiration for Hulga

(D) something that she finds both appealing and intimidating

(E) a socially embarrassing anachronism

60. We learn from the excerpt that Joy is all of the following EXCEPT

(A) highly educated

(B) purposely rude

(C) an intellectual snob

(D) conventionally feminine in her tastes

(E) intolerant of people who do not engage in self-examination

Section 2

TIME: 2 Hours
3 Essay Questions

QUESTION 1. *(Suggested time — 40 minutes. This question counts one-third of the total essay-section score.)* Read carefully the following poem by Vita Sackville-West. Then write an essay in which you analyze the various stages in the development of the speaker's thought process, concentrating especially on (a) her attitudes toward "the greater cats" and (b) the speaker's perception of the similarities and differences between man and "the greater cats." Support your analysis with specific references to the poem.

THE GREATER CATS

The greater cats with golden eyes
Stare out between the bars.
Deserts are there, and different skies,
And night with different stars.
5   They prowl the aromatic hill,
And mate as fiercely as they kill
And hold the freedom of their will
To roam, to live, to drink their fill;
But this beyond their wit know I:
10   Man loves a little, and for long shall die.

Their kind across the desert range
Where tulips spring from stones,
Not knowing they will suffer change
Or vultures pick their bones.
15   Their strength's eternal in their sight,
They rule the terror of the night,
They overtake the deer in flight,
And in their arrogance they smite;
But I am sage, if they are strong:
20   Man's love is transient as his death so long.

Yet oh what powers to deceive!
My wit is turned to faith,
And at this moment I believe
In love, and scout[1] at death.

<pre>
25   I came from nowhere, and shall be
        Strong, steadfast, swift, eternally:
        I am a lion, a stone, a tree,
        And as the Polar star in me
        Is fixed my constant heart on thee.
30   Ah, may I stay for ever blind
      With lions, tigers, leopards, and their kind.
</pre>

1. scoff

"King's Daughter," by Vita Sackville-West, Section IX.

QUESTION 2. *(Suggested time — 40 minutes. This question counts one-third of the total essay-section score.)* "Setting" is a term that denotes the locale and historical time in which action occurs in a narrative work. Setting can be used for various purposes in novels and plays (to help establish "meaning," to establish atmosphere, to contribute to themes, and so forth), and is more important in some works than in others. Discuss the importance and uses of setting in one of the following works or another of comparable quality that is appropriate for the question. Do not write about a film or a television program.

The Scarlet Letter	*Catch-22*
Henderson the Rain King	*Portrait of the Artist as a Young Man*
The Jungle	*Intruder in the Dust*
Sister Carrie	*Moll Flanders*
David Copperfield	*The Return of the Native*
Invisible Man	*Moby Dick*
The Grapes of Wrath	*The Glass Menagerie*
My Antonia	*The Cherry Orchard*
Nineteen Eighty-Four	*Main Street*
A Midsummer Night's Dream	*The Tempest*
Candide	

QUESTION 3. *(Suggested time – 40 minutes. This question counts one-third of the total essay-section score.)* In the following selection, Oliver Goldsmith discusses "sentimental" comedy and "laughing" comedy. Write an essay in which you describe his views on the two and discuss the strategies and devices he uses to argue for the superiority of one over the other.

AN ESSAY ON THE THEATRE;
or,
A COMPARISON BETWEEN LAUGHING AND SENTIMENTAL COMEDY
By OLIVER GOLDSMITH
(Westminster Magazine, for December, 1772)

The theatre, like all other amusements, has its fashions and its prejudices: and when satiated with its excellence, mankind begin to mistake change for improvement. For some years tragedy was the reigning entertainment; but of late it has entirely given way to comedy, and our best efforts are now exerted in these lighter kinds of composition. The pompous train, the swelling phrase, and the unnatural rant, are displaced for that natural portrait of human folly and frailty, of which all are judges, because all have sat for the picture.

But as in describing nature it is presented with a double face, either of mirth or sadness, our modern writers find themselves at a loss which chiefly to copy from; and it is now debated, whether the exhibition of human distress is likely to afford the mind more entertainment than that of human absurdity?

Comedy is defined by Aristotle to be a picture of the frailities of the lower part of mankind, to distinguish it from tragedy, which is an exhibition of the misfortunes of the great. When comedy, therefore, ascends to produce the characters of princes or generals upon the stage, it is out of its walks, since low life and middle life are entirely its object. The principal question, therefore, is whether, in describing low or middle life, an exhibition of its follies be not preferable to a detail of its calamities? Or, in other words, which deserves the preference, — the weeping sentimental comedy so much in fashion at present, or the laughing, and even low comedy, which seems to have been last exhibited by Vanbrugh and Cibber?

If we apply to authorities, all the great masters in the dramatic art have but one opinion. Their rule is, that as tragedy displays the calamities of the great, so comedy should excite our laughter by ridiculously exhibiting the follies of the lower part of mankind. Boileau, one of the best modern critics, asserts, that comedy will not admit of tragic distress: —

'Le comique, ennemi des soupirs et des pleurs,
N'admet point dans ses vers de tragiques douleurs.'[1]

Nor is this rule without the strongest foundation in nature, as the distresses of the mean by no means affect us so strongly as the calamities of the great. When tragedy exhibits to us some great man fallen from his height, and struggling with want and adversity, we feel his situation in the same manner as we suppose he himself must feel, and our pity is increased in proportion to the height from which he fell. On the contrary, we do not so strongly sympathise with one born in humbler circumstances, and encountering accidental distress: so that while we melt for Belisarius,[2] we scarcely give halfpence to the beggar who accosts us in the street. The one has our pity; the other our contempt. Distress, therefore, is the proper object of tragedy, since the great excite our pity by their fall; but not equally so of comedy, since the actors employed in it are originally so mean, that they sink but little by their fall.

Since the first origin of the stage, tragedy and comedy have run in distinct channels, and never till of late encroached upon the provinces of each other. Terence, who seems to have made the nearest approaches, always judiciously stops short before he comes to the downright pathetic; and yet he is even reproached by Caesar for wanting the *vis comica*. All the other comic writers of antiquity aim only at rendering folly or vice ridiculous, but never exalt their characters into buskined pomp, or make what Voltaire humorously calls *a tradesman's tragedy*.

Yet notwithstanding this weight of authority, and the universal practice of former ages, a new species of dramatic composition has been introduced, under the name of *sentimental* comedy, in which the virtues of private life are exhibited, rather than the vices exposed; and the distresses rather than the faults of mankind make our interest in the piece. These comedies have had of late great success, perhaps from their novelty, and also from their flattering every man in his favorite foible. In these plays almost all the characters are good, and exceedingly generous; they are lavish enough of their *tin* money on the stage; and though they want humor, have abundance of sentiment and feeling. If they happen to have faults or foibles, the spectator is taught, not only to pardon, but to applaud them, in consideration of the goodness of their hearts; so that folly, instead of being ridiculed, is commended, and the comedy aims at touching our passions without the power of being truly pathetic. In this manner we are likely to lose one great source of entertainment on the stage; for while the comic poet is invading the province of the tragic muse, he leaves her lovely sister quite neglected. Of this, however, he is no way solicitous, as he measures his fame by his profits.

But it will be said, that the theatre is formed to amuse mankind, and that it matters little, if this end be answered, by what means it is obtained. If mankind find delight in weeping at comedy, it would be cruel to abridge them in that or any other innocent pleasure. If those pieces are denied the name of comedies, yet call them by any other name and, if they are delightful, they are good. Their success, it will be said, is a mark of their merit, and it is only abridging our happiness to deny us an inlet to amusement.

These objections, however, are rather specious than solid. It is true, that amusement is a great object of theatre, and it will be allowed that these sentimental pieces do often amuse us; but the question is, whether the true comedy would not amuse us more? The question is, whether a character supported throughout a piece, with its ridicule still attending, would not give us more delight than this species of bastard tragedy, which only is applauded because it is new?

A friend of mine, who was sitting unmoved at one of these sentimental pieces, was asked how he could be so indifferent? 'Why, truly,' says he, 'as the hero is but a tradesman, it is indifferent to me whether he be turned out of his counting-house on Fish Street Hill, since he will still have enough left to open shop in St. Giles's.'

The other objection is as ill-grounded; for though we should give these prices another name, it will not mend their efficacy. It will continue a kind of *mulish* production, with all the defects of its opposite parents, and marked with sterility. If we are permitted to make comedy weep, we have an equal right to make tragedy laugh, and to set down in blank verse the jests and repartees of all the attendants in a funeral procession.

But there is one argument in favor of sentimental comedy, which will keep it on the stage, in spite of all that can be said against it. It is, of all others, the most easily written. Those abilities that can hammer out a novel are fully sufficient for the production of a sentimental comedy. It is only sufficient to raise the characters a little; to deck out the hero with a riband, or give the heroine a title; then to put an insipid dialogue, without character or humor, into their mouths, give them mighty good hearts, very fine clothes, furnish a new set of scenes, make a pathetic scene or two with a sprinkling of tender melancholy conversation through the whole, and there is no doubt but all the ladies will cry, and all the gentlemen applaud.

Humor at present seems to be departing from the stage, and it will soon happen that our comic players will have nothing left for it but a fine coat and a song. It depends upon the audience whether they will actually drive those poor merry creatures from the stage, or sit at a play as gloomy as at the Tabernacle.[3] It is not easy to recover an art when once lost; and it will be but a just punishment, that when, by our being too fastidious, we have banished humor from the stage, we should ourselves be deprived of the art of laughing.

1. *L'Art Poétique.* chant III. 'Comedy, enemy of sighs and tears, by no means admits of tragic distress in its lines.'

2. The story ran that Belisarius, once the illustrious Byzantine general of the sixth century, became in old age a blind beggar, asking food from door to door.

3. Whitefield's Tabernacle in London, where George Whitefield (1714–1770), founder of the Calvinistic Methodists, had preached.

TEST 2

ANSWER KEY

1.	(C)	16.	(D)	31.	(D)	46.	(B)
2.	(A)	17.	(D)	32.	(C)	47.	(D)
3.	(D)	18.	(A)	33.	(D)	48.	(A)
4.	(E)	19.	(B)	34.	(A)	49.	(E)
5.	(A)	20.	(E)	35.	(B)	50.	(E)
6.	(D)	21.	(C)	36.	(C)	51.	(C)
7.	(C)	22.	(E)	37.	(B)	52.	(B)
8.	(B)	23.	(C)	38.	(D)	53.	(C)
9.	(E)	24.	(D)	39.	(C)	54.	(B)
10.	(A)	25.	(E)	40.	(E)	55.	(D)
11.	(B)	26.	(B)	41.	(A)	56.	(B)
12.	(B)	27.	(D)	42.	(B)	57.	(C)
13.	(C)	28.	(B)	43.	(E)	58.	(A)
14.	(E)	29.	(C)	44.	(A)	59.	(E)
15.	(D)	30.	(A)	45.	(E)	60.	(D)

DETAILED EXPLANATIONS OF ANSWERS

TEST 2

Section 1

1.   **(C)**   The sense of the sentence is that the love of sublunary lovers cannot endure absence because absence removes those things (physical attributes) which constitute their love ("it").

2.   **(A)**   The speaker is addressing the beloved, from whom he will be parted for a period of time. The end of the poem makes clear his intention to return. In fact, Donne addressed this poem to his wife on the occasion of his trip to the Continent in 1612.

3.   **(D)**   The speaker says he wants their parting to be silent, to cause no stir, much like the deaths of virtuous men who also make no noise.

4.   **(E)**   The deaths of virtuous men are so quiet that "their sad friends do say/ The breath goes now, and some say, No"; that is, their transition from life to death is so peaceful that friends who are attending them cannot determine the exact moment of death.

5.   **(A)**   The speaker says it would be a "profanation" of their "joys" to "tell the laity our love"; that is, it would cheapen their love by broadcasting it to the general public through loud displays of sorrow at parting.

6.   **(D)**   Again, he suggests that their parting should be unnoticed and silent, like the "trepidation of the spheres," which involves great motion but cannot be readily seen and is therefore regarded as harmless.

7.   **(C)**   Sublunary lovers cannot bear to be parted because absence removes "those things" (eyes, lips, hands) that constitute their love.

8.   **(B)**   In contrast to sublunary lovers, the speaker and his beloved can bear to be parted because their love is not made up only of "those things," such as eyes, lips, and hands, that constitute the love of sublunary lovers.

178

9.   **(E)**   The comparison in lines 21-24 is of the souls of the speaker and his beloved to gold that expands but does not break (i.e., to gold that can be stretched and beaten very thin without breaking).

10.   **(A)**   A conceit is an elaborate comparison between apparently unlike things — in this case, the souls of the two lovers to stiff twin compasses.

11.   **(B)**   In the comparison, the speaker's soul is compared to the "traveling foot" of a compass (the foot that actually draws the circle) and the beloved's soul is compared to the fixed foot of a compass (the one that remains stationary in the center of the circle).

12.   **(B)**   Like the fixed foot of a compass that leans toward the traveling foot when it moves, her soul leans toward his when it moves. The conceit compares their souls, not their love, to the feet of a compass.

13.   **(C)**   "That" in line 32 and "the other" in line 28 both refer to the traveling foot of a compass (the speaker's soul).

14.   **(E)**   Literally, the firmness of the stationary compass foot assures that the circle will be drawn perfectly; metaphorically, keeping in mind that the beloved's soul is the stationary compass foot, her "firmness" (faithfulness, resolve) makes him "end where I begun" (i.e., come home).

15.   **(D)**   The tone of the poem is one of seriousness despite its intellectually clever wit. Its wit does not make it comic since it does not seek to evoke laughter, nor is there anything to suggest that it is not to be read at face value (that is, it is not ironic or sarcastic). The tone, though serious, is controlled and assured; it is not desperate.

16.   **(D)**   A dramatic monologue is a poem in which a single speaker addresses one or more listeners at some significant moment in the speaker's life. In this case, Ulysses addresses his mariners, asking them to join him in further adventures before "death closes all."

17.   **(D)**   The speaker, Ulysses, is elderly, which we know from his comment (line 26) that "little remains" to him of life, and from the last section of the poem, in which he laments that "much" has been taken from him by time, as well as from his comment that "you and I are old" (line 49).

18.   **(A)**   Although Ulysses mentions Telemachus, his wife, the general population of Ithaca, and the gods, his words are directed chiefly to his mariners, as line 45 makes clear. They have shared past adventures with him, and he now asks them to join him again in additional heroic exploits.

19. **(B)** Ulysses is referring to himself, saying that it is of no good to him to stay home by the hearth with an aged wife and rule a barbaric people when he is used to adventure and still capable of additional exploits and personal growth.

20. **(E)** Ulysses is bored and restless in his role as king of Ithaca. His past life of worldwide heroic adventure has made him an energetic quester who "cannot rest from travel." His previous experience has expanded his horizons and enriched his life, but it has also made it impossible for him to "pause" or to "rust, unburnished"; hence he needs to continue "to strive, to seek, to find." He does not value safety, nor has his desire for spiritual growth diminished. Home and family are less important to him than the need to test further his will. His experience has made his subjects strangers, but he feels kinship with his mariners, who share his values and desires.

21. **(C)** Lines 4 and 5 make it clear that he regards the majority of his subjects as savages, an idea that is elaborated upon in lines 36–38, in which Ulysses describes the task of the King of Ithaca — making "mild a rugged people" who can slowly be subdued to usefulness and goodness.

22. **(E)** Telemachus is portrayed as loving, dutiful, patient, prudent — in short, an able administrator well-suited to civilize an uncivilized race, but also a man "of common duties," best fitted to household duties. He is not at all like Ulysses; Telemachus has virtues, certainly, but lacks Ulysses' restless, questing nature.

23. **(C)** Ulysses' pride surfaces several times in the poem. He says "I am become a name" (line 11), that he is honored by all he has met (line 15), that his men and he "strove with gods" (line 53); one can also argue that there is pride in his belief that it is a waste of his time to remain in Ithaca to rule because he sees himself suited to a greater calling.

24. **(D)** Either explicitly or implicitly, Ulysses suggests that Telemachus has the virtues of patience, prudence, and gentleness (lines 36–41) as well as piety (lines 41–42), but he does not suggest that Telemachus is imaginative. Imagination seems to be Ulysses' domain, not Telemachus'.

25. **(E)** The unexplored world recedes forever through the arch of experience, forever beckoning Ulysses to follow, exploring the margins yet undiscovered. Because all experience is such an arch to Ulysses, his quest can never end.

26. **(B)** Ulysses wants additional knowledge (line 31), additional experience (lines 19–23 and elsewhere), to test his will (lines 69–70), and to discover new worlds (line 57), but there is no mention of the desire to add to his kingdom by conquering new lands.

27. **(D)**   From context, it is clear that Ulysses means he is widely known as someone who is "always roaming with a hungry heart" (line 12) and that he is "honored" by men in much of the known world.

28. **(B)**   He says that life piled on life is insignificant and that little remains to him "of one" (i.e., of life).

29. **(C)**   Ulysses says that time has robbed his mariners and him of much, including some of their strength, but what remains is the "will" to "strive, to seek, to find, and not to yield" — in short, determination.

30. **(A)**   Time has robbed him of much (lines 65–66) and is something that brings "eternal silence" (line 27); hence it is both destructive and threatening, something that makes the need for further adventure all the more pressing.

31. **(D)**   In this analogy, James compares the king to the body's head and his subjects to the other parts of the body. The head provides directions and the rest of the body (the "members") carries out those directions.

32. **(C)**   The sense of the sentence is that if one body part is diseased, the other parts must care for and cure it; "if otherwise" (if it cannot be cured), it must be cut off so that it does not infect others.

33. **(D)**   James argues that nature supports his contention that subjects must not resist their king no matter how irrational his behavior may seem. As evidence, he mentions storks and "many sorts of beasts and fowls" whose offspring never resist their parents. The one exception is that of vipers, who do resist their parents, leading James to conclude that any person who behaves similarly by resisting his king has a "viperous nature" (line 48).

34. **(A)**   In the second paragraph, James compares the king to a father (and his subjects to his children). All of the details in this paragraph relate to this central metaphor.

35. **(B)**   The chief metaphor in the third paragraph compares the king to the body's head and the king's subjects to the body; paragraph three develops one of the two primary metaphors introduced in paragraph one.

36. **(C)**   The sense of the sentence is that the body may, for its well-being ("for the weal of it"), strike off a diseased head. For James, however, well-being could never be the actual result, since no body can live without a head.

37. **(B)**   The first paragraph introduces two analogies: the king is compared to a father and his subjects to children, and the king is compared to a head and his

subjects to the parts of the body. Paragraph two develops the first of these analogies, and paragraph three develops the second of the analogies.

38. **(D)** All three paragraphs are part of the same argument — namely, that the king may do whatever he pleases and his subjects have no right to resist him.

39. **(C)** James does not believe that monarchs need to have the consent of those they govern or that kings can be challenged when they act irrationally. He believes that revolutions are never justified, nor does he have any concern for public good when it conflicts with self-interest. Both of James' analogies are designed to show that the king may do absolutely whatever he pleases and that no one has the right to rebel against him, even when his behavior appears irrational and abusive.

40. **(E)** James uses the examples of storks and other creatures who never turn on their parents when their parents treat them with violence to argue for the necessity of absolute obedience of the king's subjects.

41. **(A)** James' argument in the first three paragraphs proceeds entirely by analogy.

42. **(B)** The essay is not informal or personal, nor does it describe or celebrate. Its sole purpose is to persuade citizens that they owe absolute obedience to the king.

43. **(E)** In the last paragraph, James introduces an "if *x*, then *y*" proposition. If children can lawfully rise up against their father, and if the body can find good reason to cut off the head, then the king's subjects may rebel and replace their king. For James, of course, there are no conditions under which children can lawfully rise up against their father, nor can there ever be reason for the body to cut off the head.

44. **(A)** The excerpt expresses an extreme view of the right of kings — that they may do anything they please with impunity. James in fact believed in the divine right of kings.

45. **(E)** The sense of the sentence is that people may rebel and depose their king when they please and "upon respects" (based on considerations) that give them sufficient cause.

46. **(B)** Mrs. Freeman's facial expressions are described in terms of driving a vehicle. Her expressions are "neutral," "forward and reverse"; her "forward expression was steady and driving like the "advance of a heavy truck"; her eyes follow "a yellow line down the center" of a story; she seldom needs to come "to a complete stop," and so forth.

47. **(D)** The images suggest that Mrs. Freeman is earth-bound. She stands there "as real as several grain sacks thrown on top of each other," and her forward expression is steady "like the advance of a heavy truck."

48. **(A)** A simile is a comparison using "like" or "as." Mrs. Freeman's presence is described as being as "real as several grain sacks."

49. **(E)** Mrs. Freeman seldom feels the need to retract a statement. When she is clearly wrong about something, she is no longer present in spirit, and will not say anything or will only say something that is on another subject..

50. **(E)** The author uses omniscient narration; that is, she moves freely into and out of the thoughts and minds of her characters. We learn what characters think as well as what they say.

51. **(C)** Joy feels superior to the "good country people" who surround her. Her actions are calculated to offend and annoy them, and she prides herself on her differences from them.

52. **(B)** As Joy recognizes, her mother is not a person who engages in self-examination (lines 74–77). Mrs. Hopewell *is* anti-intellectual (judging from her attitude toward Joy's education), naively optimistic and conventional (judging from her simplistic platitudes and concern for what one can say to neighbors, to say nothing of her name), and self-assured (judging from the faith she has in her own judgment about people).

53. **(C)** Although Hulga is rude, what really bothers Mrs. Hopewell is Joy's abnormality. She worries that Joy has never had any "normal good times" (line 28), that every year Hulga "grew less like other people" (line 72–73), and that she cannot explain Joy's Ph.D. in philosophy to other people (lines 82–85).

54. **(B)** Mrs. Hopewell is partially correct in believing that Joy changed her name to Hulga because Hulga was the ugliest name Joy could think of. That was the original impulse in Joy's name change, but there were other, more complex motives, chiefly having to do with Joy's association of the name Hulga with Vulcan, the lame blacksmith.

55. **(D)** Joy regards her name change as her most creative act because she is able to turn her mother's dust from Joy to the ugliness of Hulga. Hence her "creativity" is based in spite.

56. **(B)** Mrs. Hopewell means that each year Joy becomes more eccentric, less like other people, more idiosyncratic — "bloated, rude, and squint-eyed."

57. **(C)** Joy's outburst was caused by Mrs. Hopewell's remark that "a smile never hurt anyone," a platitude that causes Joy to question whether her mother ever engages in self-examination (rather than simply mouthing simplistic phrases).

58. **(A)** Mrs. Hopewell believes it "was nice for girls to go to school to have a good time" (lines 54–60), but is disturbed by the fact that Joy had taken her education seriously and had "gone through" to acquire a Ph.D. in philosophy. To Mrs. Hopewell, that is not the "point" of "school."

59. **(E)** Mrs. Hopewell regards Hulga's Ph.D. as both embarrassing (one cannot tell others that "'My daughter is a philosopher'") and anachronistic ("That was something that had ended with the Greeks and Romans").

60. **(D)** We know that Joy has a Ph.D. in philosophy, enjoys being rude to people to whom she feels superior, and is intolerant of people like her mother who do not engage in self-examination. Her tastes are decidedly not conventional or feminine — "she didn't like dogs or cats or birds or flowers or nature or nice young men. She looked at nice young men as if she could smell their stupidity" (lines 87–89).

Section 2

Essay 1

The speaker in "The Greater Cats" both feels superior to and envies the cats. She is conscious of her greater wisdom, but yearns for their ability to act without regard to any sense of mortality.

In the first stanza, the speaker contrasts the cats' "wit" with her own. They mate fiercely and assert their will boldly, without regard to consequences. In contrast, she knows that man "for long shall die," while loving for only a short time. This knowledge causes her, as the rest of the poem makes clear, to behave more self-consciously — to love less fiercely and to assert her will less boldly.

The second stanza develops further the thought process began in the first. The cats have no sense of mortality ("Their strength's eternal in their sight"), and this ignorance gives them an "arrogance." In contrast, the speaker is acutely aware of her mortality and of the transient nature of love.

The major shift in the poem's thought process occurs at the beginning of the third stanza. The speaker consciously decides to deceive herself, to repress her consciousness of mortality, in order to behave like the greater cats and pledge her love fiercely and eternally to the "thee" to whom the poem is addressed. Even at the moment she claims to have rejected knowledge ("wit") in favor of faith, however, she is aware of the difficulty or impossibility of such conscious self-deception, as the final two lines make clear when she expresses the hope that she may "stay for ever blind" like the cats. The poem concludes, then, with a resolve to behave like the greater cats, but even the resolve itself reveals her returning or continuing sense of mortality.

Essay 1 — Comments

This question asks the student to analyze the *development* of the speaker's thought process, focusing particularly on the speaker's attitude toward the greater cats and on the speaker's perception of similarities and differences between the greater cats and man. By asking the student to analyze the various stages in the development of the speaker's thoughts, the question suggests that the speaker's thoughts change; hence one of the primary tasks in writing this essay is to identify and explain the changes.

In the sample essay, the writer begins with a general statement about the speaker's mixed, almost contradictory attitude toward the cats based on a reading of the entire poem. The speaker both envies and feels superior to the cats. The second sentence explains why the speaker feels superior and what it is that the speaker envies in the cats. The writer then explains the speaker's thought process stanza by stanza.

The writer recognizes that the first two stanzas develop the contrast between the speaker's sense of mortality and the cats' lack of any sense of mortality; the writer notes that this difference leads to differences in behavior, particularly in expressions of love. In the third paragraph, the writer points out that the major shift of thought in the poem occurs at the beginning of the third stanza, and explains what that shift is (the speaker's determination to deceive herself). What is particularly good about this sample essay is that it does not stop here; instead, the writer recognizes that the speaker is aware that such self-deception cannot be complete, not because the speaker says so, but because the speaker's choice of language indicates that she is conscious of the impossibility of disregarding knowledge simply through an act of will.

The sample essay is relatively brief, but it does successfully all of the things that the question asks the student to do.

Essay 2

Setting is crucially important in *Henderson the Rain King* because Saul Bellow uses it in various significant ways — to help establish meaning, to define character, to contribute to themes, and as an important ingredient in the protagonist's self-discovery. Bellow's use of setting draws attention to itself in that it violates our usual expectations about time and place in fiction.

Henderson the Rain King is a novel of character formation, and deals essentially with Henderson's spiritual quest. The protagonist abandons the familiar setting of his privileged American life in Connecticut in favor of unfamiliar settings that facilitate the process of self-discovery or self-definition that lies at the heart of the novel.

Henderson's life in America, a society of material excess, leads to depression, rage, and finally to the conclusion that he's not fit to live among men. Hence he leaves for Africa, seeking a pre-social world where he can confront directly his need to define his own "being" or self. Much of Henderson's travel is mental or internal as well as actual; hence the Africa he encounters is both a real place and a psychic and mythic landscape. This Africa of legendary time and mythic space is a place where the actual and the imaginary meet (and therefore the ideal setting for Henderson's process of self-discovery) as well as a prehistoric place with no social entanglements where Henderson can confront nature directly.

Besides being appropriate to Henderson's spiritual quest, the African setting presents several models of society that shape the characters of the people who live in them, which in turn aids Henderson's process of self-definition. For example, he encounters a matriarchal, passive society (the Arnewi) that fosters such qualities as goodness and acceptance. As appealing as this unambitious society is, Henderson's time in this setting helps him recognize that his nature is not suited to such a society, and that to pretend otherwise would impede his process of self-discovery.

Henderson also encounters a patriarchal world of violence, change, and action (the Wariri). His time in this society teaches him much about achieving a "state of being, not becoming," and gets him to recognize and accept certain aspects of his nature. Ultimately, however, neither of these settings or societies can satisfy Henderson's need.

On his flight back to America, Henderson recognizes that his own nature is not that of the cow-like Arnewi or lion-like Wariri, but similar to a fairground bear he remembers from the past (both are "sad humorists"). Hence he returns to society with increased knowledge and acceptance of self, and the lessons he learns in Bellow's imaginary Africa play a major role in his development.

Essay 2 — Comments

This "free-choice" question asks the student to analyze both the importance and the uses of setting in a novel or play. The question provides some help in directing the student to significant concerns in composing the essay. Students should note that setting refers to both time and place, and can be used for various purposes, some of which are suggested in the question, thus suggesting some possible directions essays might take. If the student elects to write on a work not listed in the question, care should be taken to select a work in which setting plays a significant role.

The writer of the sample essay chose *Henderson the Rain King*, which is a particularly rich choice for the purposes of this question. It is also an especially difficult choice because Bellow's use of setting poses unusually difficult questions. In the opening paragraph, the writer recognizes that setting is particularly important in Bellow's novel, lists some of the uses of setting in *Henderson the*

Rain King, and alerts the reader to the fact that Bellow's use of setting is unusual.

The writer organizes his essay around the difficult task of trying to explain how setting relates to the essential action of the novel — the protagonist's process of self-definition or self-discovery. The writer of the essay accomplishes two primary tasks — explaining the role of setting in the novel's "movement" as a whole (from society to a pre-social world and back to society) while also showing how some of the specific settings in the novel function. The writer notes that the novel moves from a realistic setting in a particular time in America to the legendary time and mythic space of an unspecified locale in Africa that is particularly well-suited to the timeless, fundamental spiritual quest that occupies most of the book. The fourth and fifth paragraphs briefly discuss two African settings in order to show how these settings influence character in the novel and to illustrate how setting influences the protagonist's process of self-discovery. *Henderson the Rain King* is a complex novel that cannot be exhaustively discussed in a thirty-five minute essay; hence the writer chooses only a few significant details to demonstrate both the importance and the uses of setting in the work. Nonetheless, the writer demonstrates an understanding of the essential nature of the novel and the ways in which setting contributes to it.

Essay 3

Oliver Goldsmith advances two primary arguments in trying to persuade the reader that laughing comedy is superior to sentimental comedy, and he employs various strategies, including the appeal to authority, personal anecdote, and the use of humor, to strengthen his case.

One of his main arguments concerns the proper subject matter of comedy and the related question of "mulish" genres. Underlying this argument is the assumption that comedy ought to depict "human folly and frailty." Goldsmith appeals to Aristotle to establish the proper subject of comedy ("low life and middle life") and to Boileau to argue that comedy should depict the follies rather than the calamities of "low and middle life." Laughing comedy does the the former, sentimental comedy the latter; in so doing, sentimental comedy invades the province that properly belongs to tragedy, thereby producing a mulish hybrid that is neither comic nor tragic. Goldsmith argues that such works violate the universal practice of all former ages.

Goldsmith's second major argument is that laughing comedy is more entertaining or amusing than sentimental comedy. The latter depicts the virtues and distresses of private life whereas laughing comedy exposes the vices and ridicules the faults of mankind. Goldsmith acknowledges that some sentimental works entertain audiences; his chief contention is simply that laughing comedy is *more* amusing, which he confirms by personal anecdote. Ultimately, sentimental comedy seeks to evoke tears for the suffering of virtuous characters, whereas laughing comedy seeks to evoke laughter at mankind's foibles. Goldsmith uses this difference in purpose to conclude his argument humorously. If people prefer to be as solemn and "gloomy" at theatrical comedies as they are in listening to a Calvinist sermon, they deserve to be punished by losing the ability to laugh.

Essay 3 — Comments

This question asks the student to do two things — to describe Goldsmith's views of laughing and sentimental comedy and to discuss the various strategies and devices he uses to argue that one is superior to the other. The assignment is not particularly difficult *if* the student reads Goldsmith's essay carefully, paying particular attention to the distinctions Goldsmith makes between laughing and sentimental comedy. Goldsmith does not offer definitions of the two at the beginning of his essay; only gradually does Goldsmith's attitude toward the two emerge. The student also needs to think critically about the self-conscious devices Goldsmith uses while reading the essay; some aspects of the essay that at first may seem digressive are actually parts of the strategies Goldsmith employs to persuade readers.

In the sample essay, the writer makes it clear that he has understood the overall structure and point of view of the essay and has recognized some of the devices or strategies Goldsmith uses. The writer says that Goldsmith has two primary arguments concerning the superiority of laughing comedy. The writer's second paragraph analyzes one of those arguments, while the third paragraph analyzes the other. Both also point out secondary persuasive strategies, such as appeals to authority, personal anecdote, and humor.

In order to explain Goldsmith's two main arguments, it is necessary to understand both the subject matter and the ends of laughing and sentimental comedy. Hence the writer points out that laughing comedy deals with the follies of "low and middle life" and seeks to evoke laughter at man's frailties, whereas sentimental comedy deals with the calamities and virtues of private life and seeks to evoke tears for the suffering of virtuous characters. Once this distinction is understood, Goldsmith's two main arguments (one having to do with the proper subject matter of comedy, the other focusing on whether the ridiculing of faults is more amusing than displays of distress and virtue) can be placed in their proper context. The sample essay is relatively brief, but explains all of the essential distinctions in Goldsmith's essay.

THE ADVANCED PLACEMENT EXAMINATION IN

English Literature & Composition

TEST 3

1. Ⓐ Ⓑ Ⓒ Ⓓ Ⓔ
2. Ⓐ Ⓑ Ⓒ Ⓓ Ⓔ
3. Ⓐ Ⓑ Ⓒ Ⓓ Ⓔ
4. Ⓐ Ⓑ Ⓒ Ⓓ Ⓔ
5. Ⓐ Ⓑ Ⓒ Ⓓ Ⓔ
6. Ⓐ Ⓑ Ⓒ Ⓓ Ⓔ
7. Ⓐ Ⓑ Ⓒ Ⓓ Ⓔ
8. Ⓐ Ⓑ Ⓒ Ⓓ Ⓔ
9. Ⓐ Ⓑ Ⓒ Ⓓ Ⓔ
10. Ⓐ Ⓑ Ⓒ Ⓓ Ⓔ
11. Ⓐ Ⓑ Ⓒ Ⓓ Ⓔ
12. Ⓐ Ⓑ Ⓒ Ⓓ Ⓔ
13. Ⓐ Ⓑ Ⓒ Ⓓ Ⓔ
14. Ⓐ Ⓑ Ⓒ Ⓓ Ⓔ
15. Ⓐ Ⓑ Ⓒ Ⓓ Ⓔ
16. Ⓐ Ⓑ Ⓒ Ⓓ Ⓔ
17. Ⓐ Ⓑ Ⓒ Ⓓ Ⓔ
18. Ⓐ Ⓑ Ⓒ Ⓓ Ⓔ
19. Ⓐ Ⓑ Ⓒ Ⓓ Ⓔ
20. Ⓐ Ⓑ Ⓒ Ⓓ Ⓔ
21. Ⓐ Ⓑ Ⓒ Ⓓ Ⓔ
22. Ⓐ Ⓑ Ⓒ Ⓓ Ⓔ
23. Ⓐ Ⓑ Ⓒ Ⓓ Ⓔ
24. Ⓐ Ⓑ Ⓒ Ⓓ Ⓔ
25. Ⓐ Ⓑ Ⓒ Ⓓ Ⓔ
26. Ⓐ Ⓑ Ⓒ Ⓓ Ⓔ
27. Ⓐ Ⓑ Ⓒ Ⓓ Ⓔ
28. Ⓐ Ⓑ Ⓒ Ⓓ Ⓔ
29. Ⓐ Ⓑ Ⓒ Ⓓ Ⓔ
30. Ⓐ Ⓑ Ⓒ Ⓓ Ⓔ
31. Ⓐ Ⓑ Ⓒ Ⓓ Ⓔ
32. Ⓐ Ⓑ Ⓒ Ⓓ Ⓔ
33. Ⓐ Ⓑ Ⓒ Ⓓ Ⓔ
34. Ⓐ Ⓑ Ⓒ Ⓓ Ⓔ
35. Ⓐ Ⓑ Ⓒ Ⓓ Ⓔ
36. Ⓐ Ⓑ Ⓒ Ⓓ Ⓔ
37. Ⓐ Ⓑ Ⓒ Ⓓ Ⓔ
38. Ⓐ Ⓑ Ⓒ Ⓓ Ⓔ
39. Ⓐ Ⓑ Ⓒ Ⓓ Ⓔ
40. Ⓐ Ⓑ Ⓒ Ⓓ Ⓔ
41. Ⓐ Ⓑ Ⓒ Ⓓ Ⓔ
42. Ⓐ Ⓑ Ⓒ Ⓓ Ⓔ
43. Ⓐ Ⓑ Ⓒ Ⓓ Ⓔ
44. Ⓐ Ⓑ Ⓒ Ⓓ Ⓔ
45. Ⓐ Ⓑ Ⓒ Ⓓ Ⓔ
46. Ⓐ Ⓑ Ⓒ Ⓓ Ⓔ
47. Ⓐ Ⓑ Ⓒ Ⓓ Ⓔ
48. Ⓐ Ⓑ Ⓒ Ⓓ Ⓔ
49. Ⓐ Ⓑ Ⓒ Ⓓ Ⓔ
50. Ⓐ Ⓑ Ⓒ Ⓓ Ⓔ
51. Ⓐ Ⓑ Ⓒ Ⓓ Ⓔ
52. Ⓐ Ⓑ Ⓒ Ⓓ Ⓔ
53. Ⓐ Ⓑ Ⓒ Ⓓ Ⓔ
54. Ⓐ Ⓑ Ⓒ Ⓓ Ⓔ
55. Ⓐ Ⓑ Ⓒ Ⓓ Ⓔ
56. Ⓐ Ⓑ Ⓒ Ⓓ Ⓔ
57. Ⓐ Ⓑ Ⓒ Ⓓ Ⓔ
58. Ⓐ Ⓑ Ⓒ Ⓓ Ⓔ
59. Ⓐ Ⓑ Ⓒ Ⓓ Ⓔ
60. Ⓐ Ⓑ Ⓒ Ⓓ Ⓔ

AP EXAMINATION IN ENGLISH LITERATURE AND COMPOSITION

TEST 3
Section 1

TIME: 60 Minutes
60 Questions

DIRECTIONS: *This test consists of selections from literary works and questions on their content, form, and style. After reading each passage or poem, choose the best answer to each question and blacken the corresponding space on the answer sheet.*

NOTE: Pay particular attention to the requirement of questions that contain the words NOT, LEAST, or EXCEPT.

QUESTIONS 1–15 are based on the following passage. Read the passage carefully before choosing your answers.

It was there that, several years ago, I saw him for the first time; and the sight pulled me up sharp. Even then he was the most striking figure in Starkfield, though he was but the ruin of a man. It was not so much his great height that marked him, for the "natives" were easily singled out by
5 their lank longitude from the stockier foreign breed: it was the careless powerful look he had, in spite of a lameness checking each step like the jerk of a chain. There was something bleak and unapproachable in his face, and he was so stiffened and grizzled that I took him for an old man and was surprised to hear that he was not more than fifty-two. I had this from
10 Harmon Gow, who had driven the stage from Bettsbridge to Starkfield in pre-trolley days and knew the chronicle of all the families on his line.
  Harmon drew a slab of tobacco from his pocket, cut off a wedge and

pressed it into the leather pouch of his cheek. "Guess he's been in Starkfield too many winters. Most of the smart ones get away."

15 Though Harmon Gow developed the tale as far as his mental and moral reach permitted there were perceptible gaps between his facts, and I had the sense that the deeper meaning of the story was in the gaps. But one phrase stuck in my memory and served as the nucleus about which I grouped my subsequent inferences: "Guess he's been in Starkfield too

20 many winters."

Before my own time there was up I had learned to know what that meant. Yet I had come in the degenerate day of trolley, bicycle and rural delivery, when communication was easy between the scattered mountain villages, and the bigger towns in the valleys, such as Bettsbridge and

25 Shadd's Falls, had libraries, theatres and Y. M. C. A. halls to which the youth of the hills could descend for recreation. But when winter shut down on Starkfield, and the village lay under a sheet of snow perpetually renewed from the pale skies, I began to see what life there—or rather its negation—must have been in Ethan Frome's young manhood.

30 I had been sent up by my employers on a job connected with the big power-house at Corbury Junction, and a long-drawn carpenters' strike had so delayed the work that I found myself anchored at Starkfield—the nearest habitable spot—for the best part of the winter. I chafed at first, and then, under the hypnotising effect of routine, gradually began to find a

35 grim satisfaction in the life. During the early part of my stay I had been struck by the contrast between the vitality of the climate and the deadness of the community. Day by day, after the December snows were over, a blazing blue sky poured down torrents of light and air on the white landscape, which gave them back in an intenser glitter. One would have

40 supposed that such an atmosphere must quicken the emotions as well as the blood; but it seemed to produce no change except that of retarding still more the sluggish pulse of Starkfield. When I had been there a little longer, and had seen this phase of crystal clearness followed by long stretches of sunless cold; when the storms of February had pitched their

45 white tents about the devoted village and the wild cavalry of March winds had charged down to their support, I began to understand why Starkfield emerged from its six months' siege like a starved garrison capitulating without quarter. Twenty years earlier the means of resistance must have been far fewer, and the enemy in command of almost all the lines of access

50 between the beleaguered villages; and, considering these things, I felt the sinister force of Harmon's phrase: "Most of the smart ones get away." But if that were the case, how could any combination of obstacles have hindered the flight of a man like Ethan Frome?

From ETHAN FROME *by Edith Wharton (New York: Charles Scribner's Sons, 1911)*

1. The phrase "checking each step like the jerk of a chain" (lines 6–7) is best interpreted to mean that Ethan

    (A) had served time on a chain gang

    (B) moved about with uncertainty and timidity

    (C) dragged along the dead weight of his injured leg

    (D) was obviously one of the "stockier" breed

    (E) bore the characteristics of a corrupt and criminal past

2. The phrase "singled out by their lank longitude" (lines 4–5) evokes the

    (A) tall stature of the town "natives"

    (B) sailing history of the townfolk

    (C) prejudice "natives" had for their own kind

    (D) animosity shown toward the "natives" by the foreigners in town

    (E) "natives'" superiority over the foreign breed

3. The phrase "the storms of February pitched their white tents" (lines 44–45) presents an example of

    (A) soliloquy   (D) ambiguity

    (B) paradox   (E) dramatic irony

    (C) personification

4. The narrator came to understand that life in the village was negated primarily because

    (A) the townfolk were unsociable

    (B) the long drawn carpenters' strike

    (C) of the absence of the smart ones who got away

    (D) of the degenerate influences of trolley, bicycle and rural delivery

    (E) of the psychological isolation created by the weather

5. The image of a "starved garrison" (line 47) is a reference to the

    (A) beleaguered strikers

    (B) shortage of food in the village

(C)   militaristic nature of village life

(D)   emotionally drained townfolk

(E)   presence of government troops in the vicinity

6.   In context, which of the following supports Harmon Gow's observation "Guess he's been in Starkfield too many winters" (lines 13–14)?

(A)   Ethan's being the town's most striking figure

(B)   Ethan's great height

(C)   Ethan's careless, powerful look

(D)   Ethan's bleak and unapproachable face

(E)   Ethan's awareness of Gow's opinion of him

7.   In context, the phrase "degenerate day" (line 22) is best interpreted to mean

(A)   a time when winters were more severe

(B)   a time of inferior trolley and mail service

(C)   an earlier time of restricted communication between villages

(D)   the time when winter clamped down on the village

(E)   a time of modern worldly influence on the village

8.   The final paragraph of the passage (lines 30–53) serves primarily to

(A)   relate how the narrator passed the winter

(B)   illustrate Harmon Gow's comment about "too many winters"

(C)   summarize the factors blocking Ethan's departure

(D)   demonstrate the innate prejudice of Harmon Gow

(E)   explain the folly of those who got away

9.   In the final paragraph, the narrator has difficulty

(A)   adjusting to the social life of the village

(B)   understanding the villagers' joy at the approach of spring

(C)   appreciating the beauty of the season

(D)   comprehending the situation in the village in an earlier day

(E)   reconciling the weather and its effect on the villagers

10. In context, the "enemy" (line 49) most likely represents

    (A) the degenerate influence of the world

    (B) the hypnotizing effect of winter routine

    (C) impassable snow and ice

    (D) striking carpenters

    (E) marauding cavalry

11. It can be inferred from the passage that

    (A) the narrator remained a stranger to the villagers

    (B) modern life had continued to pass the village by

    (C) the severe winters strengthened the bonds of the community

    (D) unusual circumstances compelled Ethan to stay there

    (E) Ethan enjoyed a warm relationship with the villagers

12. Which of the following best describes the narrator's view of the villagers at the end of the passage?

    (A) Closely knit community

    (B) A collection of weather beaten, phlegmatic individuals

    (C) A collection of inbred individuals who distrust strangers

    (D) Stout-hearted victors over nature

    (E) A collection of gossip mongers

13. The tone of the first paragraph is best described as

    (A) cynical glee   (D) feigned sympathy

    (B) sympathetic curiosity (E) worshipful awe

    (C) mild sarcasm

14. In lines 44–50 the narrator uses language that might best describe a

    (A) famine   (D) medieval tournament

    (B) Bedouin encampment   (E) horse race

    (C) hostile invasion

15.   All of the following represent figurative language EXCEPT

    (A)   "the most striking figure in Starkfield" (lines 2–3)

    (B)   "the leather pouch of his cheek" (line 13)

    (C)   "his mental and moral reach" (lines 15–16)

    (D)   "I found myself anchored at Starkfield" (line 32)

    (E)   "pitched their white tents" (line 44–45)

QUESTIONS 16–32 are based on the following poem. Read the poem carefully before choosing your answers.

Ode on Indolence
John Keats [1795–1821]
They toil not, neither do they spin.

One morn before me were three figures seen,
    With bowed necks, and joined hands, side-fac'd;
And one behind the other stepp'd serene,
    In placid sandals, and in white robes grac'd;
5 They pass'd, like figures on a marble urn,
    When shifted round to see the other side;
      They came again; as when the urn once more
Is shifted round, the first seen shades return;
    And they were strange to me, as may betide
10   With vases, to one deep in Phidian lore.

How is it, shadows! that I knew ye not?
    How came ye muffled in so hush a mask?
Was it a silent deep-disguisèd plot
    To steal away, and leave without a task
15 My idle days? Ripe was the drowsy hour;
    The blissful cloud of summer-indolence
      Benumb'd my eyes; my pulse grew less and less;
Pain had no sting, and pleasure's wreath no flower:
    O, why did ye not melt, and leave my sense
20   Unhaunted quite of all but—nothingness?

A third time pass'd they by, and, passing, turn'd
    Each one the face a moment whiles to me;
Then faded, and to follow them I burn'd

And ach'd for wings because I knew the three;
25 The first was a fair maid, and Love her name;
    The second was Ambition, pale of cheek,
    And ever watchful with fatigued eye;
The last, whom I love more, the more of blame
    Is heap'd upon her, maiden most unmeek,—
30   I know to be my demon Poesy.

They faded, and, forsooth! I wanted wings:
    O folly! What is Love? and where is it?
And for that poor Ambition! it springs
    From a man's little heart's short fever-fit;
35 For Poesy!—no,—she has not a joy,—
    At least for me,—so sweet as drowsy noons,
        And evenings steep'd in honied indolence;
O, for an age so shelter'd from annoy,
    That I may never know how change the moons,
40   Or hear the voice of busy common-sense!

And once more came they by;—alas! wherefore?
    My sleep had been embroider'd with dim dreams;
My soul had been a lawn besprinkled o'er
    With flowers, and stirring shades, and baffled beams:
45 The morn was clouded, but no shower fell,
    Tho' in her lids hung the sweet tears of May;
        The open casement press'd a new-leav'd vine,
    Let in the budding warmth and throstle's lay;
O shadows! 'twas a time to bid farewell!
50   Upon your skirts had fallen no tears of mine.

So, ye three ghosts, adieu! Ye cannot raise
    My head cool-bedded in the flowery grass;
For I would not be dieted with praise,
    A pet-lamb in a sentimental farce!
55 Fade softly from my eyes, and be once more
    In masque-like figures on the dreamy urn;
        Farewell! I yet have visions for the night,
And for the day faint visions there is store;
    Vanish, ye phantoms! from my idle spright,
60 Into the clouds, and nevermore return!

16. The three figures pictured in lines 1–20 are best described as which of the following?

   (A) Hypocritical and false   (D) Mirthful and carefree

   (B) Solemn and ghostly   (E) Scholarly and reclusive

   (C) Pious and cheerful

17. The speaker of the poem is pictured chiefly as a

   (A) collector of Greek artifacts

   (B) terminally ill patient

   (C) leisured person

   (D) diligent gardener

   (E) hard-working poet

18. In line 8, the phrase "the first seen shades return" is best taken to mean which of the following?

   (A) Shadows cast by the vases

   (B) Greeks risen from the dead

   (C) Shadows made by the rising sun

   (D) Strange new shades of color

   (E) Ghostly visitors

19. The relationship between lines 1–10 and lines 25–30 is best described as which of the following?

   (A) Lines 1–10 establish a thesis; lines 25–30 refute it

   (B) Lines 1–10 present a description; lines 25-30 enlarge on it

   (C) Lines 1–10 present a rule; lines 25–30 propose an exception to it

   (D) Lines 1–10 pose a question; lines 25–30 answer it

   (E) Lines 1–10 begin a narrative; line 25-30 conclude it

20. In lines 15–20 the speaker chiefly desires to

   (A) die of love

   (B) confront the ghosts of his past

    (C)   uncover the plot against him

    (D)   capitalize on the fruitful hour

    (E)   vegetate his time away

21.   The change referred to in lines 23–24 is described as one from

    (A)   frivolity to exertion

    (B)   seriousness to lethargy

    (C)   restraint to freedom

    (D)   sinfulness to piety

    (E)   straightforwardness to subtlety

22.   In lines 31–40 the speaker regards his three visitors as

    (A)   manifestations of his fevered brain

    (B)   messengers inspired by love

    (C)   opponents blocking his ability to write

    (D)   reminders of his own mortality

    (E)   antagonists disturbing his sweet inertia

23.   The main point made about the three visitors in lines 32–36 is that they

    (A)   no longer inspire him to practice his craft

    (B)   represent types of folly poets ought to avoid

    (C)   foreshadow his reinvolvement in his craft

    (D)   evoke positive memories of past encounters with him

    (E)   offered enticements that rendered him senseless

24.   Lines 42–50 suggest that the speaker

    (A)   relishes all aspects of his present situation

    (B)   keeps himself occupied by working in the garden

    (C)   was disappointed by the approach of bad weather

    (D)   desires urgently to leave his present location

    (E)   keeps his tears of disappointment to himself

25. In lines 51–56, the speaker does which of the following?

    (A) Qualifies his previous position

    (B) Anticipates an objection to his argument

    (C) Summarizes his previous argument

    (D) Digresses from the main point of the poem

    (E) Begins to comment on a new subject

26. In line 48, the phrase "throstle's lay" most likely refers to

    (A) leafy tree branches

    (B) blossoms of nearby trees

    (C) wind driven rain

    (D) darkened shadows of the trees

    (E) song bird's notes

27. According to the speaker, the three "visitors" entice him with all of the following EXCEPT

    (A) commendation

    (B) poetic artistry

    (C) romance

    (D) contentment

    (E) fame

28. In lines 41–50, the speaker attempts to do which of the following?

    (A) Chastize the reader

    (B) Demonstrate his poetic power

    (C) Summarize his argument

    (D) Draw an analogy

    (E) Recount an anecdote

29. A more conventional, but still accurate, replacement for "store" in line 58 would be

    (A) a need

    (B) a supply

    (C) a time

    (D) a scarcity

    (E) room enough

30. According to the speaker, all of the following are true of indolence EXCEPT

(A) bodily suffering disappears

(B) the ego enjoys applause

(C) no tribulations disturb the soul

(D) the heart is free of aspiration

(E) the affections remain unexcited

31. The phrase,"Tho' in her lids hung the sweet tears of May" (line 46) presents an example of

(A) dramatic irony   (D) personification

(B) run-on line   (E) paradox

(C) a lament

32. This poem is written in which of the following?

(A) Rime royal   (D) Ballad meter

(B) Iambic pentameter   (E) Heroic couplets

(C) Trochaic hexameter

QUESTIONS 33–45 are based on the following passage. Read the passage carefully before choosing your answers.

How ruinous a farm has man taken, in taking himself! How ready is the house every day to fall down, and how is all the ground overspread with weeds, all the body with diseases! where not only every turf, but every stone bears weeds; not only every muscle of the flesh, but every bone of
5 the body, has some infirmity; every little flint upon the face of this soil, has some infectious weed, every tooth in our head, such a pain as a constant man is afraid of, and yet ashamed of that fear, of that sense of pain. How dear, and how often a rent does Man pay for this farm ! he pays twice a day, in double meals, and how little time he has to raise his rent!
10 How many holy days to call him from his labor! Every day is half-holy day, half spent in sleep. What reparations, subsidies, and contributions he is put to, besides his rent! What medicines besides his diet! and what inmates he is fain to take in, besides his own family, what infectious diseases, from other men! Adam might have had Paradise for dressing and
15 keeping it; and then his rent was not improved to such a labor, as would

have made his brow sweat; and yet he gave it over; how far greater a rent
do we pay for this farm, this body, who pay ourselves, who pay the farm
itself, and cannot live upon it! Neither is our labor at an end, when we have
cut down some weed, as soon as it sprung up, corrected some violent and
20 dangerous accident of a disease, which would have destroyed speedily;
nor when we have pulled up that weed, from the very root, recovered
entirely and soundly, from that particular disease; but the whole ground is
of an ill nature, the whole soil ill disposed; there are inclinations, there is a
propenseness to diseases in the body, out of which without any other
25 disorder, diseases will grow, and so we are put to a continual labor upon
this farm, to a continual study of the whole complexion and constitution of
our body. In the distempers and diseases of soils, sourness, dryness,
weeping, any kind of barrenness, the remedy and the physic, is, for a great
part, sometimes in themselves; sometimes the very situation relieves
30 them; the hanger of a hill, will purge and vent his own malignant moisture;
and the burning of the upper turf of some ground (as health from cauteriz-
ing) puts a new and vigorous youth into that soil, and there rises a kind of
Phoenix out of the ashes, a fruitfulness out of that which was barren
before, and by that, which is the barrennest of all, ashes. And where the
35 ground cannot give itself physic, yet it receives physic from other grounds,
from other soils, which are not the worse, for having contributed that help
to them, from marl in other hills, or from slimy sand in other shores:
grounds help themselves, or hurt not other grounds, from whence they
receive help. But I have taken a farm at this hard rent, and upon those
40 heavy covenants, that it can afford itself no help; (no part of my body, if it
were cut off would cure another part; in some cases it might preserve a
sound part, but in no case recover an infected) and, if my body may have
any Physic, any Medicine from another body, one man from the flesh of
another man (as by Mummy, or any such composition), it must be from a
45 man that is dead, and not, as in other soils, which are never the worse for
contributing their marl, or their fat slime to my ground. There is nothing in
the same man, to help man, nothing in mankind to help one another (in this
sort, by way of Physic) but that he who ministers the help, is in an ill case,
as he that receives it would have been, if he had not had it; for he from
50 whose body the Physic comes, is dead. When therefore I took this farm,
undertook this body, I undertook to drain, not a marsh, but a moat, where
there was, not water mingled to offend, but all was water; I undertook to
perfume dung, where no one part, but all was equally unsavory; I undertook to make such a thing wholesome, as was not poison by any manifest
55 quality, intense heat, or cold, but poison in the whole substance and in the
specific form of it. To cure the sharp accidents of diseases, is a great work;
to cure the disease itself is a greater; but to cure the body, the root, the

occasion of diseases, is a work reserved for the great Physician, which he does never any other way, but by glorifying these bodies in the next world.

"Meditation XXII," by John Donne

33.   The passage contains all of the following rhetorical devices EXCEPT

(A)   repetition   (D)   analogy

(B)   rhetorical question   (E)   hyperbole

(C)   allusion

34.   It can be inferred from the passage that the speaker would agree with which of the following statements about the human body?

(A)   Man's infirmities come from both inside and outside the body

(B)   An illness patiently endured earns heavenly rewards

(C)   Health is ultimately a matter of bodily discipline

(D)   Cures are often achieved in one part of the body by amputating another part

(E)   Bodily perfection is a matter of healthy diet and prudent medical care

35.   In lines 8–12, the speaker uses language that might describe the problems of

(A)   owning real estate   (D)   a country parson

(B)   a country physician   (E)   a sharecropper

(C)   a rent collector

36.   The speaker is concerned that his farm may

(A)   yield more crops than he can consume

(B)   not be as productive as his neighbors

(C)   be an unwise business investment

(D)   possess insufficient marl and slimy sand

(E)   defy his efforts to live on it

37.   It is most likely that the constant man is "ashamed of that fear" (line 7) because

(A)   neighbors will guess he bought a poor farm

(B)   bearing pain uncomplainingly is considered manly

(C)   infirmities of the body are his heritage from Adam

(D)   infectious weeds will lower the productivity of the land

(E)   impending poverty awaits the incompetent farmer

38.   The comparison in lines 8–18 of the afflictions of life with rent suggest that these afflictions are all of the following EXCEPT

(A)   inexorable   (D)   efficacious

(B)   physically tiring   (E)   threatening

(C)   unrewarding

39.   In lines 14–16, the speaker suggests that the rent Adam owed for Paradise

(A)   was dependent on his ability to clothe himself adequately

(B)   was rejected because he failed to improve his surroundings

(C)   was obtainable for a minimum of physical effort

(D)   exceeded the rent we pay for our bodies

(E)   .was beyond his physical capability to achieve

40.   The sentence beginning "Neither is our labor" (lines 18–27) supports the speaker's proposition that the body

(A)   achieves an immunity as it recovers its health

(B)   is wearied by the unending need to remove weeds

(C)   has a predisposition toward disease

(D)   unites its entire constitution against the invasion of disease

(E)   should be weeded of sin and temptation regularly

41.   "It" in line 44 refers to

(A)   Mummy (line 44)   (D)   Physic (line 43)

(B)   body (line 43)   (E)   farm (line 39)

(C)   flesh (line 43)

42.   A more conventional, but still accurate, replacement for "improved" in line 15 would be

(A)   increased   (D)   cultivated

(B)   corrected   (E)   limited

(C)   promoted

43.   At the conclusion, the speaker finds that he

   (A)   was able to improve the condition of the farm

   (B)   faced problems of intense heat and cold

   (C)   overcame a problem with food poisoning

   (D)   successfully managed a reclamation of the farm

   (E)   undertook an impossible task

44.   Which of the following best describes the function of the last sentence in the passage?

   (A)   It provides an answer to the dilemma presented in the passage.

   (B)   It refutes the argument developed in the passage.

   (C)   It digresses from the main argument of the passage.

   (D)   It provides a metaphorical application of the image of the farm.

   (E)   It makes a change from figurative language to literal language.

45.   Which of the following seems LEAST compatible with the speaker's concept of the human body?

   (A)   Predilection to disease as innate

   (B)   Perfection arrives through strenuous effort

   (C)   Expenditures always exceed income

   (D)   Infirmities plague every aspect

   (E)   Assistance from within is available

QUESTIONS 46–60 are based on the following poem. Read the poem carefully before choosing your answers.

> Enlarge my life with multitude of days!
> In health, in sickness, thus the suppliant prays;
> Hides from himself his state, and shuns to know,
> That life protracted is protracted woe.

5   Time hovers o'er, impatient to destroy,
     And shuts up all the passages of joy;
     In vain their gifts the bounteous seasons pour,
     The fruit autumnal, and the vernal flower;
     With listless eyes the dotard views the store,
10 He views, and wonders that they please no more;
     Now pall the tasteless meats, and joyless wines,
     And Luxury with sighs her slave resigns.

         Unnumbered maladies his joints invade,
     Lay siege to life and press the dire blockade;
15 But unextinguished avarice still remains,
     And dreaded losses aggravate his pains;
     He turns, with anxious heart and crippled hands,
     His bonds of debt, and mortgages of lands;
     Or views his coffers with suspicious eyes,
20 Unlocks his gold, and counts it till he dies.
     But grant, the virtues of a temperate prime
     Bless with an age exempt from scorn or crime;
     An age that melts with unperceived decay,
     And glides in modest innocence away;
25 Whose peaceful day Benevolence endears,
     Whose night congratulating Conscience cheers;
     The general favorite as the general friend:
     Such age there is, and who shall wish its end?

         Yet even on this her load Misfortune flings,
30 To press the weary minutes' flagging wings;
     New sorrow rises as the day returns,
     A sister sickens, or a daughter mourns.
     Now kindred Merit fills the sable bier,
     Now lacerated Friendship claims a tear;
35 Year chases year, decay pursues decay,
     Still drops some joy from withering life away;
     New forms arise, and different views engage,
     Superfluous lags the veteran on the stage,
     Till pitying Nature signs the last release,
40 And bids afflicted Worth retire to peace.

         But few there are whom hours like these await,
     Who set unclouded in the gulfs of Fate.

         The teeming mother, anxious for her race,
     Begs for each birth the fortune of a face:
45 Ye nymphs of rosy lips and radiant eyes,
     Whom Pleasure keeps too busy to be wise,

Whom Joys with soft varieties invite,
By day the frolic, and the dance by night;
Who frown with vanity, who smile with art,
50 And ask the latest fashion of the heart;
What care, what rules your heedless charms shall save,
Each nymph your rival, and each youth your slave?
Against your fame with Fondness Hate combines,
The rival batters, and the lover mines.
55 With distant voice neglected Virtue calls,
Less heard and less, the faint remonstrance falls;
Tired with contempt, she quits the slippery reign,
And Pride and Prudence take her seat in vain.
In crowd at once, where none the pass defend,
60 The harmless freedom, and the private friend.
The guardians yield, by force superior plied:
To Interest, Prudence; and to Flattery, Pride.
Now Beauty falls betrayed, despised, distressed,
And hissing Infamy proclaims the rest.
65   Where then shall Hope and Fear their objects find?
Must dull Suspense corrupt the stagnant mind?
Must helpless man, in ignorance sedate,
Roll darkling down the torrent of his fate?
Must no dislike alarm, no wishes rise,
70 No cries invoke the mercies of the skies?
Inquirer, cease; petitions yet remain,
Which Heaven may hear, nor deem religion vain.
Still raise for good the supplicating voice,
But leave to Heaven the measure and the choice.

From "The Vanity of Human Wishes," Samuel Johnson

46. In the first section of the poem (lines 1–12), the speaker seeks to convey a feeling of

(A) contentment   (D) lamentation

(B) weariness   (E) deliverance

(C) resignation

47. In context, "hovers" (line 5) suggest that time

(A) eagerly awaits an opportunity to end life

(B) stands still when life's end nears

(C)   indifferently awaits life's end

(D)   helplessly observes life's approaching end

(E)   abhors the senseless destruction of life

48.   The speaker gives metaphorical significance to which of the following?

I.   Passages (line 6)   III.   Seasons (line 7)

II.   Gifts (line 7)   IV.   Store (line 9)

(A)   I and II only   (D)   I, II and IV only

(B)   III and IV only   (E)   I, II, III, IV

(C)   I, II and III only

49.   Line 16 is best understood to mean which of the following?

(A)   Medical failures aggravate his condition.

(B)   Cumulative effects of disease increase his pain.

(C)   Business setbacks worsen his pain.

(D)   Deaths of close friends depress him.

(E)   Losses occasioned by blockades depress him.

50.   In lines 13–16 greed is compared to

(A)   an invasion   (D)   combat casualties

(B)   a besieged town   (E)   a naval blockade

(C)   a consuming flame

51.   The speaker's description of a virtuous life (lines 21–40) emphasizes all of the following EXCEPT its

(A)   tranquil days   (D)   gentle aging

(B)   untroubled sleep   (E)   undiminished joys

(C)   loss of loved ones

52.   In lines 29-30 "Yet even to this … flagging wings" suggests that

(A)   virtue flings aside Misfortune's load

(B)   virtue is not exempt from troubles

(C)   time and patience will exhaust misfortune

(D)   misfortune is a bird of prey

(E)   minutes grow weary waiting for misfortune

53.   Because "Misfortune" (line 29) enters every life, all of the following occur
       EXCEPT

       (A)   the body grows more decrepit

       (B)   the importance of our roles increase

       (C)   our fame fades

       (D)   old friends die

       (E)   each day brings new woes

54.   In line 38, "Superfluous" functions as which of the following?

       (A)   An adjective modifying "veteran" (line 38)

       (B)   An adverb modifying "engage" (line 37)

       (C)   An adjective modifying "stage" (line 38)

       (D)   An adjective modifying "lags" (line 38)

       (E)   An adverb modifying "lags" (line 38)

55.   In lines 41–42, the speaker compares

       (A)   the wicked to the dividing waters

       (B)   the virtuous to ships

       (C)   the virtuous to clear skies

       (D)   the wicked to passing hours

       (E)   salvation to a water passage

56.   In the poem, beauty is, for the speaker, all of the following EXCEPT

       (A)   fickle   (D)   conceited

       (B)   jealous   (E)   hedonistic

       (C)   undefiled

57.   Lines 55–64 can best be described as a

       (A)   restatement of an earlier argument

       (B)   metaphorical digression on beauty

(C) summary of the speaker's thesis

(D) warning on the dangers of beauty

(E) counterargument to the section on the virtuous life

58. In the last section of the poem, the speaker implies that petitions made to Heaven are unacceptable if they

(A) call down the mercy of the skies

(B) express concern for the fortunes of fate

(C) are unheard in Heaven

(D) corrupt the stagnant mind

(E) call for specific favors

59. It can be inferred that the speaker's attitude toward the suppliant at the beginning of the poem and the sensuous beauties near the end is one of

(A) mild amusement   (D) uncritical awe

(B) measured disapproval   (E) violent hostility

(C) fond admiration

60. The poem is an example of which of the following verse forms?

(A) Heroic couplet   (D) Free verse

(B) Terza rima   (E) Blank verse

(C) Ballad meter

Section 2

TIME: 2 Hours
          3 Essay Questions

QUESTION 1. *(Suggested time — 40 minutes. This question counts one-third of the total essay-section score.)* Read the passage below carefully. Then write an essay explaining the narrator's attitude toward the "speaker" and analyzing the techniques the narrator uses to define the "speaker's" character.

> "Now, what I want is Facts. Teach these boys and girls nothing but Facts. Facts alone are wanted in life. Plant nothing else, and root out everything else. You can only form the minds of reasoning animals upon Facts: nothing else will ever be of any service to them. This is the principle on which I bring up my own children, and this is the principle on which I bring up these children. Stick to Facts, sir!"
>
> The scene was a plain, bare, monotonous vault of a school-room, and the speaker's square forefinger emphasized his observations by underscoring every sentence with a line on the schoolmaster's sleeve. The emphasis was helped by the speaker's square wall of a forehead, which had his eyebrows for its base, while his eyes found commodious cellarage in two dark caves, overshadowed by the wall. The emphasis was helped by the speaker's voice, which was inflexible, dry, and dictatorial. The emphasis was helped by the speaker's hair, which bristled on the skirts of his bald head, a plantation of firs to keep the wind from its shining surface, all covered with knobs, like the crust of a plum pie, as if the head had scarcely warehouse-room for the hard facts stored inside. The speaker's obstinate carriage, square coat, square legs, square shoulders—nay, his very neck-cloth, trained to take him by the throat with an unaccommodating grasp, like a stubborn fact, as it was—all helped the emphasis.
>
> "In this life, we want nothing but Facts, sir; nothing but Facts!"
>
> The speaker, and the schoolmaster, and the third grown person present, all backed a little, and swept with their eyes the inclined plane of little vessels then and there arranged in order, ready to have imperial gallons of facts poured into them until they were full to the brim.

From Hard Times *by Charles Dickens*

QUESTION 2. *(Suggested time — 40 minutes. This question counts one-third of the total essay-section score.)* Read the following poem carefully. Then write a

well-organized essay in which you discuss the attitude of the narrator towards
fame and death. Through careful analysis of the language and imagery, show how
the narrator's attitude is conveyed.

TO AN ATHLETE DYING YOUNG

The time you won your town the race
We chaired you through the market-place;
Man and boy stood cheering by,
And home we brought you shoulder-high.

To-day, the road all runners come,
Shoulder-high we bring you home,
And set you at your threshold down,
Townsman of a stiller town.

Smart lad, to slip betimes away
From fields where glory does not stay
And early though the laurel grows
It withers quicker than the rose.

Eyes the shady night has shut
Cannot see the record cut,
And silence sounds no worse than cheers
After earth has stopped the ears:

Now you will not swell the rout
Of lads what wore their honours out,
Runners whom renown outran
And the name died before the man.

So set, before its echoes fade,
The fleet foot on the sill of shade,
And hold to the low lintel up
The still-defended challenge-cup.

And round that early-laurelled head
Will flock to gaze the strengthless dead,
And find unwithered on its curls
The garland briefer than a girl's.

QUESTION 3. (*Suggested time — 40 minutes. This question counts one-third of the total essay-section score.*)

Leo Tolstoy once wrote, "All happy families are like one another; each unhappy family is unhappy in its own way." Select a literary work that portrays an unhappy family. Write an essay in which you explain the source of the family's unhappiness and the uniqueness of its misery.

You may choose your essay on a work from the list below or choose another work of comparable literary merit. Do not base your essay on a movie, television program or other adaptions of a work. Avoid plot summary.

Death of a Salesman	*Hard Times*
The Metamorphosis	*A Doll's House*
Wuthering Heights	*The Little Foxes*
Cry, the Beloved Country	*Native Son*
Ethan Frome	*Raisin in the Sun*
Too Late the Phalarope	*Hamlet*
A Long Day's Journey into Night	*Macbeth*
Nicholas Nickleby	*The Jungle*
Desire Under the Elms	*Oedipus Rex*
All My Sons	*King Lear*

TEST 3

ANSWER KEY

1.	(C)	16.	(B)	31.	(D)	46.	(B)
2.	(A)	17.	(C)	32.	(B)	47.	(A)
3.	(C)	18.	(E)	33.	(E)	48.	(D)
4.	(E)	19.	(B)	34.	(A)	49.	(C)
5.	(D)	20.	(E)	35.	(E)	50.	(C)
6.	(D)	21.	(A)	36.	(E)	51.	(E)
7.	(E)	22.	(E)	37.	(B)	52.	(B)
8.	(B)	23.	(A)	38.	(D)	53.	(B)
9.	(E)	24.	(A)	39.	(C)	54.	(A)
10.	(C)	25.	(C)	40.	(C)	55.	(B)
11.	(D)	26.	(E)	41.	(D)	56.	(C)
12.	(B)	27.	(D)	42.	(A)	57.	(D)
13.	(B)	28.	(C)	43.	(E)	58.	(E)
14.	(C)	29.	(B)	44.	(A)	59.	(B)
15.	(A)	30.	(B)	45.	(B)	60.	(A)

DETAILED EXPLANATIONS OF ANSWERS

TEST 3

Section 1

1. **(C)** Answer (A) is incorrect because it comes from a failure to recognize and understand the simile "like the jerk of a chain," which may suggest a chain gang, but which is not meant to be taken literally. Answer (B) is incorrect because it is inconsistent with previous observation by the narrator about "the careless, powerful look" Ethan had. Answer (C) is correct because his physical handicap creates a noticeable contrast with his "careless, powerful look." Answer (D) is incorrect because Ethan is clearly identified as one of the taller "natives." Answer (E) is incorrect because it, too, stems from a misreading of the line just as answer (A) does.

2. **(A)** Answer (A) is a correct interpretation of the figurative expression "lank longitude." Only this interpretation makes sense in the context where the "natives" are compared to the shorter and heavier "foreign breed" who have recently settled there. Answer (B) is incorrect because it interprets "longitude" in a sailing context, which it does not have here. Answer (C) is incorrect because nothing in the passage supports the idea of the "natives" being prejudiced towards their own kind. Answer (D) and (E) are incorrect because they are unsupported in the passage.

3. **(C)** Answer (A) is incorrect because a soliloquy is a device used in dramas and not in novels. Answer (B) is incorrect because the phrase is not a self-contradicting proposition. Answer (C) is correct. The storms are described as though they are humans going about the erecting of tents. Answer (D) is incorrect because ambiguity implies confusion about the situation and no such confusion exists in the phrase. Answer (E) is incorrect because dramatic irony is a statement made by a character that ironically describes the character's fate later in the story. That is not the case here.

4. **(E)** Answer (A) is incorrect because, although the passage mentions the lack of vitality and recreation in the community, it does not accuse the townfolk of

unsociability. Answer (B) is incorrect because the narrator does not link the two in his passage. Answer (C) is incorrect because their leaving the town was caused by the lack of village life and not the cause of it. Answer (D) is incorrect because the narrator mentions these as softening factors on the negating forces of the weather. Answer (E) is correct and is supported by lines 41–48.

5. **(D)** Answer (A) is incorrect because the strikers are not mentioned again after the narrator states that the strike kept him in Starkfield for the winter. Their conditions during the strike are not mentioned. Answer (B) is incorrect because the passage indicates that the villagers are undergoing an emotional starvation rather than a physical starvation. Answers (C) and (E) are incorrect because they are based on a misreading of the word garrison. The phrase is used figuratively in the passage, not literally. Answer (D) is correct because the long, confining winter has imprisoned the villagers.

6. **(D)** Answer (A) is incorrect because Ethan's appearance is more a matter of genetics, i.e., his size and height, than it is due to his residence in the town. Answer (B) is incorrect because it is contradicted by lines 3–4. Answer (C) is incorrect because Ethan retains these aspects of his appearance in spite of his personal history. Answer (D) is correct because the look on his face is a direct result of his personal history. Answer (E) is incorrect because the passage does not support it.

7. **(E)** Answer (A) is incorrect because it is not supported by anything in the passage. The word "degenerate" carries moral overtones unsuitable for describing weather in this passage. Answer (B) is incorrect because these artifacts of the outside culture are not degenerate in and of themselves as much as the cultural changes they encourage and convey. Answer (C) is incorrect because it is contrary to the meaning of lines 23–24. Answer (D) is incorrect because it erroneously connects the new age and the recurring season of winter. Answer (E) is correct because the trolley, the bicycle and rural mail delivery opened the village to outside corrupting influences that had not been experienced previously.

8. **(B)** Answer (A) is incorrect because only one sentence (lines 33–35) focuses on the narrator. Answer (B) is correct because the narrator's intent is signalled in lines 50–51. Answer (C) is incorrect because the narrator's offers descriptions as reasons why Ethan should have left long ago. Answer (D) is incorrect because Gow's statement about the winters is shown to be accurate. Answer (E) is incorrect because it substantiates the correctness of their decision to leave Starkfield.

9. **(E)** Answer (A) is incorrect because the narrator makes no references to the social life, at all. Answer (B) is incorrect because lines 46–48 contradict it. Answer (C) is incorrect because the narrator's descriptions reflect an infatuation with the clear blue days of mid-winter. Answer (D) is incorrect because lines 48–50 contradict it. Answer (E) is correct because lines 35–37 and 39–42 support it.

10. **(C)** Answer (A) is incorrect because the narrator speaks of an earlier day when the means of transportation were more limited in winter and, therefore, the influences of the outside world were also limited. Answer (B) is incorrect because this is an effect brought on the village by the winter. Answer (C) is correct because the narrator uses military siege imagery to describe the hold that winter has on the village. Answer (D) is incorrect because in the passage the carpenters are not a factor of any importance. Answer (E) is incorrect because it is based on a literal reading of figurative language used to describe winter.

11. **(D)** Answer (A) is incorrect because the narrator struck up some kind of relationship with Herman Gow. Answer (B) is incorrect because the narrator mentions the power house, the trolley, the bicycle and rural delivery. Answer (C) is incorrect because it is contradicted by "the deadness of the community" and the exodus of "the smart ones." Answer (D) is correct because it is supported by lines 52–53. Answer (E) is incorrect because line 33 indicates that the community possessed a closed and guarded personality.

12. **(B)** Answer (A) is incorrect because it is contradicted by lines 36–37. Answer (B) is correct because it is supported by lines 41–42 and 46–48. Answer (C) is incorrect because nothing in the passage gives support for either of these two assertions. Answer (D) is incorrect because winter exhausts them rather than invigorates them. Answer (E) is incorrect because Herman Gow is not a gossip. He is terse and reticent.

13. **(B)** Answer (A) is incorrect because the narrator expresses no amusement toward Ethan and there is no distrust expressed towards Ethan's motives. Answer (B) is correct because the sight of Ethan pulls the narrator up sharply and arouses his curiosity. Answer (C) is incorrect because the narrator expresses no sarcasm towards Ethan. He does not view Ethan as someone deserving criticism. Answer (D) is incorrect because Ethan's appearance intrigues the narrator but he has yet to learn anything about the man to evoke sympathy. Answer (E) is incorrect because the narrator is struck by this unusual man but there is nothing in his description to suggest a worshipful attitude.

14. **(C)** Answer (A) is incorrect in that it is derived from a limited focus on the word "starved." Answer (B) is incorrect because it is suggested by the pitching of tents but not supported by "cavalry" and "garrison." Answer (C) is correct because the narrator uses figurative language of a city besieged by a military assault. Answer (D) is incorrect because the tents and horses do not constitute a tournament. Answer (E) is incorrect because the connection with horses is in a military sense not a horse racing sense.

15. **(A)** Answer (A) is correct because there is no figurative language in this phrase. All the other answers contain figurative language.

16. **(B)** Answer (A) is incorrect because the three figures assert nothing about which they can be hypocritical or false about. They merely appear. Answer (B) is correct because it is supported by "stepp'd serene," "shades," "shadows," and "unhaunted quiet of all." Answer (C) is incorrect because although their white robes may suggest piety, there is no detail which supports "cheerful." Answer (D) is incorrect because it is contradicted by details like "bowed neck" and "stepp'd serene." Answer (E) is incorrect because nothing about their description hints at learning, nor does their general deportment support reclusiveness or being withdrawn.

17. **(C)** Answer (A) is incorrect because the speaker describes figures as though they were carved on a marble urn, but it is a figurative expression and not a real urn. Answer (B) is incorrect because it is based on a misreading of lines 17–20. Answer (C) is correct because Love, Ambition, and Poesy come to tempt him to abandon his summer indolence. Answer (D) is incorrect because it stems from a misreading of lines 43–48 in which the speaker describes his soul in terms of a beautiful garden. Answer (E) is incorrect because the three figures want to motivate the speaker to write, but he resists the temptation.

18. **(E)** Answer (A) is incorrect because there is no actual urn. The speaker merely likens them to the figures on an urn. Answer (B) is incorrect because there is no mention of Greek dead in the poem. Answer (C) is incorrect because there is no sun mentioned or implied in the opening stanza. Answer (D) is incorrect because "shades" in this context means ghosts from his past. Answer (E) is correct because it accurately depicts the ghostly aspect the three figures convey.

19. **(B)** Answer (A) is incorrect because the first stanza is entirely descriptive. Answer (B) is correct because the first stanza describes them and lines 25–30 specify who they are. Answer (C) is incorrect because no rule is presented in the first stanza. Answer (D) is incorrect because no question is posed in the first stanza. Answer (E) is incorrect because although the opening stanza does begin a story, it is not concluded in lines 25–30.

20. **(E)** Answer (A) is incorrect because the phrase "my pulse grew less and less" indicates just how drugged he was with the day's indolence. Answer (B) is incorrect because it stems from a misreading of "unhaunted" which in this context refers to the intrusion of the three figures on his leisure. Answer (C) is incorrect because the speaker offers the idea of a plot as one reason why they have appeared to him and he explains what that plot could be. Answer (D) is incorrect because "ripe" in this context does not mean fruitful but that it is the perfect time for nonproductive activity. Answer (E) is correct because it is supported by lines 19–20 where the speaker says that he wants to be haunted by nothingness. In other words, he wants to do nothing at all.

21. **(A)** Answer (A) is correct and is supported by lines 15–17. Answer (B) is incorrect because the change described is closer to the opposite of this movement. Answer (C) is incorrect because the demands of the three figures all imply a loss of freedom and the undertaking of pursuits which are very demanding. Answer (D) is incorrect. Although the speaker "ach'd for wings," they were not wings of an angel but wings of poetic inspiration. There was nothing pious or holy about them. Answer (E) is incorrect because nothing in the poem supports this movement.

22. **(E)** Answer (A) is incorrect because it stems from a misreading of line 34. Ambition arises from the heart's fever-fit and not the brain's. Answer (B) is incorrect because the speaker does not love in this poem. Love appears to him as a motivator urging him to write poetry. Answer (C) is incorrect because the the visitors represent reasons why he should be writing poetry. Answer (D) is incorrect because the speaker is unconcerned about the brevity of life or the certainty of death in this stanza. Answer (E) is correct because the speaker states that the three visitors cannot offer him anything equal to the indolence he luxuriates in.

23. **(A)** Answer (A) is correct because the speaker dismisses each as though these old and tried reasons for creating poetry can no longer work their magic on him. Answer (B) is incorrect because the visitors represent the three principal reasons why poets write. Answer (C) is incorrect because the speaker is immune to the powers of his visitors and will not become reinvolved in his craft. Answer (D) is incorrect because the visitors fail to do this, which makes them ineffective in their task. Answer (E) is incorrect because the enticements of love and ambition were unable to reach him. They want to interrupt senselessness not induce it.

24. **(A)** Answer (A) is correct because the speaker's description of his state and condition is rife with satisfaction. Answer (B) is incorrect because the lawn is a metaphor for the speaker's soul and not a real lawn at all. Answer (C) is incorrect because the speaker comments on the clouded morning but calmly notes that no showers followed. If they did, they would only bring on the beauties of May. Answer (D) is incorrect because it comes from a misreading of line 49. The speaker wants the visitors to leave as he is well satisfied with his current situation. Answer (E) is incorrect because it comes from a misreading of line 50. The speaker has no plans to shed tears; therefore, no tears have fallen on the skirts of his ghostly visitors.

25. **(C)** Answer (A) is incorrect because the speaker has been most consistent in his rejection of the three visitors and what they stand for. Answer (B) is incorrect because the time for anticipation is past. The speaker has refused to "be dieted with praise" which is a restatement of an old rejection of ambition. Answer (C) is correct because the speaker repeats the image of the urn with which he opened the poem. Answer (D) is incorrect because it is not supported by the

context of the poem. Answer (E) is incorrect because customarily new subjects are not introduced this late in a work, and none are introduced here.

26. **(E)** Answer (A) is incorrect because the open window lets in warmth but not the actual branches themselves. Line 47 states that the window pressed against a vine not a tree branch. Answer (B) is incorrect because no blossoms are mentioned, only "the budding warmth." Answer (C) is incorrect because the stanza states that the day is cloudy but line 45 states "no shower fell." Answer (D) is incorrect because the cloudy days do not produce distinct shadows. "Shadows" in line 49 is a reference to the three visitors. Answer (E) is correct because lay in this stanza means song and bird song is a usual element of a summer morning.

27. **(D)** Answer (A) is incorrect because line 53 states that he will not be "dieted with praise." Answer (B) is incorrect because lines 28–30 have him recognize his "demon Poesy" or in other words the challenge of his craft. Answer (C) is incorrect because the speaker recognizes one of the visitors as "Love" in line 25. Answer (D) is correct because this is what the speaker would have to give up if he heeded the visitor's call. Answer (E) is incorrect because this is the ultimate goal ambition strives for.

28. **(C)** Answer (A) is incorrect because the poem does not address the reader in this or any other stanza. Answer (B) is incorrect because although the lines reveal the poet's great talent, the speaker is intent on stating the reasons why the visitors will fail. Answer (C) is correct because in these lines the speaker sets down the sundry reasons why he cannot abandon his indolence to take up writing poetry. Answer (D) is incorrect because no point by point comparison is offered as would be necessary to create an analogy. Answer (E) is incorrect because the speaker does not tell a story in these lines.

29. **(B)** Answer (A) and (D) are incorrect because if this were the situation, the speaker would not bid the visitors to leave him. He would have need of them. Answer (B) is the correct answer because the context indicates that the speaker has no shortage of day visions. Answer (C) is incorrect because the speaker is not stating that a suitable time for day visions exists. He is stating that there are enough available for his needs. Answer (E) is incorrect because this choice implies a possible shortage of day visions, which is not the case.

30. **(B)** Answer (A) is incorrect because it is declared in line 18. Answer (B) is correct because this is contradicted by line 53, where the speaker rejects praise. Answer (C) is incorrect because it is supported by lines 38–40 and line 50. Answer (D) is incorrect because lines 33–34 chide Ambition for the feverish hopes it engenders in the heart. Answer (E) is incorrect because it is supported by line 32.

31. **(D)** Answer (A) is incorrect because this a device commonly found in

drama in which characters make ironic statements that come back to haunt them. Answer (B) is incorrect because the comma at the end of line 45 and at the end of this line make this line an end-stopped line. Answer (C) is incorrect because this literary form is a poem expressing great grief that is very intense and personal. This is not the case with this poem. Answer (D) is correct because it attributes to the "Morning" the human act of crying. Answer (E) is incorrect because a paradox is a self-contradictory statement and this is not.

32. **(B)** Answer (A) is incorrect because Rime royal is a seven line, iambic pentameter stanza and this is not. Answer (B) is correct because the lines of this poem contain five iambic feet. Answer (C) is incorrect because the lines are too short to be hexameter. Answer (D) is incorrect because Ballad meter has alternating lines of three and four feet. Answer (E) is incorrect because this poem does not rhyme every two lines.

33. **(E)** Answer (A) is incorrect because repetition is evident in numerous places, especially those involving the word "how." Answer (B) is incorrect because the opening sentence is a rhetorical question. Answer (C) is incorrect because line 56 contains an allusion to the story of the Phoenix. Answer (D) is incorrect in that the extensive comparison of the body to the farm is an analogy. Answer (E) is correct because the passage does not contain language which is consciously exaggerated for effect.

34. **(A)** Answer (A) is correct because lines 12–14 and 22–25 support it. Answer (B) is incorrect in that the speaker focuses on the causes of bodily disease and he does not express himself on its merits or demerits. Answer (C) is incorrect because the speaker is convinced that even our best efforts are no guarantee against disease, lines 18–25. Answer (D) is incorrect because lines 40–41 contradict this assertion. Answer (E) is incorrect because lines 57–59 state that perfection is only attainable in the next world.

35. **(E)** Answer (A) is incorrect in that the speaker is unconcerned with the problem of collecting rent. Answer (B) is incorrect because it arises from a misunderstanding of the health statements in the passage. Answer (C) is incorrect because it is based on a misreading of the lines in question which state the problem as one of paying the rent, not collecting it. Answer (D) is incorrect because it arises from a misunderstanding of "holy days" which the speaker intends to be understood as days of no labor. Answer (E) is correct because the body is compared to a farm being used by a sharecropper who must not only raise enough crops to survive on but he must also raise an additional amount to pay the rent.

36. **(E)** Answer (A) is incorrect because the speaker fears that it contains enough problems to render him bankrupt. Answer (B) is incorrect because nowhere in the passage does the speaker worry about competing with others. Answer

(C) is incorrect because the speaker is not concerned about making a profit from his farm. He wants to perfect it and free it from troubles. Answer (D) is incorrect because these are conditions of the soil which the speaker claims can be cured with outside help unlike the illness of the human body which he claims cannot be helped. Answer (E) is correct because it is supported by lines 16–18 and lines 43–45.

37. **(B)** Answer (A) is incorrect. The farm is an analogy for the body and does not exist as a real tangible object in the passage. Answer (B) is correct because the relatively everyday pain of a toothache, though it may be severe, should not daunt a man because he is supposed to be able to bear greater pain uncomplainingly. Answer (C) is incorrect because this concept is never mentioned in the immediate context of lines 7–8. Answers (D) and (E) are incorrect because although these conditions are true of a real farm and the analogous farm which the speaker refers to here, they are not the direct cause of fear referred to in line 7.

38. **(D)** Answer (A) is incorrect because man cannot abandon paying the rent, i.e., feeding himself, if he is to live and survive as expressed in lines 8–9. Answer (B) is incorrect because it is supported by line 11. Answer (C) is incorrect because the speaker states in lines 16–18 that the rent we must pay for life and its troubles usually exceeds our ability to survive. Answer (D) is correct because the cares and tribulations that afflict the living are not regarded as healthful by the speaker of the passage. Answer (E) is incorrect because the speaker views the tribulations of life as life-threatening by including in the rent he pays for life the dangerous and infectious diseases, lines 13–14.

39. **(C)** Answer (A) is incorrect because it is inconsistent with the story of Adam in Genesis and it arises from a misreading of "dressing" in line 14, which in this context means keeping in proper order. Answer (B) is incorrect because Adam is the one who does the rejecting as indicated in line 16. Answer (C) is correct because it is supported by lines 15–16 which states that it would not have made his brow sweat. Answer (D) is incorrect and arises from a misreading of lines 16–17. Our rent is greater than that needed to retain Adam in Paradise. Answer (E) is incorrect because line 15 indicates that the speaker sees the body as continually vulnerable to the onslaughts of disease.

40. **(C)** Answer (A) is incorrect because this is against the intent of the passage. There is no immunity against disease. Answer (B) is incorrect because it interprets the analogous situation of the body and farm literally. Answer (C) is the correct because "it" is supported by lines 23–25. Answer (D) is incorrect because the speaker sees the body as continually vulnerable to disease. Answer (E) is incorrect because the intent of the speaker is to stress the physical infirmities of the body not the spiritual ones.

41. **(D)** Answer (A) is incorrect because Mummy names the source of the help and not the help or "Physic" itself. Answers (B), (C) and (E) are all incorrect because they are not the antecedents of "it" in this sentence. Answer (D) is correct because "it," in the thinking of the times, refers to the only medicines or help available to the living from that of another body.

42. **(A)** Answer (A) is correct because the meaning of the line is that the labor required of Adam to remain in Paradise would not have required him to even sweat. To earn his bread by the sweat of his brow was one of the punishments suffered by Adam after he was expelled from Paradise. Answer (B) is incorrect because the required labor was already appropriate and, therefore, did not need to be correct, only performed. Answer (C) is incorrect for essentially the same reason (B) is wrong. Answer (D) is incorrect. While the principal analogy of the passage is a comparison between the body and a farm, the rent is not taken from any crop or product the body produces, but the feeding and care required to keep the body/farm healthy. Answer (E) is incorrect. It is contradictory to the sense of the statement. This word limited seems to make sense if it replaces "improved" but it expresses a meaning opposite to the intention of the author.

43. **(E)** Answers (A) and (D) are incorrect because they both contradict the final section of the meditation, which maintains that the body can only be improved in the next life. Answer (B) is incorrect because line 55 states that heat and cold were not factors. Answer (C) is incorrect because it arises from a misreading of line 55. Answer (E) is correct because it is supported by lines 53–56, which imply that the body is innately corrupt and unperfectable in this life.

44. **(A)** Answer (A) is correct because writer wants to convince the reader that our corrupt bodies can achieve perfection only in the next life. Answer (B) is incorrect because the last sentence does not refute the argument of the passage. Answer (C) is incorrect because the entire passage is a preparation for the truth of the final sentence. Answer (D) is incorrect because the images are of a diseased body and curing by a physician, and not related to the farm analogy. Answer (E) is incorrect because no such change takes place.

45. **(B)** Answer (A) is incorrect because it is supported by lines 23–24. Answer (B) is correct because it is contradicted by lines 57–59. Answer (C) is incorrect because it is supported by lines 16–18. Answer (D) is incorrect because it is supported by line 5. Answer (E) is incorrect because it is supported by lines 39–40.

46. **(B)** Answer (A) is incorrect because it is contradicted by the sense of lines 5–6. Answer (B) is correct because the pleasures of the past have lost their power and no longer please, as is indicated in line 6. The resulting mood is one of despondency. Answer (C) is incorrect because it is contradicted by lines 3–4 and 10. The verb "resigns" in line 12 describes the action taken by "Luxury" toward

the suppliant, not vice versa. Answer (D) is incorrect because although the pleasures of life have been dulled by age, there is nothing in the passage to suggest that the suppliant is bewailing his loss. Answer (E) is incorrect because the suppliant's senses have been stated by over indulgence and age, but the desire for pleasure is as strong as ever. He has not accepted his current situation.

47. **(A)**   Answer (A) is correct because it is supported by the second half of the line which describes time as being "impatient" to destroy the suppliant. Answer (B) is incorrect because time is pictured as waiting to pounce. Its passage had not been abated. Answer (C) is incorrect because it is contradicted by the word "impatient" in the second half of the line. Answer (D) is incorrect because the figurative implications of the word hovers suggests a bird of prey awaiting an opportunity to strike. Answer (E) is incorrect because it is not supported by the context of the passage.

48. **(D)**   Choice I is a metaphor for the mental and physical outlets of physical pleasure. Choice II is a metaphor for the products of the harvest season. Choice III is used in a literal sense for the different times of the year. Choice IV is used as a metaphor for the whole display of nature's gifts through out the year. The only answer that contains the three metaphorical expressions is Answer (D).

49. **(C)**   Answer (A) is incorrect because the suppliant's problems are not derived from bad medical treatment. They derive from disease and old age. Answer (B) is incorrect because the intent of the line is to focus on his greed not on his increasing pain. Answer (C) is correct because bad financial news makes his physical suffering all the more intense. This idea is further developed in lines 17–18. Answer (D) is incorrect because the losses are not individuals, as in war causalities, but financial losses. Answer (E) is incorrect because the blockades are metaphorical and not actual.

50. **(C)**   Answers (A) and (B) are incorrect because "maladies" or diseases invade his joints, not avarice. Answer (C) is correct and is supported by the word "unextinguished" in line 15. Answer (D) is incorrect because his financial set-backs are described as such, not his greed. Answer (E) is incorrect because the "maladies" press the blockade, not his greed.

51. **(E)**   Answer (A) is incorrect because it is supported by line 25, "peaceful days." Answer (B) is incorrect because it is supported by line 26, "congratulating conscience cheers" the nights. Answer (C) is incorrect because it is supported by line 32, "or a daughter mourns." Answer (D) is incorrect because it is supported by lines 23–24, "unperceived decay." Answer (E) is correct because the sense of line 36 is that "some" joys are still experienced, but the word "some" implies a decrease in number from previous days.

52. **(B)** Answer (A) is incorrect because it is contradictory to the intended meaning of the lines. Answer (B) is correct because the lines offer the idea that problems arise in life whether that life is virtuous or not. Answer (C) is incorrect because misfortune, according to the speaker, is part of the fabric of life. Nothing seems to exhaust it. Answer (D) is incorrect because it arises from a misreading of the word "wings" as though it relates to misfortune when it really relates to "minutes." Answer (E) is incorrect because time at the end of a life is weary even though misfortune strikes.

53. **(B)** Answer (A) is incorrect because it is supported by line 35, "decay pursues decay." Answer (B) is correct because it is contradicted by line 38, which implies that the old is replaced by the new. Answer (C) is incorrect because it is supported by line 33, which pictures "Merit" or fame as being laid out in a funeral display, meaning that it has died. Answer (D) is incorrect because it is supported by line 34, "Friendship claims a tear" as old companions die off. Answer (E) is incorrect because it is supported by line 31, which states the fact clearly.

54. **(A)** Answer (A) is correct because it identifies that the veteran of life, one who has lived to a great age, is unneeded, superfluous. Answer (B) is incorrect because "superfluous" is an adjective not an adverb. Answer (C) is incorrect because it is contrary to the sense of the statement. Answer (D) is incorrect because adjectives do not modify verbs. Answer (E) is incorrect because superfluous is not an adverb.

55. **(B)** Answer (A) is incorrect because the lines do not refer to the selfish and wicked, but to the virtuous. Answer (B) is correct because the "few" in line 41 refers to the "Worth" in line 40 which represent the virtuous. Answer (C) is incorrect because "unclouded" means that ships are unshaded by the storms that customarily wait over the gulf between life and death. Answer (D) is incorrect because no such comparison is made within these lines. Answer (E) is incorrect because the lines picture the virtuous as ships riding at anchor in the gulf of fate awaiting the breeze, etc., that will carry them on to the next life.

56. **(C)** Answer (A) is incorrect because it is supported by lines 51–52, "Each youth your slave." Answer (B) is incorrect because it is supported by the beginning of line 52, "Each nymph your rival." Answer (C) is correct because it is contradicted by lines 63-64, "Beauty falls betrayed." Answer (D) is incorrect because it is supported by line 49, "Who frown with vanity." Answer (E) is incorrect because it is supported by lines 46–47, which describe beauty as one eagerly engaged in the pursuit of pleasure.

57. **(D)** Answer (A) is incorrect because the lines detail the process whereby beauty abandons virtue and travels toward infamy. This is not an argument made earlier in the passage. Answer (B) is incorrect because the lines are not a digression. The lines personify human qualities in the manner of an allegory, but the meaning is very closely related to the theme the speaker has been developing.

Answer (C) is incorrect because the lines do not summarize. They detail the process of moral decay that beauty may undergo. Answer (D) is the correct answer because the lines describe the process whereby physical beauty may succumb to temptation. Answer (E) is incorrect because this section of the poem takes up a new issue: the dangers inherent in physical beauty. It does not constitute a counterargument but a further development of the theme.

58. **(E)** Answer (A) is incorrect because in line 70 the speaker raises the question, "Should no cries be raised to the skies?" The act itself is not considered unacceptable by the speaker. Answer (B) is incorrect because in line 69 the phrase "Must no dislike alarm," questions whether mankind can not properly ask Heaven about events which bring fear and worry. The implied answer in lines 73–74 is that the petitions can most certainly be raised, but Heaven alone will decide which outcome is best. Answer (C) is incorrect because it arises from a misreading of the beginning of line 72. Answer (D) is incorrect because in line 66 the speaker raises the question, "Are humans to express no curiosity about the future?" This is a question raised by the speaker, and not a fault attributed to those who make petitions to Heaven. Answer (E) is correct because it is supported by line 74.

59. **(B)** Answer (A) is incorrect because the speaker does not laugh nor smile at them. They have earned his disfavor because of their foolish actions. Answer (B) is correct because the speaker points out how each group has gone astray. How each finds little happiness in the lives that they lead. He notes their errors for the reader. Answer (C) is incorrect because the speaker does not admire these individuals nor does he express any fondness toward them. He is highly critical of their foolishness. Answer (D) is incorrect because the speaker is not uncritical of these individuals. He views them as individuals who are caught up in the vanity of human desires. Answer (E) is incorrect because the speaker highlights the folly both groups engage in, but he does not advocate their deaths or sufferings.

60. **(A)** Answer (A) is correct. Heroic couplets have five accents per line and every two lines rhyme, as is the case with this poem. Answer (B) is incorrect. Terza rima consists of three line stanzas. This poem has stanzas of much greater length. Answer (C) is incorrect. The lines in this poem have five accented syllables, while ballad meter alternates lines of four and three accents each. Answer (D) is incorrect. Free verse lines are of uneven length, whereas the lines of this poem are of equal length and rhyme. Answer (E) is incorrect. Blank verse may have the same number of accents per line as this poem but lacks rhyme.

Section 2

Essay 1

In this passage, the narrator's attitude towards the speaker is unsympathetic. The narrator draws a portrait of a stuffy, straight-edged, no-deviation-from-the-facts, knows-everything kind of man. This is a man who cannot see any beauty in life. He has pushed all the fascination and mystery out of life, and replaced it with facts. So many facts are inside him, he looks as though he is going to burst.

The narrator observes, "The speaker's square forefinger emphasized his observations by underscoring every sentence with a line on the schoolmaster's sleeve." The way the speaker uses his mind there is one set of rules that he lives by and he has no intention of deviating from them. He means every word he speaks with all his being.

The narrator makes wonderful use of the word "square." It is used to describe the speaker's finger, the "square wall" of his forehead, his "square coat," "square legs," and "square shoulders." It creates a clear picture of a person, chiseled out of rock, no roundness to him, no softness. He is just a hard, straight-path, all facts kind of man. This impression is further developed by the phrases the narrator uses to describe the speaker's eyes: "while his eyes found commodious cellarage in two dark caves, overshadowed by the wall." No smile or twinkle will ever find their way into this man's eyes.

The narrator describes the speaker's voice as "dry, inflexible and dictatorial," as is perfectly suitable for a man of facts. The speaker's neckcloth has him by the throat in an "unaccommodating grasp," as if to show that should he somehow let a nonfact slip out, it would strangle him.

Ironically, the narrator has this man of facts preach his message by using figurative language. The speaker states that, "Facts alone are wanted in life. Plant nothing else, and root out everything else." Even he cannot stick to the facts to describe the importance of facts. This detail tells us that the narrator detests this prophet of facts.

The narrator's portrait of the speaker is unflattering and critical. The narrator has achieved this effect through his repetition of the word "square," the details describing his eyes and his voice, and the ironic placement of figurative language in the mouth of a man of facts. He is, in short, an emotionless automaton.

Essay 1 — Comments

This essay accurately interprets the narrator's attitude toward the speaker in the passage. It reveals a perceptive understanding of the narrator's deliberate undercutting of the speaker's credibility as a man of fact by salting his speech with figurative language. There is a thorough discussion of the narrator's use of the word "square" and the psychological portrait it creates. While the writer does not discuss the cumulative effect created by the repetition of sentences beginning with the phrase, "The emphasis was helped" being made about the speaker's eyes and his neckcloth. The writer demonstrates stylistic maturity through the effective listing of descriptors in sentence two. On the whole the writing displays an effective command of sentence structure, diction and organization.

Essay 2

In "To an Athlete Dying Young," the narrator feels that death is a blessing to the young athlete. The narrator believes this because he knows that glory and fame are only temporary. They soon pass on and disappear.

The narrator in the first stanza remembers when the young athlete won the race and everyone "chaired" him through the town. In the second stanza the narrator describes how the same crowd now carries the athlete's coffin on their shoulders, in the same manner that they carried him triumphantly into the town on their shoulders in the past. Instead of lamenting over the untimely death of the athlete, the narrator surprisingly praises the youth for being smart enough to die before his glory faded. He points out to the youth that although fame came to him early in life, it disappears more quickly than does the rose, the symbol for beauty.

In the fourth stanza, the narrator states that now that the youth is dead, he will never see his record cut. Since the dead cannot hear, "After earth has stopped the ears," neither will the youth hear the cheers that will go up when his record is broken. Had the youth lived, the narrator points out in stanza five, then he would have joined the group of sad men who have outlived their fame and glory. Athletes whose names were known everywhere are now unknown because their reputations died before they did. The were the "Runners whom renown outran."

In the final two stanzas, the narrator tells the youth that he died unbeaten. Around him "the strengthless dead" will "flock" to gaze at the "unwithered" victory laurel that crowns his head for all eternity. In life athletic fame and ability last no longer than beauty in a girl. However, his fame will last because he died young.

The narrator is convinced that that fame and glory do not last. The dead athlete has now become a "townsman of a stiller town" and by joining the dead, he avoids the sad fate of all the living has-beens who once tasted glory and now live on in obscurity. The narrator completes the image of this "stiller town" by picturing the athlete's grave as the doorway to his new home.

The narrator broadens the scope of the poem by including the rose in stanza three and the reference to the girl in the last stanza. These two items serve as a counterpoint to athletic fame and ability symbolized by the victory laurel in the same stanzas. The narrator sees both of these qualities as transitory and fleeting. Knowing this, his attitude is to enjoy fame and beauty while they last because they are not eternal, unless we die like the athlete in this poem. Life is not eternal, and neither is strength nor swiftness nor beauty.

Essay 2 — Comments

This essay contains an accurate and perceptive analysis of the narrator's attitude toward fame and death. It reveals the writer's clear understanding of the poem, and it deals effectively with the "stiller town" imagery, including the two town processions that occur in the first two stanzas. The writer recognizes the parallel that the poet draws between the ephemeral athletic prowess of young man and the equally emphemeral beauty of young women. The discussion includes appropriate examples of diction and symbols used in the poem. It demonstrates stylistic maturity thorough an effective command of sentence structure, diction and organization. The writer has a command of a wide range of the elements of effective writing.

Essay 3

Shakespeare's *Hamlet* is a literary work that portrays an unhappy family. The source of this family's unhappiness is Claudius. It is a unique story of murder for lust, greed and vengence.

In order to become king, Claudius murdered his own brother. He further complicates matters by marrying his brother's wife, Gertrude, the queen. This arrangement can lead to nothing but disaster, and it does.

Hamlet, Gertrude's son and Claudius' nephew, resents his mother's hasty marriage that followed so quickly on his father's death. This situation is the initial reason for Hamlet's unhappiness at the opening of the play. Unhappiness turns into a desire for revenge when Hamlet learns from his father's ghost that Claudius murdered him.

King Claudius is the center of all the misery bestowed upon the family. His lust led him to murder his brother, and his treachery indirectly leads to the murders of Rosenkrantz and Guildenstern, two former classmates of Hamlet. Upon learning that Hamlet knows the truth, Claudius sets up an exhibition duel between Hamlet and Laertes, the son of Polonius, whom Hamlet murdered. The duel is devised to kill Hamlet and rid the king of an avenging menace. Unfortunately, the plan backfires. Hamlet ends up killing Laertes and vice versa. Gertrude dies after she sips a poisoned drink Claudius meant for Hamlet. Claudius could have stopped her, but his fear of revealing himself to Hamlet keeps him silent. Claudius dies by Hamlet's last thrust of vengence.

This is definitely a unique story. The family is royal and possessed of all the strange, distorted motives that accompany royalty. Claudius has corrupted everyone and everything, so much so that there was no turning back once he began to satisfy his wicked desires. His lust tempted a queen to commit adultery, and it made him murder his brother and marry his sister-in-law. Hamlet's misery over his murdered father and newly married mother could only be lessened by the death of the man who started it all. The unhappiness of the family was incurable. The family never achieved any kind of bonding. Its members remained strangers to each other from beginning to end.

Essay 3 — Comments

This essay accomplishes both requirements of the question. It correctly identifies the source of the family's unhappiness, and, more importantly, it explains the uniqueness of its misery. While it does summarize the plot of the play, it does not do it slavishly. The actions of the characters are explained in detail sufficient enough to understand motivation and cause and effect, but it avoids a blow-by-blow retelling of the plot. The essay gives ample evidence that the writer understood both the story and the question. It does so through an effective command of sentence structure, diction and organization. It reveals the writer's ability to control a wide range of the elements of effective writing.

THE ADVANCED PLACEMENT EXAMINATION IN

English Literature & Composition

TEST 4

1. Ⓐ Ⓑ Ⓒ Ⓓ Ⓔ
2. Ⓐ Ⓑ Ⓒ Ⓓ Ⓔ
3. Ⓐ Ⓑ Ⓒ Ⓓ Ⓔ
4. Ⓐ Ⓑ Ⓒ Ⓓ Ⓔ
5. Ⓐ Ⓑ Ⓒ Ⓓ Ⓔ
6. Ⓐ Ⓑ Ⓒ Ⓓ Ⓔ
7. Ⓐ Ⓑ Ⓒ Ⓓ Ⓔ
8. Ⓐ Ⓑ Ⓒ Ⓓ Ⓔ
9. Ⓐ Ⓑ Ⓒ Ⓓ Ⓔ
10. Ⓐ Ⓑ Ⓒ Ⓓ Ⓔ
11. Ⓐ Ⓑ Ⓒ Ⓓ Ⓔ
12. Ⓐ Ⓑ Ⓒ Ⓓ Ⓔ
13. Ⓐ Ⓑ Ⓒ Ⓓ Ⓔ
14. Ⓐ Ⓑ Ⓒ Ⓓ Ⓔ
15. Ⓐ Ⓑ Ⓒ Ⓓ Ⓔ
16. Ⓐ Ⓑ Ⓒ Ⓓ Ⓔ
17. Ⓐ Ⓑ Ⓒ Ⓓ Ⓔ
18. Ⓐ Ⓑ Ⓒ Ⓓ Ⓔ
19. Ⓐ Ⓑ Ⓒ Ⓓ Ⓔ
20. Ⓐ Ⓑ Ⓒ Ⓓ Ⓔ

21. Ⓐ Ⓑ Ⓒ Ⓓ Ⓔ
22. Ⓐ Ⓑ Ⓒ Ⓓ Ⓔ
23. Ⓐ Ⓑ Ⓒ Ⓓ Ⓔ
24. Ⓐ Ⓑ Ⓒ Ⓓ Ⓔ
25. Ⓐ Ⓑ Ⓒ Ⓓ Ⓔ
26. Ⓐ Ⓑ Ⓒ Ⓓ Ⓔ
27. Ⓐ Ⓑ Ⓒ Ⓓ Ⓔ
28. Ⓐ Ⓑ Ⓒ Ⓓ Ⓔ
29. Ⓐ Ⓑ Ⓒ Ⓓ Ⓔ
30. Ⓐ Ⓑ Ⓒ Ⓓ Ⓔ
31. Ⓐ Ⓑ Ⓒ Ⓓ Ⓔ
32. Ⓐ Ⓑ Ⓒ Ⓓ Ⓔ
33. Ⓐ Ⓑ Ⓒ Ⓓ Ⓔ
34. Ⓐ Ⓑ Ⓒ Ⓓ Ⓔ
35. Ⓐ Ⓑ Ⓒ Ⓓ Ⓔ
36. Ⓐ Ⓑ Ⓒ Ⓓ Ⓔ
37. Ⓐ Ⓑ Ⓒ Ⓓ Ⓔ
38. Ⓐ Ⓑ Ⓒ Ⓓ Ⓔ
39. Ⓐ Ⓑ Ⓒ Ⓓ Ⓔ
40. Ⓐ Ⓑ Ⓒ Ⓓ Ⓔ

41. Ⓐ Ⓑ Ⓒ Ⓓ Ⓔ
42. Ⓐ Ⓑ Ⓒ Ⓓ Ⓔ
43. Ⓐ Ⓑ Ⓒ Ⓓ Ⓔ
44. Ⓐ Ⓑ Ⓒ Ⓓ Ⓔ
45. Ⓐ Ⓑ Ⓒ Ⓓ Ⓔ
46. Ⓐ Ⓑ Ⓒ Ⓓ Ⓔ
47. Ⓐ Ⓑ Ⓒ Ⓓ Ⓔ
48. Ⓐ Ⓑ Ⓒ Ⓓ Ⓔ
49. Ⓐ Ⓑ Ⓒ Ⓓ Ⓔ
50. Ⓐ Ⓑ Ⓒ Ⓓ Ⓔ
51. Ⓐ Ⓑ Ⓒ Ⓓ Ⓔ
52. Ⓐ Ⓑ Ⓒ Ⓓ Ⓔ
53. Ⓐ Ⓑ Ⓒ Ⓓ Ⓔ
54. Ⓐ Ⓑ Ⓒ Ⓓ Ⓔ
55. Ⓐ Ⓑ Ⓒ Ⓓ Ⓔ
56. Ⓐ Ⓑ Ⓒ Ⓓ Ⓔ
57. Ⓐ Ⓑ Ⓒ Ⓓ Ⓔ
58. Ⓐ Ⓑ Ⓒ Ⓓ Ⓔ
59. Ⓐ Ⓑ Ⓒ Ⓓ Ⓔ
60. Ⓐ Ⓑ Ⓒ Ⓓ Ⓔ

AP EXAMINATION IN
ENGLISH LITERATURE
AND COMPOSITION

TEST 4

Section 1

TIME: 60 Minutes
             60 Questions

DIRECTIONS: *This test consists of selections from literary works and questions on their content, form, and style. After reading each passage or poem, choose the best answer to each question and blacken the corresponding space on the answer sheet.*

NOTE: Pay particular attention to the requirement of questions that contain the words NOT, LEAST, or EXCEPT.

<u>QUESTIONS 1–13.</u> Read the following poem carefully before you choose your answers.

> MY SOUL. I summon to the the winding ancient stair;
> Set all your mind upon the steep ascent,
> Upon the broken, crumbling battlement,
> Upon the breathless starlit air,
> 5 Upon the star that marks the hidden pole;
> Fix every wandering thought upon
> That quarter where all thought is done:
> Who can distinguish darkness from the soul?
>
> MY SELF. The consecrated blade upon my knees
> 10 Is Sato's ancient blade, still as it was,
> Still razor-keen, still like a looking glass

Unspotted by the centuries;
That flowering, silken, old embroidery, torn
From some court lady's dress and round
15   The wooden scabbard bound and wound,
Can, tattered, still protect, faded adorn.

MY SOUL. Why should the imagination of a man
Long past his prime remember things that are
Emblematical of love and war?
20   Think of ancestral night that can,
If but imagination scorn the earth
And intellect its wandering
To this and that and t'other thing,
Deliver from the crime of death and birth.

25   MY SELF. Montashigi, third of his family, fashioned it
Five hundred years ago, about it lie
Flowers from I know not what embroidery –
Heart's purple – and all these I set
For emblems of the day against the tower
30   Emblematical of the night,
And claim as by a soldier's right
A charter to commit the crime once more.

MY SOUL. Such fullness in that quarter overflows
And falls into the basin of the mind
35   That man is stricken deaf and dumb and blind,
For intellect no longer knows
Is from the Ought, or Knower from the Known –
That is to say, ascends to Heaven;
Only the dead can be forgiven;
40   But when I think of that my tongue's a stone.

MY SELF. A living man is blind and drinks his drop.
What matter if the ditches are impure?
What matter if I live it all once more?
Endure that toil of growing up;
45   The ignominy of boyhood; the distress
Of boyhood changing into man;
The unfinished man and his pain
Brought face to face with his own clumsiness;

The finished man among his enemies? –
50   How in the mane of Heaven can he escape

That defiling and disfigured shape
The mirror of malicious eyes
Casts upon his eyes until at last
He thinks that shape must be his shape?
55 And what's the good of an escape
If honor find him in the wintry blast?

I am content to live it all again
And yet again, if it be life to pitch
Into the frog-spawn of a blind man's ditch,
60 A blind man battering blind men;
Or into that most fecund ditch of all,
The folly that man does
Or must suffer, if he woos
A proud woman not kindred of his soul.

65 I am content to follow to its source
Every event in action or in thought;
Measure the lot; forgive myself the lot!
When such as I cast out remorse
So great a sweetness flows into the breast
70 We must laugh and we must sing,
We are blest by everything,
Everything we look upon is blest.

"A Dialogue of Self and Soul," *by William Butler Yeats*

1. The titles "My Self" and "My Soul," where they occur, indicate

    (A) which is being addressed by the poet

    (B) which is being defined

    (C) which is the favorite option of the poet at that point in time

    (E) which is speaking

    (E) which is playing devil's advocate to the other

2. In the poem, which of the following best describes the relationship between "My Self" and "My Soul?"

    (A) The soul is the essence of the self.

    (B) The soul's aims are in opposition to those of the self.

(C) The soul controls the self.

(D) The self controls the soul.

(E) The soul and the self avoid each other.

3. Which of the following devices is dominant in the first stanza (to line 8)?

(A) extended metaphor   (D) extended questioning

(B) repeated simile   (E) an expanded synecdoche

(C) personification

4. The "consecrated blade" (line 9) given to the poet by a Japanese named Sato is best interpreted as a symbol of

(A) a life of passion.

(B) a life ordered by courtly manner.

(C) a life "consecrated" by religious devotion.

(D) a life wounded and "tattered" by old age.

(E) a life ordered by attention to ancient commandments.

5. The sword and the tower stand in symbolic opposition as do

(A) the court lady's dress and the tattered scabbard

(B) death and birth

(C) day and night

(D) the blind man and the drunkard

(E) the ditch and the staircase

6. Lines 19–23 suggest that

(A) not even the darnkess of night can protect man from original sin.

(B) the use of the intellect is a protection against the mistakes of the imagination.

(C) a mind that wanders "to this and that ..." can scorn the earth.

(D) death and birth are scornful crimes against the human spirit.

(E) a spiritual life can save man from a life concerned only with death and birth.

7. Which of the following best states the Self's premise in stanza 6?

    (A) Each stage of life carries with it great unpleasantness.

    (B) Childhood is a time of great turmoil.

    (C) Old age is a time of realization and honor.

    (D) What others think of you is of no importance.

    (E) Blind men live lives of misery.

8. The "wintry blast" (line 56) is a metaphor for

    (A) hate

    (B) insensitivity from others

    (D) old age

    (D) insensitivity to others

    (E) troubled times

9. The images presented in the seventh stanza can best be understood to mean:

    (A) life casts us into different roles.

    (B) the shape of things to come cannot be discerned by anyone.

    (C) we often believe we are as others see us.

    (D) it is difficult to stand alone.

    (E) it is better not to judge others lest they judge us.

10. Which of the following best sums up what is said by the Self in stanza 8 ("I am content to live it all again")?

    (A) It is better to die than to live the life of the blind.

    (B) Life is not worth it if the blind lead the blind.

    (C) Without the love of a proud woman, life is worthless.

    (D) Living is worthwhile, no matter what the emotional costs.

    (E) Life is worthwhile only if men avoid folly.

11. Which of the following does the Self consider to be the "secret" to enjoying life?

    (A) Trusting God to help you avoid the perils of evil.

(B)   Avoiding the "life of the blind" at all costs.

(C)   Allowing for mistakes to be made along the way.

(D)   Not allowing yourself to feel guilty over past wrongs.

(E)   Being content to live the life of a mere mortal.

12.   The last three lines have the effect of

(A)   trivializing the Self's argument.

(B)   elevating the Self's argument into the realm of the Soul's.

(C)   transcending the difficulties of the argument by elation.

(D)   expanding the Self's argument.

(E)   providing a break in the regular rhyme of the poem.

13.   The structure of the poem suggests that

(A)   the Soul has won the argument.

(B)   the Self has won the argument.

(C)   both the Self and the Soul have come to a greater understanding.

(D)   neither the Self nor the Soul have altered their positions.

(E)   the poet will incorporate the opposing arguments as he continues his life.

QUESTIONS 14–29. Read the following passage carefully before you choose your answers.

The great fault of a modern school of poetry is that it is an experiment to reduce poetry to a mere effusion of natural sensibility; or what is worse, to divest it both of imaginary splendor and human passion, to surround the meanest objects with the morbid feelings and devouring egotism of the
5 writers' own minds. Milton and Shakespeare did not so understand poetry. They gave a more liberal interpretation both to nature and art. They did not do all they could to get rid of the one and the other, to fill up the dreary void with the Moods of their own Minds. They owe their power over the human mind to their having had a deeper sense than others of human life.
10 But to the men I speak of there is nothing interesting, nothing heroical, but themselves. To them the fall of gods or of great men is the same. They do not enter into the feeling. They cannot understand the terms. They are even debarred from the last poor, paltry consolation of an unmanly triumph

over fallen greatness; for their minds reject, with a convulsive effort and
15 intolerable loathing, the very idea that there ever was, or was thought to
be, anything superior to themselves. All that has ever excited the attention
and admiration of the world, they look upon with the most perfect indifference; and they are surprised to find that the world repays their indifference
with scorn. "With what measure they mete, it has been meted to them
20 again."

Shakespeare's imagination is of the same plastic kind as his conception of character or passion. "It glances from heaven to earth." Its movement is rapid and devious. It unites the most opposite extremes: or, as
Puck says, in boasting of his own feats, "puts a girdle round about the
25 earth in forty minutes." He seems always hurrying from his subject, even
while describing it; but the stroke, like the lightning's, is sure as it is
sudden. He takes the widest possible range, but from that very range he
has his choice of the greatest variety and aptitude of materials. He brings
together images the most alike, but placed at the greatest distance from
30 each other; that is, found in circumstances of the greatest dissimilitude.
From the remoteness of his combinations, and the celerity with which they
are effected, they coalesce the more indissolubly together.

From "On Shakespeare and Milton," by William Hazlitt

14. The primary distinction made in the first paragraph is one between

(A) the poetry of the senses and the poetry of imagination.

(B) the modern school of poetry and that of Shakespeare and Milton.

(C) the poetry of Shakespeare and the poetry of Milton.

(D) the poetry of egotism and the poetry of sensibility.

(E) the modern school of poetry and the poetry of human mood.

15. Which of the following best describes the function of the first sentence in the
first paragraph?

(A) It sarcastically provides evidence of the critic's intention.

(B) It establishes the critic as an authority.

(C) It clearly states the topic which the rest of the passage elucidates.

(D) It directly addresses a common misconception to prepare the ground
for a discussion of the critic's main topic.

(E) It advances an accepted viewpoint that therefore does not need extensive support in the rest of the paragraph.

16. The critic cited here seems particularly upset by what he terms the modernist's

    (A) "moods"   (D) "human passion"

    (B) "morbid feelings"   (E) "intolerable loathing"

    (C) "egotism"

17. In context, the sentence "They gave a more liberal interpretation both to nature and art" (line 6) suggests which of the following?

    (A) Shakespeare and Milton did not espouse the political conservatism of the modernists.

    (B) Shakespeare and Milton were tolerant in matters concerning nature and art.

    (C) Shakespeare and Milton did not understand poetry in the same way as the modernists.

    (D) The modernists had a greater right to their viewpoints than the Romantics.

    (E) The modern age is one of egotism.

18. The passage suggests that Classical Tragedy would not be of interst to the "modern school" because they

    (A) pay too much attention to their superiors and not enough to themselves.

    (B) do not see any difference between "the fall of gods or of great men."

    (C) they hate anything that holds the "admiration of the world."

    (D) they cannot deal with the scorn the critical world has for them.

    (E) they feel compelled to substitute their own "dreary world" for the real thing.

19. The author brings closure to his first paragraph by

    (A) stating that the modernists are as surprised at their reception as he is at their views.

    (B) implying that Biblical injunctions are still in force, even though the modernists may be unbelievers.

    (C) implying that the rest of the world is as indifferent to the modernists as they are to it.

(D) implying that the rest of the world scorns the modernists as much as he does.

(E) stating that there is nothing "heroical" in the modernist position.

20. Stylistically, the second paragraph is best characterized by the repeated use of

(A) descriptive adjectives   (D) assonance

(B) action verbs   (E) metaphor

(C) metaphor

21. The structure of the second paragraph is such that

(A) most of the following sentences reinforce the contentions of the first sentence.

(B) the final sentence has been arrived at inductively.

(C) the central theme of the paragraph is stated in the middle of the paragraph.

(D) it relies heavily for contextual meaning on the statements of the first paragraph.

(E) each sentence is dependent on the previous one in establishing meaning.

22. The critic demonstrates his admiration for Shakespeare in the second paragraph by

(A) using images from literary critics to reinforce his argument.

(B) praising Shakespeare repeatedly for doing simple tasks well.

(C) using occasional quotes from Shakespeare's poetry.

(D) speaking of Shakespeare's works in the same manner as he speaks of Milton's.

(E) describing Shakespeare's importance in grandiose terms such as "celerity."

23. The "girdle round about the earth" (lines 24–25) is best understood as

(A) Shakespeare's universal appeal.

(B) Shakespeare's ability to give form to indiscriminate images.

(C) Shakespeare's ability to discuss all topics.

(D) Shakespeare's capacity to bring together extremes.

(E) Shakespeare's ability to communicate quickly using appropriate symbols.

24. The critic suggests light criticism of Shakespeare for his

(A) almost "plastic" conception of character.

(B) need to bring dissimilar images together.

(C) deviousness in character protrayal.

(D) hurrying from one subject to another.

(E) attempting to explain too much in his writing.

25. At the end of the second paragraph, the critic distinguishes between similar images and

(A) dissimilar meanings.   (D) indissoluble combinations.

(B) indissoluble materials.   (E) dissimilar circumstances.

(C) dissimilar ranges.

26. The critic focuses the reader's attention on Shakespeare by

(A) giving a plethora of examples from his works.

(B) the repeated use of pronouns for reference.

(C) making exaggerated claims as to the writer's genius.

(D) describing the Bard with Latin-based words of praise.

(E) attempting to describe Shakespeare's imagination.

27. The use of the words "dissimilitude" and "indissolubly" has the effect of

(A) providing closure with the opening contention in the first sentence of the second paragraph.

(B) providing poetic consonance that is appropriate to the discussion of Shakespeare's works.

(C) providing a point of contrast to concepts of similarity as advanced in the preceding sentences.

(D) providing parallelism between the ideas contained in the two sentences.

(E) providing a further description of the range of Shakespeare's writing.

28. Hazlitt's two paragraphs might best be distinguished by which of the following stylistic changes?

(A) A shortening of sentence length.

(B) Increased use of punctuation.

(C) Decreased attention to his opening contention.

(D) Increased attention to the foibles of the "modern school."

(E) Decreased use of descriptive adjectives.

29. The development of the argument in paragraphs one and two can best be described as

(A) moving from the specific to the general.

(B) moving from the speculative to the abstract.

(C) moving from the general to the specific.

(D) moving from the specific to the speculative.

(E) moving from contention to speculation.

QUESTIONS 30–39. Read the following poem carefully before you choose your answers.

The Leap

The only thing I have of Jane MacNaughton
Is one instant of a dancing-class dance.
She was the fastest runner in the seventh grade,
My scrapbook says, even when boys were beginning
5 To be as big as the girls,
But I do not have her running in my mind,
Though Frances Lane is there, Agnes Fraser,
Fat Betty Lou Black in the boys-against-girls
Relays we ran at recess: she must have run

10 Like the other girls, with her skirts tucked up
So they would be like bloomers,
But I cannot tell; that part of her is gone.
What I do have is when she came,
With the hem of her skirt where it should be

15 For a young lady, into the annual dance
     Of the dancing class we all hated, and with a light
     Grave leap, jumped up and touched the end
     Of one of the paper-ring decorations

     To see if she could reach it. She could.
20 And reached me now as well, hanging in my mind
     From a brown chain of brittle paper, thin
     And muscular, wide-mouthed, eager to prove
     Whatever it proves when you leap
     In a new dress, a new womanhood, among the boys
25 Whom you easily left in the dust
     Of the passionless playground. If I said I saw
     In the paper where Jane MacNaughton Hill,

     Mother of four, leapt to her death from a window
     Of a downtown hotel, and that her body crushed-in
30 The top of a parked taxi, and that I held
     Without trembling a picture of her lying cradled
     In that papery steel as though lying in the grass,
     One shoe idly off, arms folded across her breast,
     I would not believe myself. I would say
35 The convenient thing, that it was a bad dream
     Of maturity, to see that eternal process

     Most obsessively wrong with the world
     Come out of her light, earth-spurning feet
     Grown heavy: would say that in the dusty heels
40 Of the play ground some boy who did not depend
     On speed of foot, caught and betrayed her.
     Jane, stay where you are in my first mind:
     It was odd in that school, at that dance.
     I and the other slow-footed yokels sat in corners
45 Cutting rings out of drawing paper

     Before you leapt in your new dress
     And touched the end of something I began,
     Above the couples struggling on the floor,
     New men and women clutching at each other
50 And prancing foolishly as bears: hold on
     To that ring I made for you, Jane —
     My feet are nailed to the ground

By dust I swallowed thirty years ago —
While I examine my hands.

"The Leap," by James Dickey. Copyright 1964 by James Dickey. Reprinted from POEMS 1957–1967 by permission of University Press of New England.

30. In this poem, the speaker is mainly

   (A) interpreting and reevaluating a past event.

   (B) struggling to create an image.

   (C) examining the mystery of death.

   (D) reminiscing about his school days.

   (E) asserting his individualism.

31. The first stanza of the poem serves to

   (A) set the tone.

   (B) establish the poem's main symbols

   (C) set Jane apart from others.

   (D) contrast the speaker with Jane.

   (E) introduce the speaker's envy of Jane.

32. The phrases "a new womanhood" (line 24) and "New men and women" (line 49) refer to

   (A) children acting like adults.

   (B) graduates of the dancing school.

   (C) adults looking back on their childhoods.

   (D) the "yokels" making paper ring decorations.

   (E) all of the above.

33. By pairing the words "light" and "Grave" (lines 16, 17) to describe Jane's first leap, the speaker

   (A) unknowingly contradicts himself.

   (B) tells how he saw her leap then and now.

   (C) places her leap out of time.

    (D)   tells how her leap seemed carefree but was seriously executed.

    (E)   compares her first leap to her "second" one.

34.   "That eternal process / Most obsessively wrong with the world" (lines 36–37) is

    (A)   youth.   (D)   age.

    (B)   time.   (E)   death.

    (C)   memory.

35.   Jane's first leap seems to represent _____ while her second leap seems to represent _____ .

    (A)   the past; the present

    (B)   aspiration and achievement; frustration of hopes and dreams

    (C)   immortality; mortality

    (D)   Both (A) and (C)

    (E)   Both (B) and (C)

36.   Besides the leap, the other dominant symbol in this poem is/are

    (A)   the scrapbook (line 4).

    (B)   the paper-ring decorations (line 18).

    (C)   the new dress (line 24).

    (D)   the picture (line 31).

    (E)   the speaker's hands (line 54).

37.   Which of the following are true of lines 50–54?

    I.   They show the speaker acknowledging the fact that despite his yearnings, he can only travel in memory, not time.

    II.   They show the speaker, differentiating between his image of Jane and the actual, physical Jane in the newspaper story.

    III.   They show the speaker certifying his connection to Jane.

    (A)   I only   (D)   II and III only

    (B)   II only   (E)   I, II, and III

    (C)   I and II only

38. The break in the poem which occurs every nine lines

    (A) creates suspense.

    (B) divides the poem into stanzas, each concentrating on a clearly definable subject.

    (C) shows where the speaker tries to gather his thoughts.

    (D) makes the poem flow more easily.

    (E) All of the above

39. As the speaker recalls Jane's first leap he says that she "reached me now as well" (line 20). This serves to

    (A) begin the movement in the poem that will take it into present time.

    (B) reveal the speaker's secret love for Jane.

    (C) demonstrate a feeling of nostalgia for the friendship that the speaker had with Jane.

    (D) help the speaker realize that Jane loved him.

    (E) transfer the focus of the poem from Jane to the speaker.

QUESTIONS 40–47. Read the following poem carefully and then answer the questions.

> Behold her, single in the field,
> Yon solitary Highland lass!
> Reaping and singing by herself;
> Stop here, or gently pass!
> 5 Alone she cuts and binds the grain,
> And sings a melancholy strain;
> O listen! for the Vale profound
> Is overflowing with the sound.
>
> No Nightingale did ever chaunt
> 10 More welcome notes to weary bands
> Of travelers in some shady haunt,
> Among Arabian sands;
> A voice so thrilling ne'er was heard
> In springtime from the Cuckoo bird,
> 15 Breaking the silence of the seas
> Among the farthest Hebrides.

Will no one tell me what she sings?
Perhaps the plaintive numbers flow
For old, unhappy, far-off things,
20 And battles long ago;
Or is it some more humble lay,
Familiar matter of today?
Some natural sorrow, loss, or pain,
That has been, and may be again?

25 Whate'er the theme, the Maiden sang
As if her song could have no ending;
I saw her singing at her work,
And o'er the sickle bending –
I listened, motionless and still;
30 And, as I mounted up the hill,
The music in my heart I bore,
Long after it was heard no more.

by William Wordsworth

40. The first stanza is stylistically dominated by

    (A)   agrarian imagery.   (D)   images of solitude.

    (B)   Scots dialect.   (E)   spatial allusions.

    (C)   lyrical references.

41. The comment that "No Nightingale did ever chaunt / More welcome notes" (lines 9–10) implies that the speaker

    (A)   knows he is ignoring the meaning of the song in favor of its context.

    (B)   is afraid he is being deceived by his inability to understand the words of the song.

    (C)   is not yet aware of his inability to understand the words of the song.

    (D)   is already bothered by the "melancholy" nature of the song.

    (E)   is charmed by the "melancholy" nature of the song.

42. The basic structure of stanza three relies on

    (A)   a listing of the possibilities of the lass' sorrows.

    (B)   a listing of the possibilities of the lass' songs.

    (C)   a movement through the time of possibilities.

(D)   a movement through emotions of possibilities.

(E)   a movement through space of the songs' concerns.

43.   In context, the word "numbers" (line 18) is best interpreted to mean

(A)   the repeated movements of her sickle.

(B)   the words of her song.

(C)   the number of sheafs she binds with each song.

(D)   syllables.

(E)   many pieces of music (as in "let's hear the next number").

44.   The use of the word "plaintive" implies that the song is one that reflects

(A)   a need to complain.

(B)   a legal problem.

(C)   the problems involved in leading a simple life close to nature.

(D)   the problems of an agrarian life.

(E)   suffering and woe.

45.   In the last stanza, Wordsworth implies that

(A)   the girl has spent much of her life in song.

(B)   the girl will spend much of her life working.

(C)   work will keep the girl satisfied the rest of her life.

(D)   song is what makes the girl's work satisfying.

(E)   neither work nor song will ever lighten the girl's emotional burden.

46.   Wordsworth's statement at the end of the poem ("…as I mounted up the hill,/ The music in my heart I bore,") might best be paraphrased as:

(A)   Her song made a strong impression.

(B)   It was tragic to see a young life wasted in manual labor.

(C)   Even though I am well-known, I remember her ordinary life.

(D)   As I grew older, I took her song and her story with me.

(E)   Even though my ideas are lofty ones, I respect the virtues of hard work.

47. The solitary reaper might best be interpreted as

    (A) a symbol of Death.

    (B) a symbol of the passage of time.

    (C) a symbol of loneliness.

    (D) a symbol of human labor.

    (E) a symbol of the burden of life's sorrows.

QUESTIONS 48–60. Read the following passage carefully and then answer the questions.

    She had suffered badly during the period of poverty. Nothing, however, could shake the curious, sullen, animal pride that dominated each member of the family. Now, for Mabel, the end had come. Still she would not cast about her. She would follow her own way just the same. She would
5   always hold the keys of her own situation. Mindless and persistent, she endured from day to day. Why should she think? Why should she answer anybody? It was enough that this was the end, and there was no way out. She need not pass any more darkly along the main street of the small town, avoiding every eye. She need not demean herself any more, going into the shops and buying the cheapest food. This was at an end. She thought of
10 nobody, not even of herself. Mindless and persistent, she seemed in a sort of ecstasy to be coming nearer to her fulfillment, her own glorification, approaching her dead mother, who was glorified.

    In the afternoon, she took a little bag, with shears and sponge and a small scrubbing-brush, and went out. It was a gray, wintry day, with
15 saddened dark green fields and an atmosphere blackened by the smoke of foundries not far off. She went quickly, darkly along the causeway, heeding nobody, through the town to the churchyard.

    There she always felt secure, as if no one could see her, although as a matter of fact she was exposed to the stare of everyone who passed along
20 under the churchyard wall. Nevertheless, once under the shadow of the great looming church, among the graves, she felt immune to the world, reserved within the thick churchyard wall as in another country.

    Carefully, she clipped the grass from the grave, and arranged the pinky-white, small chrysanthemums in the tin cross. When this was done,
25 she took an empty jar from a neighboring grave, brought water, and carefully, most scrupulously sponged the marble headstone and coping-stone.

    It gave her sincere satisfaction to do this. She felt in immediate contact with the world of her mother. She took minute pains, went through the park

30   in a state bordering on pure happiness, as if in performing this task she
came into a subtle, intimate connection with her mother. For the life she
followed here in the world was far less real than the world of death she
inherited from her mother.

"The Horse Dealer's Daughter," from The Complete Short Stories of D.H. Lawrence, *Vol.
II, by D.H. Lawrence. Reprinted by permission of Viking-Penguin, Inc.*

48.   Which of the following best summarizes the subject of the first paragraph of
the passage?

   (A)   The debilitating effect of poverty on a family.

   (B)   The liberating effects of impoverishment.

   (C)   The ability of hope to overcome the debilitating effects of poverty.

   (D)   The ecstasy that results when death is imminent.

   (E)   The insanity caused by total despair.

49.   The tone of the author toward Mabel is

   (A)   sympathetic.   (D)   patronizing.

   (B)   sarcastic.   (E)   uninterested.

   (C)   horrified.

50.   The author implies that Mabel's questioning

   (A)   is an act of information gathering.

   (B)   is an expression of self-doubt.

   (C)   is a defiant expression of self-assurance.

   (D)   is simply an attempt by the author to indicate what she is thinking.

   (E)   is an attempt by the author to gain the reader's sympathy for her
situation.

51.   The attainment of glory is associated in Mabel's mind with

   (A)   the attainment of riches.

   (B)   the loss of riches.

   (C)   the pursuit of spiritual immortality.

   (D)   the arrival of death.

   (E)   the triumph of the individual mind.

52. Mabel's liberation from misery is based mostly on the fact that she

    (A)   no longer has to contend with poverty.

    (B)   is full of a sullen pride, like the rest of her family.

    (C)   no longer thinks of herself.

    (D)   has grown closer to her dead mother.

    (E)   no longer has to demean herself when she goes to town.

53. The second paragraph of this selection is remarkable stylistically in that it

    (A)   portrays a woman more involved with death than with life.

    (B)   sustains a pattern of death imagery almost throughout.

    (C)   concentrates on seemingly unimportant minor details.

    (D)   uses natural description to portray Mabel's despair.

    (E)   is written in a style unlke the surrounding paragraphs.

54. The author's placement of the description of Mabel's bag in the same paragraph with the description of the landscape

    (A)   underscores the stylistic challenges the author typically presents to the reader.

    (B)   indicates that Mabel is as intent on eliminating the grime of her life as she is in "scrubbing" the soot off her mother's grave.

    (C)   foreshadows her impending suicide.

    (D)   is meant to indicate the disorder of her mind; no well-adjusted person would go out in this weather.

    (E)   reinforces the picture of Mabel as a character who gives no outward indication of her "dark" intentions.

55. The third paragraph of this passage ("There she always...") (line 19) presents the reader with the basic contradiction that

    (A)   Mabel beleves the graveyard will not hide her; she is more obvious to the prying public when she goes there.

    (B)   Mabel feels immune from the world even though she is more exposed to it.

    (C)   Mabel can feel most alive surrounded by a world of death.

(D)   Mabel can only find independence by communing with the spirit of her dead mother.

(E)   Mabel can only feel secure within the insecure and threatening world of death.

56.   The details supplied in the description of the graveyard clearing indicate that

(A)   Mabel has not cleaned the grave in a long time.

(B)   Mable is unique in cleaning her mother's grave.

(C)   cleaning her mother's grave is a fulfilling, even happy task.

(D)   it is unusual for Mabel to clean the grave alone.

(E)   headstone cleaning is a seasonal occurrence.

57.   Mabel enjoys cleaning her mother's grave because

(A)   she believes she is defying the world of death by entering its confines.

(B)   she is able to escape her real world of troubles by contemplating the afterlife.

(C)   she feels she is returning all the favors her mother did for her when she was alive

(D)   she enjoys the park-like atmosphere of the graveyard.

(E)   she comes in contact with the more real world of death.

58.   The churchyard wall represents for Mabel

(A)   the boundary between the living and the dead.

(B)   a border between her native land and that of foreigners.

(C)   a mere physical obstacle of little consequence.

(D)   a forbidding symbol of death.

(E)   a religious boundary, representing hallowed ground.

59.   Which of the following best describes the movement in this passage?

(A)   From the crowded world of her house to the solitary world of the graveyeard.

(B)   From the careworn world of the town to the carefree world of death.

(C)   From the solitary world of her house to communion with her mother at the graveyard.

(D)   From the earthly connections of her house to the otherworldly in the graveyard.

(E)   From the critical world of the town to the liberating world of the graveyard.

60.   In line 16, "saddened dark green fields" is an example of which of the following?

(A)   Hyperbole

(B)   Irony

(C)   Personification

(D)   Apostrophe

(E)   Metaphor

Section 2

TIME: 2 Hours
3 Essay Questions

QUESTION 1. *(Suggested time — 40 minutes. This question counts one-third of the total essay-section score.)* Read the following poem carefully. Then write an essay in which you analyze how the speaker of the poem portrays the larger world to "my love" — the nature of this portrayal, the manner in which it is reinforced by the poet's choice of words, and in what ways this sometimes harsh portrayal is qualified. Develop your essay with specific references to the text of the poem.

Lay Your Sleeping Head, My Love

Lay your sleeping head, my love,
Human on my faithless arm;
Time and fevers burn away
Individual beauty from
Thoughtful children, and the grave
Proves the child ephemeral:
But in my arms till break of day
Let the living creature lie,
Mortal, guilty, but to me
The entirely beautiful.

Soul and body have no bounds:
To lovers as they lie upon
Her tolerant enchanted slope
In their ordinary swoon,
Grave the vision Venus sends
Of supernatural sympathy,
Universal love and hope;
While an abstract insight wakes
Among the glaciers and the rocks
The hermit's sensual ecstasy.

Certainty, fidelity
On the stroke of midnight pass
Like vibrations of a bell,
And fashionable madmen raise
Their pedantic boring cry:

Every farthing of the cost,
All the dreaded cards foretell,
Shall be paid, but from this night
Not a whisper, not a thought,
Not a kiss nor look be lost.

Beauty, midnight, vision dies:
Let the winds of dawn that blow
Softly round your dreaming head
Such a day of sweetness show
Eye and knowing heart may bless,
Find the mortal world enough;
Noons of dryness see you fed
By the involuntary powers,
Nights of insult let you pass
Watched by every human love.

QUESTION 2. *(Suggested time — 40 minutes. This question counts one-third of
the total essay-section score.)* The passage quoted below is the opening of
Thoreau's persuasive essay "Civil Disobedience." Read the passage carefully.
Then write an essay in which you analyze the strategies or devices (organization,
diction, tone, use of detail) that make Thoreau's appeal compelling and effective
for his educated audience.

I heartily accept the motto, — "That government is best which governs
least"; and I should like to see it acted up to more rapidly and systemati-
cally. Carried out, it finally amounts to this, which also I believe, — "That
government is best which governs not at all"; and when men are prepared
for it, that will be the kind of government which they will have. Government is at best but an expedient; but most governments are usually, and all
governments are sometimes, inexpedient. The objections which have been
brought against a standing army, and they are many and weighty, and
deserve to prevail, may also at last be brought against a standing government. The government itself, which is only the mode which the people
have chosen to execute their will, is equally liable to be abused and
perverted before the people can act through it. Witness the present Mexican war, the work of comparatively a few individuals using the standing
government as their tool; for, in the outset, the people would not have
consented to this measure.

This American government — what is it but a tradition, though a recent one, endeavoring to transmit itself unimpaired to posterity, but each instant losing some of its integrity? It has not the vitality and force of a single living man; for a single man can bend it to his will. It is a sort of wooden gun to the people themselves. But it is not the less necessary for this; for the people must have that idea of government which they have. Governments show thus how successfully men can be imposed on, even impose on themselves, for their own advantage. It is excellent, we must all allow. Yet this government never of itself furthered any enterprise, but by the alacrity with which it got out of its way. It does not keep the country free. It does not settle the West. It does not educate. The character inherent in the American people has done all that has been accomplished; and it would have done somewhat more, if the government had not sometimes got in its way. For government is an expedient by which man would fain succeed in letting one another alone; and, as has been said, when it is most expedient, the governed are most let alone by it. Trade and commerce, if they were not made of India rubber, would never manage to bounce over the obstacles which legislators are continually putting in their way; and, if one were to judge these men wholly by the effects of their action and not partly by their intentions, they would deserve to be classed and punished with those mischievous persons who put obstructions on the railroads.

But to speak practically and as a citizen, unlike those who call themselves no-government men, I ask for, not at once no government, but at once a better government. Let every man make known what kind of government would command his respect, and that will be one step toward obtaining it.

From Civil Disobedience *by Henry David Thoreau*

QUESTION 3. (*Suggested time — 35 minutes. This question counts one-third of the total essay-section score.*) In great literature writers often create cultural, governmental, and other social situations in order to make important and even revolutionary statements on the nature of humanity. Choose a work of literary merit in which the author creates such a situation. In a well-organized essay, define that situation and the statement the author is making, and explain how the author's choice of that situation contributes to the effective communication of the statement.

The following titles are listed as suggestions. You may base your essay on one of them or choose another work of equivalent literary merit on which to write.

A Separate Peace   *The Grapes of Wrath*

Crime and Punishment   *All My Sons*

The Stranger

A Tale of Two Cities

Catch-22

Julius Caesar

Nineteen Eighty Four

Brave New World

Lord of the Flies

Les Misérables

Death of a Salesman

Slaughterhouse Five

Native Son

Inherit the Wind

Macbeth

Gulliver's Travels

Animal Farm

Catcher in The Rye

TEST 4

ANSWER KEY

1. (D)	16. (C)	31. (C)	46. (D)
2. (B)	17. (B)	32. (B)	47. (E)
3. (A)	18. (B)	33. (D)	48. (D)
4. (A)	19. (D)	34. (E)	49. (A)
5. (C)	20. (B)	35. (E)	50. (C)
6. (E)	21. (A)	36. (B)	51. (D)
7. (A)	22. (C)	37. (E)	52. (C)
8. (C)	23. (D)	38. (A)	53. (B)
9. (C)	24. (D)	39. (A)	54. (B)
10. (D)	25. (E)	40. (D)	55. (B)
11. (D)	26. (B)	41. (C)	56. (C)
12. (C)	27. (D)	42. (C)	57. (E)
13. (B)	28. (A)	43. (D)	58. (B)
14. (B)	29. (C)	44. (E)	59. (D)
15. (C)	30. (A)	45. (B)	60. (C)

DETAILED EXPLANATIONS OF ANSWERS

TEST 4

Section 1

1. **(D)** "My Self" and "My Soul" are negated in a dialogue with each other which reflects the poet's psychic conflict. The titles can be understood as if they were character names repeated in a script, signifying which is speaking at a given time. There is no function implied by the titles (as in (C) and (E)), nor does the dialogue reveal they are concerned with defining themselves, (B). They are addressing each other directly and therefore (A) does not apply.

2. **(B)** The soul is summoning the poet away from a life of action and passion (self) and toward one of wisdom and reflection. The debate revolves around these opposing claims. Neither yet controls the other, or there would be no free debate; by the same token, (E) is not the best choice, as this active give and take implies that neither avoids the other.

3. **(A)** Here, the "winding ancient stair" is a metaphor for spiritual ascent. This metaphor is extended in lines 2 and 3, ("steep ascent / broken battlement") after which the life of contemplation is compared to the arrival at a place of "starlit air" at the top of the "winding stair." There are no similes in the stanza — no comparisons using like or as; nor is there any questioning. Any personification is obscure and most likely to break down under scrutiny, as the image is too complex. Synecdoche could be a possibility with any particular image (e.g., saying "50 sails" for "50 ships" — the part represents the whole), but is not worth considering when images are not in isolation.

4. **(A)** The Soul in the next stanza refers to Sato's blade as "emblematical of love and war" (line 19). This is the slanted view of the opposition. The Self interprets it as somewhat tattered on the outside, but still "razor-keen" in its capabilities, especially considering that the poet is older (although the opposition refers to the poet in the next stanza as "long past his prime" (line 18)).

5. **(C)** The Soul urges the Self to "Think of ancestral night" (line 20) and, in

257

the fourth stanza, the Self sets flowers "for emblems of the day against the tower / Emblematical of the night," in effect, accepting the Soul's challenge. The voices that were first opposed now share a common syllogism: the life of the tower is to the life of the sword as night is to day.

6.   **(E)**   This argument of the Soul in opposition to that of the Self restates its basic premise that a life devoted to action and passion can lead men into folly, while a life of contemplation (the Soul) can transcend this limited existence. There is much that is traditional in this argument, especially given the social constraints and propriety of the Victorian Age.

7.   **(A)**   This stanza is a catalog of miseries of every stage of life; no stage is without its "ignominy." This is a given in the Self's argument. The question, "Is life worth it?" is what is important.

8.   **(C)**   Images of winter are traditionally meant to signify old age and approaching death. This use is best seen historically in the Shakespearean Sonnets (see "That Time of Year Thou Mayst In Me Behold") and is honored by poets to the present day.

9.   **(C)**   In this complex series of images, the poet describes the inescapability of a victim of "malicious eyes" believing that what others think of him is an accurate picture of what he really is. It is eyes meeting eyes in a "mirror" image that ultimately is defiling and disfiguring.

10.   **(D)**   The Self, beginning in Stanza B, is reaffirming the value of life and living — with all of man's foibles, with all the folly into whose grip fall the lives of men, and even with — and this is one of the worst fates, says the poet — the bad luck of a man's falling in love with "a woman not kindred of his soul."

11.   **(D)**   The poet says: "When ... I cast out remorse / So great a sweetness flows ..." Forgiveness of self, then, is the secret, and forgiveness means not permitting yourself to feel guilty or to dwell on past wrong. (E) has little meaning in the context of the poem. (B) and (C) are close, but wide of the mark; they do not account for feelings after a deed is done. Similarly, God may absolve past wrongs, but there is no indication from the poem that he will help people avoid them; free will remains operative.

12.   **(C)**   The poet ends on a decidely "up" note. Without remorse, he is liberated from second thoughts about life. The world becomes good and experience worthwhile.

13.   **(B)**   The structure of the poem suggests that the Self has gotten the last word — in fact, four times as many words as the last statement by the Soul. The elated

tone in the last three lines differs somewhat from the tortured images of stanza 6. The poet, therefore, seems to embed his conclusions in the final lines of the poem.

14. **(B)** The first paragraph distinguishes between the "modernists" (here, the Romantics), who, Hazlitt says, are egotistical, and Milton and Shakespeare, who have a "deeper sense of human life."

15. **(C)** The entire paragraph deals with a discussion of the faults of the modernists in comparison to Shakespeare and Milton. The critic assumes an authoritative tone throughout. He provides no evidence in this first sentence, but rather an unconventional opinion.

16. **(C)** This line is from the middle of the first paragraph: "But to the men I speak of there is nothing interesting, nothing heroical, but themselves." This is the central point of an almost visceral dispute between Hazlitt and the "modern school," which he condemns as "egotism" at the end of his first sentence.

17. **(B)** According to the critic, Shakespeare and Milton were not determined "to get rid of" nature and art, introducing as much of their own personal views into their art as did the "modern school." Instead, they have a "deeper," and, by inference, "wider" understanding of human life — a greater tolerance in general.

18. **(B)** The key to tragedy, especially Classical Tragedy (the principles of which Shakespeare followed closely), is that a being of great or lofty station is brought down to a much lower level. A lesser personage — an "average" person — would not be a candidate for tragedy because he or she has less distance to fall. The modernists, says Hazlitt, are indifferent to the various distances different stations in life entail, and therefore, they would not be interested in Classical Tragedy.

19. **(D)** The critic brings a sense of closure (bringing to an and) to the ideas in his first paragraph by referencing and magnifying the scorn he has for the modernists in his statement that "the world repays their indifference with scorn" — in effect, stating, "It is not just myself who feels this way, but everybody."

20. **(B)** The second paragraph, while it does employ some metaphor and simile (i.e., "like the lightning's") is characterized by the use of action verbs: glances, unites, hurrying, takes, brings, etc.

21. **(A)** Each of the sentences gives examples of the contention in the first sentence that "Shakespeare's imagination is of the same plastic kind ...." Thus the fact that his imagination "unites ... puts a girdle ...takes the widest possible range" etc., all stand in support of the "plastic" contention. Contrary to statement (E), this paragraph is also interesting structurally because each sentence following the first

can stand independently as an example.

22. **(C)** Pope has said that poetry is "what oft was thought, but ne'er so well expressed." Hazlitt here shows his admiration for Shakespeare by using the Bard's own words instead of his own. There are no images here from other critics; he recognizes that Shakespeare has accomplished complex tasks. "Celerity" is not a word of importance (like "celebrity"), but rather a word that describes quickness.

23. **(D)** Hazlitt wants to emphasize the point that Shakespeare is able to embrace and unite even "opposite extremes": "He brings together images ... placed at the greatest distance from each other."

24. **(D)** Hazlitt qualifies this muted criticism by stating that, although he hurries from describing his subject, his descriptions remain accurate ("but the stroke, like the lightning's, is sure as it is sudden.")

25. **(E)** Hazlitt finds it remarkable that Shakespeare can so easily bring together similar images "found in circumstances of the greatest dissimilitude." It is this that provides the "coalescence" that is the genius of Shakespeare's writing, according to the author.

26. **(B)** Hazlitt's paragraph succeeds because he is able to successfully employ a difficult strategy: the repeated use of the pronoun "he." Indeed, "he" appears as the first word in three succeeding sentences — something most English teachers would normally caution against.

27. **(D)** The words are almost opposite in meaning; the first refers to dissimilarity, and the second refers to a lack of distinction — close to a fusing of various elements. Hazlitt contends that Shakespeare was able to "coalesce" images of the first description into the material of the second. His use of similar-sounding words provides a bridge between sentences with seemingly opposite thrusts.

28. **(A)** The first paragraph is marked by the joining of independent clauses using semicolons. The second paragraph is marked by many shorter sentences. The effect of the first is to emphasize the speculative nature of his inquiry, while the effect of the second is to underscore the factual "proof" he is providing for his contentions.

29. **(C)** The two paragraphs move from a brief and general contention about the "modern school" in comparison to Shakespeare and Milton, toward specific discussion of a specific quality of Shakespeare's writing (plasticity), not inconsistent with what was said in the opening sentences.

30. **(A)** In "The Leap," the speaker takes a seemingly ordinary event from his

past (Jane MacNaughton's leap at the dance recital) and attempts to interpret and inject meaning into it. At the time it originally happened, the leap was not of any great significance; now, after reading of her "second" leap, the speaker tries to make sense of "the only thing [he has] of Jane MacNaughton" (line 1). His disbelief at the news of her suicide (lines 26–34) causes him to go back in his memory and examine what he "has" of her: an image of a "light / Grave leap" (lines 16–17), much different from one of her "lying cradled / In that papery steel" (lines 31–32). (B) is incorrect, since his image of Jane is already formed and with him; we never see him struggling to create it. While the speaker does comment on death, its mystery is not the focus of the poem, so (C) is wrong. (D) is incorrect because the poem is far more than a simple reminiscence and (E) is wrong because nowhere in the poem does the speaker "assert his individualism."

31. **(C)** By describing her as "the fastest runner in the seventh grade … even when boys were beginning / To be as big as the girls," (lines 3–5) and excluding her from the list of girls whom he has "running in [his] mind," (line 6) the speaker sets Jane apart as someone different and, as we discover, special. The poem lacks any easily or clearly definable tone, so (A) is wrong. The first stanza does not establish the poem's main symbols (the leaps and the paper chain), so (B) is wrong. The speaker does contrast himself with Jane, but not in this stanza, so (D) is wrong. Finally, (E) is wrong because we are never led to believe that the speaker is in any way envious of Jane.

32. **(B)** The action of the past occurs at the graduation recital of a dancing school. We know this because the speaker refers to the dancers as "new men and women" — "new" because they presumably now know how to dance. (We are told by the speaker, however, that although they are "new men and women," many spend their time at the recital "prancing foolishly as bears" (line 50) rather than leaping like the graceful Jane.) All of the other choices do not fit the definition of "new" in this context and are incorrect.

33. **(D)** The work "light" refers to something careful and whimsical, while the word "grave" refers to something deadpan and serious. By pairing the two (and placing them on different lines) the speaker is able to show us two sides of Jane's first leap; the outer, "light" side associated with the act and its appearance, and the inner, "grave" side associated with the skill required to perform such an act. By placing "light" at the end of one line and "Grave" at the beginning of the next, the speaker forces a slight pause between the two words, thus heightening their contrast. (A) is wrong because nowhere else does the speaker contradict himself, and it is doubtful that he would here. (B) is wrong because he is viewing her leap only as he saw it then, thirty years ago; here he is only relating, not interpreting, the event; (C) is wrong for the same reason — he is keeping her leap "in" time, i.e., viewing it through the lens of himself as a child, not putting it into a new context.

(E) is incorrect because the speaker has not yet addressed Jane's "second" leap.

34. **(E)**   The speaker is both confused and bitter about Jane's suicide; he cannot believe that it even happened and wishes that he could simply refer to it as "a bad dream" (line 35). Death, like all of the other choices, is an "eternal process," but it is also the correct answer because of the speaker's labeling of it as something "Most obsessively wrong with the world." The speaker takes no issue with youth, time, memory, or age — only death, for including Jane in its "obsession."

35. **(E)**   Jane's first leap at the recital stuck in the speaker's mind; obviously it was important to him and symbolized/stood for something, although at the time he may have been unaware of what that something was. He examines, as an adult, the first leap and tries to determine what it was/is so important to him (lines 15–26, 44–50), without much success, until he describes himself as a "slow-footed yokel" sitting outside the action. Here it becomes clear that Jane, and her first leap, represented what the speaker wanted to but could not be: graceful, talented, and artistic. The second leap is ironic because while the first leap made her "immortal" (in the speaker's mind) this leap destroys her and reminds us of her human, and thus ephemeral, nature. It illustrates that the greatest achievements and highest hopes can be frustrated, and that we, as humans, cannot transcend our mortality, no matter how graceful or artistic we may seem. Therefore (E) is correct, since it incorporates these two meanings of the leap. (A) is incorrect because while the two leaps do occur in the past and present, they do not represent these abstractions.

36. **(B)**   We are told by the speaker that Jane leapt to touch the end of one of the paper-ring decorations which he had made (lines 44–46); from this we can infer that the paper-ring is a symbol of connection or linkage. To further understand this symbol, we must look at what is being "connected." We are told that the paper is "brittle" (line 21) and that the craftsmen are "slow-footed yokels" who "sat in corners" (line 44) and are "easily left in the dust" (line 25); in other words, the non-artists, the underachievers who can only watch talent and never possess it. The speaker is one of this group, and it is his paper chain which connects them to the artistic Jane, who invigorates the "passionless playground" (line 26) with her "earth-spurning" (line 38) feet. The paper-link decoration symbolizes a way in which those who cannot "leap" can take part in artistic creation and, ultimately, achievement. A poem, painting, or any work of art for that matter is a similar "link," in which the audience is "connected" to, and invited to take part in, artistic achievement. All of the other choices are not dominant symbols in the poem, and are therefore incorrect.

37. **(E)**   All three of the numbered statements are correct. I is correct because we see him asking Jane to "hold on" to his paper ring, as if to save her from the fate of her second leap. The fact that his feet are "nailed to the ground / By dust [he]

swallowed thirty years ago," shows his feeling of helplessness and desire to help Jane if he only could. II is also correct for similar reasons, i.e., the speaker knows that his image of Jane will never "die," but by asking her to "hold on" to his ring he is addressing the unartistic, frustrated Jane who leapt to her death. III is correct because in the last line of the poem we see the speaker examining his hands — the hands that made the paper ring which connected him to her; by examining his hands, he is certifying that such a connection took place.

38. **(A)** The break which occurs every nine lines creates suspense not of nail-biting type, but rather a "what will happen next" question in the reader's mind. After the first stanza, the question which forms in the reader's mind is "How did she run?" After stanza two, the question is "Why did she leap?" Stanza three ends with the reader thinking, "What did you see in the paper?" Stanza four ends with the question "What eternal process?" Finally, stanza five ends with "What was odd?" (B) is incorrect because while certain issues are discussed in certain stanzas, there are no clear-cut labels or "definable subjects" for each stanza. (C) is incorrect because the stanzas end in mid-thought, not at the ends of complete thoughts. (D) is incorrect because the poem would flow just as well without the breaks every nine lines.

39. **(A)** The most obvious indicator of the beginning of a movement away from memory and into present time is, of course, the use of the word "now." This line is the start of a transition that will allow the speaker to make observations on life that are beyond mere memory. (B) is incorrect because the speaker's reflectiveness, we later learn, is due to the contrast of the two leaps rather than a realization of romantic love. (C) is incorrect because there is nothing in particular in the poem that indicates that Jane and the speaker were anything more than classmates. (D) is incorrect because the speaker knows that Jane did not make her first leap for him but rather for her "new womanhood." (E) is incorrect because the speaker never really becomes the focus of the poem in the same way that Jane is in the beginning.

40. **(D)** While there are elements of each of the above, by far the most common image is that of solitude. Wordsworth logs four "aloneness" descriptions in five lines. It is to his credit that he does not repeat himself. It is also interesting to note the repetition of "sing" and its variants resemble "single" as well.

41. **(C)** Wordsworth's comments imply that he is not yet bothered by his inability to understand the words of the song. In the next stanza, he is perturbed by this inability. Though he has previously recognized the song as "melancholy," the evident beauty of the scenery (the context) has evidently obscured this fact and he is not concerned. Curiously, he is not consciously aware that he is being deceived, nor is he afraid of being deceived. His first impression is a strong one, and the only thing he is concerned with.

42. **(C)** Although at first it may not seem apparent, Wordsworth structures this stanza by a movement through time from "long ago" to "today" to "May be again." He hangs on this structure his list of possibilities of what she is singing and why she is singing it.

43. **(D)** Surprisingly, the contextual meaning is close to the slangy, modern use in (E) — which seems to derive from a very old use of "number" in reference to meter, and especially the syllables of poetry. Wordsworth does not refer to the girl as singing many tunes — rather he refers to "her song."

44. **(E)** This accepted meaning of "plaintive" is reinforced by the use of "unhappy" and "natural sorrow" in the following lines, and brings a new dimension to the significance of the girl's song.

45. **(B)** Wordsworth parallels work and song, and interjects the line "As if her song could have no ending" between the two discussions. The implication is that she sings as if she will be bent forever over her sickle working.

46. **(D)** Climbing the hill seems to be a reference to growing older, continuing on the journey through life, rather than to a social station, or a description of his physical journey. That the song made a lasting impression is evidenced by Wordsworth's creation of this poem. Interestingly, this is one of the few poems he wrote that is not based on a personal experience, but rather on a scene from Wilkinson's Tour of Scotland."

47. **(E)** The girl's story, as Wordsworth imagines it, is one in which the memory of sorrow remains long after the sorrowful incident. The girl is a "reaper" of unhappiness as we all are, gathering and assuming burdens as she, like the poet, continues living and working.

48. **(D)** Mabel is in a state of "ecstasy," not because she is impoverished, or because she is in despair, but because she has decided to "end it all" and kill herself. There are strong hints throughout this passage, yet a casual reader might think she is speaking of the "end," meaning, perhaps, eviction from her property. By the time she thinks about being near her mother in the graveyard, however, the meaning should be clear.

49. **(A)** The author describes Mabel's actions in careful detail, stressing her pleasurable bond to death and her new found self-control. The author does not sound disparaging or repulsed; rather Mabel is presented in a sympathetic light, inviting emotional response from the reader.

50. **(C)** Mabel's self-questioning expresses her new-found defiance, and her growing independence from the onus of responding to the prejudices of the wider world. When Lawrence asks: "Why should she answer anybody?" we can hear the

tragically directed Mabel saying: "I don't have to answer you or anybody," as she walks down the "dark main street of the small town."

51. **(D)**   Mabel looks forward to her death, says Lawrence, as a personal fulfillment and "glorification," and as a way of getting closer to her mother — not just in a physical sense as she cleans up at the graveyard, but in a spiritual way as well.

52. **(C)**   It is surprising, or so Lawrence implies, that a person who is about to commit suicide thinks "of nobody, not even of herself." Yet, it might be precisely this feeling that provides the sensation of liberation and which actually allows her to contemplate suicide.

53. **(B)**   Lawrence presents us with a machine-gun procession of depressing images: "gray, wintry ... saddened, dark green ... blackened by the smoke." Along with this are the depressing images of foundries and graveyards.

54. **(B)**   Mabel has already decided on the path she will take to eliminate her troubles. The brief description of Mabel and her bag seems almost medical. Perhaps she is gone to perform an operation — and in this sense it might be an omen. But Lawrence places this description next to the smoky and depressing landscape: Mabel will clean the headstone, Mabel will wipe her own slate clean.

55. **(B)**   Lawrence points out that Mabel is more obvious to the public in the graveyard than she imagines herself to be: yet she feels immune.

56. **(C)**   Cleaning her mother's grave gave her "sincere satisfaction." Lawrence implies that this task is performed often.

57. **(E)**   Lawrence states in the last line: "For the life she followed here in the world was far less real than the world of death she inherited from her mother." Thus a trip to the graveyard and a contemplation of death is not an escape from the "real" world, but a return to the more real world her mother left to her.

58. **(B)**   Lawrence states: "She felt reserved within the thick churchyard wall as in another country." It is a difficult concept for the reader to understand fully until he or she confronts the concept again in the last paragraph quoted in this passage.

59. **(D)**   What is indicated here is a general and gradual separation from the living and a removal to the world of the dead. There is also specific movement discerned within the general: that is, a shift from all the ties (not just with the bothersome people of the town, but with the suffering members of her family) toward one original bond, not just with her mother, but with the world of death.

60. **(C)**   Personification involves assigning human qualities to inanimate objects as is done by describing the dark green fields as "saddened." The correct answer is (C) personification.

Section 2

Essay 1

In W.H. Auden's "Lay Your Sleeping Head, My Love," the speaker presents to "my love" (who appears to be a child for whom he cares deeply) a dismal picture of the wider world. Auden does this effectively by reinforcing this picture with appropriate images and individual words. He does give the child some hope at the end; however, the speaker seems intent on preventing "my love" from growing up with false illusions.

In the first stanza, the speaker refers to his own arm as "faithless." It soon becomes obvious that he has lost faith in the human goodness, and in the lasting nature of "beauty" (he says it "proves ephemeral"). He does not absolve "my love" from these darker aspects of being human, for he calls "my love" both "mortal" and "guilty." The speaker's choice of words here is almost Biblical, and brings to mind original sin — in this case, the human "sin" of frailty that is brought out in the rest of the poem.

In the second stanza, the speaker appears to be qualifying his dark view when he says "soul and body have no bounds / To lovers." This, he hopes, might be reassuring to "my love," yet he calls love an "ordinary swoon," and, while he seems to feel that love has almost magical powers ("abstract insight"), by the third stanza he is cautioning "my love" that both "certainty" and "fidelity" can pass "Like vibrations of a bell."

The deliberate use of the bell image reinforces his portrayal of love as temporary, for however beautiful the bell's sound might be, we recognize it will fade away unless struck again. The wider world, the speaker says, is full of madmen and hermits, yet even they can feel "sensual ecstasy" — even the hermit can be woken — even the madman can be inspired to raise a cry. The use of a hermit and a madman gives reinforcement to the idea that the world is not populated entirely by happy people, but that even they — as threatening as they might be to "my love" — have human capacities for love.

Thus, by the final stanza, the speaker has created an unsentimental picture of the larger world. He has admitted he is little better than the rest, and has cautioned "my love" that he or she too is human. Even so, he can "bless" "my love" / can wish that all "nights of insult" the child might experience be tempered by a "human love" which, though fleeting, can be a powerful and special healing force at the time it is experienced.

Essay 1 — Explanation

This essay is well written: it demonstrates a command of syntax, organization, and diction. It also demonstrates that the writer has effectively analyzed how the speaker portrays the world, and defines the nature of this portrayal as well as the manner in which the portrayal is reinforced. Finally, it clearly states the poet's qualifications to this portrayal and effectively uses specific references from the text of the poem.

Essay 2

Thoreau begins his essay, "Civil Disobedience," by offering his audience a well-known motto: the government is best which governs least. Starting with an idea like this, associated in the public mind with founding fathers like Thomas Jefferson, enables Thoreau to demonstrate to his audience that he and they are in some agreement.

Next, he grabs their attention further by advancing a notion that doubtless, shocked the educated minds he was trying to convince: that a government is best which governs not at all. At the risk of seeming an anarchist, he quickly says that this is the ideal state, and that men will come to want this in time. He does not call for the overthrow of the government which was then engaged in the Mexican War, though he does register his disapproval. This may have been omitted on purpose, as he is arguing for a greater point, and is attempting to sound reasonable after knowing he must have shocked many.

Thoreau then enters a highly rational discourse on the questionable necessity of government. His tone here is one of reason and concern. He is meeting his intelligent audience on their own terms. He is not some wild-eyed revolutionary, as his diction seems to convey, but rather an honest citizen asking probing and sincere questions.

Perhaps his most convincing argument is his contention that it is not the government itself which educates the populace, or settles frontier territories; it is the people, and, to the extent that government involves itself in these affairs, that involvement is often obstructive. Thoreau's strategy here is to indirectly praise his audience, for they are the American people, and they are credited, rather than their government, with the heroic acts of the pioneers, and with cultural enhancement.

Thoreau also interjects a bit of humor at the end of the second paragraph, as if to lighten the heavy load of what the audience might think are still highly critical contentions. He compares "legislators" to "mischievous persons" who would often derail the trail of progress rather than assist it.

Now that he has made his preliminary case, and has shown his audience he can be reasonable, he retreats, it seems, a little bit farther to the real point of his persuasive piece: that all he wants is a better government. This is similar to his opening statement, in that it is designed to pose a common point of agreement between himself and his audience. By the end of this passage, then, Thoreau has succeeded in gaining his audience's attention, finding "common ground," advancing an argument using examples and reasoning, and concluding with a retreat from radicalism and a simple call for reform. These must have been very effective strategies for Thoreau's highly educated and skeptical audience, who were already having doubts about the government's misadventures in the Mexican War.

Essay 2 — Explanation

This essay is well written. It indicates a command of diction, syntax, and organization. In addition, it identifies and discusses a number of persuasive strategies, and recognizes how these strategies were meant to persuade an educated audience.

Essay 3

In the novel *Lord of the Flies,* William Golding creates a particular situation in order to make an important statement on the nature of humanity.

Golding sets his epic in a future time. The world appears to be at war, although this war is only a background concern of the novel. Golding chooses, instead, to communicate his message by creating a microcosm of the wider world on a desert island which is the scene of a crash landing of a choral group from an English boy's school. He has evidently chosen these characters to represent the best of the "civilized" world, and created a crash landing to ask the question: how civilized are people when they are left on their own to either survive or perish?

At first it appears that the boys will be able to survive using the "civilized" tools of representative government (under their elected leader, Ralph) and division of labor. The aim of this temporary government is very logical: help the boys to survive until they can be rescued, and encourage that rescue by maintaining a signal fire. Unfortunately one of the older boys, Jack, is power-hungry, and knows that what the younger boys really want is to play "hunting games" and have "fun."

Golding has created a situation in which the conflict between Ralph and Jack really represents a conflict between the forces of civilization and the forces of savagery. It is central to the message Golding wishes to communicate that the forces of savagery win out, and the boys would have destroyed each other on the island had not a passing ship seen their "signal fire": the smoke from the vegetation on the island after Jack and his hunters set it on fire in an effort to smoke out Ralph and kill him. Even the military officer (involved in a war himself) who discovers them cannot believe how quickly they became savages.

Golding has communicated the idea that "civilized" people — everyone — is really only a short step away from the savagery that typically expresses itself in warfare and killing. His shocking message is effectively communicated because Golding has chosen a plot, set characters, and setting that will work throughout the novel to deliver this one powerful revelation.

Essay 3 — Explanation

This essay is well written. It demonstrates a command of syntax, organization, and diction, and defines both the situation the author creates, and the important statement he is making. It also explains how the author's choice of situation contributes to the communication of his statement.

THE ADVANCED PLACEMENT EXAMINATION IN

English Literature & Composition

TEST 5

1. Ⓐ Ⓑ Ⓒ Ⓓ Ⓔ
2. Ⓐ Ⓑ Ⓒ Ⓓ Ⓔ
3. Ⓐ Ⓑ Ⓒ Ⓓ Ⓔ
4. Ⓐ Ⓑ Ⓒ Ⓓ Ⓔ
5. Ⓐ Ⓑ Ⓒ Ⓓ Ⓔ
6. Ⓐ Ⓑ Ⓒ Ⓓ Ⓔ
7. Ⓐ Ⓑ Ⓒ Ⓓ Ⓔ
8. Ⓐ Ⓑ Ⓒ Ⓓ Ⓔ
9. Ⓐ Ⓑ Ⓒ Ⓓ Ⓔ
10. Ⓐ Ⓑ Ⓒ Ⓓ Ⓔ
11. Ⓐ Ⓑ Ⓒ Ⓓ Ⓔ
12. Ⓐ Ⓑ Ⓒ Ⓓ Ⓔ
13. Ⓐ Ⓑ Ⓒ Ⓓ Ⓔ
14. Ⓐ Ⓑ Ⓒ Ⓓ Ⓔ
15. Ⓐ Ⓑ Ⓒ Ⓓ Ⓔ
16. Ⓐ Ⓑ Ⓒ Ⓓ Ⓔ
17. Ⓐ Ⓑ Ⓒ Ⓓ Ⓔ
18. Ⓐ Ⓑ Ⓒ Ⓓ Ⓔ
19. Ⓐ Ⓑ Ⓒ Ⓓ Ⓔ
20. Ⓐ Ⓑ Ⓒ Ⓓ Ⓔ
21. Ⓐ Ⓑ Ⓒ Ⓓ Ⓔ
22. Ⓐ Ⓑ Ⓒ Ⓓ Ⓔ
23. Ⓐ Ⓑ Ⓒ Ⓓ Ⓔ
24. Ⓐ Ⓑ Ⓒ Ⓓ Ⓔ
25. Ⓐ Ⓑ Ⓒ Ⓓ Ⓔ
26. Ⓐ Ⓑ Ⓒ Ⓓ Ⓔ
27. Ⓐ Ⓑ Ⓒ Ⓓ Ⓔ
28. Ⓐ Ⓑ Ⓒ Ⓓ Ⓔ
29. Ⓐ Ⓑ Ⓒ Ⓓ Ⓔ
30. Ⓐ Ⓑ Ⓒ Ⓓ Ⓔ
31. Ⓐ Ⓑ Ⓒ Ⓓ Ⓔ
32. Ⓐ Ⓑ Ⓒ Ⓓ Ⓔ
33. Ⓐ Ⓑ Ⓒ Ⓓ Ⓔ
34. Ⓐ Ⓑ Ⓒ Ⓓ Ⓔ
35. Ⓐ Ⓑ Ⓒ Ⓓ Ⓔ
36. Ⓐ Ⓑ Ⓒ Ⓓ Ⓔ
37. Ⓐ Ⓑ Ⓒ Ⓓ Ⓔ
38. Ⓐ Ⓑ Ⓒ Ⓓ Ⓔ
39. Ⓐ Ⓑ Ⓒ Ⓓ Ⓔ
40. Ⓐ Ⓑ Ⓒ Ⓓ Ⓔ
41. Ⓐ Ⓑ Ⓒ Ⓓ Ⓔ
42. Ⓐ Ⓑ Ⓒ Ⓓ Ⓔ
43. Ⓐ Ⓑ Ⓒ Ⓓ Ⓔ
44. Ⓐ Ⓑ Ⓒ Ⓓ Ⓔ
45. Ⓐ Ⓑ Ⓒ Ⓓ Ⓔ
46. Ⓐ Ⓑ Ⓒ Ⓓ Ⓔ
47. Ⓐ Ⓑ Ⓒ Ⓓ Ⓔ
48. Ⓐ Ⓑ Ⓒ Ⓓ Ⓔ
49. Ⓐ Ⓑ Ⓒ Ⓓ Ⓔ
50. Ⓐ Ⓑ Ⓒ Ⓓ Ⓔ
51. Ⓐ Ⓑ Ⓒ Ⓓ Ⓔ
52. Ⓐ Ⓑ Ⓒ Ⓓ Ⓔ
53. Ⓐ Ⓑ Ⓒ Ⓓ Ⓔ
54. Ⓐ Ⓑ Ⓒ Ⓓ Ⓔ
55. Ⓐ Ⓑ Ⓒ Ⓓ Ⓔ
56. Ⓐ Ⓑ Ⓒ Ⓓ Ⓔ
57. Ⓐ Ⓑ Ⓒ Ⓓ Ⓔ
58. Ⓐ Ⓑ Ⓒ Ⓓ Ⓔ
59. Ⓐ Ⓑ Ⓒ Ⓓ Ⓔ
60. Ⓐ Ⓑ Ⓒ Ⓓ Ⓔ

AP EXAMINATION IN ENGLISH LITERATURE AND COMPOSITION

TEST 5

Section 1

TIME: 60 Minutes
60 Questions

DIRECTIONS: This test consists of selections from literary works and questions on their content, form, and style. After reading each passage or poem, choose the best answer to each question and blacken the corresponding space on the answer sheet.

NOTE: Pay particular attention to the requirement of questions that contain the words NOT, LEAST, or EXCEPT.

QUESTIONS 1–16 are based on the following passage. Read carefully before choosing your answers.

Prologue Spoken by Mr. Garrick[1]
AT THE OPENING OF THE THEATRE ROYAL, DRURY LANE, 1747

> When Learning's triumph o'er her barbarous foes
> First reared the stage, immortal Shakespeare rose;
> Each change of many-colored life he drew,
> Exhausted worlds, and then imagined new:
> 5 Existence saw him spurn her bounded reign,
> And panting Time toiled after him in vain.
> His powerful strokes presiding Truth impressed,
> And unresisted Passion stormed the breast.
>   Then Jonson came, instructed from the school

10 To please in method and invent by rule;
His studious patience and laborious art
By regular approach essayed the heart;
Cold Approbation gave the lingering bays,
For those who durst not censure, scarce could praise.
15 A mortal born, he met the general doom,
But left, like Egypt's kings, a lasting tomb.
        The wits of Charles found easier ways to fame,
Nor wished for Jonson's art, or Shakespeare's flame;
Themselves they studied; as they felt, they writ;
20 Intrigue was plot, obscenity was wit.
Vice always found a sympathetic friend;
They pleased their age, and did not aim to mend.
Yet bards like these aspired to lasting praise,
And proudly hoped to pimp in future days.
25 Their cause was general, their supports were strong,
Their slaves were willing, and their reign was long:
Till Shame regained the post that Sense betrayed,
And Virtue called Oblivion to her aid.
        Then, crushed by rules, and weakened as refined,
30 For years the power of Tragedy declined;
From bard to bard the frigid caution crept,
Till Declamation roared while Passion slept;
Yet still did Virtue deign the stage to tread;
Philosophy remained though Nature fled;
35 But forced at length her ancient reign to quit,
She saw great Faustus lay the ghost of Wit;
Exulting Folly hailed the joyous day,
And Pantomime and Song confirmed her sway.
        But who the coming changes can presage,
40 And mark the future periods of the stage?
Perhaps if skill could distant times explore,
New Behns,² new Durfeys, yet remain in store;
Perhaps where Lear has raved, and Hamlet died,
On flying cars new sorcerers may ride;
45 Perhaps (for who can guess the effects of chance?)
Here Hunt may box, or Mahomet may dance.³
        Hard is his lot that, here by fortune placed,
Must watch the wild vicissitudes of taste;
With every meteor of caprice must play,
50 And chase the new-blown bubbles of the day.
Ah! let not censure term our fate our choice,

The stage but echoes back the public voice;
The drama's laws, the drama's patrons give.
For we that live to please, must please to live.
55   Then prompt no more the follies you decry,
As tyrants doom their tools of guilt to die;
'Tis yours this night to bid the reign commence
Of rescued Nature and reviving Sense;
To chase the charms of Sound, the pomp of Show,
60 For useful Mirth and salutary Woe;
Bid scenic Virtue from the rising age,
And Truth diffuse her radiance from the stage.

—*Samuel Johnson*

1. David Garrick, the famous actor, had become joint patentee and manager of Drury Lane Theatre.
2. Aphra Behn (1640–89), first Englishwoman to earn her living by writing. Thomas Durfey (1653–1723), satirist and writer of songs and plays.
3. Edward Hunt, a popular pugilist; Mahomet, a tightrope dancer.

1. "Time" in line 6 is an example of

    (A) invocation   (D) synecdoche

    (B) apostrophe   (E) metaphor

    (C) personification

2. The primary purpose of the first 38 lines is to

    (A) provide a critical history of English drama up to 1747

    (B) argue that English drama has steadily declined since Shakespeare's time

    (C) prove that tragedy is a nobler genre than comedy

    (D) demonstrate that current English drama is stronger than in any period since Shakespeare's time

    (E) show that diversity of forms leads to increased excellence in drama

3. In line 4, "exhausted" is

    (A) an adjective meaning tired

    (B) a verb meaning to consume entirely

    (C) an adjective meaning empty

(D) a verb meaning to tire completely

(E) an adjective meaning used up

4. Which of the following statements most accurately states the poem's contrast of Shakespeare and Jonson?

   (A) Jonson is regarded as a superior dramatist, largely because he had the advantage of learning from Shakespeare's mistakes.

   (B) The poem can find nothing in Jonson to praise because Shakespeare's artistry overshadows that of all other dramatists.

   (C) Both are praised, Shakespeare for depicting truth and passion, Jonson for his inventiveness and originality.

   (D) Jonson is praised for his craftsmanship, but Shakespeare receives greater praise for his imagination and passion.

   (E) Jonson's plays achieved a fleeting popularity, but there is no longer any reason to read them, whereas Shakespeare's plays are immortal.

5. In line 13, "bays" can best be taken to mean

   (A) ridicule   (D) imitation

   (B) obscurity   (E) fame

   (C) passion

6. Line 16 contains a

   (A) simile   (D) pathetic fallacy

   (B) paradox   (E) conceit

   (C) metaphor

7. The poem's chief objection to the plays of the comic dramatists who wrote during the reign of Charles I is that

   (A) their plots were not sufficiently interesting

   (B) they were too interested in general causes

   (C) they lacked wit

   (D) they did not address social issues

   (E) they encouraged vice

8. Which of the following ideas is found in lines 21–23?

    (A) The Restoration comic dramatists did not try to change their ways.

    (B) Shakespeare and Jonson achieved greater popularity than the Restoration comic dramatists.

    (C) The Restoration comic dramatists were not critical of their society.

    (D) The pride of the Restoration comic dramatists led them to desire immediate but not future fame.

    (E) The Restoration comic dramatists were pleased with themselves when elderly.

9. The speaker attributes the decline of tragedy chiefly to

    (A) an overemphasis on didacticism or moralizing

    (B) the choice of unnaturally violent subject matter

    (C) an emphasis on passion at the expense of philosophy

    (D) the absence of talented playwrights

    (E) a slavish adherence to conventional rules of decorum

10. In lines 34–38, the speaker's primary criticism is that

    (A) subject matter appropriate to tragedy was being used in other genres

    (B) tragedians no longer observed ancient, classical rules of tragedy

    (C) playwrights inappropriately introduced wit into tragedy

    (D) audiences began to regard such things as ghosts as ridiculous in tragedies

    (E) tragedians foolishly decided to compete for audiences with such entertainments as pantomime shows and concerts

11. In line 36, "she" refers to

    (A) Virtue   (D) Tragedy

    (B) Nature   (E) Folly

    (C) Passion

12. In line 38, "her" refers to

    (A) Tragedy   (D) Nature

    (B) Declamation   (E) Folly

    (C) Virtue

13. The main purpose of lines 39–62 is to

    (A) try to predict the future course of drama

    (B) appeal to the audience to change its taste

    (C) lament the difficult role of the critic

    (D) argue that the stage should be more carefully regulated by the government

    (E) assert the superiority of modern modes of drama to earlier dramatic forms

14. In line 54, "we" is best understood to refer to

    (A) critics   (D) the drama's patrons

    (B) members of the court   (E) members of the audience

    (C) playwrights and actors

15. The speaker says that the rules of drama ultimately derive from

    (A) classical Greece and Rome

    (B) decisions of playwrights

    (C) truth and virtue

    (D) public taste

    (E) nature

16. The poem is written in which of the following verse forms?

    (A) Blank verse   (D) Ballad meter

    (B) Heroic couplet   (E) Free verse

    (C) Rhyme royal

QUESTIONS 17–30 are based on the following poem. Read carefully before choosing your answers.

Journey of the Magi

"A cold coming we had of it,
Just the worst time of the year
For a journey, and such a long journey:
The ways deep and the weather sharp,
5   The very dead of winter."[1]
And the camels galled, sore-footed,
     refractory,
Lying down in the melting snow.
There were times we regretted
The summer palaces on slopes, the terraces,
10 And the silken girls bringing sherbet.
Then the camel men cursing and grumbling
And running away, and wanting their liquor
     and women,
And the night-fires going out, and the lack of
     shelters,
And the cities hostile and the towns
     unfriendly
15 And the villages dirty and charging high
     prices:
A hard time we had of it.
At the end we preferred to travel all night,
Sleeping in snatches,
With the voices singing in our ears, saying
20 That this was all folly.
Then at dawn we came down to a temperate
valley,
Wet, below the snow line, smelling of
vegetation;
With a running stream and a water mill
     beating the darkness,
And three trees on the low sky,
25 And an old white horse galloped away in the
     meadow.
Then we came to a tavern with vine-leaves
over the lintel,
Six hands at an open door dicing for pieces
     of silver,

And feet kicking the empty wineskins.
But there was no information, and so we
    continued
30 And arrived at evening, not a moment too soon
Finding the place; it was (you may say)
    satisfactory.

All this was a long time ago, I remember,
And I would do it again, but set down
This set down
35 This: were we led all that way for
Birth or Death? There was a Birth, certainly,
We had evidence and no doubt. I had seen
    birth and death,
But had thought they were different; this
Birth was
Hard and bitter agony for us, like Death, our
    death.
40 We returned to our places, these Kingdoms,
But no longer at ease here, in the old
    dispensation,
With an alien people clutching their gods.
I should be glad of another death.

1. "A cold ... winter," adapted from a nativity sermon by the seventeenth-century preacher Lancelot Andrewes (1555–1626).

"Journey of the Magi" from Collected Poems 1909–1962, *copyright 1936 by Harcourt Brace Jovanovich, Inc., © 1964, 1963 by T.S. Eliot, reprinted by permission of the publisher.*

17. The speaker is

    (A)   the poet himself

    (B)   one of the disciples

    (C)   a pagan prince

    (D)   one of the three wise men

    (E)   a modern man visiting Bethlehem

18. The speaker is

    (A)   a young child

(B)   an adolescent

(C)   a young adult

(D)   an elderly man

(E)   speaking from beyond the grave

19.   The poem is divided into three sections: I (lines 1–20), II (lines 21–31), III (lines 32–43). Which of the following statements best expresses the relationships among the three parts?

(A)   Each describes a separate but related event.

(B)   Parts I and II describe an event; Part III describes the effects of that event.

(C)   Part I describes an event; Parts II and III are a meditation on that event.

(D)   Part I presents a thesis; Parts II and III supply evidence supporting it.

(E)   Parts I and II offer one point of view; Part III refutes that point of view.

20.   Which of the following statements is LEAST accurate?

(A)   Part III is more meditative than Part I.

(B)   The major shift in tone and subject matter occurs at line 32.

(C)   Part II is more self-reflective than Part III.

(D)   Part II combines description and allusion or symbol.

(E)   Part I is more descriptive than Part III.

21.   In line 6, "refractory" is

(A)   an adjective meaning docile

(B)   an adverb meaning slowly

(C)   an adjective meaning unmanageable

(D)   a verb meaning stopped

(E)   an adjective meaning determined

22.   Lines 9 and 10

(A)   describe sights seen during the journey

(B)   provide examples of the corrupt, luxurious world the speaker wants to change

(C)   are memories of things the magi sometimes longed for during their journey

(D)   describe scenes the magi hope to find at the end of their journey

(E)   are examples of the temptations the magi must resist if they are to see Christ

23.   The images in lines 21–23 suggest

(A)   decay   (D)   indifference

(B)   death   (E)   renewal

(C)   alienation

24.   The images in lines 24-27 can best be described as

(A)   signs of the random, chaotic nature of daily life

(B)   foreshadowings of disastrous events in Christ's life and death

(C)   emblems of man's general depravity

(D)   allusions to significant events preceding Christ's birth

(E)   signals of man's inability to recognize significant events while they are occurring

25.   In line 30, "not a moment too soon" chiefly

(A)   refers to the magi arriving shortly before Christ's birth

(B)   indicates the speaker's fear of the dark

(C)   indicates the exasperated state of mind of the speaker at the time

(D)   alerts the reader to the speaker's skepticism about the holiness of the event he has come to witness

(E)   alludes to the speaker's imminent death

26.   The repetition ("set down/ This set down/ This") in lines 33–35 chiefly

(A)   emphasizes that the following question is the primary issue with which the speaker is concerned

(B)   signals the reader that the speaker's mind is wandering

(C)   indicates that the speaker is uncertain what primary question or prob-
       lem he wishes to pose

(D)   emphasizes that the speaker is both angry and resentful

(E)   indicates that the speaker would not make the journey again

27. The speaker's remark that "this Birth was/ Hard and bitter agony for us, like
     Death, our death" (lines 38-39) can best be understood to mean that

     (A)   Christ's birth reminded them of their own mortality

     (B)   they suffered great hardships during their journey

     (C)   they anticipated Christ's eventual crucifixion

     (D)   Christ's birth made them realize that pain accompanies all great
            achievements

     (E)   Christ's birth destroyed their belief in their pagan religion

28. The speaker says that he "would do it again" (line 33) presumably because

     (A)   the event was spiritually important to him

     (B)   he now knows more about hitherto unknown lands

     (C)   it has made him a more politically astute king

     (D)   it was his only opportunity to see Christ

     (E)   it gave him a form of fame that he would not otherwise have achieved

29. "Another death" in the last line of the poem refers to the death of

     (A)   the other magi

     (B)   memory

     (C)   the speaker

     (D)   Christ

     (E)   the gods of the "alien people"

30. The poem is an example of which of the following verse forms?

     (A)   Blank verse   (D)   Ballad meter

     (B)   Villanelle   (E)   Free verse

     (C)   Terza rima

It is too little to call man a little world; except God, man is dimunitive
to nothing. Man consists of more pieces, more parts, than the world; than
the world doth, nay, than the world is. And if these pieces were extended
and stretched out in man as they are in the world, man would be the giant
5 and the world the dwarf; the world but the map, and the man the world. If
all the veins in our bodies were extended to rivers, and all the sinews to
veins of mines, and all the muscles that lie upon one another to hills, and
all the bones to quarries of stones, and all the other pieces to the proportion
of those which correspond to them in the world, the air would be too little
10 for this orb of man to move in, the firmament would be but enough for this
star. For as the whole world hath nothing to which something in man doth
not answer, so hath man many pieces of which the whole world hath no
representation. Enlarge this meditation upon this great world, man, so far
as to consider the immensity of the creatures this world produces. Our
15 creatures are our thoughts, creatures that are born giants, that reach from
east to west, from earth to heaven, that do not only bestride all the sea and
land, but span the sun and firmament at once: my thoughts reach all,
comprehend all.

Inexplicable mystery! I their creator am in a close prison, in a sick
20 bed, anywhere, and any one of my creatures, my thoughts, is with the sun,
and beyond the sun, overtakes the sun, and overgoes the sun in one pace,
one step, everywhere. And then as the other world produces serpents and
vipers, malignant and venomous creatures, and worms and caterpillars,
that endeavor to devour that world which produces them, and monsters
25 compiled and complicated of divers parents and kinds, so this world, our
selves, produces all these in us, producing diseases and sicknesses of all
those sorts; venomous and infectious diseases, feeding and consuming
diseases, and manifold and entangles diseases made up of many several
ones. And can the other world name so many venomous, so many consum-
30 ing, so many monstrous creatures, as we can diseases, of all these kinds? O
miserable abundance, O beggarly riches! How much do we lack of having
remedies for every disease when as yet we have not names for them?

But we have a Hercules against these giants, these monsters: that is the
physician. He musters up all the resources of the other world to succor
35 this, all nature to relieve man. We have the physician but we are not the
physician. Here we shrink in our proportion, sink in our dignity in respect
of very mean creatures who are physicians to themselves. The hart that is
pursued and wounded, they say, knows an herb which, being eaten, throws
off the arrow: a strange kind of vomit. The dog that pursues it, though he is

40 subject to sickness, even proverbially knows his grass that recovers him.
    And it may be true that the drugger is as near to man as to other creatures;
    it may be that obvious and present simples, easy to be had, would cure
    him; but the apothecary is not so near him, nor the physician so near him,
    as they two are to other creatures. Man hath not that innate instinct to
45 apply these natural medicines to his present danger, as those inferior
    creatures have. He is not his own apothecary, his own physician, as they
    are. Call back therefore thy meditation again, and bring it down. What's
    become of man's great extent and proportion, when himself shrinks
    himself and consumes himself to a handful of dust? What's become of his
50 soaring thoughts, his compassing thoughts, when himself brings himself
    to the ignorance, to the thoughtlessness of the grave? His diseases are his
    own, but the physician is not, he hath them at home, but he must send for
    the physician.

—John Donne

31. The central metaphor in the first paragraph is a comparison of

     (A) Man and God

     (B) Earth and heaven

     (C) Man and the world

     (D) Man's mental and physical attributes

     (E) God and nature

32. Which of the following can best be substituted for "answer" (line 12)
     without changing the author's meaning?

     (A) Surpass   (D) Repudiate

     (B) Correspond   (E) Aspire

     (C) Correct

33. Which of the following statements most nearly expresses the main idea of
     the first paragraph?

     (A) Man is God-like.

     (B) Man is a macrocosm .

     (C) Man imitates small worlds.

     (D) Man is a microcosm.

     (E) Man is small and insignificant.

34. The "other world" (line 29) refers to

    (A) hell

    (D) the world of nature

    (B) man's inner self

    (E) the Garden of Eden

    (C) the firmament

35. "Miserable abundance" (line 31) refers to

    (A) human diseases

    (B) man's flawed intellect

    (C) monstrous creatures in nature

    (D) temptations that lead to excess

    (E) the richness and limitations of language

36. In line 31, "beggarly riches" is an example of

    (A) apostrophe

    (D) synecdoche

    (B) invocation

    (E) paradox

    (C) dead metaphor

37. The author's metaphor in the second paragraph suggests that sickness and malignant creatures are alike chiefly in that both

    (A) are unpleasant and unexpected presences

    (B) violate the natural order of things

    (C) are complex and difficult to understand

    (D) dangerous but necessary aspects of the natural world

    (E) destroy that which produces them

38. Which of the following statements best expresses the idea in the author's comment in lines 35–36 ("we are not the physician")?

    (A) Doctors are ineffective.

    (B) Man cannot cure himself.

    (C) Few of us are doctors.

    (D) Few of us understand medical practices.

    (E) Men generally do not like doctors.

39. In line 39, "it" refers to

    (A) health   (D) hart

    (B) sickness   (E) man

    (C) grass

40. In line 40, "his grass that recovers him" can best be understood to mean

    (A) what to eat to cure himself

    (B) how to avoid trouble

    (C) how to regain what he has lost

    (D) that his reason has certain limitations

    (E) that he must rely on others

41. "Him" (line 43) refers to

    (A) apothecary   (D) drugger

    (B) dog   (E) God

    (C) man

42. "They" (line 44) refers to

    (A) animals   (D) giants

    (B) men in general   (E) medicines

    (C) apothecaries and physicians

43. "Thy" (line 47) refers to

    (A) man   (D) death

    (B) physician   (E) the author

    (C) the reader

44. The last paragraph chiefly

    (A) supplies additional proof of the main argument in paragraph one

    (B) answers the philosophical question posed in the first two paragraphs

    (C) supplies a specific example to support the general assertion made in paragraph two

(D)   qualifies and at least partially rebuts the main idea expressed in paragraph one

(E)   cites an exception to the general rule stated in paragraph two

45.   The author most likely wrote this meditation

(A)   when preparing to leave for a journey

(B)   while trying to decide whether to enter the priesthood

(C)   during an attack of illness

(D)   after receiving a bill from an incompetent physician

(E)   while contemplating suicide

46.   This passage can best be described as a meditation on

(A)   the superiority of the natural to the human world

(B)   the state of medicine in the author's time

(C)   man's relationship to God

(D)   the human condition

(E)   religious uncertainty

QUESTIONS 47–60 are based on the following passage. Read carefully before choosing your answers.

Knowing that Mrs. Mallard was afflicted with a heart trouble, great care was taken to break to her as gently as possible the news of her husband's death.

It was her sister Josephine who told her, in broken sentences, veiled
5   hints that revealed in half concealing. Her husband's friend Richards was there, too, near her. It was he who had been in the newspaper office when intelligence of the railroad disaster was received, with Brently Mallard's name leading the list of "killed." He had only taken the time to assure himself of its truth by a second telegram, and had hastened to forestall any
10   less careful, less tender friend in bearing the sad message.

She did not hear the story as many women have heard the same, with a paralyzed inability to accept its significance. She wept at once, with sudden, wild abandonment, in her sister's arms. When the storm of grief had spent itself she went away to her room alone. She would have no one
15   follow her.

There stood, facing the open window, a comfortable, roomy armchair.

Into this she sank, pressed down by a physical exhaustion that haunted her body and seemed to reach into her soul.

20 She could see in the open square before her house the tops of trees that were all aquiver with the new spring life. The delicious breath of rain was in the air. In the street below a peddler was crying his wares. The notes of a distant song which some one was singing reached her faintly, and countless sparrows were twittering in the eaves.

25 There were patches of blue sky showing here and there through the clouds that had met and piled above the other in the west facing her window.

She sat with her head thrown back upon the cushion of the chair quite motionless, except when a sob came up into her throat and shook her, as a child who has cried itself to sleep continues to sob in its dreams.

30 She was young, with a fair, calm face, whose lines bespoke repression and even a certain strength. But now there was a dull stare in her eyes, whose gaze was fixed away off yonder on one of those patches of blue sky. It was not a glance of reflection, but rather indicated a suspension of intelligent thought.

35 There was something coming to her and she was waiting for it, fearfully. What was it? She did not know; it was too subtle and elusive to name. But she felt it, creeping out of the sky, reaching toward her through the sound, the scents, the color that filled the air.

Now her bosom rose and fell tumultuously. She was beginning to
40 recognize this thing that was approaching to possess her, and she was striving to beat it back with her will — as powerless as her two white slender hands would have been.

When she abandoned herself a little whispered word escaped her slightly parted lips. She said it over and over under her breath: "Free, free,
45 free!" The vacant stare and the look of terror that had followed it went from her eyes. They stayed keen and bright. Her pulses beat fast, and the coursing blood warmed and relaxed every inch of her body.

She did not stop to ask if it were not a monstrous joy that held her. A clear and exalted perception enabled her to dismiss the suggestions as
50 trivial.

She knew that she would weep again when she saw the kind, tender hands folded in death; the face that had never looked save with love upon her, fixed and gray and dead. But she saw beyond that bitter moment a long procession of years to come that would belong to her absolutely. And
55 she opened and spread her arms out to them in welcome.

There would be no one to live for during those coming years; she would live for herself. There would be no powerful will bending her in that blind persistence with which men and women believe they have a

right to impose a private will upon a fellow-creature. A kind intention or a
60 cruel intention made the act seem no less a crime as she looked upon it in
that brief moment of illumination.

And yet she had loved him — sometimes. Often she had not. What did
it matter! What could love, the unsolved mystery, count for in face of this
possession of self-assertion which she suddenly recognized for the strong-
65 est impulse of her being.

"Free! Body and soul free!" she kept whispering.

Josephine was kneeling before the closed door with her lips to the
keyhole, imploring for admission. "Louise, open the door! I beg; open the
door — you will make yourself ill. What are you doing, Louise? For
70 heaven's sake open the door."

"Go away. I am not making myself ill." No; she was drinking in a very
elixir of life through that open window.

Her fancy was running riot along those days ahead of her. Spring
days, and summer days, and all sorts of days that would be her own. She
75 breathed a quick prayer that life might be long. It was only yesterday she
had thought with a shudder that life might be long.

She arose at length and opened the door to her sister's importunities.
There was a feverish triumph in her eyes, and she carried herself unwit-
tingly like a goddess of Victory. She clasped her sister's waist, and
80 together they descended the stairs. Richards stood waiting for them at the
bottom.

Some one was opening the front door with a latchkey. It was Brently
Mallard who entered, a little travel-stained, composedly carrying his grip-
sack and umbrella. He had been far from the scene of accident, and did not
85 even know there had been one. He stood amazed at Josephine's piercing
cry; at Richards' quick motion to screen him from the view of his wife.

But Richards was too late.

When the doctors came they said she had died of heart disease — of
joy that kills.

"The Story of an Hour" by Kate Chopin. From <u>The Complete Works of Kate Chopin</u>,
edited by Per Seyersted. Published by Louisiana State University Press.

47. Which of the first five sentences contains foreshadowing? Sentence number

   (A) one   (D) four

   (B) two   (E) five

   (C) three

48. All of the following are instances of irony EXCEPT

I.   the lines on Mrs. Mallard's face indicating repression

II.   Josephine's belief that Mrs. Mallard is making herself ill

III.   the doctor's belief that Mrs. Mallard died of joy at seeing her husband alive

IV.   Mrs. Mallard's anticipation of freedom and long life as she descends the stairs

(A)   I only

(B)   I and III only

(C)   IV only

(D)   II and III only

(E)   II and IV only

49.   Mrs. Mallard's initial reaction to news of her husband's death can best be described as

(A)   hypocritical

(B)   sincere grief

(C)   uncomprehending

(D)   calculated to deceive others

(E)   puzzled

50.   The details in the fifth paragraph (lines 19–23) suggest

(A)   sorrow

(B)   triviality

(C)   rebirth

(E)   alienation

(D)   death

51.   Mrs. Mallard's joy at being free is first presented as something that she

(A)   has long desired

(B)   resists

(C)   believes is monstrous

(D)   is ashamed of

(E)   struggles to create

52.   Mrs. Mallard's initial thoughts of freedom are depicted as

(A)   an external force that overpowers her

(B)   an immediate reaction to news of Brently Mallard's death

(C)   a manifestation of her self-centeredness

(D)   the result of a deliberate reasoning process

(E)   influenced by Josephine and Richards' presence

53. The kind of narration used in the story is

    (A) unreliable first-person   (D) objective

    (B) stream of consciousness   (E) unreliable third-person

    (C) limited omniscience

54. Which of the following LEAST accurately describes Brently Mallard?

    (A) Faithful   (D) Loving

    (B) Abusive   (E) Tender

    (C) Filled with good intentions

55. In her "brief moment of illumination" (line 61), Mrs. Mallard's criticism is chiefly directed at

    (A) Brently Mallard

    (B) the bonds of marriage

    (C) herself

    (D) society's expectations of widows

    (E) her prior lack of educational opportunities

56. In line 60, "it" refers to

    (A) the conditions of life

    (B) the sexual obligations of marriage

    (C) lack of privacy in marriage

    (D) unequal employment opportunities for women

    (E) one person's will being dominated by another

57. Mrs. Mallard thinks that it did not matter whether or not she had loved Brently Mallard because

    (A) death had separated them forever

    (B) time will obliterate her memory of him

    (C) her new sense of self makes her past life with him seem insignificant

    (D) he had never made clear to her whether he loved her

    (E) love is a mystery which can never be solved

58. Mrs. Mallard's most important discovery is

    (A) that she is capable of living without Brently

    (B) that she never loved Brently

    (C) that people do not understand her

    (D) her need for self-assertion

    (E) her desire to escape from society

59. Line 79 contains

    (A) personification   (D) an apostrophe

    (B) a simile   (E) an invocation

    (C) a paradox

60. Which of the following statements about the last sentence of the story is LEAST accurate?

    (A) The author implies that Mrs. Mallard's death is just punishment for the "monstrous joy" she experienced earlier.

    (B) No character left alive at the end of the story fully understands Mrs. Mallard's death.

    (C) Mrs. Mallard has experienced great joy that intensifies her shock at seeing Brently alive.

    (D) The doctors are wrong in believing that Mrs. Mallard died of joy at seeing Brently alive.

    (E) The effectiveness of the last sentence depends on the reader understanding events more completely than the other characters who witness them.

Section 2

TIME: 2 Hours
            3 Essay Questions

QUESTION 1. *(Suggested time — 40 minutes. This question counts one-third of the total essay-section score.)* Read carefully the following poem. Then write an essay analyzing the various stages in the poem's "argument." Consider how the speaker's choice of images, allusions, and other devices of language re-enforce his argument. Your essay should take into account the poem's overall structure.

To His Coy Mistress

            Had we but world enough, and time,
        This coyness, lady, were no crime.
        We would sit down, and think which way
        To walk, and pass our long love's day.
5   Thou by the Indian Ganges' side
        Shouldst rubies find; I by the tide
        Of Humber would complain.¹ I would
        Love you ten years before the flood,
        And you should, if you please, refuse
10   Till the conversion of the Jews.
        My vegetable love should grow
        Vaster than empires and more slow,
        An hundred years should go to praise
        Thine eyes, and on thy forehead gaze;
15   Two hundred to adore each breast,
        But thirty thousand to the rest;
        An age at least to every part,
        And the last age should show your heart.
        For, lady, you deserve this state,
20   Nor would I love at lower rate.
            But at my back I always hear
        Time's winged chariot hurrying near;
        And yonder all before us lie
        Deserts of vast eternity.
25   Thy beauty shall no more be found,
        Nor, in thy marble vault, shall sound
        My echoing song; then worms shall try
        That long-preserved virginity,

And your quaint honor turn to dust,
30 And into ashes all my lust:
The grave's a fine and private place,
But none, I think, do there embrace.
        Now therefore, while the youthful hue
Sits on thy skin like morning dew,
35 And while thy willing soul transpires[2]
At every pore with instant fires,
Now let us sport us while we may,
And now, like amorous birds of prey,
Rather at once our tune devour
40 Than languish in his slow-chapped[3] power.
Let us roll all our strength and all
Our sweetness up into one ball,
And tear our pleasures with rough strife
Thorough the iron gates of life:
45 Thus, though we cannot make our sun
Stand still, yet we will make him run.

—Andrew Marvell

1. "Complain" implies songs of plaintive love.
2. Breathes forth. "Instant fires"; immediate, present enthusiasm.
3. Slow-jawed.

QUESTION 2. *(Suggested time — 40 minutes. This question counts one-third of the total essay-section score.)* Minor characters in literary works can be used for various purposes by authors. Choose two minor characters from one of the following works (or another of comparable quality that is appropriate for the question) and examine the ways in which they contribute to the work from which they come. Do not write about a film or television program. Some questions to think about in writing your essay: Why are these characters included? How are they used by their authors? To what aspects of their work do they contribute? How would this work be different if these characters were not present?

Native Son	*Antigone*
Hamlet	*Jude the Obscure*
Macbeth	*The Great Gatsby*
A Doll's House	*The House of Seven Gables*
Hard Times	*The Importance of Being Earnest*
Tartuffe	*The Way of the World*

The Catcher in the Rye   *Volpone*

To Kill a Mockingbird   *Vanity Fair*

Tom Jones   *Major Barbara*

The Awakening   *Madame Bovary*

Gulliver's Travels   *Oedpius Rex*

QUESTION 3. *(Suggested time — 40 minutes. This question counts one-third of the total essay-section score.)* In the selection below from *Leviathan*, Thomas Hobbes distinguishes between Right of Nature and Law of Nature. Write an essay in which you explain Hobbes' distinction between the two. What are the relationships between them?

From *Part 1, Chapter 14. Of the First and Second Natural Laws*

The Right of Nature, which writers commonly call *jus naturale,* is the liberty each man hath to use his own power as he will himself for the preservation of his own nature, that is to say, of his own life; and consequently of doing anything which in his own judgment and reason he shall
5 conceive to be the aptest means thereunto.

By Liberty is understood, according to the proper signification of the word, the absence of external impediments, which impediments may oft take away part of a man's power to do what he would, but cannot hinder him from using the power left him according as his judgment and reason
10 shall dictate to him.

A Law of Nature *(lex naturalis)* is a precept or general rule found out by reason, by which a man is forbidden to do that which is destructive of his life or taketh away the means of preserving the same; and to omit that by which he thinketh it may be best preserved. For though they that speak
15 of this subject use to confound *Jus* and *Lex, Right* and *Law*; yet they ought to be distinguished, because Right consisteth in liberty to do or to forbear, whereas Law determineth and bindeth to one of them: so that Law and Right differ as much as obligation and liberty, which in one and the same matter are inconsistent.
20 And because the condition of man (as hath been declared in the precedent chapter) is a condition of war of every one against every one, in which case every one is governed by his own reason, and there is nothing he can make use of that may not be a help unto him in preserving his life against his enemies: it followeth that in such a condition every man has a
25 right to every thing, even to one another's body. And therefore as long as this natural right of every man to every thing endureth, there can be no

security to any man (how strong or wise soever he be) of living out the time which nature ordinarily alloweth men to live. And consequently it is a precept, or general rule of reason, *That every man ought to endeavor*
30 *peace as far as he has hope of obtaining it; and when he cannot obtain it, that he may seek and use all helps and advantages of war.* The first branch of which rule containeth the first and fundamental law of nature, which is *to seek peace and follow it.* The second, the sum of the right of nature, which is, *by all means we can to defend ourselves.*

35   From this fundamental law of nature, by which men are commanded to endeavor peace, is derived this second law: *That a man be willing, when others are so too, as far-forth as for peace and defence of himself he shall think necessary, to lay down this right to all things, and be contented with so much liberty against other men as he would allow other men against*
40 *himself.* For as long as any man holdeth this right of doing anything he liketh, so long are all men in the condition of war. But if other men will not lay down their right, as well as he, then there is no reason for anyone to divest himself of his. For that were to expose himself to prey (which no man is bound to) rather than to dispose himself to peace. This is that law of
45 the Gospel: *Whatsoever you require that others should do to you, that do ye to them.*

TEST 5

ANSWER KEY

1. (C)	16. (B)	31. (C)	46. (D)
2. (A)	17. (D)	32. (B)	47. (A)
3. (B)	18. (D)	33. (B)	48. (A)
4. (D)	19. (B)	34. (D)	49. (B)
5. (E)	20. (C)	35. (A)	50. (C)
6. (A)	21. (C)	36. (E)	51. (B)
7. (E)	22. (C)	37. (E)	52. (A)
8. (C)	23. (E)	38. (B)	53. (C)
9. (E)	24. (B)	39. (D)	54. (B)
10. (A)	25. (C)	40. (A)	55. (B)
11. (D)	26. (A)	41. (C)	56. (E)
12. (E)	27. (E)	42. (A)	57. (C)
13. (B)	28. (A)	43. (E)	58. (D)
14. (C)	29. (C)	44. (D)	59. (B)
15. (D)	30. (E)	45. (C)	60. (A)

DETAILED EXPLANATIONS OF ANSWERS

TEST 5

Section 1

1.   **(C)**   Personification is the attribution of human qualities to a non-human thing or abstraction. Here the abstraction Time is depicted as toiling after Shakespeare in vain.

2.   **(A)**   The first thirty-eight lines provide a critical history of English drama from Shakespeare up to 1747 as a preliminary to Johnson's appeal to audiences to alter current dramatic taste. He does not view the history of English drama as one of steady decline; though Shakespeare may be England's greatest playwright, others (such as Ben Jonson) have made significant, different contributions.

3.   **(B)**   The line means that Shakespeare thoroughly depicted known worlds and then went on to depict imaginary worlds. He consumed entirely known worlds and then imagined new ones.

4.   **(D)**   Johnson praises Shakespeare for his imagination (line 4), truth (line 7), and passion (line 8). Jonson is praised, somewhat less enthusiastically, for his craftsmanship; he "pleases by method" and "invents by rule," but nonetheless left "a lasting tomb" (i.e., monument by which he will be remembered).

5.   **(E)**   The sense of the sentence is that although praise of Jonson is less enthusiastic than of Shakespeare, such approval has given him lasting fame ("lingering bays").

6.   **(A)**   A simile is a comparison using "like" or "as." The simile in line 16 is that Jonson, like Egypt's kings, left a lasting tomb.

7.   **(E)**   Johnson complains that the Restoration comic dramatists were sympathetic friends to "vice" (line 21) and that their wit was often "obscenity" (line 20).

8.   **(C)**   Johnson says that the Restoration comic dramatists pleased audiences in their own time and did not seek to improve or criticize their society (line 22).

They were popular, sought lasting fame (line 24), and were strongly supported in their own time (line 25).

9. **(E)** In lines 29–30, Johnson says that tragedy declined because it was "crushed by rules" (i.e., it relied too heavily on accepted rules drawn from critics and past practice rather than being daringly imaginative). As it became more "refined" (more rule-bound), it became weaker.

10. **(A)** Johnson says that subject matter that had long been the province of tragedy (such as the tale of Faustus) became subject matter for farce and pantomime; hence tragedy at last abandoned her "ancient reign."

11. **(D)** Tragedy saw her subject matter (in this case, Faustus) used in other, inappropriate genres.

12. **(E)** Folly welcomed the joyous day when tragedy's proper subject matter was used in other genres; Folly's influence or reign ("sway") is strengthened by Pantomime and Song.

13. **(B)** In lines 39–62, Johnson says that no one can predict the future history of drama, but that the stage echoes public taste. Hence he appeals to audiences to alter their taste by preferring Nature, Sense, Virtue, and Truth to "the charms of Sound" and "the pomp of Show."

14. **(C)** Line 54 means that theater people (actors and playwrights) live to please audiences and that they can survive only if they succeed in pleasing audiences. Hence the "we" in line 54 are those (actors, playwrights) whose main function is to please audiences.

15. **(D)** Lines 52-53 say that audiences determine the laws of drama, and that plays simply reflect the "public voice" (i.e., what the audience desires).

16. **(B)** The poem is written in rhyming couplets of iambic pentameter (heroic couplets).

17. **(D)** The speaker is one of the magi, the wise men from the east, who journeyed to Bethlehem to see the infant Christ.

18. **(D)** The speaker is recalling events during his journey to Bethlehem, which took place many years earlier, as line 32 makes clear.

19. **(B)** Parts I and II describe the journey of the magi to Bethlehem; Part III consists of the speaker's reflections on the significance of that journey.

20. **(C)** Part I primarily describes conditions the magi encountered on their journey; Part II continues the description, but introduces images or symbols of

things that were to play a part in Christ's life; Part III is by far the most meditative section, as the speaker discusses the implications of the events and their effect on him. The major shift occurs at the beginning of line 32, as the speaker turns from an account of the journey itself to reflections on its importance.

21. **(C)** "Refractory" is an adjective modifying camels, meaning the camels were unmanageable.

22. **(C)** The magi made their journey during the dead of winter. Discouraged by the harsh conditions, the magi sometimes regretfully recalled scenes that contrast with the conditions they encounter during the winter journey (i.e., summer palaces, silken girls bringing sherbet).

23. **(E)** The images in these lines (vegetation, running stream) suggest renewal.

24. **(B)** These images suggest various significant events in Christ's life and crucifixion. The three trees suggest the crucifixion; the dicing for silver suggests the thirty pieces of silver paid to Judas for betraying Christ as well as the gambling of soldiers at the foot of the cross for Jesus' garments. The white horse is probably an allusion to the end of the world (mentioned in the Biblical book of Revelations, in passages alluding to the end of the world).

25. **(C)** "Not a moment too soon" reflects the speaker's exasperation with the harsh conditions encountered during the journey, which he is glad to complete. The magi arrived well after Christ's birth, and of course the speaker lived for many more years.

26. **(A)** The repetition (the only instance of such a device in the poem) indicates that this is the single most important question the speaker has been struggling with. The remainder of the poem seeks to answer the question (were we led all that way for birth or death?).

27. **(E)** The speaker means that Christ's birth fundamentally altered the lives of the magi, who were no longer comfortable with their old, pagan religion or in the kingdoms from which they came. They now view their people as "aliens" clutching gods that have lost their meaning for the magi.

28. **(A)** Although the event was "hard and bitter agony" to him, the speaker says he would do it again, presumably because he has discovered a greater faith or truth than in "the old dispensation" (his former pagan religion).

29. **(C)** The speaker suggests that he would welcome death in order to be rid of his uneasiness in living among an alien people whose religion no longer is meaningful to him. He is a wiser man, but not a "happier" one.

30. **(E)** Free verse is verse whose meter is irregular in some respect or whose

rhythm is not metrical. The poem is not rhymed, nor does it employ a regular meter.

31. **(C)** Donne's *Meditation* is built on the Renaissance notion of man as a microcosm (a little world), analogous to the big world outside (the macrocosm), except that Donne reverses the idea, temporarily arguing that man is the macrocosm and the world outside the microcosm. The first paragraph develops the comparison of man and the world, arguing that man is larger, more complete, than the world.

32. **(B)** The line means that the outside world does not contain anything to which some part of man does not correspond (put another way, some part of man corresponds to everything in the outside world).

33. **(B)** In the first paragraph, Donne plays with the idea that man is the macrocosm and the outside world the microcosm. See number 31, above.

34. **(D)** Line 29 asks rhetorically whether the outside world (the world of nature) can produce as many monstrous, venomous creatures as man can produce diseases. In his comparison of man and the outside world, man's diseases correspond to the outside world's venomous creatures.

35. **(A)** Donne means that man himself produces an abundance of diseases, but it is an unwelcome abundance. Hence "miserable abundance" refers to human diseases.

36. **(E)** A paradox is a statement that is seemingly contradictory or opposed to common sense but that is nonetheless true in context. How can riches be "beggarly"? Only in context can the paradox be explained: "riches" refers to the diseases man produces, and these diseases of course make him "poor" (hence the riches are only apparent).

37. **(E)** In the metaphor in the second paragraph, man's diseases are compared to the other world's "serpents and vipers, malignant and venomous creatures, and worms and caterpillars." The latter seek to devour the world that produces them, much as human diseases seek to destroy the humans who produce them.

38. **(B)** Donne means that man has produced men who are physicians, but cannot cure himself. Unlike the hart or dog, who seem to know instinctively cures for certain diseases, man does not have the ability to rely on himself for cures. He must turn to others for help.

39. **(D)** "It" refers to the hart (deer) that the dog pursues, discussed in the preceding sentence.

40. **(A)** The sentence means that the dog, according to proverb, knows what grass to eat to cure himself when sick.

41. **(C)**   The line means that physicians and apothecaries are not as similar to men in general as they are to those creatures in nature (such as harts and dogs) who know remedies for illnesses. Hence the line means they are not so near man ("him") as they are to other creatures.

42. **(A)**   "They" refers back to "those inferior creatures" (lines 45–46), which are the animals in nature who are their own physician (hart, dog).

43. **(E)**   The author addresses himself, saying that he must alter the earlier part of his meditation, in which he praised man as superior to the outside world. The fact that man is not his own physician, in contrast to some "inferior creatures" in the outside world, forces him to qualify his earlier praise of man's stature.

44. **(D)**   See number 43, above. Donne says that his earlier celebration of man's "great extent and proportion" must be qualified because man himself, through his diseases, "shrinks himself and consumes himself to a handful of dust" (through death). Despite his soaring thoughts, man brings himself to "the thoughtlessness of the grave."

45. **(C)**   Donne wrote this meditation during an attack of illness, which can be deduced from the subject matter of the *Meditation*.

46. **(D)**   The *Meditation* attempts to assess the human condition. It begins by defining man as a macrocosm, praising especially man's comprehensiveness of thought. The author seeks to define man in relation to the outside world and to assess his value in relation to it. He later qualifies his assessment of man, based on man's inability to be his own physician. Throughout the Meditation, Donne attempts to assess what the conditions of being human are.

47. **(A)**   The information that Mrs. Mallard is "afflicted with a heart trouble" foreshadows her death by heart attack at the end of the story.

48. **(A)**   Irony involves disparity between what is said and what is meant, what is expected and the actual outcome, or what is understood by a character and what is understood by the audience or reader. Hence it is ironic that Josephine believes Mrs. Mallard is making herself ill through grief while we know she is experiencing joy, and ironic that the doctors think Mrs. Mallard died of joy at seeing her husband alive while we know that the shock that kills her does not result from joy at his being alive. Mrs. Mallard's expectations for the future are also ironically misplaced when she descends the staircase, losing both her freedom and her life at once upon Brently's return.

49. **(B)**   Her immediate reaction to his death is one of sincere grief. It is only later that she experiences joy at the realization that she is free.

50. **(C)**   The details all suggest rebirth — new spring life, trees reviving from

the winter, sparrows twittering, spring rain, the sound of a song. All are indications of life reviving and continuing.

51. **(B)** Lines 35–42 make it clear that this new feeling of joy (through the recognition of freedom) is something that she senses with fear and which she strives "to beat ... back with her will."

52. **(A)** Lines 30–42 indicate that Mrs. Mallard is passive. Her gaze indicates "a suspension of intelligent thought." The thought of freedom is a "thing that was approaching to possess her." In short, the author presents the idea of freedom as something external to her that approaches and overpowers her, not as something she consciously seeks.

53. **(C)** Limited omniscient narration allows the writer to move in and out of the thoughts of some but not all of the characters at will. In this story, we are given inside views of Mrs. Mallard, but we do not know the thoughts of all of the characters.

54 **(B)** Lines 51–53 portray Brently Mallard as tender, kind, and loving, not abusive or distant or faithless, and lines 59–60 suggests that he was well-intentioned. The fact that Mr. and Mrs. Mallard had a conventionally "good" marriage is part of what gives the story its interest.

55. **(B)** Her criticism is directed at marriage in general, which allows men and women to believe they "have a right to impose a private will upon a fellow-creature." The generalizing language ("men and women," not Brently specifically; a "fellow-creature," not Mrs. Mallard) indicates the general nature of the criticism.

56. **(E)** The "crime" to which Mrs. Mallard refers is the "act" of one person imposing a "private will upon a fellow-creature." Regardless of whether the intention in doing so is "kind" or "cruel," the act is still a "crime."

57. **(C)** "What did it matter" whether she had loved him since love does not "count" in the face of "this possession of self-assertion which she suddenly recognized as the strongest impulse of her being." Having learned what is most important to her, Mrs. Mallard considers all things trivial.

58. **(D)** Outweighing all other matters is Mrs. Mallard's discovery that the need for "self-assertion" was "the strongest impulse of her being." Whether she loved Brently, whether she can live comfortably without him, and all other issues are secondary to her recognition of the desire for self-assertion.

59. **(B)** A simile is a comparison using "like" or "as." The simile in line 79 is Mrs. Mallard carrying herself "like a goddess of Victory."

60. **(A)** We have seen that Mrs. Mallard experiences great joy, but it is not the joy of seeing her husband alive. Instead, her joy at being free causes shock when

that freedom is suddenly taken away as her husband returns alive. No character in the story understands the nature of Mrs. Mallard's joy and the sudden reversal of that joy; the effectiveness of the last sentence depends on our understanding what the other characters do not understand.

Section 2

Essay 1

Andrew Marvell's "To His Coy Mistress" is a poem of seduction in which the speaker attempts to persuade his mistress to give in to his desires. There are three major sections to the poem, which form the three parts of his argument. The poem is structured as an "if x, then y" syllogism, but is not logically valid.

In the first section (the "if x, then y" proposition), the speaker argues that his mistress' coyness would be acceptable if they had unlimited time and space for him to woo her at a slow pace. The speaker's images and allusions are global, suggest unlimited time and leisure, depict time as a comforting friend, and seek to compliment her (as part of his seduction strategy). For example, she could be in India and he in England, and he could love from before the Biblical flood and she could refuse until just before the Last Judgment. His "vegetable" love could grow slowly, with vast amounts of time to praise each of her attractions, since she deserves such slow praise.

The second section (lines 21–32) asserts, however, that they do not have unlimited time. The images and allusions in this section are graphic and are designed to frighten, and time is depicted as man's destroyer, not something that nurtures him. The songs, rubies, and hearts of the first section are replaced by deserts, vaults, graves, and devouring worms. The speaker argues that time is hurrying on, that "deserts of vast eternity" lie ahead, that his lust will turn to ashes, and that her "quaint" honor will turn to dust in her tomb. Most graphically, the virginity that she has protected from him will be violated by worms after her death. Finally, he adds ironic understatement to his argument in the closing couplet of section two (lines 31–32).

In the final section (lines 33-46), he concludes that she should submit to him because they lack "world enough and time." The images swerve back from the cold marble of the tomb to the warmth of moist, living flesh, and then urge the lovers, "like amorous birds of prey," to become active, to devour time rather than be passively devoured by time. Again the lovers' relationship to time changes. Although they cannot stop time, they can be so active that the sun must run to keep up with them.

As persuasive as the speaker may sound, his argument is invalid. In logic, a valid conclusion can follow only when the minor premise affirms the conditions in the first half ("If we had world enough and time") of the "if x, then y" proposition. The speaker's minor premise ("we do not have world enough and time") denies those conditions. Hence no conclusion can follow logically, although the speaker has built an apparently logical case and made a strong emotional appeal.

Essay 1 — Explanation

The question asks the student to do two things: to analyze the poem's primary argument and to discuss how such things as images and allusions are used to support the poem's main argument. To write an acceptable essay, the student must recognize that there are several stages in the speaker's argument, and that the different stages (three) use different means to achieve their ends. A good essay will recognize that there are three stages to the speaker's argument; an excellent essay will recognize the form of those three stages, including knowing that the argument takes the form of an invalid syllogism.

In the sample essay, the writer's first paragraph defines the purpose of the poem ("a poem of seduction"), makes clear that the poem has three parts, and identifies the specific form of argument the speaker uses (an invalid "if x, then y" syllogism).

The next three paragraphs analyze the three sections of the poem. In addition to explaining *what* the argument is in each section, the writer provides selected illustrations of *how* the speaker carries out his argument. The writer recognizes, for example, that the first section of the poem uses images that are appropriate to the argument (images of slow growth, reenforcing the idea that her coyness would be fine if they had all the time in the world), as well as images that comfort and reassure. The writer also recognizes that part of the speaker's strategy is to flatter his reluctant mistress. Similarly, in discussing section two, the writer recognizes that the images change to cold, threatening, and graphic depictions of objects associated with death and sterility. The speaker's strategy has changed from complimenting to trying to frighten; hence the language and the images of the poem change to suit that purpose. In discussing the third section, the writer recognizes that the images change again. As the writer notes, all three sections deal with the relationship of the lovers to time. In the final section, the speaker uses images that urge the lovers to use time actively, rather than be victimized by time.

In the final paragraph, the writer explains why the apparently logical argument of the poem is in fact logically invalid while still acknowledging the emotional persuasiveness of the poem.

One of the strengths of this essay is that the first paragraph establishes the major points to be addressed in the essay and indicates clearly that the student has understood the poem's overall structure. The rest of the essay elaborates on the subjects introduced in the first paragraph.

Essay 2 — *The Way of the World*

Many Restoration comic dramatists establish subtle hierarchies in distinguishing among characters in their plays. Characters range from those who are closest to the ideal or most admirable, through various gradations, to those who are furthest from the ideal or least admirable. Most of these comedies of manners seek

303

to ridicule human failings. They do so by assuming an ideal mode of life based on a code of manners by which the actions and worthiness of individual characters are judged. Usually this code is highly sophisticated, clearly defined, and artificial, involving such concerns as wit, ability to manipulate, control of emotion, and the supremacy of reason. Most comedies of manners contain a sophisticated couple who engage in a battle of wit and who most nearly approximate the ideal. Minor characters are often used both to help define the ideal and as foils for the leading couple.

In William Congreve's *The Way of the World*, Witwoud and Fainall are minor male characters whose shortcomings make audiences appreciate more fully the virtues of the play's leading male character, Mirabell. Witwoud and Fainall, however, fall short of the ideal for strikingly different reasons.

As his name suggests, Witwoud is a false wit. He strives to be witty, but — in contrast to Mirabell — fails. He is not a gross dunce, but his attempts at wit lack the originality or Mirabell's wit; his wit is described by others in the play as borrowed scraps of other folks' wit. Further, he lacks Mirabell's sense of proportion, restraint, and timing. His attempts at wit are excessive and frequently inappropriate to the occasion. Finally, his comparisons or similitudes often annoy others, rather than pleasing or amusing them.

Unlike Witwoud, Fainall is nearly Mirabell's equal in wit, but he lacks Mirabell's common decency. He also lacks Mirabell's foresight and ability to dissemble. Fainall is condemned in the play on moral grounds — not because he engages in sexual intrigue, as does Mirabell, but because he actively seeks to harm admirable characters for personal gain. His presence in the play signals an increasing concern for ethical matters in the comedy of manners. He also falls short of Mirabell in areas more traditionally associated with the comedy of manners. His scheme to gain control of his wife's fortune is defeated by Mirabell's "counter-scheme," which evinces greater foresight. Finally, Mirabell is better able to manipulate others, partly because he is a better dissembler; in Mirabell's case, these skills are used for benign, not malignant, purposes.

The shortcomings of Witwoud and Fainall help establish, by negative examples, what the ideal should be. The flaws of Witwoud and Fainall make audiences more aware of Mirabell's strengths.

Essay 2 — Explanation

This "free response" question asks the student to explain how an author uses two minor characters in whatever work the student chooses to discuss. The question does not call for plot summary or simply a description of the two minor characters. It asks *how* the two minor characters are used — that is, what does their presence contribute to the work? In order to write a good essay, the student must know *what* the two minor characters contribute and *how* they contribute. The student must exercise care in the selection of the two characters to be discussed. They are not to be the principal characters in the work, but they must have a significant enough role to contribute something substantial to the work.

In the sample essay, the writer has chosen two characters from a Restoration comedy of manners, William Congreve's *The Way of the World*. Because *The Way of the World* belongs to a genre that has a fairly specific set of conventions and characteristics, the student elected to explain something of what a Restoration comedy of manners is in order to show how the two minor characters function in the play.

After explaining some of the values operating in the Restoration comedy of manners and the way in which Restoration comic dramatists typically establish hierarchies of characters, the writer identifies two ways in which minor characters are often used in these plays (as foils and as a means of establishing an ideal of behavior which the leading character usually comes closer to fulfilling). The writer then identifies the two characters to be discussed, and analyzes them in the terms set out in the first paragraph. Notice that the writer did not pick two characters who function in the same way in the play; instead, the writer picked two characters who fall short of an assumed ideal, but who fall short for very different reasons. Hence the student is better able to demonstrate a more complete understanding of the play and to illustrate a broader range of functions of minor characters. In discussing Witwoud and Fainall, the student demonstrates awareness of why each is in the play, how each serves as a foil to the play's leading male character, how the shortcomings of each helps define an ideal that neither achieves, and even manages to show how the presence of one of them indicates a change taking place in the drama of the period. The essay, then, is consistent in its treatment of the two characters, but discriminates between the two, showing that the two contribute in different but equally important ways.

Essay 3

Hobbes distinguishes between the Right of Nature, which basically looks only to self-interest, and the Law of Nature, which looks to the common good. But because self-interest ultimately depends on the common good, the Law of Nature must take priority over the Right of Nature.

By "Right of Nature," Hobbes means the liberty to preserve one's life through any means the individual's reason deems necessary. Under the Right of Nature, no external force may restrain man from taking any action he pleases to defend or preserve himself.

In contrast, a Law of Nature is based not on liberty, but obligation, and forbids man to do things that would destroy his life or destroy the means of preserving his life. Both Right and Law derive from reason, but the former derives from an individual's reason whereas the latter derives from a broader perspective.

To fully understand the relationship between the two, it is necessary to understand Hobbes' conception of the human condition. Because he believes man's natural condition is a state of war, it follows that the Right of Nature would entitle men to destroy one another, in which case individual and group security are impossible. Hence a broader perspective is needed to create security. That broader perspective suggests that all men should pursue peace, which is Hobbes' first Law of Nature. Only when peace cannot be achieved may the Right of Nature — to protect oneself — be exercised. Furthermore, Hobbes derives a second Law of Nature from the first; in order to preserve peace and protect himself, man must be willing to give up unrestrained liberty if he wishes others to give up unrestrained liberty in their actions toward him. What Hobbes argues for, then, is a social contract which recognizes not only the desirability but the necessity of subordinating individual self-interest to the group interest even from the narrow perspective of self-preservation. In a constant state of war in which each individual does as he pleases, no individual will prosper. Hence the Right of Nature cannot take priority over the Law of Nature if chaos is to be avoided.

Essay 3 — Explanation

This question asks the student to explain the distinction between two concepts in a fairly difficult essay and to explain the writer's conception of the relationship between the two concepts. The student must understand the selection from Hobbes' *Leviathan* in order to write a good essay, but must do more than simply summarize what Hobbes says. There are several stages in Hobbes' explanation, and the student must demonstrate understanding of those stages. Moreover, the two concepts spring from certain assumptions and depend on other background ideas that must be explained or clarified. Finally, the relationship between the two concepts is more subtle than first appears, and the student must make sure that he clarifies that relationship.

In the sample essay, the writer provides a brief explanation of the essential difference between Law of Nature and Right of Nature and states the ultimate relationship between the two in the first paragraph. The second paragraph then explains, in clear, contemporary English and in more detail, what Hobbes means by Right of Nature. The third paragraph explains what Hobbes means by Law of Nature, contrasting the source of the Law of Nature with the source of the Right of Nature. The relationship between the two, briefly stated in the writer's first paragraph (that the Law of Nature must take priority over the Right of Nature because self-interest ultimately depends on the common good), is complex, involving several steps; hence the writer appropriately spends more time on this aspect of the question than on any other part in the essay. The writer explains that the relationship between the two depends on an understanding of a prior concept (Hobbes' conception of the human condition) and on several conclusions that follow from that concept. Finally, the writer restates the central argument of the excerpt in language that Hobbes might not recognize but that makes Hobbes' chief position clear. Only by tracing the several stages of Hobbes' argument can the student arrive at an adequate explanation of the two concepts that the question asks the student to analyze.

THE ADVANCED PLACEMENT EXAMINATION IN

English Literature & Composition

TEST 6

1. Ⓐ Ⓑ Ⓒ Ⓓ Ⓔ	21. Ⓐ Ⓑ Ⓒ Ⓓ Ⓔ	41. Ⓐ Ⓑ Ⓒ Ⓓ Ⓔ
2. Ⓐ Ⓑ Ⓒ Ⓓ Ⓔ	22. Ⓐ Ⓑ Ⓒ Ⓓ Ⓔ	42. Ⓐ Ⓑ Ⓒ Ⓓ Ⓔ
3. Ⓐ Ⓑ Ⓒ Ⓓ Ⓔ	23. Ⓐ Ⓑ Ⓒ Ⓓ Ⓔ	43. Ⓐ Ⓑ Ⓒ Ⓓ Ⓔ
4. Ⓐ Ⓑ Ⓒ Ⓓ Ⓔ	24. Ⓐ Ⓑ Ⓒ Ⓓ Ⓔ	44. Ⓐ Ⓑ Ⓒ Ⓓ Ⓔ
5. Ⓐ Ⓑ Ⓒ Ⓓ Ⓔ	25. Ⓐ Ⓑ Ⓒ Ⓓ Ⓔ	45. Ⓐ Ⓑ Ⓒ Ⓓ Ⓔ
6. Ⓐ Ⓑ Ⓒ Ⓓ Ⓔ	26. Ⓐ Ⓑ Ⓒ Ⓓ Ⓔ	46. Ⓐ Ⓑ Ⓒ Ⓓ Ⓔ
7. Ⓐ Ⓑ Ⓒ Ⓓ Ⓔ	27. Ⓐ Ⓑ Ⓒ Ⓓ Ⓔ	47. Ⓐ Ⓑ Ⓒ Ⓓ Ⓔ
8. Ⓐ Ⓑ Ⓒ Ⓓ Ⓔ	28. Ⓐ Ⓑ Ⓒ Ⓓ Ⓔ	48. Ⓐ Ⓑ Ⓒ Ⓓ Ⓔ
9. Ⓐ Ⓑ Ⓒ Ⓓ Ⓔ	29. Ⓐ Ⓑ Ⓒ Ⓓ Ⓔ	49. Ⓐ Ⓑ Ⓒ Ⓓ Ⓔ
10. Ⓐ Ⓑ Ⓒ Ⓓ Ⓔ	30. Ⓐ Ⓑ Ⓒ Ⓓ Ⓔ	50. Ⓐ Ⓑ Ⓒ Ⓓ Ⓔ
11. Ⓐ Ⓑ Ⓒ Ⓓ Ⓔ	31. Ⓐ Ⓑ Ⓒ Ⓓ Ⓔ	51. Ⓐ Ⓑ Ⓒ Ⓓ Ⓔ
12. Ⓐ Ⓑ Ⓒ Ⓓ Ⓔ	32. Ⓐ Ⓑ Ⓒ Ⓓ Ⓔ	52. Ⓐ Ⓑ Ⓒ Ⓓ Ⓔ
13. Ⓐ Ⓑ Ⓒ Ⓓ Ⓔ	33. Ⓐ Ⓑ Ⓒ Ⓓ Ⓔ	53. Ⓐ Ⓑ Ⓒ Ⓓ Ⓔ
14. Ⓐ Ⓑ Ⓒ Ⓓ Ⓔ	34. Ⓐ Ⓑ Ⓒ Ⓓ Ⓔ	54. Ⓐ Ⓑ Ⓒ Ⓓ Ⓔ
15. Ⓐ Ⓑ Ⓒ Ⓓ Ⓔ	35. Ⓐ Ⓑ Ⓒ Ⓓ Ⓔ	55. Ⓐ Ⓑ Ⓒ Ⓓ Ⓔ
16. Ⓐ Ⓑ Ⓒ Ⓓ Ⓔ	36. Ⓐ Ⓑ Ⓒ Ⓓ Ⓔ	56. Ⓐ Ⓑ Ⓒ Ⓓ Ⓔ
17. Ⓐ Ⓑ Ⓒ Ⓓ Ⓔ	37. Ⓐ Ⓑ Ⓒ Ⓓ Ⓔ	57. Ⓐ Ⓑ Ⓒ Ⓓ Ⓔ
18. Ⓐ Ⓑ Ⓒ Ⓓ Ⓔ	38. Ⓐ Ⓑ Ⓒ Ⓓ Ⓔ	58. Ⓐ Ⓑ Ⓒ Ⓓ Ⓔ
19. Ⓐ Ⓑ Ⓒ Ⓓ Ⓔ	39. Ⓐ Ⓑ Ⓒ Ⓓ Ⓔ	59. Ⓐ Ⓑ Ⓒ Ⓓ Ⓔ
20. Ⓐ Ⓑ Ⓒ Ⓓ Ⓔ	40. Ⓐ Ⓑ Ⓒ Ⓓ Ⓔ	60. Ⓐ Ⓑ Ⓒ Ⓓ Ⓔ

AP EXAMINATION IN ENGLISH LITERATURE AND COMPOSITION

TEST 6

Section 1

TIME: 60 Minutes
60 Questions

DIRECTIONS: *This test consists of selections from literary works and questions on their content, form, and style. After reading each passage or poem, choose the best answer to each question and blacken the corresponding space on the answer sheet.*

NOTE: Pay particular attention to the requirement of questions that contain the words NOT, LEAST, or EXCEPT.

QUESTIONS 1-12. Read the following poem carefully before you choose your answers.

DO NOT GO GENTLE INTO THAT GOOD NIGHT

Do not go gentle into that good night,
Old age should burn and rave at close of day;
Rage, rage against the dying of the light.

Though wise men at their end know dark is right,
5 Because their words had forked no lightning they
Do not go gentle into that good night.

Good men, the last wave by, crying how bright
Their frail deeds might have danced in a green bay,

Do not go gentle into that good night.

10 Wild men who caught and sang the sun in flight,
And learn, too late, they grieved it on its way,
Do not go gentle into that good night.

Grave men, near death, who see with blinding sight
Blind eyes could blaze like meteors and be gay,
15 Rage, rage against the dying of the light.

And you, my father, there on the sad height,
Curse, bless, me now with your fierce tears, I pray.
Do not go gentle into that good night.
Rage, rage against the dying of the light.

1. In the first stanza, the poet is addressing

    (A) the general audience.

    (B) wise men, good men, wild men, and grave men.

    (C) older people.

    (D) people of public notoriety.

    (E) "my father."

2. In the context of the first stanza, lines 2 and 3 express the belief that

    (A) old people should be less complaining.

    (B) old people should vent their anger regularly, and thus prolong their lives.

    (C) old people should fight against death in every way.

    (D) old people should fight against losing the will to live.

    (E) old people should be expected to be bitter and disappointed.

3. In the second stanza the poet implies that

    (A) wise men cannot accept death, and so they must protest.

    (B) wise men always knew that their voices could not stop death, and so they accept it.

    (C)   no wise person would willingly go gently into death.

    (D)   wise men accept the rightness of death, but they protest anyway.

    (E)   wise men feel frustrated that they could not expose death to the "light" of the truth they sense.

4.   The "dying of the light" (lines 3, 15, 19) refers metaphorically to

    (A)   the passage of time.

    (B)   the aging of the body.

    (C)   the aging of the spirit.

    (D)   death.

    (E)   the loss of the will to live.

5.   The use of the word "rage" throughout the poem has the greatest effect in

    (A)   increasing the emotional intensity of the statement.

    (B)   providing closure at the end of every stanza.

    (C)   providing "stock" figures with a vivid emotional reaction.

    (D)   providing the poet's audience with a clear statement of the poem's message.

    (E)   reinforcing the "curse" of the last stanza.

6.   "Good men," (line 7) the poet implies, are best noted for

    (A)   their having done "frail deeds."

    (B)   the extent of their rage.

    (C)   their tendency to join wise men ("the last wave") in anger.

    (D)   the extent to which their deeds are recognized by others ("danced," etc.).

    (E)   the extent of their regret at not being recognized.

7.   The fifth stanza is notable for its evident

    (A)   hyperbole   (D)   sexual innuendo

    (B)   irony   (E)   paradox

    (C)   synecdoche

8. Stanza four indicates that "Wild men" are those who

    (A) attempt to alter the laws of nature.

    (B) try to live life as if "there was no tomorrow."

    (C) do not respect the wisdom of their elders.

    (D) do not trust anyone but themselves.

    (E) at the point of death, realize they have never really lived.

9. The poem indicates that the poet's father

    (A) is at the same time wise, good, wild, and near death.

    (B) is old, only.

    (C) is already dead.

    (D) is watching his son prepare for death.

    (E) is already raging against death.

10. The poet "pray(s)" to his father to "bless" him because the poet implies he

    (A) is near death himself.

    (B) is afraid of death.

    (C) is in need of a last blessing from his father.

    (D) knows he will have to face death sometime in the future.

    (E) is unsure of his own feelings about death.

11. The battle of color and light within each of the four middle stanzas has the effect of

    (A) portraying life as good, and death as evil.

    (B) emphasizing the ongoing conflict between good and evil.

    (C) underscoring the frustration each individual feels as he confronts death.

    (D) reinforcing the cosmic imagery throughout.

    (E) imbuing the confrontation with a vivid, "living" quality.

12. The poet's lyrical style is characterized mostly by

    (A) the use of easily identifiable images.

    (B) regular use of contrasting colors.

(C)   personification.

(D)   repetition of vowel sounds.

(E)   repetition of words and phrases.

QUESTIONS 13–28. Read the following passage carefully before you choose your answers.

The points that I particularly wish to make about Yeats' development are two. The first, on which I have already touched, is that to have accomplished what Yeats did in the middle and later years is a great and permanent example — which poets-to-come should study with reverence
5   — of what I have called Character of the Artist: a kind of moral, as well as intellectual, excellence. The second point, which follows naturally after what I have said in criticism of the lack of complete emotional expression in his early work, is that Yeats is preeminently the poet of middle age. By this I am far from meaning that he is a poet only for middle-aged readers:
10   the attitude towards him to younger poets who write in English, the world over, is enough evidence to the contrary. Now, in theory, there is no reason why a poet's inspiration or material should fail, in middle age or at any time before senility. For a man who is capable of experience finds himself in a different world in every decade of his life; as he sees it with
15   different eyes, the material of his art is continually renewed. But in fact, very few poets have shown this capacity of adaptation to the years. It requires, indeed, an exceptional honesty and courage to face the change. Most men either cling to the experiences of youth, so that their writing becomes an insincere mimicry of their earlier work, or they leave their
20   passing behind, and write only from the head, with a hollow and wasted virtuosity. There is another and even worse temptation: that of becoming dignified, or becoming public figures with only a public existence — coat-racks hung with decorations and distinctions, doing, saying, and even thinking and feeling only what they believe the public expects of them.
25   Yeats was not that kind of poet: and it is, perhaps, a reason why young men should find his later poetry more acceptable than older men easily can. For the young men can see him as a poet who in his work remained in the best sense always young, who even in one sense became young as he aged. But the old, unless they are stirred to something of the honesty with
30   oneself expressed in the poetry, will be shocked by such a revelation of what a man really is and remains. They will refuse to believe that they are like that.

You think it horrible that lust and rage
Should dance attendance upon my old age;

35 They were not such a plague when I was young:
   What else have I to spur me into song?

  These lines are very impressive and not very pleasant, and the sentiment has recently been criticized by an English critic whom I generally
respect. But I think he misread them. I do not read them as a personal
40 confession of a man who differed from other men, but of a man who was
essentially the same as most other men; the only difference is in the
greater clarity, honesty, and vigor. To what honest man, old enough, can
these sentiments be entirely alien? They can be subdued and disciplined
by religion, but who can say that they are dead? Only those to whom the
45 maxim of La Rochefoucauld applies: "When our vices abandon us, we
flatter ourselves with the belief that it is we who are abandoning them."
The tragedy of Yeat's epigram is all in the last line.

13. According to Eliot, Yeats' achievements later in life

  (A) are a testament to the character of the artist.

  (B) are a testimony to his moral excellence.

  (C) are in contrast to the obscurity of his younger days.

  (D) are examples of intellectual and emotional excellence.

  (E) are important to middle-aged readers.

14. Eliot indicates that the poet Yeats

  (A) did not begin writing until later in life.

  (B) did not achieve fame until later in life.

  (C) did not enjoy his success until middle age.

  (D) did not achieve full poetic inspiration until middle age.

  (E) did not realize his potential until he began writing about middle age.

15. Which of the following best describes the function of the first sentence of
the paragraph?

  (A) It simply states the main thesis of the paragraph.

  (B) It provides a transition statement from the last paragraph.

  (C) It establishes the credibility of the author as a noted critic.

(D) It demonstrates that the author is aware his previous arguments may seem weak.

(E) It provides a summing up of previously determined attitudes.

16. In context, the statement "Now, in theory, there is no reason why a poet's inspiration or material should fail, in middle age or at any time before senility" (lines 11–13) suggests which of the following?

(A) Yeats and other poets used this theory as a defense against criticism.

(B) Yeats used this theory as an excuse.

(C) Eliot is praising Yeats for not having "failed."

(D) Many poets' inspiration and material blossom in middle age.

(E) Many poets' inspiration and material fail in middle age, and these poets use this observation to excuse their failure.

17. According to the passage, the key to retaining poetic inspiration lies in

(A) remaining young at heart.

(B) adapting well to the aging process.

(C) leaving the "experiences of youth" behind.

(D) remaining "capable of experience."

(E) avoiding the trappings of a "public existence."

18. "Public figures" (line 22) are often "coat-racks" (lines 22–23) because they

(A) are public "skeletons" of their previous selves.

(B) are sensitive to contemporary poetic and public "fashion."

(C) are dignified, rigid, and uninspired.

(D) are only fit to remain in the "back rooms" of poetry's "house."

(E) are content to behave according to public whim.

19. Eliot determines that young men find Yeats' later poetry more acceptable than older men do because

(A) younger men have not yet achieved Yeats' level of emotional maturity.

(B) younger men see the older Yeats as a contemporary.

(C) Yeats was too far ahead of his time for his own generation to understand him.

(D)   Yeats was emotionally immature.

(E)   younger men relate to Yeats' disdain for the older writer.

20.   The function of Yeats' epigram as it appears in the passage is to

(A)   provide the reader with an example of what older critics find upsetting in Yeats' poetry.

(B)   provide Eliot with a writing sample upon which he can base further commentary.

(C)   indicate the language which the critic Eliot later cites finds so offensive.

(D)   indicate that Eliot can speak with authority as one familiar with Yeats' sentiment.

(E)   provide evidence that what others have said was Yeats' purpose is really not.

21.   In his use of Yeats' epigram, Eliot implies that older men refuse to believe that

(A)   their way of life is inferior to Yeats.

(B)   Yeats' "song" is the equal of theirs.

(C)   they must attract a younger audience to retain popularity.

(D)   they remain governed by the same "lust and rage" (line 33) as is Yeats.

(E)   they are jealous of the accolades of Yeats' younger audience.

22.   Yeats' epigram is "not very pleasant," Eliot implies, because

(A)   though its sentiment is impressive, its poetic sounds are not.

(B)   its sentiment is vulnerable to valid criticism.

(C)   its sentiment is shocking and universal.

(D)   its poetry is too "vigorous" for the sentiment to be conveyed.

(E)   its sentiment is uncomfortably confessional.

23.   Eliot refers to La Rochefoucauld's maxim as

(A)   a reason why so many critics have misunderstood Yeats.

(B)   the philosophical tenet behind Yeats' poetic attitude.

(C)   the tragic result of his critics' attacks.

    (D)   a misreading of Yeats' philosophy.

    (E)   an example of dishonest reflection upon the aging process.

24.   La Rochefoucauld's maxim implies that those who urge moderate, unpassionate behavior

    (A)   are hypocrites.

    (B)   are unaware of the dynamics of aging.

    (C)   are criticizing others for what they themselves believe.

    (D)   are indirectly ignoring the teachings of religion.

    (E)   are resentful of youth.

25.   In the context of the passage, Eliot refers to "an English critic" (line 38) at this point in his argument because

    (A)   he wishes to reinforce his argument.

    (B)   he wants to appear fair in his discussion of this controversial figure.

    (C)   he feels he must recognize widespread critical disapproval of Yeats' poetry.

    (D)   he wishes to use his discussion of Yeats to discredit the well-known critic.

    (E)   he seeks to identify this critic with those who "flatter themselves."

26.   Eliot implies that the "tragedy of Yeats' epigram" (line 47) is that

    (A)   readers will never understand his poetry.

    (B)   younger readers will refuse to empathize with Yeats' contentions as they grow older.

    (C)   Yeats himself felt the pathetic nature of his situation.

    (D)   Yeats felt most of mankind was in the same sad situation.

    (E)   expressions of lust became the only motive for Yeats' poetry.

27.   The development of the argument can best be described as progressing from.

    (A)   dispute to agreement.

    (B)   assertion to proof.

    (C)   general to specific.

(D) assertive to concessional.

(E) objective description to subjective opinion.

28. Taken as a whole, the passage is best described as

(A) a praise of Yeats by Eliot with input from others.

(B) a defense of Yeats' critics by Eliot.

(C) a descriptive passage that makes use of concrete examples.

(D) an argument developed through the use of supposition.

(E) a technical discussion for students of Yeats' poetry.

QUESTIONS 29-40. Read the following poem carefully before you choose your answers.

IMMORTAL AUTUMN

I speak this poem now with grave and level voice
In praise of autumn of the far-horn-winding fall
I praise the flower-barren fields the clouds the tall
Unanswering branches where the wind makes sullen noise

5 I praise the fall it is the human season now
No more the foreign sun does meddle at our earth
Enforce the green and thaw the frozen soil to birth
Nor winter yet weigh all with silence the pine bough

But now in autumn with the black and outcast crows
10 Share we the spacious world the whispering year is gone
There is more room to live now the once secret dawn
Comes late by daylight and the dark unguarded goes

Between the mutinous brave burning of the leaves
And winter's covering of our hearts with his deep snow
15 We are alone there are no evening birds we know
The naked moon the tame stars circle at our eaves

It is the human season on this sterile air
Do words outcarry breath the sound goes on and on
I hear a dead man's cry from autumn long since gone

20 I cry to you beyond this bitter air.

29. The title and the first line of this poem indicates that the poet intends to speak

    (A) in defense of autumn.

    (B) in praise of the passing of the seasons.

    (C) with reference to death.

    (D) with reference to the resurrection inherent in nature.

    (E) with sarcasm.

30. The unpunctuated, run-on sentences the poet introduces in the first stanza are designed to

    (A) accommodate the long catalog of praiseworthy autumnal images.

    (B) approximate an ungrammatical and rustic country accent.

    (C) reinforce the images of tired nature the poet presents.

    (D) reflect the almost breathless excitement the season brings to the poet.

    (E) underscore the "nature in chaos" themes the poet advances.

31. In the second stanza the poet surprises the reader most by

    (A) continuing to speak in the first person.

    (B) continuing to speak in unpunctuated, run-on sentences.

    (C) praising a season that is rarely praised.

    (D) expressing relief at the passage of summer.

    (E) expressing a dread of approaching winter.

32. In identifying fall as "the human season," (line 17) the poet

    (A) personifies his delivery of autumn images

    (B) indicates a shift in thematic intention

    (C) places human life within a traditional natural framework

    (D) make an allusion to a famous Shakespearean sonnet

    (E) indicates a continuation of his thematic intention

33. According to the speaker, the sun is "foreign" (line 6) because

    (A) it does not originate in the earth

    (B) it destroys the "green" with its strong rays

(C)   it throws the light of truth where it is better not to know

(D)   it disturbs the "human season" by causing plants to grow

(E)   its lessening strength brings on winter

34.   In the third stanza, the poet implies that humans are similar to

(A)   the "spacious world" (line 10)

(B)   the "secret dawn" (line 11)

(C)   the passing of the "whispering year" (line 10)

(D)   the "dark unguarded" (line 12)

(E)   the "outcast crows" (line 9)

35.   The phrase, "There is more room to live now" (line 11) suggests that

(A)   the lack of leaves provides more room for human movement

(B)   the late dawn provides a greater opportunity to view beauty

(C)   the increasing darkness provides man with a more fitting world

(D)   the fading year reminds humans that they have much left to accomplish

(E)   harvest time provides man and crows both with sustenance

36.   In stanza four the speaker is doing which of the following?

(A)   Indicating that man is a destroyer of nature

(B)   Indicating that man is afraid of winter

(C)   Indicating that man is isolated in an unfamiliar world

(D)   Indicating that man is in communion with the universe

(E)   Indicating that man is helping the earth to prepare for winter

37.   The phrase "It is the human season on this sterile air" (line 17) implies that

(A)   man's thoughts and creations are really barren of meaning.

(B)   man lives in a world which threatens his very existence.

(C)   autumn's air is crisp and beneficial to human health.

(D)   nature in autumn poses no interference to human wishes.

(E)   man lives in the sight of the other creatures of the universe.

38. In the context of the poem, "words outcarry breath" (line 18) because

    (A)   humans have the gift of memory by which they recall the words of those who have passed on.

    (B)   there is nothing in the air to stop them.

    (C)   great thoughts exceed the limitations of short lives.

    (D)   life is a more powerful force than death.

    (E)   the pen can commit "immortal" thoughts to paper.

39. Which of the following BEST paraphrases the meaning of the last line?

    (A)   I hear my own dead man's scream in this bitter air.

    (B)   I hear again the dead man's cry I heard in a previous autumn.

    (C)   I mourn for someone who has died before me.

    (D)   Life was not as empty for me in the past as it is now.

    (E)   The human season is the season of death.

40. Which of the following best describes the poem AS A WHOLE?

    (A)   An artful reversal of traditional images.

    (B)   An elegy to the human race.

    (C)   A confessional in first person.

    (D)   A didactic treatment of "man's inhumanity to man."

    (E)   An energetic rebuttal to advocates of the "death in life" philosophy.

QUESTIONS 41-49. Read the following passage carefully and then answer the questions.

"I'd like to clear away the lion business," Macomber said. "It's not very pleasant to have your wife see you do something like that."

I should think it would be even more unpleasant to do it, Wilson thought, wife or no wife, or to talk about it having done it. But he said, "I
5 wouldn't think about that any more. Any one could be upset by his first lion. That's all over."

But that night after dinner and a whisky and soda by the fire before going to bed, as Francis Macomber lay on his cot with the mosquito bar over him and listened to the night noises it was not all over. It was neither
10 all over nor was it beginning. But more than shame he felt cold, hollow fear in him. The fear was still there like a cold slimy hollow in all the

emptiness where once his confidence had been and it made him feel sick. It was still there with him now.

15 It had started the night before when he had wakened and heard the lion roaring somewhere up along the river. It was a deep sound and at the end there were sort of coughing grunts that made him seem just outside the tent, and when Francis Macomber woke in the night to hear it he was afraid. He could hear his wife breathing quietly, asleep. There was no one to tell he was afraid, nor to be afraid with him, and, lying alone, he did not
20 know the Somali proverb that says a brave man is always frightened three times by a lion; when he first sees his track, when he first hears him roar and when he first confronts him. Then while they were eating breakfast by lantern light out in the dining tent, before the sun was up, the lion roared again and Francis thought he was just at the edge of camp.

25 "Sounds like an old-timer," Robert Wilson said, looking up from his kippers and coffee. "Listen to him cough."

"Is he very close?"

"A mile or so up the stream."

"Will we see him?"

30 "We'll have a look."

"Does his roaring carry that far? It sounds as though he were right in camp."

"Carries a hell of a long way," said Robert Wilson. "It's strange the way it carries. Hope he's a shootable cat. The boys said there was a very
35 big one about here."

"If I get a shot, where should I hit him," Macomber asked, "to stop him?"

"In the shoulders," Wilson said. "In the neck if you can make it. Shoot for bone. Break him down."

40 "I hope I can place it properly," Macomber said.

"You shoot very well," Wilson told him. "Take your time. Make sure of him. The first one in is the one that counts."

41. Which of the following best indicates the subject of the passage?

(A) Dealing with the apprehension of an impending confrontation.

(B) Coping with life in the wild.

(C) Dealing with a previous failure of courage.

(D)   Coping with marital difficulties.

(E)   Dealing with culture shock in a new situation.

42.   Macomber's reflections reveal that the fledgling hunter is

(A)   uneasy about what his wife would think of his actions if she knew the truth.

(B)   angry at his wife for not having been with him when he needed her most.

(C)   afraid of his wife and what she will say about his cowardly actions.

(D)   embarrassed about his actions while his wife was looking on.

(E)   afraid that his cowardly actions in front of his wife have eroded his self-confidence.

43.   The passage implies that Macomber first became fearful

(A)   when he confronted his first lion.

(B)   when he realized his wife was looking on as he confronted his first lion.

(C)   when he suspected that only he was afraid of the impending confrontation.

(D)   when he was eating breakfast just before the hunt.

(E)   only afterwards, when he fully realized the shame of what he had done.

44.   The passage is most stylistically notable for

(A)   clear and precise descriptions of time placement.

(B)   clear and precise descriptions of fear.

(C)   clear and precise descriptions of geography and climate.

(D)   clear and precise descriptions of camp life.

(E)   clear and precise descriptions of the sounds of nature.

45.   The chief effect of Hemingway's seemingly casual attention to punctuation and sentence length in this passage is to

(A)   contribute to a "stream of consciousness" atmosphere.

(B)   indicate that the personalities he is describing are marginally educated.

(C)   indicate that Macomber's emotional turmoil is great.

(D)   imply that these passages are not as important as those that will come later.

(E)   create a sense of detachment in the reader.

46.   Which of the following best sums up the contrast between Macomber's attitude about his confrontation and that expressed by the Somali proverb?

(A)   Macomber is afraid, while the Somali proverb praises the "brave man."

(B)   Macomber is afraid, while the Somali proverb speaks of reasonable and prudent caution.

(C)   Macomber is really afraid of his wife's perceptions, not the lion.

(D)   Macomber thinks he is a coward, but the Somali proverb would indicate that he could still be a "brave man."

(E)   Macomber's cowardice renders him unable to appreciate the Somali wisdom.

47.   Throughout the passage, Hemingway implies that the most important difference between Macomber and Wilson is that

(A)   Wilson is brave while Macomber is a coward.

(B)   Macomber is dependent on his wife, while Wilson lives independently.

(C)   Wilson is African while Macomber is an outsider.

(D)   Macomber is expressive, while Wilson is more restrained.

(E)   Wilson is experienced, while Macomber is inexperienced.

48.   The nature of the dialogue between the men at the end of the passage is most indicative of

(A)   Macomber's limited attention and Wilson's complete absorption.

(B)   Macomber's curiosity and Wilson's casual interest.

(C)   Macomber's fear and Wilson's bravery.

(D)   Wilson's delight and Macomber's dread.

(E)   Macomber's limited experience and Wilson's complete knowledge.

49. Macomber's comment that the lion's roar "sounds as though he were right in camp," (lines 31–32) implies that Macomber

    (A)   is woefully inexperienced in lion hunting.

    (B)   is not as yet sensitized to the atmospheric conditions of East Africa.

    (C)   is very apprehensive about the impending confrontation.

    (D)   has already determined that he will act in a cowardly manner.

    (E)   is not aware of the possibility that this lion is not "a shootable cat."

QUESTIONS 50-60. Read the following poem carefully and then answer the questions.

THE LOST LEADER
1

Just for a handful of silver he left us,
    Just for a riband to stick in his coat —
Found the one gift of which fortune bereft us,
    Lost all the others she lets us devote;
5 They, with the gold to give, doled him out silver,
    So much was theirs who so little allowed:
How all our copper had gone for his service!
    Rags — they were purple, his heart had been proud!
We that had loved him so, followed him, honored him,
10   Lived in his mild and magnificent eye,
Learned his great language, caught his clear accents,
    Made him our pattern to live and to die!
Shakespeare was of us, Milton was for us,
    Burns, Shelley, were with us — they watch from their graves!
15 He alone breaks from the van and the freemen
    — He alone sinks to the rear and the slaves!

2

We shall march prospering — not through his presence;
    Songs may inspirit us — not from his lyre;
Deeds will be done — while he boasts his quiescence,
20   Still bidding crouch whom the rest bade aspire;
Blot out his name, then, record one lost soul more,
    One task more declined, one more footpath untrod,
One more devils'-triumph and sorrow for angels,
    One wrong more to man, one more insult to God!
25 Life's night begins: let him never come back to us!

There would be doubt, hesitation and pain,
Forced praise on our part — the glimmer of twilight,
    Never glad confident morning again!
Best fight on well, for we taught him — strike gallantly,
30   Menace our heart ere we master his own;
Then let him receive the new knowledge and wait us,
    Pardoned in heaven, the first by the throne!

—*Robert L. Browning.*

50. The speaker implies that their "leader"

    (A)   physically deserted his friends — he died.

    (B)   politically alienated his friends.

    (C)   spiritually abandoned his friends.

    (D)   verbally hurt his friends.

    (E)   cheated his friends out of money.

51. According to the speaker, the leader has

    (A)   received attractive compensation for his actions.

    (B)   actually donated a "gift" as well as betrayed them.

    (C)   already lost much of what was given to him.

    (D)   received less than what he originally imagined for his actions.

    (E)   lost more than he has gained.

52. The reference to "purple" (line 8) indicates that

    (A)   the gifts attained were at the price of great bloodshed.

    (B)   the leader does not realize how angry his former admirers are.

    (C)   it was false pride that led him to accept the honors.

    (D)   the honors were bestowed by royalty.

    (E)   he now appears to his friends as a jester in comic costume.

53. The speaker believes that the leader

    (A)   should stop comparing himself to other famous authors.

    (B)   should not be treated by the rich and powerful as they have treated the other authors listed.

(C)   should not be considered on the same literary level as the others.

(D)   has destroyed his chances of ever again being viewed on the same literary level as the others.

(E)   has departed from the social and political heritage of the other writers.

54.   Which of the following do the opening four lines of stanza 2 best suggest about the leader's advice?

(A)   His advice is no longer inspirational; in fact, the old followers are doing the opposite of their former leader.

(B)   His advice may still be inspirational, but his deeds are not.

(C)   His advice is only valid when given by someone else.

(D)   His followers will use his example to subvert the government.

(E)   His advice is the same at it was before.

55.   Which of the following best paraphrases lines 13 and 14?

(A)   Shakespeare believed as we did, Milton wished us well, and Burns and Shelley agreed with us.

(B)   Shakespeare was from the same class as we are, Milton wished us well, and Burns and Shelley agreed with us.

(C)   Shakespeare had a similar political philosophy, Milton would have been sympathetic, and Burns and Shelley were our friends.

(D)   Shakespeare was from the same class as we are, Milton's work was useful to us, and Burns and Shelley agreed with him.

(E)   Shakespeare had a similar political philosophy, Milton agreed with him, and Burns and Shelley were our friends.

56.   The speaker implies that from this point onward

(A)   it is better that the leader continues to offend, than that he tries to reconcile with his old friends.

(B)   it would be easier to let the devil triumph than to reverse the friends' attitude toward the leader.

(C)   it is better that the leader stay away from them than return and expect to be praised again.

(D)   it is more painful to praise the leader now than it would be to endure the devil's triumph.

(E)   it is easier to curse the twilight than to praise the leader now.

57. In the context of the rest of the poem, which of the following seems most likely to be the speaker's intention in lines 21-24?

    (A) To give serious advice to former admirers.

    (B) To present a series of curses, given half-seriously.

    (C) To give a somewhat exaggerated description indicating the seriousness of the complaint.

    (D) To excuse the public praise the leader had lately received.

    (E) To give a message to the literary establishment that not every one admires the leader as they do.

58. In the last four lines of the poem, the speaker is most likely implying that

    (A) a blow has been dealt to his and his friends' creative endeavors from which they will never recover.

    (B) the leader's transgressions will have little effect on their continuing efforts.

    (C) the leader's actions have been more of a blow to his reputation than to their efforts.

    (D) even though the leader is discredited, he has taught them valuable lessons.

    (E) in registering a protest, there is a chance they can save the leader from himself.

59. The meaning of the last two lines of the poem is intentionally obscured

    (A) by the confusing implication that one who insulted God can still end up in heaven.

    (B) by the dual implication of the word "throne."

    (C) by the dual implication of the word "pardoned."

    (D) by the evident wish that the leader will "wait" for the speaker in heaven.

    (E) by the evident supposition that the speaker will be going to heaven.

60. Which of the following contain an example of personification?

    (A) lines 1-2   (D) lines 23-24

    (B) lines 3-4   (E) lines 31-32

    (C) lines 11-12

Section 2

TIME: 2 Hours
3 Essay Questions

QUESTION 1. *(Suggested time — 40 minutes. This question counts one-third of the total essay-section score.)* Read the following poem carefully. Then write an essay in which you analyze how the poet employs images of nature to support his central theme. Develop your essay with specific references to the text of the poem.

The Wind and the Rain
I

That far-off day the leaves in flight
Were letting in the colder light.
A season-ending wind there blew
That, as it did the forest strew,
5 I leaned on with a singing trust
And let it drive me deathward too.
With breaking step I stabbed the dust,
Yet did not much to shorten stride.
I sang of death—but had I known
10 The many deaths one must have died
Before he came to meet his own!
Oh, should a child be left unwarned
That any song in which he mourned
Would be as if he prophesied?
15 It were unworthy of the tongue
To let the half of life alone
And play the good without the ill.
And yet 'twould seem that what is sung
In happy sadness by the young,
20 Fate has no choice but to fulfill.

II

Flowers in the desert heat
Contrive to bloom
On melted mountain water led by flume
To wet their feet.
25 But something in it still is incomplete.
Before I thought the wilted to exalt
With water I would see them water-bowed.
I would pick up all ocean less its salt,

And though it were as much as cloud could bear
30   Would load it onto cloud,
And rolling it inland on roller air,
Would empty it unsparing on the flower
That past its prime lost petals in the flood
(Who cares but for the future of the bud?),
35   And all the more the mightier the shower
Would run in under it to get my share.

'Tis not enough on roots and in the mouth,
But give me water heavy on the head
In all the passion of a broken drouth.

40   And there is always more than should be said.

As strong as rain without as wine within,
As magical as sunlight on the skin.

I have been one no dwelling could contain
When there was rain;
45   But I must forth at dusk, my time of day,
To see to the unburdening of skies.
Rain was the tears adopted by my eyes
That have none left to stay.

From the <u>Poetry of Robert Frost</u> *edited by Edward Connery Lathem. Copyright © 1969 by Holt, Rinehart and Winston, copyright 1942 by Robert Frost, © 1970 by Lesley Frost Ballantine. Reprinted by permission of Henry Holt and Company, Inc.*

QUESTION 2. *(Suggested time — 40 minutes. This question counts one-third of the total essay-section score.)* The passage below is the opening of a short story. Read the passage carefully. Then write an essay in which you define the stylistic techniques by which the author attempts to create an atmosphere of horror. Refer to the text of the passage where ever appropriate.

During the whole of a dull, dark, and soundless day in the autumn of
the year, when the clouds hung oppressively low in the heavens, I had been
passing alone, on horseback, through a singularly dreary tract of country,
and at length found myself, as the shades of the evening drew on, within
5   view of the melancholy House of Usher. I know not how it was — but,
with the first glimpse of the building, a sense of insufferable gloom
pervaded my spirit. I say insufferable; for the feeling was unrelieved by
any of that half-pleasurable, because poetic, sentiment with which the
mind usually receives even the sternest natural images of the desolate or
10   terrible. I looked upon the scene before me — upon the mere house, and

the simple landscape features of the domain — upon the bleak walls — upon the vacant eye-like windows — upon a few rank sedges — and upon a few white trunks of decayed trees — with an utter depression of soul which I can compare to no earthly sensation more properly to the after-dream of the reveller upon opium — the bitter lapse into every-day life — the hideous dropping off of the veil. There was an iciness, a sinking, a sickening of the heart — an unredeemed dreariness of thought which no goading of the imagination could torture into aught of the sublime. What was it — I paused to think — what was it that unnerved me in the contemplation of the House of Usher?

From "The Fall of The House of Usher" by Edgar Allan Poe

QUESTION 3. *(Suggested time — 40 minutes. This question counts one-third of the total essay-section score.)* In great literature, authors often seize upon the plight of one particular character to represent a more general concern of humanity. In a well organized essay, explain how an author of one of the works below accomplishes this. Avoid plot summary. Refer to a specific character and his specific concerns with textual references, then identify the more general concern which is represented.

The following titles are listed as suggestions. You may base your essay on one of them or choose another work of equivalent literary merit.

The Grapes of Wrath	*Manchild in the Promised Land*
Catch-22	*Exodus*
Julius Caesar	*Pale Fire*
Macbeth	*Moby Dick*
Waiting for Godot	*The Scarlet Letter*
Antigone	*The Red Badge of Courage*
The American Dream	*Mourning Becomes Electra*
The Stranger	*Who's Afraid of Virginia Woolf?*
The Sun Also Rises	*The Assistant*
The Great Gatsby	

TEST 6

ANSWER KEY

1. (E)	16. (E)	31. (D)	46. (D)
2. (C)	17. (D)	32. (B)	47. (E)
3. (D)	18. (E)	33. (D)	48. (E)
4. (D)	19. (B)	34. (E)	49. (C)
5. (A)	20. (B)	35. (C)	50. (B)
6. (A)	21. (D)	36. (C)	51. (E)
7. (E)	22. (C)	37. (B)	52. (D)
8. (B)	23. (A)	38. (B)	53. (E)
9. (E)	24. (A)	39. (A)	54. (A)
10. (D)	25. (C)	40. (C)	55. (C)
11. (C)	26. (D)	41. (C)	56. (A)
12. (E)	27. (B)	42. (E)	57. (C)
13. (D)	28. (A)	43. (C)	58. (E)
14. (D)	29. (C)	44. (A)	59. (B)
15. (B)	30. (C)	45. (C)	60. (B)

DETAILED EXPLANATIONS
OF ANSWERS

TEST 6

Section 1

1. **(E)** It may appear, on a quick and careless reading, that the poet is addressing wise men, good men, etc., but he is not. He is noting each of them in each of the stanzas as examples of others who do not go gently. He is addressing his father — as we find out in the last stanza. The confusion here may stem from Thomas' use of "And you …" in the last stanza. Read the first and last stanza together without the middle stanzas and hear the difference.

2. **(C)** Thomas' message is perhaps unexpected. Acceptance of death is not the issue; rather, protest is encouraged. Maintaining the will to live is not enough; old people should rage against it in every possible way.

3. **(D)** Thomas honors seemingly contradictory notions: that death can be accepted and protested at the same time by "wise" minds. The reason why they do this ("because their words" … etc.) is metaphorical and open to wider interpretation.

4. **(D)** While the image is used just before this and then later in the poem in conjunction with the passage of the sun across the sky, it is repeated throughout as a metaphor for dying and death. It is interesting to note that, like "winter," "sunset" is usually taken to mean this, at least since Shakespeare's time ("In me thou sees the setting of the sun …") yet Thomas uses the metaphor in a way that is both interesting and lyrically fresh.

5. **(A)** The repetition of "rage" serves many purposes, but its clearest purpose is to provide emotional intensity — and by an apt choice of a word which allows growing intensity with only slightly varied pronunciation of the heavy "r" which begins the word. Thomas' Welsh accent exaggerates this effect when recordings of his readings are reviewed.

6. **(A)** "Good men" are doers of deeds, although they cry "how bright / Their frail deeds might have danced." They too rage against death.

7. **(E)** In an artful dance of words, Thomas uses a contradictory phrase like "blinding sight," and the simile "Blind eyes could blaze like meteors." In addition, these dying men can be "gay" (meaning happy), and dying blind men can see (that) being blind is not as powerless a state as death. These are statements that seem to contradict common sense and yet are true — the definition of paradox.

8. **(B)** Wild men here try to catch the sun only to see the sun has continued on its path. Perhaps they lamented the passage of time. Most likely they have tried to "burn the candle at both ends" — attempting to deny and defy the fact of death, only to find that what they "sang" was really a dirge for themselves.

9. **(E)** (A) seems a likely choice at first. The poet is saying, "Look, wise men feel this way, and good men, too." He could therefore be trying to say to the father, "You are all of these — so you should rage as well." However, in the last stanza, the poet tells us that the father is crying "fierce tears" — a terse restatement of raging against the prospect of imminent death. Thus, the poem becomes almost a "cheer" for his father to continue to face death with righteous indignation.

10. **(D)** The poet asks to be "cursed," as well as "blessed," by his father's tears — symbols of inevitable death and human rage against it. It should be clear, by now, that the poet is speaking to his father (and not heavenly father — who presumably does not have to face death). Thomas regularly emphasized the continuum of life and death — the cycles — the passage of the generations. He will face death soon enough, he implies — as his father is doing now. (With horrible irony, Dylan Thomas died one year after this poem was published — at the age of 39.)

11. **(C)** In each stanza the human effort involves introducing light onto the dark stage of death. Wise men try to throw lightning; good men need light to see their deeds; wild men try to save the sun's rays; grave men find that their blind eyes can blaze in the face of darkness. Darkness, however, and therefore, death, wins out (they are each going into that "good night" — though not gently). Thus, each is frustrated in his confrontation with death.

12. **(E)** The songlike power of this poem is derived from repetition — much as in any song. Thomas, however, can be lyrical without being mindlessly repetitious (as in "singsong"). Count how many times he uses the word "rage," or the phrase "Do not," and realize this is within only a few short lines.

13. **(D)** Eliot clearly states that he will make two points. The first — intellectual excellence — is to be expected. The second — a kind of emotional poetic maturity — is surprising because of the lack of this earlier in his career.

14. **(D)** Some readers may infer that Yeats did not find notoriety until later in life, but this is not the case. His first poems were published when he was 20, and soon after he began meeting the luminaries of his age. Eliot goes to great lengths to clarify his "middle age" comment — praising the poet for intellectual excellence early in life, but stating that he did not achieve "complete emotional expression" until later.

15. **(B)** While the first sentence provide a general direction for the paragraph (that there will be two points), the thesis statement is actually in the second sentence. What Eliot does in the first sentence is provide transition from the previous paragraph. If there was no need for a transition, he could have started with sentence two. In the second sentence he says that his first point had already been "touched" upon. Therefore, his mention of "the points that I particularly wish to make" directs the reader's mind to previous material at the same time as it is directed forward to the new second point.

16. **(E)** Eliot is implying not just that middle-aged poets often do "fail," but that they often use this common observation as an excuse, as if to say, "Of course I'm not as inspired as when I was younger. No one is." Eliot believes the opposite is true of Yeats.

17. **(D)** Syntactically as well as contextually, Eliot is clearly saying that any person short of senility can be able to retain poetic inspiration — by being "capable of experience." Capability, however, is not just defined by physical ability, but by a "capacity" to adapt — to find oneself in a "different world in every decade." One can grow older without being senile and still not be capable of experiencing this phenomenon.

18. **(E)** Eliot criticizes poetry's public figures not because they are sensitive to contemporary fashion, but because they are sensitive to it ONLY, and, in addition, are more than content to behave this way and to let this govern their writing, statements, acts, and thoughts as well.

19. **(B)** Eliot contends that younger men "can see him as a poet who in his work remained in the best sense always young." Young, as defined here, relates to honesty about oneself expressed in the poetry.

20. **(B)** Eliot wishes to advance his argument in a number of ways, among

which is to make specific points about Yeats, and to take one of the clearest expressions of the poet's sentiments and defend it.

21. **(D)** This is reinforced by the discussion that follows, and also by the preceding discussion of "honesty with oneself." The notion that passions are somehow most appropriate to youth is long-standing, broken most recently by Freudian psychoanalytic philosophy, to which Yeats was an adherent.

22. **(C)** Eliot is impressed by the "lines," and originally questioned the sentiment. But he has come to believe that the epigram is not a confessional in which the poet explores the differences between himself and other poets, but rather it is an honest statement of universal traits found in all men.

23. **(A)** Eliot employs La Rochefoucauld's maxim to point out the improper foundations of "anti-lust" sentiments that motivate Yeats' critics. This maxim is used against Yeats' critics, and in outright defense of Yeats himself.

24. **(A)** Eliot believes, as does La Rochefoucauld, that criticism of "vices" arises from improper understanding. These critics base their belief on the incorrect observation that as people grow older and "wiser," they abandon their vices. This is then improperly translated into a dictum that older people should not contemplate "lustful" topics.

25. **(C)** There is a strong sense throughout that Eliot feels he is defending an unpopular idea, at least among his "older" contemporaries. A traditional rhetorical principle when endorsing an unpopular idea is to recognize the contrary position as soon as possible, and to openly respect certain of its aspects while appearing reasonable in its refutation. By doing so Eliot does not "turn off" his audience, and seems less of a renegade in his defense of his controversial subject.

26. **(D)** In the powerful last line of this passage, Eliot implies that the critics have overlooked an undercurrent in Yeats' poetry, one that is expressed in the last line of his epigram: that is that Yeats, and all aging people, have little more to motivate them in old age than they did in younger days. Eliot has already argued for the universality of Yeats' position, so the "tragedy" is not, therefore, the poet's alone.

27. **(B)** Eliot appears to move from assertion to proof, though this is more for rhetorical uses than it is coincidental. In the first sentence, Eliot says he wants to make two points. He reasons subjectively and persuasively. The superficial tone changes with the introduction of the epigram. He is now dealing with "hard facts"

from Yeats, from the "English critic," from La Rochefoucauld. Of course, he is still expressing opinion, but it appears more "proven."

28. **(A)** Eliot is actually delivering the annual Yeats Lecture to the Friends of the Irish Academy at Dublin in 1940, just after Yeats' death. He is critiquing (and praising) the poet, and using other critics' voices as foils with which he can draw further praise for his renowned friend and contemporary.

29. **(C)** Mortality and other concerns of the "grave" will be the poet's concern. This is reinforced by the death-imagery of "flower-barren fields" (line 3) and perhaps even the "far-horn-winding fall" (line 2) — an allusion to a salutory funeral tune, or perhaps even "Taps."

30. **(C)** Run-ons, even in poetry, tend to make one "breathless," not in excite-ment, but in sheer fatigue. MacLeish's use of unpunctuated cataloguing here is intentional. Branches that don't answer, fields that have no flowers in them, wind that makes only sullen noise, are reflections of the tiredness of nature. Here, lack of punctuation reinforces theme.

31. **(D)** There are a number of surprises in the second stanza. Of the possibili-ties listed here, the poet's relief at the passage of summer (and spring) is perhaps the most surprising. Fall is not as often praised as spring, but its beauty is often the subject of poetry. The fact that the poet continues first person and unpunctuated sentences may be surprising, but the tone has already been set in the first stanza.

32. **(B)** The poet had begun by saying he would speak "In praise of autumn," and listed natural images to reinforce the point in the reader's mind. He continues cataloguing in the second stanza, but a dramatic shift in intent is indicated by his introduction of fall as "the human season." (line 5). He has played a trick on the reader. He is really talking about human life. It is unclear at this point if there is the kind of one-to-one metaphor demanded by personification.

33. **(D)** The poet's (and the "human's") world is almost the reverse of what would be expected in a typical seasonal poem. The sun brings "green" growth, and in doing so, disturbs the natural human season of fall.

34. **(E)** Humans share the world of autumn with the "outcast crows," implying that humans are similarly outcast in this crow and human season. There is some identification here with "whispering year" (line 10) and daylight as it fades, but the central parallel is a concentrated and haunting one between the unwanted birds and ourselves.

35. **(C)** The speaker provides an ominous hint here that man is a creature of the night — again, a reversal of what would be expected. The fall brings more room for humans not just because the leaves are off the trees, but also because there is less daytime.

36. **(C)** While a case could be made that burning leaves is an act of destruction, it would be mitigated by the fact that the leaves are already dead and also by the poet's curious use of the laudatory word "brave." What is more evident here is that the human race is very alone and surrounded by an unfamiliar world ("there are no evening birds we know") (line 15). Even the moon is unexpectedly "naked." This image is reinforced by the notion of the previous stanza that man is somehow a creature of the night.

37. **(B)** "Sterile" refers to a "field" in which nothing lives but "sterile" also implies that man is a creature whose reproductive capabilities have been destroyed by his environment — by the same air that sustains him. Man draws his aerobic sustenance, then, from a gas which may eventually exterminate him. This foreboding is reinforced by the lines which follow.

38. **(B)** Within the context of the poem, words in this nightmarish world of autumn can exist long after life because there is nothing "alive" or flourishing in the air to stop them: The air is sterile. Lest the reader believe that these are profound or "immortal" thoughts that are traveling through the air, the poet quickly notes that they are a "dead man's cry" (line 19).

39. **(A)** The power of the poem's conclusion resides in the juxtaposition of the dead man's cry and the poet's own — and is a more personal vision than (E) would indicate. Perhaps the poet is implying that he has been dead for some time — spiritually dead — and there is nothing in his universe to stop his cry of agony from continuing on and on. That is the greatest tragedy.

40. **(C)** The exposition of the poem as it appears here seems to indicate that "Immortal Autumn" is a confessional of private agony whose origins are not explored in any specific sense, though it is placed within a larger context of the precarious position man holds among the other forces in the universe. This placement, however, is not primarily what the poem is about.

41. **(C)** While there is some apprehension about a future confrontation at the end of the passage, the passage begins with Macomber's desire to "clear away that lion business," (line 1) and then continues to dwell on Macomber's reflections about what went wrong just before. The Somali proverb underscores the indirect references to what must have been Macomber's cowardice when confronting the

lion.

42. **(E)** While Macomber was clearly embarrassed by his cowardly behavior in front of his wife, even Macomber quickly realizes that, as Wilson muses, it was "even more unpleasant to do it ... wife or no wife" (line 4). Macomber's "shame," therefore, quickly becomes fear that fills the space "where once his confidence had been" (line 12).

43. **(C)** Macomber's fear can be traced to the night before the hunt when he heard the lion roaring "somewhere up along the river," and when he realized he had no one with whom to communicate his fear. There is a strong implication, here, that, in his wife's continued sleeping, and the camp's otherwise tranquil reaction, Macomber suspects that there is something wrong with him in his fear, and that he would be ashamed to communicate his fear, even if his wife and the rest of the camp was awake. This is reinforced by Hemingway's reference to the Somali proverb.

44. **(A)** Hemingway's passage is remarkable for its clear precise descriptions of time. This is reinforced by the proper and effective breakage of paragraphs at particular demarcations. The passage begins, evidently, with a conversation at dinner. A new paragraph is then begun with, "But that night ..." and ends with the word "now." This ending is intentional and important, because the next paragraph begins with the time notation. "It had started the night before" and ends with another transition. "Then while they were eating ...."

45. **(C)** Stream of consciousness is debatable here because it is the author's voice which is telling the reader what Macomber is thinking — not Macomber's voice. Excitement is created because the reader senses Macomber's emotional turmoil. The extent of the characters' formal education does not enter the picture, and few authors would advertise the inappropriateness of segments of their writing. The seemingly casual style here is in interesting contrast to much of Hemingway's writing — noted for short sentences and therefore little need for punctuation.

46. **(D)** The answer is not necessarily obvious. There is a fine examination of words required by the reader to understand that, while the Somalis believe "a brave man is always frightened," this does not necessarily imply that anyone who is frightened may or may not be a brave man. In fact, Macomber may be a coward, but, the Somali proverb implies, he can not know this from only one confrontation with a lion.

47. **(E)** Wilson knows that "any one could be upset by his first lion" experi-

ence, and he is not threatened by the lion's roar because he knows from its "cough" it is an "old-timer," (line 25). While Wilson may be less expressive than Macomber, most of this may be due to his having been a "veteran" of many years in East Africa. (C), then, is also a remote possibility, but clearly Wilson is a European.

48. **(E)** Macomber is not inexperienced in hunting or shooting. Indeed, Wilson tells him, "You shoot very well" (line 41). It is Macomber's knowledge that is limited, and Wilson's that seems complete. It is his knowledge that he offers to Macomber. Macomber's lack of knowledge as he approaches this dangerous situation is ominous.

49. **(C)** There is no question in the reader's mind that Macomber will act in a cowardly manner, yet Macomber, at this point in time, still does not know how he will react. Heightening of the senses is one primitive response to danger, and Macomber exhibits this in this quote and throughout the passage by a heightened sense of hearing.

50. **(B)** The poem is fraught with references to the leader's betrayal of his friends — but the sentiment here is more on the side of the speaker. The leader received a number of accolades and some money from political figures, and the speaker does not like this. It does not seem that the leader ignored or turned on his old friends; rather they felt alienated from him because of his decisions.

51. **(E)** It is the speaker's idea that the leader's compensation was not much monetarily. The leader, however, does not seem disappointed with the money or awards given him. The speaker points out that while the leader "found the one gift" (line 3) he and his friends couldn't give, the leader has "lost all the others" (line 4) that they were giving him.

52. **(D)** "Purple" is commonly used in reference to royalty, and in this poem other references support this assertion (even without the knowledge that this is Browning criticizing Wordsworth for accepting money and poet laureate status from Queen Victoria) — such as the reference to the "they" who have all the money.

53. **(E)** The speaker's comments refer to the leader's social and political responsibilities and evident alteration of philosophy. The speaker and his friends have learned the leader's "great language" (line 11). Presumably the language retains its greatness, though, in the speaker's eye, the leader does not. Again, the idea here is that the leader has committed actions which the speaker does not like — though they were not intended to offend him.

54. **(A)** The leader "boasts his quiescence" (line 19). He has willingly been swallowed by "The Establishment," and his advice, no longer an inspiration, is now of the cowardly sort — the "crouching" approach.

55. **(C)** Shakespeare was "of us" — which describes common origins — philosophical and political — as this is the theme of the leader's betrayal. Milton was not from these origins, but was "for us" just the same, and Burns and Shelley — contemporaries of Browning — were followers of these beliefs while they were alive.

56. **(A)** The speaker wishes that the leader's name be "blotted out." But the key here is that, even if the leader recants and "comes back" to his old friends, things would never be the same again. Any praise given would be "forced," and therefore, the speaker implies that it is better that the leader doesn't even attempt a reconciliation.

57. **(C)** While the speaker is perhaps more serious in his curses than the modern reader might be willing to accept, it is doubtful Browning is wishing eternal damnation upon his old friend Wordsworth. The slight exaggeration in these lines is more likely to be indicative of the speaker's serious desire to register intense and deep-seated disagreement with the leader's actions. (E) is perhaps a possibility, except that the speaker has already associated the literary "mainstream" with his views, and that his anger is directed in stanza 1 at both the leader and those "with gold to give."

58. **(E)** There is a curious and perhaps difficult "twist" at the end of this poem — an indication and a hope that, by "striking gallantly" (line 29) — as the leader would have formerly — his friends may "re-master" the leader's heart. Previously, the speaker made the expected comments that he will continue "marching" without the leader. Now, the tone seems to change.

59. **(B)** The ending of the poem is abrupt and fascinating. On the surface, it might seem to be a pleasant wish that reconciliation will occur in heaven, if not sooner. On the other hand, the use of the word "throne" may be an artful and cutting reference to the leader already having received his "handful of silver" from the "throne" of Queen Victoria. In life, therefore, as he may be in death, the leader will find some way to be "first" — closest to the center of power even if it compromises his creative integrity.

60. **(B)** Personification is a figure of speech in which a thing, quality, or idea is represented as a person. Lines 3–4 refer to fortune with the pronoun "she" — representing an idea as a human being. The correct answer is (B).

designed to produce one single, shocking effect.

Poe's overall description may be said to be deductive, or proceeding from the more general aspects of the sky and the countryside, to the more specific aspects of the house itself, and how he feels as he first comes upon it. He uses the words "dull, dark, and soundless" to describe the day; he calls the country "singularly dreary."

His first sight of the House of Usher leaves him with "a sense of insufferable gloom." The house, he implies, must be more than what he is looking at — it cannot be a "mere house." The very sight of it, with its "bleak walls," and its "eye-like" windows leaves him with an icy, sickening feeling.

All of this leads the reader to expect that something horrible will happen later on in the story. This is the precise effect Poe wishes to have on his readers. In addition, the descriptions Poe offers leads the reader to wonder whether or not the supernatural is at work; whether or not the speaker has entered a realm of unreality in which anything can happen.

Poe is able to create an atmosphere of horror by designing each of his descriptions so that each contributes an emotional piece to the puzzle that will be the total emotional effect. Nothing Poe offers us in this piece is extraneous. Our minds and emotions are being manipulated by a master of the horror genre, and readers to this day continue to enjoy it.

Essay 2 — Explanation

This essay is well written. It demonstrates the writer's command of syntax, diction, and organization. In addition, this essay clearly defines stylistic techniques employed in the passage that create an atmosphere of horror, and cites specific, relevant textual examples as well.

Essay 3

Nathaniel Hawthorne in his novel *The Scarlet Letter* uses a specific problem facing his heroine as she confronts society, to represent people throughout history who have had to go on with life despite the sometimes narrow-minded opinions of their fellow citizens.

Hester Prynne is an unwed mother whose expected economic and social problems are made worse by the attitudes of her Puritan Boston neighbors, and by the fact that the father of her child is the Reverend Dimmesdale, the town's minister. Life is not easy for either of them, though Dimmesdale is able to go on with his life (at least to the casual eye), while Hester has to endure the punishment of the Scarlet A and the remarks and gossip that follow her progress through life.

Toward the end of Hester's life, Hawthorne relates that many of the townsfolk had forgotten what the Scarlet A was supposed to mean, and that they now assumed it meant "Able." Hester had learned to cope with her problem and, by good deeds and an otherwise honest life, had saved her reputation.

Hawthorne's story is illustrative of a common and larger problem: intolerance. People throughout history have chosen to interfere in other peoples' lives because they believe what is right for them must also be right for everyone else. It takes great self-confidence to endure their catcalls and social pressure, Hawthorne seems to be saying, but with the added gift of human love, the battle can be won.

Hawthorne uses Hester's predicament and her reaction to it to illustrate for all of us the problems and promise that can result when a brave and caring individual makes a conscious decision to violate some of the basic rules of a society. In doing so he presents a challenge to societies the world over: find a way to establish prudent and practical rules that do not violate the individual's right to pursue life as he or she sees fit.

Essay 3 — Explanation

This essay is well written. It indicates the writer's command of diction, syntax, and organization. In addition, it clearly identifies the character's specific problem and relates this to a more general statement by the author of what the specific problem represents within a greater context. Finally, the writer illustrates the essay with examples from the story, and does not rely on plot summary or simple statements to prove the points.

AP LITERATURE INDEX

This index lists all of the literary works mentioned in this book, in both the tests and the reviews, with references to where each work appears. The works are listed alphabetically by author's last name. This index also serves as a list of suggested reading material. By reading these works for both study and pleasure, your knowledge of literature will be expanded as well. The works are listed by page number.

INSTALLING REA's TESTware®

SYSTEM REQUIREMENTS

Pentium 75 MHz (300 MHz recommended) or a higher or compatible processor; Microsoft Windows 98 or later; 64 MB Available RAM; Internet Explorer 5.5 or higher.

INSTALLATION

1. Insert the AP English Literature & Composition TESTware® CD-ROM into the CD-ROM drive.
2. If the installation doesn't begin automatically, from the Start Menu choose the RUN command. When the RUN dialog box appears, type d:\setup (where D is the letter of your CD-ROM drive) at the prompt and click OK.
3. The installation process will begin. A dialog box proposing the directory "Program Files\REA_AP_Lit\TESTware" will appear. If the name and location are suitable, click OK. If you wish to specify a different name or location, type it in and click OK.
4. Start the AP English Literature & Composition TESTware® application by double-clicking on the icon.

REA's AP English Literature & Composition TESTware® is **EASY** to **LEARN AND USE**. To achieve maximum benefits, we recommend that you take a few minutes to go through the on-screen tutorial on your computer. The "screen buttons" are also explained here to familiarize you with the program.

SSD ACCOMMODATIONS FOR STUDENTS WITH DISABILITIES

Many students qualify for extra time to take the AP, and our TESTware® can be adapted to accommodate your time extension. This allows you to practice under the same extended time accommodations that you will receive on the actual test day. To customize your TESTware® to suit the most common extensions, visit our Website at *www.rea.com/ssd*.

TECHNICAL SUPPORT

REA's TESTware® is backed by customer and technical support. For questions about **installation or operation of your software**, contact us at:

> **Research & Education Association**
> **Phone: (732) 819-8880 (9 a.m. to 5 p.m. ET, Monday–Friday)**
> **Fax: (732) 819-8808**
> **Website: http://www.rea.com**
> **E-mail: info@rea.com**

Note to Windows XP Users: In order for the TESTware® to function properly, please install and run the application under the same computer-administrator level user account. Installing the TESTware® as one user and running it as another could cause file-access path conflicts.

USING YOUR INTERACTIVE TEST*ware*®

Exam Directions

The **Exam Directions** button allows you to review the specific exam directions during any part of the test.

Stop Test

At any time during the test or when you are finished taking the test, click on the **Stop** button. The program will advance you to the next screen.

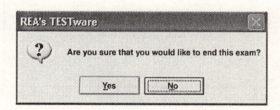

This screen allows you to quit the entire test, or return to the last question accessed prior to clicking the **Stop** button.

Back / Next Buttons

These two buttons allow you to move successfuly between questions. The **Next** button moves you to the next question, while the **Back** button allows you to view the previous question.

Mark/Q's List

If you are unsure about an answer to a particular question, the program allows you to mark it for later review. Flag the question by clicking on the **Mark** button. The **Q's List** button allows you to navigate through the questions and explanations. This is particularly useful if you want to view marked questions in Explanations Mode.

351

Writing and Scoring Your Essay

To complete the essay portion of the AP English Literature & Composition exam, use the TEST*ware*'s **Write Essay** and **Score Essay** buttons. Clicking **Write Essay** opens the essay window, shown below. When you have finished your essay, click the **Score Essay** button. Since this section is self-graded, this window will allow you to enter the essay score you believe you would receive.

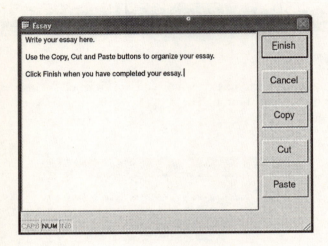

View Scores

Three score reports are available: Chart, Summary and Detail (shown below). All are accessed by clicking on the **View Scores** button in the Main Menu.

Explanations

In Explanations mode, click on the **Q & A Explanations** button to display a detailed explanation to any question. The split window shown below can be resized for easier reading.

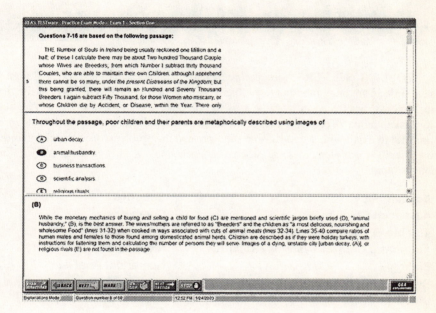

Congratulations!

By studying the reviews in this book, taking the written and computerized practice exams, and reviewing your correct and incorrect answers, you'll be well prepared for the AP English Literature & Composition exam. Best of luck from everyone at REA.

REA'S
PROBLEM SOLVERS®

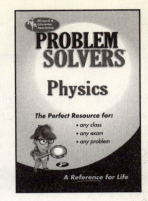
The PROBLEM SOLVERS® are comprehensive supplemental textbooks designed to save time in finding solutions to problems. Each PROBLEM SOLVER® is the first of its kind ever produced in its field. It is the product of a massive effort to illustrate almost any imaginable problem in exceptional depth, detail, and clarity. Each problem is worked out in detail with a step-by-step solution, and the problems are arranged in order of complexity from elementary to advanced. Each book is fully indexed for locating problems rapidly.

Accounting	**Genetics**
Advanced Calculus	**Geometry**
Algebra & Trigonometry	**Linear Algebra**
Automatic Control Systems/Robotics	**Mechanics**
Biology	**Numerical Analysis**
Business, Accounting & Finance	**Operations Research**
Calculus	**Organic Chemistry**
Chemistry	**Physics**
Differential Equations	**Pre-Calculus**
Economics	**Probability**
Electrical Machines	**Psychology**
Electric Circuits	**Statistics**
Electromagnetics	**Technical Design Graphics**
Electronics	**Thermodynamics**
Finite & Discrete Math	**Topology**
Fluid Mechanics/Dynamics	**Transport Phenomena**

If you would like more information about any of these books,
complete the coupon below and return it to us or visit your local bookstore.

Research & Education Association
61 Ethel Road W., Piscataway, NJ 08854
Phone: (732) 819-8880   **website: www.rea.com**

Please send me more information about your Problem Solver® books.

Name _____

Address _____

City _____ State _____ Zip _____